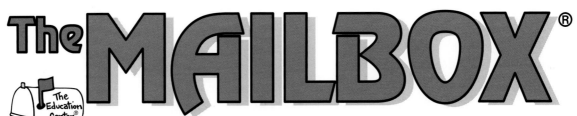

The MAILBOX®

The Idea Magazine For Teachers®

INTERMEDIATE

2001–2002

YEARBOOK

Becky S. Andrews, Managing Editor, *The Mailbox* Magazine
Deborah G. Swider, Managing Editor, *The Mailbox* Yearbook

The Education Center, Inc.
Greensboro, North Carolina

The Mailbox® 2001–2002 Intermediate Yearbook

Founding Editor in Chief: Margaret Michel
Managing Editor: Becky S. Andrews
Assistant Managing Editor: Peggy W. Hambright
Executive Director, Magazine Publishing: Katharine P. S. Brower
Editorial and Freelance Management: Karen A. Brudnak
Curriculum Director: Karen P. Shelton
Editorial Training: Irving P. Crump
Contributing Editors: Irving P. Crump, Debra Liverman, Christa New
Copy Editors: Sylvan Allen, Karen Brewer Grossman, Karen L. Huffman, Amy Kirtley-Hill, Debbie Shoffner
Traffic Manager: Lisa K. Pitts
Staff Artists: Pam Crane, Nick Greenwood, Clevell Harris, Rebecca Saunders (SENIOR ARTISTS); Theresa Lewis Goode, Ivy L. Koonce, Sheila Krill, Clint Moore, Greg D. Rieves, Barry Slate, Stuart Smith, Donna K. Teal
Cover Artist: Lois Axeman
Typesetters: Lynette Dickerson, Mark Rainey
Editorial Assistants: Terrie Head, Hope Rodgers, Jan E. Witcher
Librarian: Dorothy C. McKinney

ISBN 1-56234-505-2
ISSN 1088-5552

Printed in the United States of America.

The Education Center, Inc.
P.O. Box 9753
Greensboro, NC 27429-0753

Look for *The Mailbox*® 2002–2003 Intermediate Yearbook in the summer of 2003. The Education Center, Inc., is the publisher of *The Mailbox*®, *Teacher's Helper*®, *The Mailbox*® BOOKBAG®, and *Learning*® magazines, as well as other fine products. Look for these wherever quality teacher materials are sold, or call 1-800-714-7991.

Contents

Teacher Resource Ideas

Decorating Your Classroom on a Shoestring Budget

Creative and Inexpensive Tips From Our Subscribers

With some free or inexpensive materials and a little imagination, you can turn your classroom into an inviting learning place for kids. Just check out the following decorating ideas from our subscribers!

Shoebox Cubbies

Before the new school year begins, collect a class supply of shoeboxes. After school starts, have each student decorate the inside of a box with stickers and markers. Then use heavy tape to combine the boxes. Cover the outside of the boxes with wallpaper or Con-Tact® paper. Use these shoebox cubbies for storage, as student mailboxes, or as display cases for items that kids bring to school to share. *Kimberly A. Minafo, Carmel, NY*

Recycled Calendars

Here's a great source of beautiful posters and pictures for your classroom: last year's calendars! Ask friends and neighbors to give you their calendars instead of throwing them away. Sort the pictures according to teaching units or themes, or by season. From cartoons to museum masterpieces, you'll have scads of free artwork to decorate your classroom! *Julia Alarie—Gr. 6, Essex Middle School, Essex, VT*

Cool Suncatchers

Beautiful student-made suncatchers will brighten any classroom! Provide each student with an 8" x 8" paper square and an 8" x 8" piece of clear lightweight vinyl. First, have each student draw a simple design on the paper square. Next, have him lay his vinyl square over the design and outline the picture with a black fine-tipped permanent marker. Finally, have the student turn over the vinyl and color in the design with permanent markers. Attach these suncatchers to your windows for months of viewing pleasure! *Heather Eubank—Gr. 5, Willow Brook Elementary, Creve Coeur, MO*

Add a Little Fabric

For a quick decorating trick that will transform your classroom, head to your local fabric store. Buy fabric when it's on sale, and look for prints and solids that tie in with your teaching themes. Then use the fabric to back your bulletin boards. When a piece of fabric needs cleaning, just dip it into a sink of water and liquid soap, and then hang it on a hanger to drip-dry. For eye-catching bulletin board titles, place your letters front side down on a piece of fabric; then laminate and cut out the letters. Not only does fabric brighten up a classroom, but it also never seems to fade, show staple holes, or tear. *Terry Schneider—Gr. 5, Clarkdale-Jerome School, Clarkdale, AZ*

Just a Few Bucks

Decorating on limited funds? No problem! Check out these nifty, thrifty ideas:

- Do you have an old countertop that needs a face-lift? Cover it with marble Con-Tact® paper. (Visitors to your classroom just might think you have a brand-new countertop!)
- Buy some inexpensive sheets from a discount store and make curtains backed with Velcro® strips. These curtains can be easily removed when blinds need cleaning.
- Are your posters and large bulletin board sets squeezed between cabinets? Eliminate this unsightly storage problem by storing the large items in an outdoor-sized garbage can.
- Bring personal knickknacks from home. Baskets and air fresheners enhance the overall atmosphere of a classroom and give it a warm, welcoming feeling.

Terry Warner—Gr. 4, Brookview Elementary, Jacksonville, FL

Pam Crane

Reading Throne

Here's an inexpensive way to make students feel regal when they're reading! All you need is a white plastic lawn chair and two cans of gold spray paint. Spray-paint the chair outdoors and let it dry overnight. Hot-glue some jewels, rhinestones, or beads to the chair. If desired, add an inexpensive tie-on cushion. Now you have a special (and inexpensive!) chair for your reading center. *Michelle Curtis—Gr. 5, Preston Hollow Elementary, Plano, TX*

A Banner Idea

Add color to your classroom and create a feel-good atmosphere with this banner idea! Use die-cut letters to spell an inspirational quote. Glue the letters to a long strip of bulletin board paper. Then laminate the banner and hang it on a wall or from the ceiling. You can't beat these colorful, inspirational, and cheap space fillers! *Heather Eubank—Gr. 5, Willow Brook Elementary, Creve Coeur, MO*

In this room, it's okay to make mistakes!

Picket Fencing

Make an inexpensive classroom divider in a snap with this handy idea! Buy a nine-foot section of standard picket fencing from a home improvement store. Cut the section in half; then drill two holes at the end of each crosspiece. Put the two halves back together at a right angle and insert screws in the four holes as shown. Now you have a freestanding fence that you can use to create a special center in your classroom. For fun, decorate the fence for each season (leaves in the fall, evergreen boughs and lights in December, etc.). To store the fence, simply remove the screws to make two flat sections. *Marti Bierdeman—Gr. 5, Bolin School, East Peoria, IL*

Building a Class Community

How can you create a comfortable class community? Build it on a foundation of meaningful compliments and encouraging words with this whole-class, interactive activity!

idea by Kirsten Murphy—Grs. 5 and 6, Sycamore Elementary, Ft. Worth, TX

You are so organized!

Materials: ball of yarn, Nerf® ball, scissors, decorated shoe-box labeled "Compliment Box" with an opening cut in its lid, stack of compliment cards (similar to the sample on page 9)

Introducing the activity: Begin by sharing resources from your media center that tell about a spiderweb's design, purpose, and construction. Tell students that they will be creating a web of their own that's built of meaningful compliments and encouraging words. Then explain the difference between a meaningful compliment, such as "You always greet everyone with a nice smile," and one that's too general, such as "You are so cool." Point out that the first compliment is specific, while the other one is too vague to be of any real value.

Step 1: Create the web. Have students stand with you in a circle. Hold the loose end of the ball of yarn tightly in the fingers of one hand. Use your other hand to toss the ball to any student. Hold on to the piece of yarn and pay the catcher a specific compliment. Next, direct the catcher to unwind the ball of yarn slightly, hold the piece of yarn in one hand, toss the ball of yarn with the other hand, and give a meaningful compliment to its catcher as you did. Have students continue in this manner until everyone in the circle is holding a part of the web and the ball of yarn has been tossed back to you.

Step 2: Demonstrate how important everyone is to maintaining the web. Instruct students to hold their lengths of yarn tightly as you place a Nerf ball in the center of the web. Direct students to work together to move the ball around on the web. After five minutes or so, have students freeze. Use scissors to randomly cut several lengths of yarn. Ask the students holding those lengths to sit outside the circle. Then have the remaining students move the Nerf ball around on the web again. After five more minutes, randomly cut more yarn and have the students holding the cut lengths sit outside the circle. Continue in this manner until the web can no longer support the ball. Then have students return to their seats to discuss what happened to the web and how it relates to building a class community.

Compliments

K u d o s **G r e a t**

To Justin

From Jessie

For helping me clean up the splattered paint when I dropped the paint container on the floor during art. No one asked you to help me. You just volunteered. Thanks!

Terrific • Wow • Fantastic

Step 3: Explain how to use the compliment box. Show students the decorated box and compliment cards. Explain that whenever a student observes a classmate doing something positive that deserves recognition, he should fill out a compliment card and drop it in the box. Remind students to use the cards only for meaningful compliments, not for telling their best friends that they enjoyed being at their birthday parties or how great their shoes are! Encourage students to be on the lookout for deeds to acknowledge. Then place the compliment box and cards in a prominent place in the classroom.

Step 4: Invite staff members to fill out compliment cards. Without telling students, encourage other staff members who work with your class—such as the librarian, secretary, and school nurse—to fill out cards as well. Students will be thrilled to receive compliments from people outside the classroom. To ensure that no one gets left out, make a point of filling out at least one compliment card per student during each grading period.

Step 5: Share the compliment cards daily. Set aside a time each day for sharing the compliments on the cards. Students will enjoy hearing them even if they aren't the recipients. Present each card to its recipient as a memento to take home.

Super!

You really have a knack for writing stories!

You're a whiz at math!

Your handwriting is always so neat!

You draw horses better than anyone!

Terrific!

Way to go!

More Community-Building Ideas

• Divide students into groups of four. Give each group markers and four large triangles cut from colorful paper. Assign each group the names of four other classmates. Have the group members think of a complimentary slogan or nickname for each one. Then have them write each slogan on a banner and decorate it appropriately. Hang the banners in the classroom to build a feeling of warmth and acceptance—two necessary building blocks of a genuine class community. *Colleen Dabney, Williamsburg-JCC Public Schools, Williamsburg, VA*

• Inspire students to display attitudes and behaviors that build a sense of community with signs that fill the bill! Write messages that will encourage your students to demonstrate the actions you desire on signs of every shape and color. Then periodically display a different sign and recognize those students who demonstrate that attitude or behavior. *adapted from an idea by Nancy Curl—Gr. 6, Olson Middle School, Tabernacle, NJ*

Helping Hands

Creative Ways to Organize and Use Student Helpers

Need papers passed out? Books straightened? Boards cleaned? Then help yourself to these timesaving tips about how students can lend a helping hand!

Weekly and Yearly Jobs

Make your life easier and your classroom neater by recruiting students to perform both weekly *and* yearlong tasks. First, list all the tasks that must be done in your classroom on a regular basis. Divide the tasks into two categories: simple weekly jobs and those that a student could do with additional training. Then follow these simple steps:

- **Weekly Jobs:** Record the simple jobs on a weekly job chart. (See the sample for possible jobs.) Each week assign every child a task. If necessary, ask two students to share a job so that every child is employed.
- **Yearlong Tasks:** Consider recruiting students to perform certain jobs for the entire year. Think of tasks you do that a responsible child could be trained to tackle for you (see the list shown). Before hiring anyone for these positions of honor, observe students to identify who might make the most qualified employees. Then train the recruits accordingly. If desired, "pay" your yearlong helpers on the 15th and 30th of each month with extra-credit points so they'll learn some of the dynamics of a real-life working situation. ***Lisa Boddez—Gr. 5, St. Mary's Elementary, Vancouver, British Columbia, Canada***

Weekly Jobs
- paper distributors
- paper collectors
- bookcase organizers
- shelf straighteners
- notice monitors—remind students to take weekly/daily notices home
- floor janitors
- classroom manager—do odd jobs for the teacher
- board cleaners
- desk straighteners
- center organizers
- sink cleaners
- paper and cupboard organizers
- job chart monitor—rotate names on job chart each week

Yearlong Jobs
- absentee monitors—record, collect, and explain missed assignments for absentees
- birthday monitor—keep track of student birthdays and oversee the signing of birthday cards
- library book monitor—check a list and remind students to return books
- homework board monitor—record assignments neatly on the board as they are given

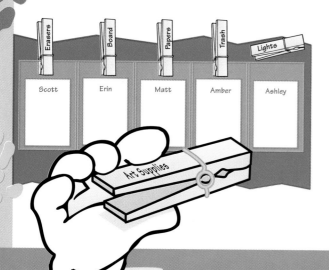

Snappy Job Assignments

Looking for a quick way to assign classroom jobs each week? Then this tip's for you! Write each student's name on the top half of an index card. Slip one card in each pocket of a pocket chart as shown. Next, write each classroom job on a separate spring-type clothespin. Then clip one clothespin to the top of each pocket. To change the job assignments, simply move the clothespins one pocket to the right from one row to the next. When you reach the last pocket, just start over at the top! ***Lynn Dunklee—Gr. 4, Danville School, Danville, VT***

HELP WANTED!

WANTED: ERRAND EXPERT
to run errands around the school. Must have a swift pace and good sense of direction.

Ann

WANTED: MAIL CARRIER
to distribute papers to classmates.

Sue

WANTED: ELECTRICIAN
needed to turn on/off lights, computers, television, etc.

Dave

Alan Kim Peter

For Hire

Seth Hope

On Vacation

Classified Helpers

Create a new interest in classroom jobs by listing them in the classifieds! Cover a bulletin board with the classified section of a newspaper and title it "Help Wanted!" Add two construction paper pockets—one labeled "For Hire" and the other "On Vacation"—to the display. Next, write each student's name on a different index card. Finally, fill the board's columns with the names and descriptions of different classroom jobs, leaving space beside each description to attach a library pocket.

Each Monday have a "manager" move the cards of students who had jobs last week into the "On Vacation" pocket. Then have him rotate the "For Hire" students' cards into the job pockets. Finally, have him move the "On Vacation" cards to the "For Hire" pocket. *Rami Parker—Gr. 4, Abita Springs Middle School, Abita Springs, LA*

Newsletter Helpers

Add another dimension to your classroom job chart by including helpers who create your weekly newsletter! In addition to the usual classroom jobs, assign the following positions: editor, math reporter, social studies reporter, language arts reporter, science reporter, and interviewer. Explain that the interviewer will interview a school employee and then write an article about this person. Each reporter will summarize what the class studied about that subject during the week, while the editor will compile the five articles into the newsletter. Not only does this idea provide important skills practice, but it also guarantees a classroom newsletter every week. *Kathy Occhioni—Gr. 4, Fairbanks Road Elementary, Churchville, NY*

Easy-to-Spot Reminders

Do you have students who sometimes forget to do their assigned classroom jobs? Solve that problem using simple visual reminders! Attach an E-Z-Up clip to each student's desk. Also write each classroom job on a separate index card. When a student is assigned a new job, have her clip that card on her desk. One quick glance reminds her that she's got a job to do! *Joyce Hovanec—Gr. 4, Glassport Elementary, Glassport, PA*

bookshelves

The Second Time Around

Using Recyclables in the Classroom

Don't throw that away! Instead, put it to good use in your classroom with the help of these recycling ideas from our readers.

Using Recyclables With Students

When studying plants, have students make root viewers from **clear plastic water tubes** collected from florists. Begin by having each student layer half a cotton ball, grass or green bean seeds, and the remaining cotton ball half in the bottom of a tube. Have the student add drops of water to dampen the cotton. Then direct him to knot one end of a 12-inch length of yarn and thread the yarn through the hole in the water tube's cap. After he attaches the cap to the tube, have the student tape the yarn to a well-lighted window. Because the seeds sprout quickly, students will get to view the entire germination process! *Louella Nygaard—Gr. 5, Isabel Bills Elementary, Colstrip, MT*

- Culminate the study of any biome by having students create terrarium-like models from **two- and three-liter plastic soda bottles.** First, cut a hand-sized hole in the side of each bottle and fill its bottom with sand. Have each student fill her terrarium with various natural and hand-made materials to represent the chosen biome. Then have her attach a paragraph describing the biome's location, terrain, and plant and animal life. *Rebecca McCright and Melissa Nuñez—Gr. 6, Washington Elementary, Midland, TX*

- Make it easy for students to draw perfect circles by saving unsolicited **CD-ROMs** that come in the mail. Collect enough for a class set. When teaching geometry or circle graphs, the disks are easy to trace anytime a circle is needed. They also make great tracers on overhead projectors, chalkboards, or whiteboards. *Lisa Hoegerman—Gr. 6, Vista Campana Middle School, Apple Valley, CA*

Teach propaganda techniques with the help of **empty product containers,** such as oatmeal boxes, spice shakers, and hair spray bottles. Divide students into groups and give each group several containers. After a group studies the advertising on its containers, have group members use art materials to turn one container into an original must-have product. Then have the group use various propaganda techniques to write television or radio ads to sell its product. *Rebecca McCright*

You'll never have a hair out of place if you use our Heavenly Hair hair spray!

- Create a file of **calendar pictures** that can be used to strengthen students' writing skills. Cut pictures from old calendars and sort them into categories: scenes (for describing settings), people (for profiling characters), and events (for writing narratives). Next, divide students into groups and give each group a different picture to write about. Display the pictures and the students' written work on a bulletin board. Also post a challenge for readers to match the written pieces with their corresponding pictures. Include an answer key for checking. *Mary Gates—Gr. 4, Huckleberry Hill School, Brookfield, CT*

- Brew endless ideas for writing prompts by clipping the unique artwork pictured on **tea bag boxes,** such as that on boxes of Celestial Seasonings tea bags. Store the clippings in a file box at a writing center. Have each student choose a clipping and write about what might have been going on before, during, and after the pictured scene. Or have her write a character sketch about a person or animal depicted in the artwork. *Kelly Cook—Gr. 5, Dana Elementary, Dana, NC*

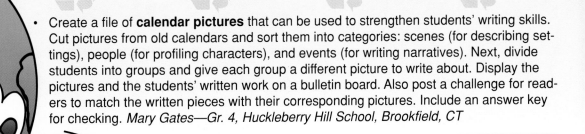

Using Recyclables to Organize Your Classroom

- Save the **tops of dried-up markers** to use as game pieces. Or use them to form cooperative groups. Just place the exact number and color of tops needed in a container. Then have each student draw out a top. *Toni O'Neil—Gr. 4, Ramsey Robertson Elementary, Harbor Beach, MI*

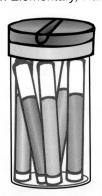

- Put empty plastic **Parmesan cheese containers** to use as marker holders. Use each container to hold a set of large or small markers. To remove a marker, simply lift or remove the hinged lid. *Sheila Wigger—Gr. 4, Clara Barton School, Alton, IL*

- Cover **Crystal Light drink mix containers and Pringles potato chip cans** with Con-Tact paper and use them to hold pencils or paintbrushes. Use **plastic trays from frozen dinners** to sort small items, such as beads or noodles, for projects. Also retrieve items that are examples of cylinders, cubes, and rectangular prisms from recycling bins to help students identify geometric solids. *Amie L. Tedeschi—Gr. 5, Triangle Day School, Durham, NC*

- Create sturdy magazine holders from 92-ounce **laundry detergent boxes.** Cut away each box top and the top two inches of each side. Make a wide cut (as shown) on one narrow end of each box. Then cover the inside and outside of the box with Con-Tact paper. *Karen Miller—Gr. 4, Happy Valley Elementary, Johnson City, TN*

Tuning Up for a Test

Creative Ways to Help Students Review for Tests

Looking for some clever techniques to help students review for an upcoming science, social studies, or other subject-area test? Then check out the following games and activities from our readers!

Who Said *That?*

When it's time for a test, students often get their facts mixed up, particularly when faced with questions about famous people in history. Was it Balboa or Magellan who named the Pacific Ocean? Did Thomas Edison or Alexander Graham Bell invent the phonograph? Encourage students to remember important information about the famous folks they study with a fun game of Who Said That?

To prepare:
1. Have each student choose a different famous person, such as an explorer, to research. Tell students to focus on the major events and accomplishments related to the person.
2. Direct each student to write a quote that his person might have said and label it with his team's name or number. Encourage the student to evaluate the person's situation and try to think like him or her. For example, Ponce de León may have said, "Let's continue to search for the Fountain of Youth in this beautiful land of flowers!" Encourage students to write creative quotes that contain historically accurate facts.

To play:
1. Collect and review students' quotes.
2. Divide students into two teams. Separate the quotes by team.
3. Read one of Team 2's quotes to Team 1 and ask, "Who said that?" If the team answers correctly, award it five points.
4. Include an additional question related to the quote for a bonus round, such as "What was the land of flowers?" Award two additional points for a correct answer.
5. Read a Team 1 quote to Team 2 and repeat Steps 3–4.

Adapt this game to review any subject-area topic. Simply have students make up quotes that inanimate objects—such as those from math, geography, or science—might say.

Betsy McQueen—Gr. 5, Branson Cedar Ridge Elementary, Branson, MO

I think this new assembly line will cut production costs.

Twister® Review

Do you have a Twister® game stored away in your classroom? Then try this fun twist to review for any subject-area test! Cut out 24 construction paper circles to match the ones on the game mat: six each of red, blue, green, and yellow. On each set of same-colored circles, write the values "10," "20," "30," "40," "50," and "60" (one per circle). Next, write a review question on the opposite side of each circle, increasing the difficulty of questions on the circles with higher point values. Place the circles on the Twister mat with the point values facing up.

To play, divide students into two teams and have the teams sit around the Twister mat. Have the first player on Team 1 spin the game spinner. The player picks up one of the six circles of the color spun, reads the question on the back of the circle, and answers it. If she's correct, her team keeps that circle. If not, she returns it to the same spot on the mat. Continue play until all 24 questions have been answered correctly. The team with the most total points at the end of the game is the winner.

Colleen Dabney, Williamsburg–JCC Public Schools, Williamsburg, VA

Testing, Testing...

You've used textbook tests, and you've created your own. Now let the test *takers* become the test *writers!* Near the conclusion of a unit, tell students that you want them to help write the test for that unit. Hold a brainstorming session during which students name all the important concepts they learned. Record their ideas on the board or on a transparency; then discuss how many items should be included on the test. With the class, decide which items are the most important and circle them. Use these items as the basis for creating your test, or invite students to help write the questions. Because your students help make the test, they'll approach the assessment with more confidence!

Julia Alarie—Gr. 6, Essex Middle School, Essex, VT

A Crackerjack Review

This easy activity can be used to review for any subject-area test—plus students can help you prepare the questions and answers. First, write 15–20 numbered review questions on an overhead transparency. Also program a matching set of index cards with the answers on one side and the numbers on the opposite side. Write "Crackerjack" on one card below the answer. Display all of the cards in the chalk tray with their numbered sides facing out.

To play, divide students into teams and appoint a recorder for each one. Have each team answer the questions on the transparency in any order and one at a time. The recorder writes down her team's answer, then goes to the matching numbered card to check it. If the answer is correct, each team member earns a sticker, a pretzel, or another small treat. If the answer card is the one labeled "Crackerjack," award each team member with a box of Cracker Jack® candied popcorn. The more correct answers, the more treats!

Margaret Wanat—Grs. 4–5, St. Eugene School, Chicago, IL

Who Wants to Shorten the Test?

What kid wouldn't want to shorten a test? In this fun adaptation of a popular TV show, students can earn the privilege of skipping up to five test questions. To prepare, have each child write ten numbered multiple-choice questions and answers about the topic, ranging from easy (1) to difficult (10). Also make up a question that students will answer to qualify as a game contestant. Just like in the show *Who Wants to Be a Millionaire*™, this question should consist of four or five items that students must list in correct time order.

On the day of the game, have each student turn in his questions as his ticket to play. To begin, copy the qualifying question on a transparency and divide the class into groups. Position a chair at the front of the classroom to serve as the hot seat. Then follow these steps:

1. Show the qualifying question to the class. Direct each student to quickly write his answer and stand when he finishes.
2. Have the Team 1 student with the correct answer and the quickest time sit in the hot seat. Ask him to answer his classmates' questions one at a time. Allow the student two lifelines: one in which he may ask for the entire class's help and another in which he is allowed 30 seconds to check his notes. For every two correct answers, award the player the privilege of skipping one nonessay question on the upcoming test.
3. When the student misses a question (or has earned five skips), have him sit down at his desk. Then ask the Team 2 student with the correct qualifying answer and the quickest time to sit in the hot seat to answer questions.
4. Continue until all qualifiers have sat in the hot seat. Then, if desired, display another qualifying question and play again.
5. At the end of the game, award each student who makes it to the hot seat with a certificate that states the number of test questions he can skip.

Jennifer Davis—Gr. 5, York Elementary, Wauseon, OH

I'd like to use a lifeline!

Let's Do Lunch!

Make lunchtime more manageable and pleasant for everyone with these handy management tips from our readers.

Lunch Count Made Easy

Make lunch count a painless procedure with this tip. Bring in a red coat hanger, a blue coat hanger, and a class supply of spring-type clothespins. Assign each student a number; then write it on a separate clothespin. When a student arrives in the morning, have him pin his clothespin to the red hanger if he wants a hot lunch or the blue hanger if he wants a cold lunch. A quick count tells you how many hot lunches to order and also who is absent that day.

Barb Wylie—Gr. 4
Terry Redlin Elementary
Sioux Falls, SD

Lunch Money Keepers

Eliminate the "I've lost my lunch money!" hassle with this handy tip. Collect a class supply of empty film canisters. Write each student's name on a separate canister. Then store the canisters in a basket near your desk. In the morning, have each student place his lunch money in his canister. When it's time for lunch, have a student helper distribute the money canisters.

Michelle Allison—Gr. 4
Palmer Elementary
Easton, PA

Lunchroom Boredom Busters

A bored kid during lunch can spell trouble. Calm restless diners by laminating several reproducible word search puzzles and brainteasers. Attach a wipe-off marker to each laminated sheet. When a student becomes a bit too fidgety at the lunch table, hand her a puzzle to solve. Bye-bye, boredom!

Patricia Dancho—Gr. 6
Apollo-Ridge Middle School
Spring Church, PA

Red Light, Green Light

Monitor lunchroom behavior with the help of a simple stoplight display. Hang three large circles—red, yellow, and green—in a vertical row on a wall in the cafeteria. If the noise level is acceptable during lunch, position the green circle atop the other two circles. If the noise level rises to an unacceptable level, caution students about their behavior by moving the yellow light to the top. If students do not heed the caution light, move the red circle to the top, indicating a period of silent lunch with no talking allowed. You'll find that just displaying the yellow light will usually motivate students to make a change in their behavior.

Sue Calaway—Gr. 5
Jack Hayes School
Monroe, LA

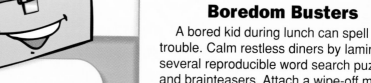

Classroom Displays

"In-vest" Some Time to Get Acquainted!

For a back-to-school display that doesn't require a big investment of time, copy the pattern on page 30 for each student. First, have the student decorate each pocket with the following: top left = favorite activity, top right = personal goal, bottom left = description of family, bottom right = favorite food. Then have him write his name on the label and color the vest with his favorite color. To encourage reading, have students color their vests and post them on the board. When a child finishes a book, have him write the book's title and author on a pocket.

Kimberly A. Minafo, Carmel, NY

Light a fire under even your most reluctant readers with this motivating display! Post a campfire made out of yellow, orange, red, and brown paper as shown. Staple a brown paper "stick" for each student around the campfire. Have each student post a cutout of her hand, labeled with her name, at the end of her stick.

Each time a student finishes a book from a different genre, have her glue a marshmallow (a white cotton ball) onto her stick. Then give her a real marshmallow to snack on. When a student reads six books (each from a different genre), reward her with a microwave s'more, made using the recipe shown.

Donna G. Pawloski—Gr. 4
Primos Elementary
Primos, PA

Microwave S'more

Put a piece of a chocolate bar on top of a graham cracker square. Place a marshmallow on top of the chocolate. Top with another graham cracker. Wrap the s'more in a paper towel; then microwave on high for 15 seconds or until the marshmallow is mushy and the chocolate is melted.

DISPLAYS

We're a Perfect Mix!

John

Noah

Rachel

Timmy

Ashley

Dina

Liz

Raul

Ben

Kevin

Tara

Theo

Heather

Max

Raul

Encourage class cooperation with this colorful display! On the first day of school, have each student fingerpaint a few designs on a bulletin board backed with white paper. While the paint dries, have each student write a paragraph explaining what he can do to mix well with his classmates this year. Once the paint has dried, have each student sign his name on the board and share his paragraph. Post the paragraphs on the display.

Heather Graley, Columbus, OH

"TACO" 'BOUT A TERRIFIC CLASS!

Deana

Robin

Maria

Tyrone

Tanner

Rosa

Lindsey

Becca

Cade

Lin

Felipe

Colby

Welcome your new class with a door display they'll "taco" 'bout for days! Post two cutout chili peppers as shown. For each student, fold a large yellow paper circle in half and label it with her name. Inside each paper taco, place a small amount of green Easter grass. Post the tacos on your classroom door for a display that's definitely hot!

Juli Engel—Gr. 4
Highlandville Elementary
Ozark, MO

Pick a peck of perfect alliteration practice with this perky fall display! Enlarge the pattern on page 32 and label it with the tongue twister shown. Then give each student an orange paper copy of page 32 to label with his own alliterative sentence. Post the pumpkins on the board along with a green paper vine and leaves.

Kimberly A. Minafo, West Babylon, NY

"Boooo-st" writing skills with a display that's also a fun art activity! Cover a small bulletin board with black paper. Add paper strips to make a window frame. Then position a table in front of the display. Place a paper tablecloth on the table along with a Halloween treat bag. Then have each student use available art materials to make a pretend piece of candy to place on the table. Also have the student make a spooky pair of paper eyes to mount in the window. For a writing extension, have students write about their curious creatures in stories or descriptive paragraphs.

Joan Groeber
Dayton, OH

DISPLAYS

Bubble away the book report blues with this squeaky-clean display! Mount a large tub like the one shown. After a student reads a book, have her complete a light blue copy of the pattern on page 31; then have her cut out the pattern and mount it on the board. Challenge the class to completely cover the board with bubbles. If desired, post this display in November to celebrate National Children's Book Week.

Rhonda Sigler—Gr. 5, Eva B. Stokely Elementary, Shiprock, NM

Want to fill your room with a spirit of thankfulness this November? Mount a turkey's head and a speech bubble as shown. Then have each student label a paper leaf cutout with a paragraph describing a person he is thankful for. Provide extra leaves for students who want to write more than one paragraph and for staff members and parents.

Merrill Watrous—Gr. 5, Fox Hollow School, Eugene, OR

Cash in on all the holiday hoopla with a display that sharpens writing skills! Mount a gift-wrapped box and a giant gift tag labeled as shown. Copy a class supply of the money pattern on page 33 onto light green paper. Have each student label a copy of the pattern with a paragraph that describes a cost-free gift he would like to give someone this holiday (for example, love, joy, helpfulness, etc.). Post the bills around the package.

Bonnie Gaynor—Gr. 5, Franklin Elementary, Franklin, NJ

For a classroom jobs display that everyone will go ape over, enlarge and color the King Kong pattern on page 33. (If desired, glue fake fur onto the cutout for a furry 3-D effect.) Mount the ape with a cityscape as shown. Next, photograph each student posing as if she is a frightened victim in the giant ape's hand. Cut out the students' bodies from the developed photos. Then laminate the cutouts. At the start of each day or week, choose two or three students to serve as your special helpers. Then use Sticky-Tac to display your helpers' cutouts in Kong's hand.

Kerry Christiano—Gr. 5, Merritt Academy, Fairfax, VA

DISPLAYS

All Aboard the Adjective Train!

Keep parts-of-speech skills on track with this bulletin board activity! Mount a train engine as shown. Have each student glue an interesting picture from an old magazine to a sheet of construction paper. Then have him label the paper with as many specific adjectives to describe the picture as possible. After the student glues two cutout wheels to the paper, direct him to add it to the adjective train as shown. All aboard!

Patty Smith—Gr. 5, Collins Middle School, Collins, MS

Increase vocabulary "snow-how" with this wintry word activity! Divide the class into pairs or groups of three. Give each group the materials listed and one overused word, such as *said, big, small, go, nice, good,* or *sad.* Instruct each group to cut out a large snowball from the white paper and label it with its word. Then explain that the group can build on this base by adding details, as long as each detail is labeled with a synonym for the overused word. Post the finished snowmen in a hallway with the title "Snowy Synonyms." Provide additional art supplies in case students discover more synonyms later to add to their snowy pals.

Julia Alarie—Gr. 6, Essex Middle School
Essex, VT

Materials: white and black construction paper, wallpaper and construction paper scraps, scissors, glue, other art materials, thesaurus

Adverbs From the Heart

Celebrate Valentine's Day with a display that sharpens parts-of-speech, dictionary, and vocabulary skills. Write each listed adverb on a cutout heart. Then divide the class into pairs. Give each twosome a heart and an unlined index card. Direct the students to look up the word in the dictionary and draw on the card a picture that illustrates the word's meaning. Encourage students to use favorite fairy-tale, cartoon, or book characters in their scene. At the bottom of the card, have the students use the adverb in a sentence about the picture (for example, "Snow White smiled *affectionately* at the dwarfs"). Then post the hearts and scenes on a bulletin board.

Mary S. Gates, Huckleberry Hill School, Brookfield, CT

Adverbs	
blissfully	joyfully
affectionately	fervently
charmingly	generously
serenely	gallantly
gently	fondly
heartily	compassionately
tenderly	cordially
merrily	sympathetically

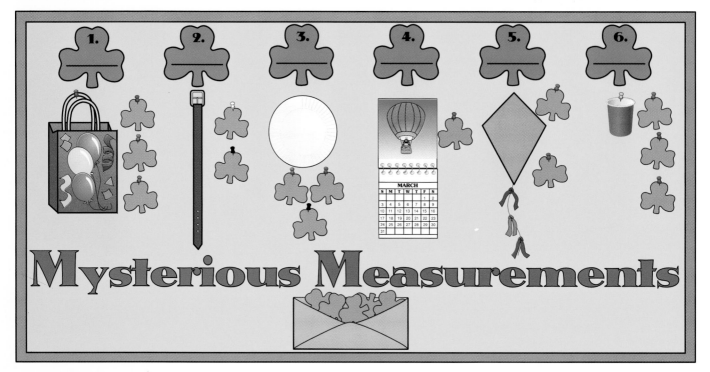

Mysterious Measurements

Here's a St. Patrick's Day display that really measures up! Display six everyday objects. Above each object, post a numbered shamrock (pattern on page 34) labeled with an appropriate measurement, such as circumference, height, or perimeter. Also display an envelope filled with shamrock cutouts. A student measures an object, writes his name and measurement on a shamrock, and pins the cutout facedown beside the item. Reward each student who correctly measures all six objects with a "pot of gold" (a paper cup filled with gold-wrapped candies).

DISPLAYS

We're Big Fans of Prefixes!

For a simply "fan-tastic" way to review word skills, have each student fold a sheet of construction paper to create a fan. Have him label each panel with a prefix and at least one word that uses it (for example, *pre-* and *preview*). Then have the student decorate the fan, scallop its edges with scissors, and staple one end together before pinning it to the board. For a fun finishing touch, let students add pictures of their favorite stars to the display.

Kimberly A. Minafo, Pomona, NY

Motivate students with a display that's a real sunny delight! Make a class supply of the sun pattern on page 34 on yellow paper. Then use one of the following ideas to encourage students that they are each "sun-body" special!

- Give each student a pattern. Have him label the pattern with his name and a skill he has achieved or improved this year.
- Write each student's name on a pattern. Then write a sentence about an area in which the student excels or has shown improvement.
- Have each student write his name on a pattern. Then divide students into small groups. Direct each group's members to swap patterns and label them with specific compliments. Be sure each student labels each group member's cutout.

Kimberly A. Minafo

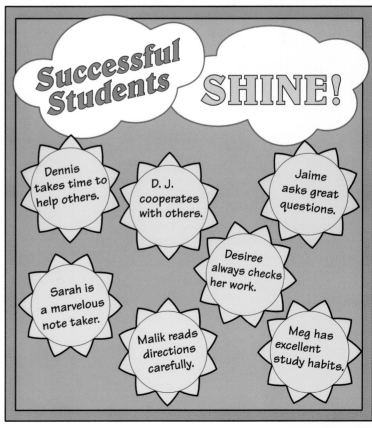

Did "somebunny" in your class do a great job on an assignment or test? Then honor that student on this super display! Post a large bunny as shown. When a student does an exceptional job on a paper, write his name on a page from a bunny-shaped notepad or on a copy of the pattern on page 35. Then staple the bunny to the display. Hop, hop, hooray!

Jennifer Mross—Grs. 5–6, Franklin Elementary, Franklin, NJ

Serve up a display that keeps track of your students' progress on writing assignments! Cover a small bulletin board with a plastic tablecloth or alternating sheets of red and white construction paper. Then write each student's name on a separate spring-type clothespin and post seven paper plates labeled as shown (adapt the writing process steps to fit your curriculum as needed). As each student works on a writing assignment, she moves her clothespin to the plate that indicates where she is in the writing process. Simple!

Lyndsey Lange—Gr. 4
Byron-Bergen Elementary
Bergen, NY

DISPLAYS

Our Earth's Health Is on the Line!

Celebrate Earth Day this April with a display that puts it all on the line! Discuss different slogans students have seen that promote Earth Day or the environment. Then have each child decorate a paper T-shirt cutout with a new slogan as shown. Clip the shirts to a clothesline suspended in a school hallway so that everyone gets the message that our earth's health is on the line!

Julie Jordan
Heritage Elementary
College Park, GA

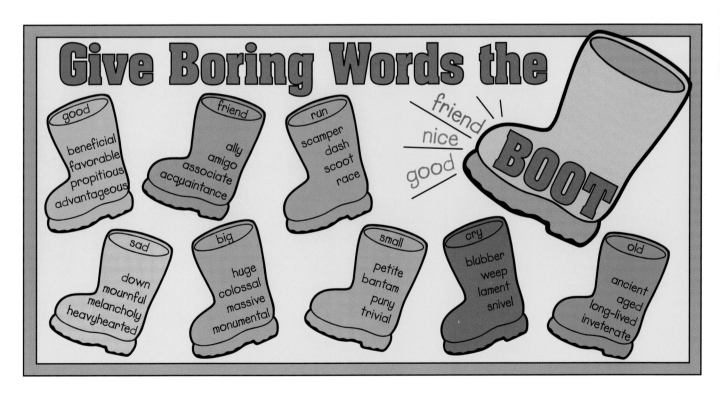

Give tired, overused words the boot with a display that acquaints students with the thesaurus. Assign each student a "tired" word such as one of those shown. Have her write the word at the top of a boot pattern (page 35). Then have her use a thesaurus to finish labeling the boot with interesting synonyms for the word.

Kimberly A. Minafo, Pomona, NY

27

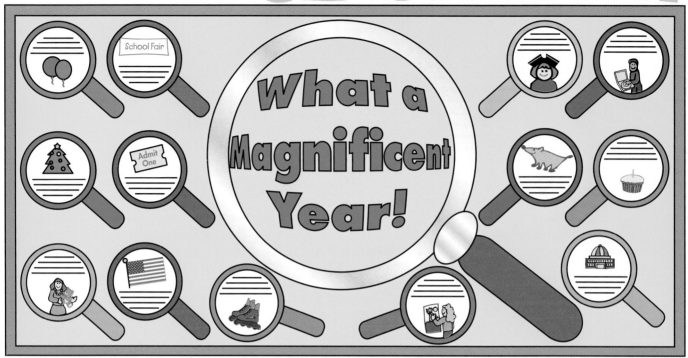

Take a closer look at the school year that's ending with this easy-to-make display! Mount on the board a large magnifying glass labeled as shown. Next, brainstorm with students a list of memorable events from the year. Have each child describe and illustrate one event on a white paper circle. Then have him glue the circle atop a slightly larger construction paper circle and add a paper handle. Magnifique!

Gaston Comeau—Gr. 5, Bridgewater Elementary, Bridgewater, Nova Scotia, Canada

What's "s'more" fun on a hot summer day than reading a good book? Toast the great books your students have read this year—and motivate an interest in summer reading—with this fun display. Have each student complete a copy of the book recommendation form on page 36 to post on the board. Add a cutout graham cracker and marshmallow, along with a chocolate candy bar wrapper. Also use the display to advertise summer reading programs available at your local library.

Colleen Dabney
Toano Middle School
Williamsburg, VA

DISPLAYS

MOVIN' ON UP!

The wheels on the bus go round and round—right to a new grade level or even to middle school for your graduating students. Celebrate their big move with this fun display. Enlarge one or more copies of the bus pattern on page 36. Cut out the windows and mount the bus on a wall or bulletin board. Next, take a photo of each student with your school's digital camera. Then cut out each printed photo and mount it inside a bus window. Also place a photo of yourself in the driver's window of each bus. If desired, laminate the buses. Then use a wipe-off marker to label each bus with the name of the grade level or school that students will head to next year.

Connie Thompson—Gr. 5
Falling Branch Elementary
Christiansburg, VA

It's easy to "sea" why everyone will want to linger at this underwater display! Have each student label an index card with a paragraph describing an important thing she learned this year. Then have the student glue her card onto a large fish shape and decorate the cutout. Post the fish on a bulletin board as shown. Adapt this idea to wrap up any unit or grading period.

Sara Gabel—Gr. 6, Governor Mifflin Intermediate School, Wyomissing, PA

Pattern

Use with the bulletin board on page 18.

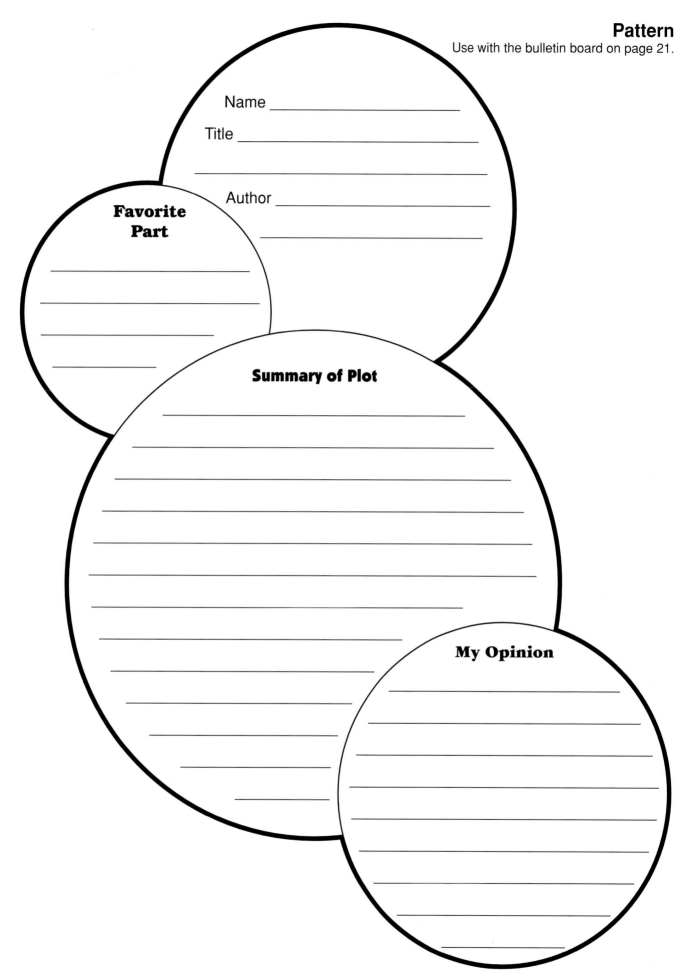

Name _____

Title _____

_____

Author _____

Favorite Part

_____

_____

_____

_____

Summary of Plot

_____

_____

_____

_____

_____

_____

_____

_____

_____

_____

My Opinion

_____

_____

_____

_____

_____

_____

Pattern

Use with the bulletin board on page 20.

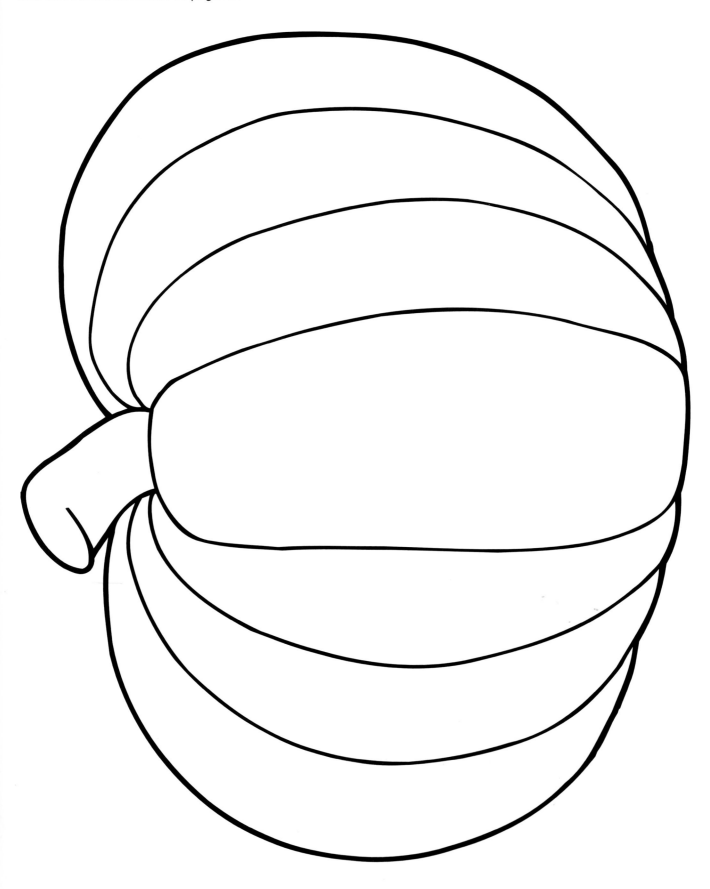

Name: _____

MOOLAH

Patterns

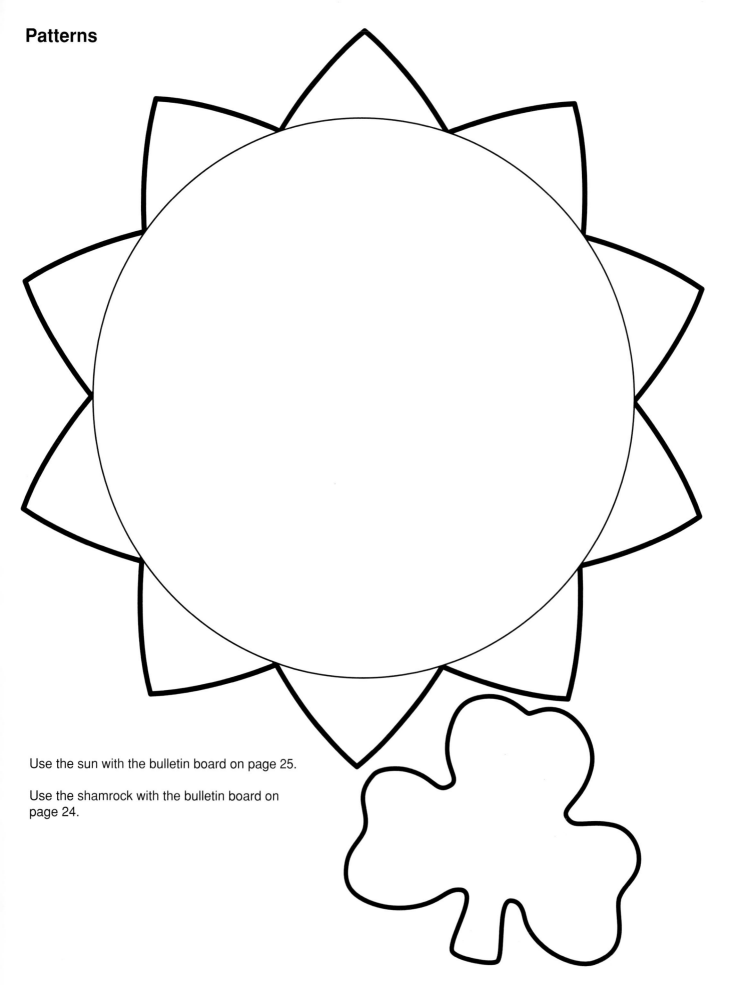

Use the sun with the bulletin board on page 25.

Use the shamrock with the bulletin board on page 24.

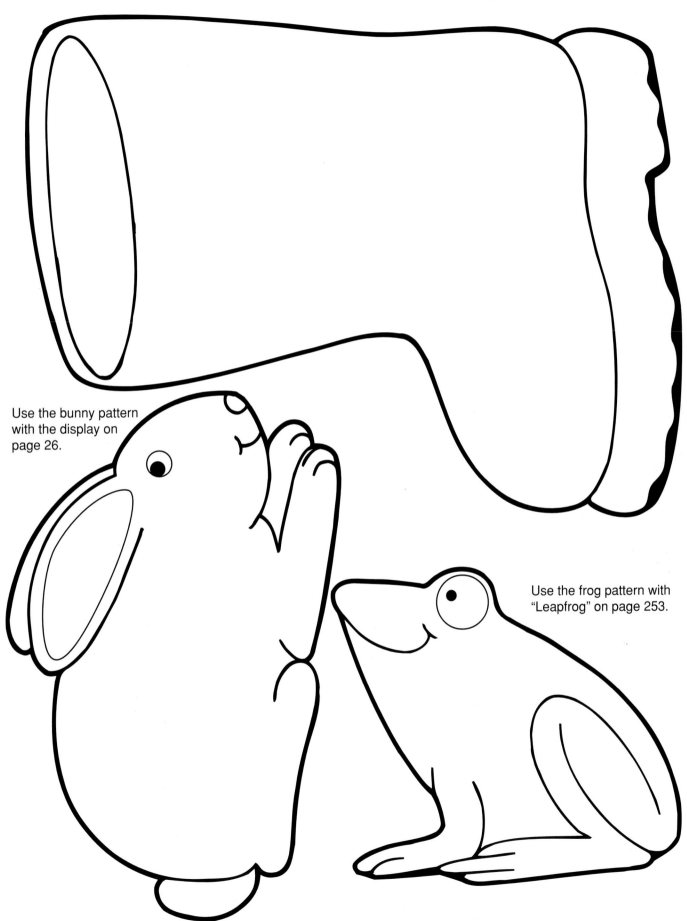

Use the bunny pattern
with the display on
page 26.

Use the frog pattern with
"Leapfrog" on page 253.

Patterns

Use the bus with the display on page 29.
Use the form with the display on page 28.

©2002 The Education Center, Inc.

Name _____

Book recommendation

TOASTING A GREAT BOOK

There's nothing that's "s'more" fun than a great book. And I have a great one for you!

Title: _____

Author: _____

Genre: _____

What the book is about: _____

Here's a picture of my favorite part of the book.

Want to find out "s'more"?
Then read the book to find out!

CHOCOLATE

©The Education Center, Inc. • *THE MAILBOX*® • *Intermediate* • June/July 2002

LANGUAGE ARTS UNITS

Voyaging With Verbs

"Sea" for yourself how exciting a voyage with verbs can be with the following skill-packed activities and reproducibles!

with ideas by Tina Cassidy, Ella Canavan Elementary, Medina, OH

Verb Collages
Skill: Recognizing action verbs

When it's time to review action verbs, dive into this fun activity! Give each student a sheet of construction paper, scissors, glue, and a discarded magazine. Direct the student to write the word *verb* in large, uppercase bubble letters on the paper as shown. Then challenge him to cut out action verbs from the magazine and glue them collage-style inside the letters. Require students to check with at least two classmates about words they are unsure of.

After the collages are complete, point out to students that not all action verbs refer to lively physical actions, such as *climb, leap, swim,* or *race.* Some describe quiet actions, such as *wonder, dream, think,* and *read.* Have students brainstorm a list of these types of verbs as you write them on chart paper. Then challenge each child to search his collage to see how many not-so-active action verbs he included.

adapted from an idea by Jill R. Bluth
Draper, UT

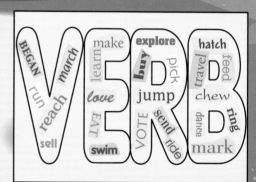

Verb Phrases (helping verbs in *italics*)

will stay	*might have* found
can crawl	*will be* singing
am leaving	*could have* spoken
had listened	*has been* whistling
should see	*has been* throwing
have heard	*would have been* skating
can look	*might have* felt
did solve	*will have been* reading
may make	*has been* breaking
must correct	*will have been* writing

Save Our Ship!
Skill: Identifying main and helping verbs

Keep verb skills afloat with a game that focuses on main and helping verbs. First, copy the life raft patterns on page 42 onto construction paper. Cut out the patterns; then label one raft "Team 1" and the other "Team 2." Next, draw the gameboard shown on the board. Place a piece of magnetic or double-sided tape on the back of each raft and attach the rafts to the board where indicated. Finally, write each verb phrase below on a strip of paper. Place the strips in a container.

To play, divide the class into two teams. Ask the first two players on Team 1 to come to the board. Have one player draw a verb phrase from the container, read it aloud, and give a sentence that uses it. Ask the second student to identify the sentence's main and helping verbs. If the student is correct, have the players move the team's raft one wave closer to the sinking ship. Then have Team 2's first two players come to the board to play. Declare the first team to get its raft to the ship the winner.

Verb Tense Puzzles
Skill: Using verb tenses correctly

If verb tenses puzzle your students, this activity is sure to conquer their confusion! Divide the class into groups of four. Ask each student to fold a sheet of paper vertically two times to create three columns; then have him fold his paper in half twice. When the student unfolds his paper, he should have 12 small boxes. Next, assign a different set of three verbs below to each student in a group. Have the student label the first row of boxes on his paper "Past," "Present," and "Future" as shown. Then have him label each remaining box with a sentence that uses one of the verbs in the correct tense (see the example; allow students to use helping verbs as needed). After the student proofreads his sentences, have him cut the boxes apart and place them in an envelope labeled with his name. Direct students in each group to swap envelopes and try to reassemble the charts correctly. Make the activity even more challenging by having each child make an additional chart that features the present, past, and future perfect tenses.

For additional practice with verb tenses, see the reproducible on page 41.

Past	Present	Future
I broke the window.	Today we are breaking our time capsules open.	I will break his record tomorrow.
She skipped home.	I am skipping rope right now.	Meg will skip in tomorrow's race.
Sean played ball on Tuesday.	He is playing soccer.	They will be playing at 10:00 tomorrow.

Verbs to Use			
ask	break	run	laugh
follow	skip	hop	leave
ride	play	say	talk

An Irregular Display
Skill: Identifying and using irregular verbs

Watch verb skills take shape with this student-made display of irregular verbs! Give each student three half sheets of construction paper, scissors, and a marker; then assign her an irregular verb, such as the ones listed. Direct the student to cut each of her construction paper sheets into an irregular shape. Have her label the three shapes with the present, past, and past participle forms of her verb. Pin the cutouts on a bulletin board as shown and discuss the verbs. Then, while students are out of the room, remove about one-third to one-half of the shapes. When students return, challenge them to identify the missing verb forms. Also use the display as a reference during writing workshops or other grammar lessons. Provide additional construction paper so students can add to the display as they think of more irregular verbs.

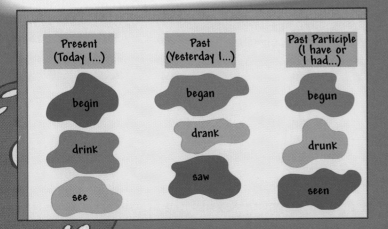

Irregular Verb Forms		
Present (Today I…)	**Past** (Yesterday I…)	**Past Participle** (I have or I had…)
begin	began	begun
break	broke	broken
bring	brought	brought
do	did	done
drink	drank	drunk
eat	ate	eaten
give	gave	given
go	went	gone
know	knew	known
lose	lost	lost
ride	rode	ridden
ring	rang	rung
rise	rose	risen
see	saw	seen
swim	swam	swum

To Be or Not to Be

Skill: Using linking verbs correctly

Unlock the mystery of linking verbs with this activity. Give each student eight index cards and a marker. Have the student label his cards with these linking verbs (one per card): *am, are, is, was, were, be, being, been.* When each student is ready, read aloud one of the sentences shown. At your signal, have each child hold up the card with the correct linking verb. Repeat with the remaining sentences.

Next, instruct each student to write five sentences on his paper, omitting the linking verb in each one. After students have finished, divide the class into groups of four. Direct one student in each group to read his sentences aloud one at a time to his group mates. Have each of the other group members hold up the appropriate card. Repeat until every student has shared his sentences. For more practice with linking verbs, see the reproducible on page 43.

Sample sentences
- This book ____ heavy. *(is)*
- I ____ so proud of you. *(am)*
- They ____ playing a game tonight. *(are)*
- The book we read yesterday ____ sad. *(was)*
- We ____ going to the park when it started to rain. *(were)*
- How long will you ____ in town? *(be)*
- Everyone was ____ quiet in the hallway. *(being)*
- It has ____ a long time since I have seen you. *(been)*

Verb Concentration

Skill: Subject-verb agreement

Concentrate on sharpening subject-verb agreement skills with this partner game. List the subjects and verbs shown below on the board. Then divide the class into pairs. Give each twosome 20 index cards and a marker. Have each pair follow the directions listed to prepare and play Verb Concentration. When each twosome has finished playing, display a copy of the answer key on the overhead projector.

Directions for each student pair:
1. Write each subject and verb on a separate index card.
2. Shuffle the cards. Then deal them facedown in a 4 x 5 grid.
3. In turn, flip two cards. If the cards make a phrase that illustrates correct subject-verb agreement, keep them and take another turn. If the cards do not match, turn them back over.
4. The game is over when no more matches can be made.
5. Check your matches using the answer key shown. Score one point for each correct match. Subtract one point for each incorrect match. The winner is the player with the higher score.

Answer Key

singular subjects *(match any singular verb in the list)*
Grandma   actress   baby
principal   firefighter

plural subjects *(match any plural verb in the list)*
twins   waiters   parrots
reporters   winners

singular verbs *(match any singular subject in the list)*
is giggling   shouted   wails
was whispering   buys

plural verbs *(match any plural subject in the list)*
play   are singing   were arguing
yell   have been jumping

Name That Verb!

It's time for you to cash in on your knowledge of verbs by playing Name That Verb! Name the correct verbs and you could walk away with the $15,000 jackpot!

1. It _____ very cold in December and January.
   is = $106, are = $112, be = $145

2. Snow _____ to fall early this morning.
   begin = $200, began = $211, begun = $256

3. I have _____ lots of traffic jams here.
   see = $309, saw = $314, seen = $321

4. Ben will _____ snowballs at Mia.
   throw = $419, threw = $439, thrown = $467

5. Karen and I _____ on our walk today.
   freeze = $516, froze = $578, frozen = $596

6. We should have _____ scarves and mittens.
   bring = $643, brings = $673, brought = $693

7. As soon as we reached home, we _____ hot cocoa.
   drink = $784, drank = $791, drunk = $799

8. One of my friends _____ on the ice.
   fall = $836, fell = $842, fallen = $851

9. I had _____ my bike for hours before I fell.
   ridden = $912, rode = $924, ride = $927

10. I will _____ to catch up with my friends.
    run = $1,007; ran = $1,009; running = $1,111

11. We had _____ the pictures by the time Dad got home.
    hang = $1,000; hung = $1,009; hanged = $1,003

12. Kevin should have _____ us a letter by now.
    written = $1,246; wrote = $1,278; write = $1,097

13. She _____ her arm in a sledding accident.
    break = $2,022; broke = $2,032; broken = $2,042

14. I have _____ skiing many times.
    go = $2,068; went = $2,078; gone = $2,088

15. Mitch has _____ to our house before.
    come = $2,745; came = $2,753; comes = $2,786

Directions: Read each sentence. Underline the verb that correctly completes the sentence. Then write that verb's value in the cash column. When you're finished, add the amounts in the cash column. If your total is $15,000, you win! If not, check your work. You may be only a few dollars away from winning the jackpot!

Cash Column

1. _____
2. _____
3. _____
4. _____
5. _____
6. _____
7. _____
8. _____
9. _____
10. _____
11. _____
12. _____
13. _____
14. _____
15. _____
TOTAL _____

Note to the teacher: If desired, provide students with calculators to help them complete this page.

41

Life Raft Patterns

Use with "Save Our Ship!" on page 38.

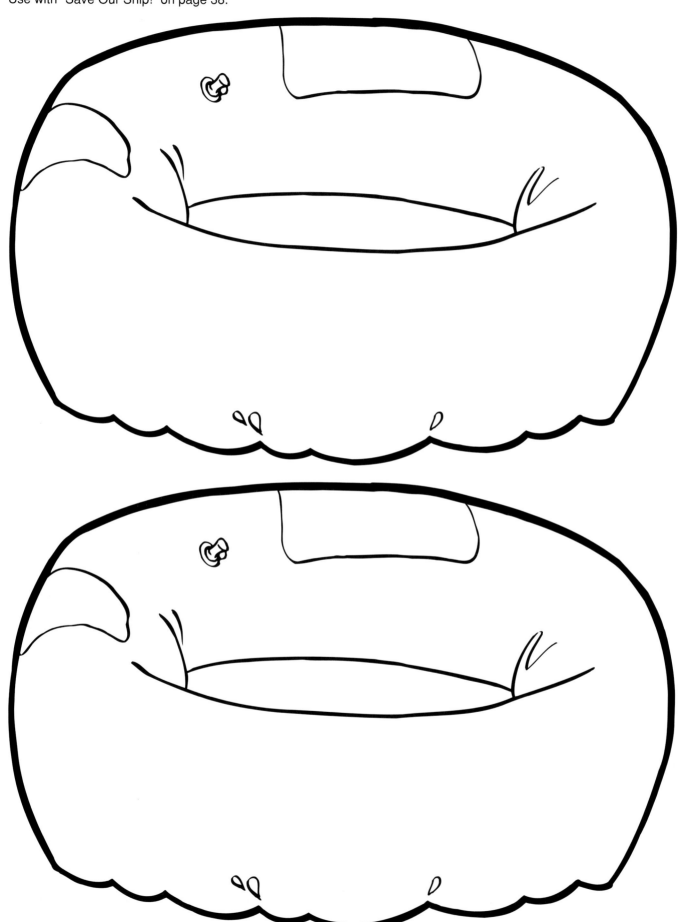

Missing Links

Did you know that not all linking verbs are forms of the verb *to be?* Well, they're not! Practice identifying some of these other linking verbs by completing Parts 1 and 2 below.

Part 1: Read each sentence and find the linking verb. Write the linking verb in the numbered link below.

1. The tiger looks tame to me.
2. Her roses smell lovely to me.
3. I grew restless waiting for the train.
4. That music sounds wonderful.
5. The bus driver seemed annoyed because we were singing.
6. Mom remained calm during the fire.
7. She became a princess when she married the prince.
8. The dessert tasted very sweet.

1.   2.   3.   4.   5.   6.   7.   8.

Part 2: Write a verb from the chain above in each blank below. Then draw an arrow to connect the two words that the verb links. See the example.

Example: The pillow <u>feels</u> soft.

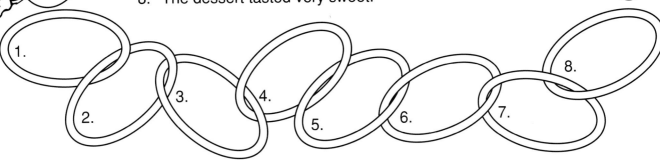

1. Mary _____ president when she won the election.

2. My mom _____ happy that I gave her the birthday present.

3. Your idea _____ great to me!

4. She _____ fantastic in her new dress.

5. The teacher _____ impatient when I forgot my homework again.

6. Those dirty socks _____ terrible!

7. Jake _____ tennis champion for many years.

8. The dinner you made _____ delicious.

Bonus Box: Circle the linking verb in Part 2 with a red crayon or marker if it is followed by a predicate adjective. Circle the linking verb in blue if it is followed by a predicate noun.

©The Education Center, Inc. • *THE MAILBOX®* • *Intermediate* • Dec/Jan 2001–2 • Key p. 306

Note to the teacher: The student will need red and blue crayons or markers to complete the Bonus Box activity.

Nailing Narrative Writing
Teaching Students to Write Well-Constructed Narratives

Help your students nail their narrative-writing assignments with the following ideas on developing good plots, settings, characters, and more.

with ideas by Isabel R. Marvin

Plot

Young writers often write themselves into a corner because they have no basic direction in mind. Help them use the following tips for developing good plots.

- Tell about only one happening or solve only one problem. In other words, tell just one story.
- Cover a short time span. Don't try to tell a story that takes a character from birth to death.
- Limit yourself to four or five different actions. Support each action with at least two details.
- Organize the story according to a logical order (i.e., describe what happens first, second, third, and so on). Be sure your story has a beginning, middle, and end.

Activity: Discuss the above tips with the class. Then challenge each student to write a one-paragraph description of a plot for a personal narrative. To help students, provide the list of suggestions shown. After everyone has finished, divide the class into pairs. Have each twosome evaluate their two plots according to the above tips. Collect the paragraphs; then meet with any student whose plot is unworkable.

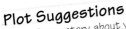

Plot Suggestions
- a funny story about your pet
- the birth of a younger sibling
- being lost or losing something you value
- a time of great joy or pain
- moving
- making or losing friends
- the effort in reaching some prize or goal
- a favorite or miserable day

Setting

A story's setting tells when and where the story is happening. Lead students to develop the setting of a story by using these techniques.

- Introduce the setting at the beginning of your story so the reader knows where and when the story takes place.
- Don't state the setting directly, such as "My story is happening in the present, and we are at home." Instead, set the stage without being obvious. For example, "Joanne awoke to see the sun shining through her bedroom window. Soon her mother would call her for breakfast." In this example, the reader is told indirectly that the setting is Joanne's bedroom in the early morning.
- Include no more than two settings in your narrative.

Activity: Choose several stories or novels that do a good job of indirectly giving the setting of the story in the opening paragraph. Read aloud each opening paragraph; then ask students to identify each story's setting. Next, list the following settings on the board: sea, desert, library, city street, classroom, fast-food restaurant, grocery store. Have each student choose one item from the board and write the first paragraph of a story with that setting. Challenge the student to inform the reader of the story's setting without actually naming it. Have each child read his paragraph aloud and challenge classmates to identify the setting. If desired, discuss details that could have been added to a paragraph to more clearly describe the setting.

Characters

If a writer has developed a character well, the reader will care about the character and his or her problem. Guide students to use these tips for developing characters with which readers can identify and empathize.
- Introduce characters at the beginning of your story.
- Limit yourself to no more than four characters.
- Show instead of tell. For example, don't tell the reader that the character is vain. Instead, show the character looking in every mirror that he walks by.

Activity: Write the following list of character traits on the board: brave, selfish, frightened, nervous, confident, cranky, determined, sad, lazy, clever, greedy. Tell each student to choose one trait and write a paragraph describing an imaginary character with this quality without directly stating it. Have partners exchange papers and try to identify the trait being developed.

Dialogue

Conversation in a story or book must be highly selective. It should either develop a character or move the plot along. Share these dialogue-writing tips with students.
- Avoid random dialogue; use dialogue to either develop a character or move the plot.
- A story shouldn't be entirely dialogue. Intersperse dialogue with action.

Activity: Make a copy of a page or short chapter from a story that contains good dialogue. Also prepare a transparency of the example. Display the transparency; then have students number each example of dialogue as you do the same on the transparency. Next, divide the class into small groups. Have each group discuss the examples and determine whether each one develops the character, moves the plot, or does both. Discuss the groups' answers together as a class.

Ending

A good writer knows the ending before he begins. If not, he might never get to the ending! Encourage students to write strong endings with the following suggestions.
- Tell how the activity ends or how the problem is solved.
- Limit the ending to two or three sentences.
- If your narrative is an imaginative story, don't solve the protagonist's problem completely by magic. Have the protagonist solve the conflict by her own efforts or accept the fact that the problem can't be solved. Also avoid solving the problem with an extreme circumstance (such as having the bad guy die or go crazy).
- If your narrative tells about something that happened to you personally, tell what you thought, felt, or learned through the experience.

Activity: Direct each student to copy the ending of a favorite story. Have the student read aloud the ending to the class and explain why he thinks it is a strong conclusion.

Sharpening Expository Writing Skills

Point the way to sharper expository writing skills with the following ready-to-use activities and reproducibles.

with ideas by Julia Alarie, Essex Middle School, Essex, VT

Expository Exposure
Skills: Reading and evaluating expository text, comparing and contrasting

Before students try to write their own expository compositions, let them get acquainted with a few good models of this type of writing. Collect a variety of expository texts, such as cookbooks, how-to books, game directions, magazine and newspaper articles that explain how to do something, and empty food boxes that include preparation directions. Divide the class into groups; then give each group several of the items, a sheet of chart paper labeled as shown, and a marker. Challenge each group to examine the items and list ways they are alike and different on the chart.

After the groups share their charts, discuss the information to the right about expository writing. Then challenge students to bring in other examples of expository text to post on a bulletin board titled "Explanation Inspiration." If desired, title another section of the board "Explanation Aggravation." Then have students bring in examples of poorly written explanations. Have each child explain why an explanation confused him before he adds it to the display.

ALIKE	DIFFERENT
Use words like "first," "then," and "next"	Some are written in paragraphs, others in numbered steps
Tell how to do something	
Give steps that are in order	

- Expository writing tells or explains how to do something.

- The writer uses transitional or linking words—such as first, then, next, and finally—to help the reader understand the order of the explanation's steps.

Picture This!
Skills: Writing directions, listening

Trying to picture a simple way for students to get their feet wet with expository writing? This activity fills the bill! In advance, make a transparency of the directions shown. Provide each student with a sheet of drawing paper and a few colored pencils. Then follow these steps:

1. Read the directions aloud. Direct students to follow each step as you read it.
2. Read the directions aloud a second time. Ask students to name the special transitional words that helped them understand the order of the steps *(first, then, next, after, finally)*.
3. Divide the class into pairs. Have the students in each twosome compare their drawings. Discuss as a class differences students observe in their pictures.
4. Display the directions on the overhead projector. Instruct each pair to cooperatively write a more explicit set of instructions that will produce more similar pictures than those compared in Step 3.
5. Have each pair read aloud its directions. Vote to select the most clearly written set.
6. Ask each student to turn over her first drawing. Then have students repeat Step 1 using the directions chosen in Step 5.
7. Have the student pairs compare their second drawings.

Directions:
First, use your colored pencils to draw a cat on your paper.
Then sketch a tree near the cat.
Next, draw a bird in the tree.
After drawing the bird, place a cloud in the sky.
Finally, add a large dog to the picture.

Scenario: Your favorite musical group has agreed to do a private concert just for your class. But word about the group's visit has leaked out. Now thousands of crazed fans will be invading your school in a matter of minutes. To keep your favorite group from being mobbed, you've decided to hide them in your school.

Directions: Write precise directions explaining how to get from your classroom to the hiding spot you selected. Don't forget to use transitional words that show the sequence of the actions that must be taken. Practice your speech so you'll be ready to give it to your famous friends before the mob arrives.

Let's Get Out of Here!
Skills: Writing and giving an expository speech

Prepare students for writing their own expository compositions with a top secret speech-making project! In advance, cut one slip of paper for each student. Label each slip with a different location in your school, such as the office, cafeteria, library, parking lot, gym, music room, or playground. Place the slips in a paper bag. Then follow these steps:

1. Ask students to name their favorite musical groups. Discuss how students would react if they found out that one of the groups was going to give a private concert for your class.
2. Have each student draw a slip from the bag. Then read or display the scenario and directions shown.
3. Provide time for students to write and practice their expository speeches.
4. Have each student give his speech without identifying the final destination. Challenge his classmates to try to name the hiding spot.

Tell Me Why
Skill: Writing an expository paragraph

If your students aren't ready to write multiparagraph expository compositions, get them started with this single-paragraph activity. To begin, ask students, "Why is it important to do homework?" Write students' responses on the board. Then challenge the class to prioritize the reasons according to importance. Next, model for students how to use the prioritized list to write an expository paragraph such as the example shown. Point out that you used the prewriting strategy of listing and prioritizing reasons to help you plan the paragraph. Also have students identify

- the topic sentence, which states the purpose of the paragraph
- the examples that explain the topic
- the use of time words—such as *first, second,* and *third*—to keep the examples in order
- the conclusion that wraps up the paragraph by restating the topic sentence

Once students have studied the model, divide the class into pairs. Have each twosome choose one of the starters shown below (making sure they both agree with the statement) and work together to write an expository paragraph.

Homework Doesn't Hurt

Even though it's sometimes a pain, doing homework is a good idea. First, homework helps you practice what you learned in school. If you didn't do homework, you might not become good at a new skill. Second, homework helps you realize when you are confused about a skill. If you can't do the homework easily, then you'll know to ask the teacher for extra help. Third, homework helps you learn to study better. For example, doing homework helps you learn to manage your time. It also helps you review what you learned in class that day. So don't complain about homework. It's actually good for you!

Include at least three reasons to explain why...
- it's hard to be a big brother or sister (or a little brother or sister)
- snow days are very exciting
- being a teacher is a challenging job
- best friends are great to have
- playing team sports can really help a child
- it's important to have computer skills

Pam Crane

47

To Be Organized or Not to Be Organized
Skill: Writing an expository paragraph

Challenge students to take a closer look at home, sweet home with this activity! Display a magazine article or book about becoming better organized. Ask students, "In which book would your bedroom more likely be featured: *Beautifully Organized Bedrooms* or *Disorganized Disasters*?" After students respond, have each child draw the chart shown on her paper. Then have her follow the steps listed below. After students share their paragraphs, encourage them to actually follow the directions. Suggest that any interested child take before and after photos of her bedroom to share with the class.

Steps:
1. Box 1: Identify the most disorganized area in your bedroom (closet, dresser drawers, desk, bookshelf, cabinet, etc.).
2. Box 2: List the steps you need to take to organize the area. Number them in a logical order.
3. Box 3: List the materials you'll need.
4. Use your planning sheet and transitional words like *first, next, after,* and *finally* to write a paragraph explaining how to organize the problem area. Include specific and descriptive details that relate to your topic.

1. Area:

2. Steps:

3. Materials:

If the Shoe Fits...Tie It!
Skills: Writing directions, revising

Ease students into more involved expository writing by focusing on familiar tasks that they do almost without thinking. Ask a student to demonstrate the art of shoe tying. After the demonstration, challenge the class to write precise directions on how to accomplish this feat. Help students brainstorm a list of related words, such as *laces, tongue, grommet,* or *knot.* Then have students work together to list the steps in order and use them to cooperatively write a paragraph.

After students are satisfied with the directions, divide the class into pairs. (Make sure that at least one child in each twosome is wearing laced shoes.) Instruct one student in each pair to read the directions aloud and the other child to follow them exactly as described. Discuss the results; then help students revise the directions. As a follow-up, have each child choose a topic shown and write his own set of directions for completing the task.

How-To Topics
- brush teeth
- make a bed
- set a table
- draw a stick person
- add 58 to 97
- check out a library book
- make microwave popcorn
- find the word *sneaker* in a dictionary

Here we are at Pencil Point Water Park!

TOUR GUIDE

Pencil Point Water Park

A Nice Place to Visit
Skills: Planning and writing an expository composition

Don't look now, but there's an expository writing activity right in your own backyard! Tell students that they have been hired by your town to plan and describe a tour to give the town's visitors. The mayor will review all plans and pick the best tour. After students follow the directions shown, have them meet in small groups to share their compositions.

Directions: The tour will start at 9:00 A.M. and end at 3:00 P.M. It will include a one-hour lunch.

1. List the must-see spots in your town, including a restaurant to visit for lunch.
2. Note how much time you'll need to spend at each spot, including travel time to and from the location.
3. From the list, choose the spots you will include on your tour. Then write an itinerary (see the example) that lists the locations in order, including time frames.
4. Write an explanation of your tour to give to your town's mayor.

Itinerary

9:00 A.M.–12:00 P.M.	Shaker Village
12:00 P.M.–1:00 P.M.	Lunch at the Cozy Café
1:00 P.M.–1:45 P.M.	Town Square and Garden
1:45 P.M.–2:30 P.M.	High Bridge Park
2:30 P.M.–3:00 P.M.	Sims Ice-Cream Parlor

Keys to Raising a Terrific Kid

Some people say, "Kids should come with a set of instructions!" Being a kid yourself, you probably know exactly what those instructions should be.

Part 1:
1. On scrap paper or the back of this page, list ten steps for raising a terrific kid.
2. Read over your list. Then number the steps to show the most logical sequence.
3. Rewrite the list in order on the lines below.

1. _____

2. _____

3. _____

4. _____

5. _____

6. _____

7. _____

8. _____

9. _____

10. _____

Part 2: On another sheet of paper, rewrite your list of steps in the form of an expository paragraph. Begin with a topic sentence that states the purpose of the paragraph. Then use transitional words like *first, second, third, then, next, after,* and *finally* to help the reader understand the sequence of steps. End your paragraph with a concluding sentence.

Bonus Box: Design a poster that illustrates one or more of the keys you listed above.

Put On a Happy Face!

Uh-oh! You're in a terrible mood. All your friends want to cheer you up. But they don't know why you're grumpy or what they can do to improve your mood. You're the only person who can clue them in. Fill in the blanks below so your friends can help you put on a happy face.

How I feel: _____

Why I feel this way: _____

_____

Steps to Cheer Me Up

First, _____

_____

Second, _____

_____

Then _____

_____

Next, _____

_____

After _____

_____

Later, _____

_____

Finally, _____

_____

By then, I'll be feeling _____ because

_____

_____

Bonus Box: Write the steps you can take to cheer up your best friend.

Note to the teacher: To provide more practice with expository writing, have each student use the information in the blanks to write an
50 expository paragraph or composition.

Examining Characters
Analyzing Characters in Literature

Take a closer look at the characters your students read about with the following literary analysis activities.

with ideas by Marcia Barton, Prairieville, LA

The Word Eater

lonely	sad
brave	smart
	angry

Baggage Check

Skills: Analyzing a character's traits, critical thinking

If you're ready to send weak literary analysis skills packing, then this hands-on activity should do the trick! After reading a story or book, divide the class into pairs. Have each pair use the materials and steps shown to create a suitcase that's packed with a favorite character's traits. Post the completed bags on a bulletin board; then challenge students to look at the traits inside each suitcase and guess the identity of the character who packed it.

Materials for each student pair: file folder, scissors, 12" x 18" sheet of brown construction paper, glue, old magazines, marker, unlined index card, tape, 4" length of yarn

Steps:

1. Trim a file folder as shown to make a suitcase shape.
2. Glue the opened suitcase shape on the brown construction paper. Cut around the suitcase to leave a small border of brown as shown. Let the glue dry.
3. Crease the suitcase at the fold. Cut a handle from the brown paper scraps and glue it to the suitcase as shown.
4. Choose a character from the story. Brainstorm at least five traits this character displayed.
5. For each trait, cut out a magazine picture that illustrates or represents that quality. (For example, a mirror could represent a character's self-centeredness.)
6. Glue each picture inside the suitcase and label it with the matching trait.
7. Fold the index card in half to make a luggage tag. Write "Who Am I?" on the front of the tag. Write the character's name on the inside.
8. Tape the tag to one end of the yarn. Tie the other end around the suitcase's handle.

Plus and Minus

Skill: Analyzing a character's traits

Use this idea to encourage students to search for both the good and not-so-good traits exhibited by a story's characters. After reading aloud the first chapter (or more) of a novel, list with students the characters encountered. On the board, draw a chart such as the one shown and label it with a character's name. Then invite students to name positive and negative traits that the character displayed as you list them on the board. Have students include the page number where the trait is described or evident.

Next, give each student an eight-inch circle of pastel construction paper. Have him fold his circle in half, open it, and draw a chart like the one on the board. Then direct the student to select one character (other than the one discussed earlier) and fill in the chart as he continues reading the book. To keep track of his chart, have the student fold the circle in half and use it as a bookmark. After students have read for several days (or have finished the book), extend this activity with "Flat or Round?" on page 52.

Jonas

−	+
frightened (p. 1)	obedient (p. 2)
apprehensive (p. 4)	careful about language (p. 3)

(Jonas)
The Giver

51

Flat or Round?

Skill: Identifying flat and round characters

Introduce the literary concept of flat and round characters with this follow-up to the "Plus and Minus" activity on page 51. A *round character* is well-developed, displays both positive and negative qualities, and undergoes change during the story. Like a cardboard cutout, a *flat character* lacks complexity and will not change or develop during the story. After students share the bookmarks they made in "Plus and Minus," discuss these questions:

- Which kind of character—flat or round—is most like a real person?
- Which famous characters in cartoons, movies, and television are flat? Which are round? Explain your choices.
- Which type makes the best main character? Why?
- Why might an author include flat characters in a story?
- How would you categorize the character you charted on your bookmark? Why?

Warning: Conflict Ahead!

Skills: Analyzing a character's conflicts, recalling story events

A good story always includes a conflict or two (or more!). Try this activity to help students analyze how characters confront and overcome obstacles. After the class finishes a story or book, divide students into groups. Have each group use the materials and steps shown to create a poster that illustrates the conflicts faced by a favorite character.

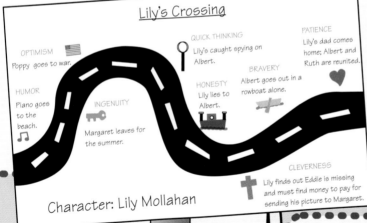

Materials for each group: sheet of poster board, markers or crayons, scissors, glue, construction paper scraps

Steps:

1. Choose a character. Brainstorm a list of the character's traits.
2. List the obstacles that your character encounters during the story. Write the conflicts in the order in which they occur, ending with the story's conclusion.
3. Make a small symbol from construction paper to represent each obstacle.
4. On the poster board, draw and color a road. Glue the obstacles in order along the road. Label each obstacle.
5. Write the character's name and the title of your book or story on the poster.
6. Decide as a group which trait(s) listed in Step 1 the character used to overcome each obstacle. Write the trait beside the obstacle.
7. Share your poster with the class.

What If...?

Skill: Analyzing the effect of a character's traits on the plot

What would have happened in *Charlotte's Web* if trusting Wilbur hadn't believed his spider friend when she said she liked him? What if Aunt Spiker and Aunt Sponge had not been horrible toward James in *James and the Giant Peach*? Challenge students to think about how a character's traits affect the plot of a story with this simple activity. With the class, choose a character and brainstorm a list of his or her character traits. Next, assign one trait to each student. Direct the student to use a thesaurus to find one or more antonyms for the trait. Then have the student write a paragraph that tells how the book (or chapter) would have ended differently if the character had displayed the opposite trait instead of the actual one. Provide time for students to share their paragraphs with the class.

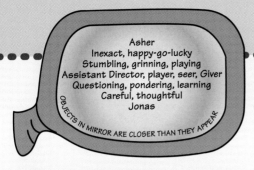

Closer Than They Appear

Skills: Identifying a foil, writing poetry

Sometimes an author will include a foil in his or her story. A *foil* is a character who sharply contrasts with the protagonist. The author includes the foil as a way to highlight traits of the main character. For example, a foil might be extremely greedy to highlight the generosity of the main character.

If the novel your class is reading includes a foil, try this activity. First, enlarge the rearview mirror pattern shown below on construction paper for each pair of students. Divide the class into pairs. Then have each twosome brainstorm ways that the foil's traits and actions call attention to those of the main character. After students share their lists, have each pair use the materials and steps shown to create a diamante poem that shows the differences between the two characters. Discuss Step 5 and why this message found on many rearview mirrors is appropriate when comparing a protagonist and a foil. *(There's a closer relationship between the main character and the foil than might appear at first.)* Post the poems on a bulletin board titled "Closer Than They Appear."

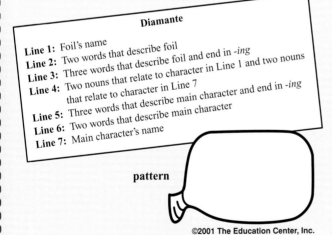

Diamante

Line 1: Foil's name
Line 2: Two words that describe foil
Line 3: Three words that describe foil and end in *-ing*
Line 4: Two nouns that relate to character in Line 1 and two nouns that relate to character in Line 7
Line 5: Three words that describe main character and end in *-ing*
Line 6: Two words that describe main character
Line 7: Main character's name

pattern

©2001 The Education Center, Inc.

Materials for each student pair: mirror pattern, 8" strip of aluminum foil, scissors, fine-point permanent marker, glue

Steps:
1. Use the form above to write a diamante about the book's main character and foil.
2. Cut a piece of aluminum foil to fit inside the mirror pattern.
3. Use the marker to copy the poem onto the foil.
4. Glue the foil on the pattern as shown.
5. Write the following along the bottom of the foil: "OBJECTS IN MIRROR ARE CLOSER THAN THEY APPEAR."

Lily

daydreamer
creative
impatient with Gram
dishonest
suspicious of Albert
lonely   unhappy
             with school
sneaky

BEFORE

caring toward Albert
daydreamer
more happy with school
more understanding of Gram
not lonely   more
                 honest

AFTER

Things Have Gotta Change!

Skills: Identifying static and changing characters, writing an explanation

Help students understand how characters change (or don't change) with this group activity. First, explain that a *static character* basically stays the same throughout the story. *Changing characters* change during the story because of what happens to them. Ask students to name characters the class has read about; then have them categorize each character as static or changing, providing evidence to support each choice.

Next, divide the class into small groups. Assign each group a character from the book students have just completed. Have each group use an overhead projector to trace two large silhouettes on white paper to represent its character. Then have the group follow these steps:
1. Cut out the silhouettes. Place them on a table facing each other.
2. Label the tracing on the left "BEFORE" and the one on the right "AFTER."
3. On the "BEFORE" silhouette, use colored pencils or markers to list traits the character displayed at the beginning of the story. On the "AFTER" shape, list traits exhibited at the end.
4. Glue the silhouettes on a large sheet of construction paper as shown. Write the character's name on the poster.

After the groups have shared their posters, have each student write a paragraph explaining the events and circumstances that caused his assigned character to change. Display these paragraphs with the posters.

Wise About Why

The famous psychologist Dr. Wilhelmina Wise spends her days explaining the "whys" of book characters' behavior. She carefully analyzes all the information provided in a novel. Then she explains why the characters behave as they do. Unfortunately, Dr. Wise is out of town today. In her absence, she wants you to do the explaining for her.

Directions: Choose a character. Write the character's name in the blank. Then fill in each column of the chart.

_____ character

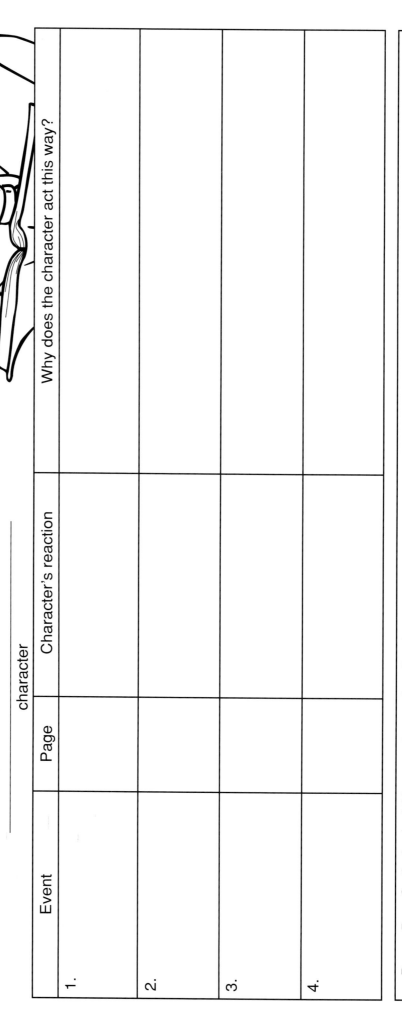

Event	Page	Character's reaction	Why does the character act this way?
1.			
2.			
3.			
4.			

Bonus Box: On the back of this page, draw a chart like the one above, leaving out the page column. Fill it in with information that tells how you reacted to a difficult time in your life and why you acted that way. Below the chart, answer these questions: Do circumstances matter? Why or why not?

Note to the teacher: Have students complete copies of this page while they read or at the conclusion of a book (or series of chapters). Provide extra copies of the page if needed.

Inside Private Eye

A good author doesn't just tell a reader what a character looks like on the outside. A good author also gives the reader information about what the character is like on the inside.

Part I:

1. Fill out the ID card for one character from your book. Draw a picture in the photo box.
2. Pretend that you are the character. On each line below, write one phrase about yourself.

	Name _____
	Age _____
	Gender _____
	Distinguishing physical traits:
	_____
	_____
Photo	_____

I like

- _____
- _____
- _____
- _____
- _____
- _____

I don't like

- _____
- _____
- _____
- _____
- _____
- _____

I believe

- _____
- _____
- _____
- _____
- _____

I dream

- _____
- _____
- _____
- _____
- _____

Part II: Continue pretending that you are the character you selected. Write one event from the book on these lines. _____

_____

On your own paper, write a letter to another character in the story. Use some of the phrases listed above to explain why you responded the way you did in that situation.

> **Bonus Box:** On the back of this page, write three phrases about yourself for each of the four boxes above. Then use the phrases to write a paragraph titled "This Is Who I Am."

Targeting Informational Text

Creative Activities on Reading Informational Text

Take aim at the skills needed to read and comprehend informational text with the following collection of creative activities. Bull's-eye!

with ideas by Kimberly A. Minafo, Pomona, NY

What Is Informational Text?

In the primary grades, students are prepared to read mainly narrative texts. As they move through the intermediate grades, they are required to read more informational text. *Informational text* refers to any reading selection that contains ideas, facts, and principles related to the biological, physical, or social world. It includes materials such as textbooks, nonfiction picture books and chapter books, articles, essays, brochures, manuals, and reference books.

Know, Show, and Go

Skills: Activating prior knowledge, summarizing, asking questions

Equip students to tackle an informational selection with this simple aid. First, give each student four index cards. Direct him to label each card at the top with one of the headings below. Then have the student tape the cards together end to end as shown.

Know, Show, and Go: All About [topic of reading selection]	I Think I Know!	It Just Goes to Show!	Where Do I Go?

Before the student reads the selection, have him label the "know" card with any prior knowledge he has about the text's topic. (If an entire group or class will read the same selection, let students share their prior knowledge before reading.) After the student finishes reading, have him summarize the selection's information on the "show" card. Then have him label the "go" card with questions he still has about the topic and resources he can use to answer them. Provide time for students to share their last two cards with the class or in small groups. If desired, challenge each student to use the resources he listed to find answers to the questions on his last card.

Reading Lifelines

- **Ask the Reader:** What have I learned or experienced that reminds me of what I'm reading?
- **50/50:** What part makes sense to me? What part is unclear?
- **Phone for Help:** What kind of help do I need? Where can I go for help?
  - Context clues
  - Reference tools
  - Text aids (print, graphics, illustrations, etc.)
  - Rereading
  - Reading parts before or after
  - Looking for signal words (*because, however, before,* etc.)
  - Looking at the organizational structure of the text (compare and contrast, cause and effect, sequence, etc.)

Who Wants to Be a Million-Dollar Reader?

Skill: Monitoring comprehension

When the going gets tough, a good reader keeps going, working around any obstacle to comprehension. Help your students learn how to confront comprehension roadblocks with this strategy, based on the popular television show *Who Wants to Be a Millionaire.* Display and discuss the poster shown. Then refer students to a brief textbook selection. Model for students how to use the poster's steps to confront a question or difficulty with the text. Then have each student read another informational selection and take notes on how she used the lifelines to monitor her comprehension. Discuss students' strategies. Then encourage students to refer to the poster each time they read an informational selection.

Text Aids

Print Features
- fonts
- boldfaced print
- colored print
- bullets
- titles
- headings
- subheadings
- italics
- labels
- captions

Graphic Aids
- diagrams
- sketches
- graphs
- figures
- maps
- charts
- tables
- timelines
- overlays

Organizational Aids
- table of contents
- index
- glossary
- preface
- pronunciation guide
- appendix

Illustrations
- photographs
- drawings
- labeled drawings
- paintings

What's It All About?

Skills: Making predictions, using text aids, setting a purpose for reading

Too often kids start an informational book without having any idea what it's about or why they're reading it. Needless to say, this cluelessness makes comprehension even more challenging! Use the following activities to help students learn to use a book's cover and other text aids to predict content and set a purpose for reading.

Activity 1:
1. Select an informational picture book and display its cover. Ask students, "What question do you think this book will answer?"
2. Have one student share his question as you write it on chart paper. Ask classmates with similar questions to share them.
3. Repeat Step 2 until each student has shared his question.
4. Have students read the book independently.
5. After reading, decide as a group which questions on the chart, if any, were answered in the book. Circle those questions.
6. Have students work together and use specific examples from the text to label a second chart with answers to the circled questions.

Activity 2:
1. Complete Steps 1–3 above.
2. Display the list of text aids shown above. Share with students that these features can help them make even more predictions about a book's content. Then point out some of the text aids in the informational book being used.
3. Have students suggest other questions the book might answer. Point out that it was easier to predict what the book would be about after examining the text aids.
4. Repeat Steps 4–6 above.

Noteworthy Outlining

Skills: Note taking, determining important information, outlining

A great way to actively process new ideas in an informational selection is by taking notes and creating an outline. But students often have a hard time with these critical skills. Give them a hand with the help of the graphic organizer on page 60. First, choose a reading selection that students can read along with you. Display a transparency of page 60 on the overhead projector. Read the directions on page 60 with students. Then model for them how to take notes on and outline the reading selection. (For the outlining steps, show students how to write a *topic outline* that contains only words and phrases rather than a more detailed sentence outline.) If desired, repeat the activity with another text selection until students are comfortable with the process. Then give each student a highlighter and have her complete a copy of the page (independently or with a partner) using a new text selection.

Defend or Detour?

Skills: Making and confirming predictions

Good readers make and confirm predictions as they read. To give students a chance to practice this important skill, choose a reading selection that has several sections. Have each student label an index card with a prediction about what she'll learn from reading the first section. After students read the section, have each child turn over her card and follow these directions:

- If you found evidence supporting your prediction, label the card "DEFEND." Then explain how the text confirmed your prediction. Give specific examples.
- If the text contradicts your prediction, label the card "DE-TOUR." Then explain what you learned that caused you to detour from your original prediction.

Provide time for students to share their cards. Then ask how they could improve their predictions. Guide students to consider using text aids (see the list on page 57) to help them. Point out any of these aids in the next section to be read. Then distribute new cards and repeat the activity.

Pass the Vocabulary Pie, Please!

Skill: Learning new vocabulary

Try this simple activity to introduce new words students might encounter in an informational selection. List on a chart any words from the selection that students may not know. As you read each word aloud, ask each child to give a thumbs-up signal if he knows the word, a thumbs-down if he doesn't know the word, and a so-so signal (see the illustration below) if he's not sure. After discussing the words' meanings, label a small paper plate for each word as shown. Ask students to help you complete each word "pie" with related words or concepts. Then have students read the selection. If desired, cut apart each plate after students have read the selection. Then challenge students to reassemble each pie correctly.

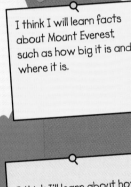

I think I will learn facts about Mount Everest, such as how big it is and where it is.

DEFEND
I could defend my prediction because I learned that the mountain is about 5½ miles high. I also learned that it is near Nepal and Tibet.

I think I'll learn about how beautiful it is on Mount Everest.

DETOUR
I think it is probably beautiful to look at, but there's a lot of danger. It's really cold. It's also very windy. Plus the air is thin and there are lots of dangerous avalanches.

What's the Plan, Stan?

Skill: Analyzing the structure of an informational selection

Authors use a variety of methods to organize informational text. Help students learn to recognize these organizational patterns using the reproducible on page 59. Have each student complete a copy of the page independently, with a partner, or in a small group. Then discuss the completed page as a class.

Next, mount eight sheets of chart paper on a bulletin board or wall. Label each chart with the name of a text pattern on page 59. As the class reads other informational selections, challenge students to identify the pattern each one uses and list it (by title) on the appropriate chart. After two weeks, tally the number of examples on each poster and discuss these questions:

- Which text pattern has the largest number of examples?
- Which text pattern(s) is used frequently for social studies selections? Science? Why do you think these patterns are used by authors of selections on these topics?
- Which type of pattern would you use if you were going to write a selection about [a topic you're currently studying]? Why?

To give students practice with analyzing the cause and effect pattern, use the reproducible graphic organizer on page 61.

What's the Plan, Stan?

Stanley J. Schlotmeyer is writing a book about the turtles of Tahiti. He knows that authors of informational materials use a variety of methods to organize their texts. But he can't decide which method to use in his book. Can you help Stan?

Organizational Patterns
- Cause and effect = **red**
- Compare and contrast = **purple**
- Description = **yellow**
- Enumeration = **green**
- Generalization = **brown**
- Problem and solution = **black**
- Question and answer = **orange**
- Sequence = **blue**

Part 1: Read each definition A–H below. Find the matching organizational pattern in the box. Then color the turtle to match.

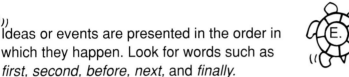

A. Ideas or events are presented in the order in which they happen. Look for words such as *first, second, before, next,* and *finally.*

B. Sometimes an author organizes text in a simple list. For example, the author may say that five points will be given about the topic. Then the author discusses each point one at a time. You can identify this pattern by words such as *first, second, third,* and so on.

C. The author makes a general statement and then supports it with specific examples. For example, the author might write "The Civil War was a time of great sadness" and then give examples that support that statement. Signal words to look for include *for example, for instance, specifically,* and *thus.*

D. In this pattern, the author explains or gives reasons for different phenomena. For example, the author might give a cause and its effects or an effect and its causes. You can identify this pattern by words such as *because, since, therefore, so,* and *for this reason.*

E. Sometimes an author will discuss two ideas, events, or items to show how they are alike and different. Watch for words such as *on the one hand, yet, but, rather, like, unlike, similarly,* and *in contrast.*

F. Sometimes an author will decide to simply ask important questions about the topic and then give the answers. You can spot this pattern by the use of words such as *who, what, why, where, when,* and *how.* Also look for question marks.

G. In this pattern, the author identifies problems and then gives possible solutions. Keep your eye out for signal words such as *propose, conclude, solution, research shows, a reason for,* and *the evidence is.*

H. This pattern uses colorful, descriptive language to help the reader visualize a process or an image. You'll find lots of descriptive details and adjectives in a selection that uses this pattern.

Part 2: Pretend that you are going to write each of the following books. On the back of this sheet, write the name of the organizational pattern you think would be best to use in each book.

a. *Calling All Kids Cookbook*
b. *Pollution: How We Can Stop It Now*
c. *Why the Sky Is Blue and Other Wonders*

d. *Dogs and Cats*
e. *Getting to Know the Rain Forest*
f. *How to Catch a Fish in Ten Easy Steps*

Note to the teacher: See "What's the Plan, Stan?" on page 58 for instructions on using this page. Students will need crayons or colored pencils to complete the activity. Point out to students that authors usually use more than one pattern to organize an informational piece of writing. However, the content in a single section of text is often organized according to a single pattern.

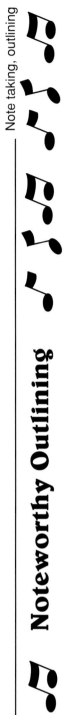

Note taking, outlining

Noteworthy Outlining

Topic: _____

To take notes on the selection:
1. Write the reading selection's topic on the line above.
2. Write each section's subtopic in a small box. Then take notes on each section as you read.
3. When you finish reading, highlight two or three of the most important ideas in each box.

To outline the selection:
1. Write each box's subtopic as a main heading (I–III) in the outline.
2. Write each box's highlighted ideas as details (A–C) in the outline.

Notes

Subtopic: _____

_____
_____
_____
_____
_____

Notes

Subtopic: _____

_____
_____
_____
_____
_____

Notes

Subtopic: _____

_____
_____
_____
_____
_____

Outline

Title: _____

I. _____

  A. _____

  B. _____

  C. _____

II. _____

  A. _____

  B. _____

  C. _____

III. _____

  A. _____

  B. _____

  C. _____

Note to the teacher: See "Noteworthy Outlining" on page 57 for instructions on using this page. Provide each student with a highlighter. If the reading selection has more than three sections, give each student an additional copy of this page.

"Paws" for the Cause

Fill in this organizer to show the cause and effect relationships in the text you are reading. Remember: Some effects may have more than one cause.

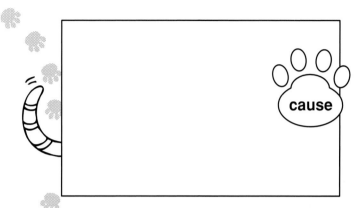

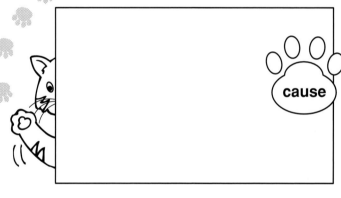

©The Education Center, Inc. • *THE MAILBOX*® • *Intermediate* • June/July 2002

Wrestling With Word Parts

Creative Activities on Prefixes, Suffixes, and Roots

Do your students wrestle with prefixes, suffixes, and roots? Then help them pin down these important word parts with the following can't-be-beat activities and reproducibles!

with ideas by Marsha Schmus, Shippensburg Area School District, Shippensburg, PA

Bright Beginning, Excellent Ending

Skills: Using affixes to form words, writing sentences

Begin and end the day with this easy-to-do word-study activity. In the morning, list three prefixes on the board (see the list of examples). Challenge each student to form a word with each prefix and then use all three words in a meaningful sentence. For example, if the prefixes *re-*, *sub-*, and *un-* are displayed, the student might write a sentence such as "I'm <u>unhappy</u> that we can't <u>revisit</u> the wonderful <u>submarine</u> exhibit." At the end of the day, list three suffixes on the board and repeat the challenge. Easy!

Prefixes	Suffixes
anti-	-al
astro-	-ble
auto-	-ed
bi-, bin-	-er
cent-	-ess
co-	-est
ex-	-ful
inter-	-ic
micro-	-ily
non-	-ing
oct-	-ist
pre-	-less
quadr-	-ly
re-	-ment
sub-	-ness
trans-	-ology
tri-	-sion
un-	-tion

A Novel Idea

Skills: Identifying words with affixes, categorizing

Use this activity to demonstrate how frequently affixes are used and how knowledge of them can help students tackle unfamiliar vocabulary. First, display a transparency of a page from your current read-aloud. Have students identify the words on the page that include affixes. Discuss each word's definition, using the meaning of the affix(es) and the context in which the word is used as tools. Next, ask each child to scan one or two pages of the book he is currently reading to find words that use prefixes and suffixes. Direct the student to list each word and its definition on his paper. Provide dictionaries for this step, if necessary.

When each student has listed several words, divide the class into groups of three or four. Give each group two sheets of chart paper, a marker, and a dictionary. Then direct the students in each group to follow the steps shown. Provide time for each group to share its chart with the class. As a variation, display a list of roots and their meanings (see page 67 for examples). Then repeat the activity, having students scan their novels for words formed from common roots.

Steps:

1. Have every group member share his or her list.
2. On one sheet of chart paper, compile a master list of the words found by your group. Check any words you're unsure of in a dictionary.
3. Brainstorm different ways to categorize the words. Choose one way.
4. On the other sheet of chart paper, draw a chart that categorizes the words in the manner you selected.
5. Decide which group member(s) will share the chart with the class.

Nouns and Verbs	Adjectives and Adverbs
frosting	thoughtful
actress	childish
bicycle	crazier
enjoyment	strangely
triangle	uncomfortable
afternoon	automatic
immigrate	extraordinarily
actor	wisely

A handy reference to use with these activities is *The New Reading Teacher's Book of Lists* by Dr. Edward Bernard Fry, Dr. Dona Lee Fountoukidis, and Jacqueline Kress Polk. You'll find detailed lists of prefixes, suffixes, and Latin and Greek roots, including their definitions and sample words.

Phony Fact

Skills: Using prefixes, suffixes, and word roots

Use this fun game of Phony Fact to give students a real workout with word parts! Post the chart shown. Also give each student or pair of students a dictionary. Invite one child to form a word using a root and at least one affix from the chart. Ask the class to decide whether the word is correct, checking a dictionary if necessary. If the word is correct, discuss its meaning and list it on the chart where indicated. If the word isn't correct, write it on the chart and determine with students why it is incorrect. Repeat the activity with three or four other words.

Next, divide the class into teams and give each team a dictionary. Challenge each team to secretly form four words not already on the chart: three correct and one incorrect. Have the team write each correct word in a sentence that explains its meaning, using a dictionary if necessary. Then have the team write a fourth sentence that defines the incorrect word. (See the example sentences.) Call on a team to read aloud its sentences in any order. Challenge each opposing team to identify the phony fact. Award a point for each correct guess. Then repeat with the remaining teams. Award bonus points or a small treat to the highest-scoring team.

1. When you <u>proclaim</u>, you declare something in public.
2. <u>Subfraction</u> is the study of the parts of the earth that are underground.
3. If you are <u>immobile</u>, you aren't able to be moved.
4. <u>Phonics</u> is the science of sound.

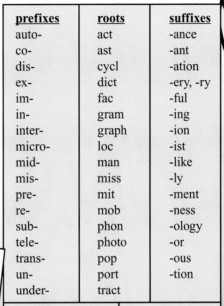

prefixes	roots	suffixes
auto-	act	-ance
co-	ast	-ant
dis-	cycl	-ation
ex-	dict	-ery, -ry
im-	fac	-ful
in-	gram	-ing
inter-	graph	-ion
micro-	loc	-ist
mid-	man	-like
mis-	miss	-ly
pre-	mit	-ment
re-	mob	-ness
sub-	phon	-ology
tele-	photo	-or
trans-	pop	-ous
un-	port	-tion
under-	tract	

correct words	incorrect words
location	popment
phonograph	mobous
photograph	

Family Photo

<u>migr</u>
(move)
migrate
immigrant
emigrate
migratory
migration

<u>phon</u>

phonograph
telephone
symphony

All in the Family

Skill: Using knowledge of roots to learn unfamiliar words

Try this weekly activity to help students learn the meanings of some common Latin and Greek roots. To prepare, cut a frame shape from poster board and label it as shown. Ask a few students to decorate the frame with markers or crayons. Then attach it to the chalkboard.

Each week, tape a sheet of chart paper on the board behind the frame. Label the paper with a root and several words that use it (see the example). Challenge students to figure out the root's meaning using the words' definitions. Also instruct students to think of other words that belong in the same family. At the end of the week, discuss students' answers and reveal the root's meaning. Then add to the chart the root's meaning and any other words suggested by students. Post the chart in the room. Also tape a new sheet of paper behind the frame so you can label it with a new root and word list on Monday. After you've displayed charts from several weeks, bind them together in a big book for students to use as a reference. For another activity on word roots, see the reproducible on page 67.

A Juicy Ending

Skill: Using suffixes to form words

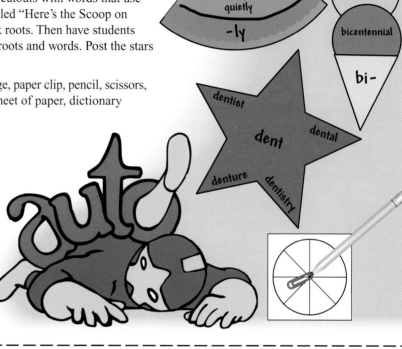

Make suffixes the center of attention with an activity that results in a "seed-sational" student-made display! Divide the class into teams. Then distribute the materials and display the steps shown. Have students staple their completed slices on a bulletin board titled "A Juicy Ending."

As a variation, reprogram the spinner pattern with prefixes. Then have students label paper cone shapes with the prefixes and ice-cream scoop cutouts with words that use them as shown. Display the cutouts on a bulletin board titled "Here's the Scoop on Prefixes." Or reprogram the spinner with Latin and Greek roots. Then have students label red, white, and blue star shapes, as shown, with the roots and words. Post the stars on a display titled "We Salute Roots!"

Materials for each team: one spinner pattern from this page, paper clip, pencil, scissors, white paper plate, green and red crayons, black marker, sheet of paper, dictionary

Steps:

1. Cut the paper plate into fourths. Draw a black line on each fourth, as shown, to make a watermelon slice.
2. Spin the paper clip as shown. Write the suffix you spin on the rounded rim of a slice. Brainstorm four words that use the suffix and list them on the paper.
3. Check the words in a dictionary to make sure they are correct.
4. After making necessary corrections, use the marker to list the words on the slice as shown.
5. Color the slice. Add black seeds with the marker.
6. Repeat Steps 2–4 three more times. If you spin a suffix you've already used, spin again.

Patterns
Use with "A Juicy Ending" above.

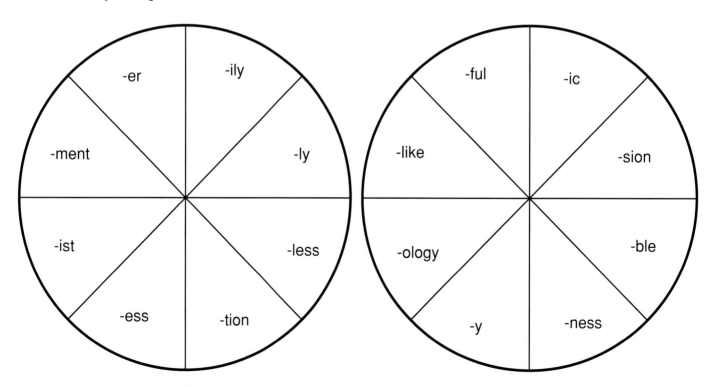

©The Education Center, Inc. • *THE MAILBOX® • Intermediate •* April/May 2002

Jumbled Journal

B. C. (Bone Crusher) Crunchwell loves two things: wrestling and writing in his journal. After his big match with Terrible Tarlton, B. C.'s head was still spinning, and his journal entries show it! Use your knowledge of prefixes and word roots to help B. C. unjumble his journal.

Prefixes
- **micro-:** small
- **auto-:** self
- **sub-:** under

Roots
- **vis, vid:** see
- **fract, frag:** break
- **aud:** hear

Directions: The underlined words in each journal entry are in the wrong blanks. Read each day's entry. Use context clues and the information in the box on the left to decide which word belongs in each blank. Then write the correct words on the numbered lines. The first one is done for you.

May 4
What would the other wrestlers say if they knew that studying (1) microscope was my hobby? While looking through my (2) microwave, I noticed a (3) microbiology that I had never seen before. My mom was so excited that she cooked me a special lunch in the (4) microorganism oven.

May 6
While waiting for my flying lessons, I began writing my (5) autopilot. Once I was in the air, I put the plane on (6) autograph to work on my draft. The plane flew (7) autobiography. If I ever want to become a famous author who is asked for his (8) automatically, I'd better set aside some time on the ground for writing!

May 9
During my (9) vision with my grandmother yesterday, it was (10) visit that her (11) evident was getting worse. She was unable to watch the (12) invisible I had brought for her. At times, she didn't even seem to see me. It was like I was (13) video! Tomorrow I'm taking her to an eye doctor.

May 11
Last night I worked on my boat models. I should have known that using (14) subject materials in the model (15) submerge would cause it to (16) substandard and never return to the surface. Using poor materials instead of good ones sure did (17) submarine me to lots of problems.

May 13
Yesterday I tripped over a (18) fragile of a chair I broke while training for my match with Terrible Tarlton. I soon learned that I had (19) fragment my foot. In my (20) fraction state, I was only able to complete a (21) fractured of the chores I needed to do.

May 16
I just got a call from the producer of a big theater. Her voice was barely (22) audition over my old telephone. She wants me to (23) audience in the theater's (24) audible for a part in a new musical about wrestling. If I get the part, I'll invite all my friends to be in the (25) auditorium.

1.   *microbiology*
2. _____
3. _____
4. _____
5. _____
6. _____
7. _____
8. _____
9. _____
10. _____
11. _____
12. _____
13. _____
14. _____
15. _____
16. _____
17. _____
18. _____
19. _____
20. _____
21. _____
22. _____
23. _____
24. _____
25. _____

Bonus Box: Write a short journal entry that B. C. might have written using these four words correctly: *preheat, pretest, preview, prescription.*

Alien Affixes

U. F. O. (Universally Feared Opponent) Jones, world-famous wrestler, needs your help! While on a training run, she found an alien spacecraft. Inside was an owner's manual. Unfortunately, parts of the manual are written in a strange extraterrestrial language. Follow the directions below to help U. F. O. read the manual and prepare for the alien driver's test!

Part 1: Read each sentence below and underline the prefix in the bold-faced word. Then number your paper 1–10 and write the meaning of each boldfaced word without using its prefix in the definition. Use the information in the box to help you.

Driving Guidelines	**Alien Vocabulary**
1. Don't touch the yellow dials because they have been **presweened** for speed.	**sweene** = to set
2. Avoid any ship from the planet Pikky since Pikky aliens are very **unrikitic.**	**stellu** = hourly
3. Discuss all flight plans with your **cozither.**	**troot** = to continue
4. Check the galatonium fuel supply **bistellu.**	**phratter** = to price
5. **Distroot** the flight if a red light starts to flash.	**zither** = pilot
6. If the engine breaks down, it can be **refeddled** with a few simple parts.	**feddle** = to build
7. The compass is the **octaplinky** shaped dial.	**rikitic** = friendly
8. Before approaching the landing pad, get **prelelluped** by the alien airport crew.	**lellup** = to approve
9. Try not to run out of gas since fuel in our galaxy is very **overphrattered.**	**grup** = to start
10. It's easy to **regrup** the engine if it doesn't turn on the first time you try.	**plinky** = side

Part 2: Below is a driver's examination from the spacecraft's planet. Answer the questions on your paper.

Driver's Exam

a. How many times in one day should you check the galatonium supply?

b. Explain the shape of the compass dial.

c. How many pilots are on the ship?

d. Are the speed dials set before, during, or after takeoff?

e. What should you do if a red light flashes during the flight?

f. If the engine breaks down, will it do any good to tow the spacecraft to a mechanic?

g. When should you let the alien airport crew know that you are landing?

h. Why should you avoid any spacecraft from the planet Pikky?

i. Why shouldn't you worry if the engine doesn't start on the first try?

j. Why should you carry extra alien cash when you travel?

©The Education Center, Inc. • THE MAILBOX® • Intermediate • April/May 2002 • Key p. 306

66   **Note to the teacher:** Have each student staple a piece of notebook paper behind this page before completing it as directed.

Seeing Stars!

Do you ever wrestle with trying to figure out the meanings of unfamiliar words? Knowing the meanings of word roots can help!

Directions: Read each sentence. Look in the box to find the boldfaced word's root. Read the root's meaning. Then, on your own paper, write a possible definition for the boldfaced word. Use the example below to help you.

Root: *Ped* means "foot."
Sentence: When you drive, watch out for **pedestrians** who are crossing the street.
Possible definition for *pedestrians:* people who travel on foot

Roots and Their Meanings

• **mob:** move	• **fug:** flee	• **surg, surr:** rise
• **cess:** go, yield	• **dict:** speak	• **anthr:** man
• **cogn:** know	• **reg:** guide, rule	• **gen:** birth, race
• **belli:** war	• **nov:** new	• **arch:** chief

1. The doctor said that the **mobility** of the man's arm would not be affected by the accident.

2. The treaty called for the **cessation** of all fighting.

3. He wasn't **cognizant** of the team's victory.

4. The bully was known for his **belligerent** attitude toward everyone.

5. The thief was a **fugitive** from the law.

6. The little girl's **diction** when she read the poem was nearly perfect.

7. That nation's **regime** is no longer in power.

8. Phyllis was a **novice** at in-line skating.

9. There is a **resurgent** interest in starting a chess club in our school.

10. He's known as a **philanthropist** who supports many charities.

11. That couple's **progeny** looks very much like them.

12. The three little pigs' **archenemy** is the Big Bad Wolf.

Bonus Box Color Code
really close = red
fairly close = blue
not very close = yellow
unsure = green

Bonus Box: Find each boldfaced word in the dictionary. Read the meanings. Then use the code to color each star according to how close your definition was to those given in the dictionary.

Note to the teacher: Use with "A Novel Idea" on page 62 and "All in the Family" on page 63. Students will need red, blue, yellow, and green crayons to complete the Bonus Box activity.

Tuning In to Multiple Meanings

Looking for cool ways to teach students about multiple-meaning words? Then tune in to the following activities, coming live to you from MMTV—Multiple-Meaning Television. Hey, turn up the volume!

by Julia Alarie—Gr. 6, Essex Middle School, Essex, VT

Word Bank

ease	poll	net	just	season
face	cast	open	key	pen
give	date	park	watch	bark
hide	arm	seal	land	back
vent	beat	throw	yard	bail
quack	mark	iron	like	admit

Can We Talk?

Skills: Writing dialogue using multiple-meaning words

Guide your students in writing dialogue as they explore words with multiple meanings. Invite students to act as guests and hosts on the popular MMTV talk show *Can We Talk?* Divide students into pairs and secretly assign each pair a word from the word bank. Have the students in each pair decide who will serve as the talk show host and who will be the guest. Then have each pair write a conversation that includes multiple meanings of the assigned word. Encourage each student to speak at least five times. Next, arrange a desk and two chairs at the front of the classroom for the show set. As each pair presents its dialogue, have the audience record the different ways a word is used.

The Yoke's on You!

Skills: Using multiple-meaning words, writing puns

Share with your students that a new comedy show, *The Yoke's on You!,* is looking for writers to create funny puns for its first episode. Explain that a *pun* is a joke that uses a play on words in a humorous way. (For example: Why was the skeleton afraid to go out on Halloween? Because he had no guts!) Mention that nearly all puns use words that have multiple meanings. Brainstorm a list of those words, such as *right, bank, band, run, stock, die, set,* and *line* (see also the word bank on this page). Then provide some introductions for students to use, such as

- What do you get when you cross a…?
- Knock, knock! Who's there?
- Why was the…?

Have students think about their puns overnight and then share their multiple-meaning laughs the next day.

Headline News, Weather, and Sports

Skills: Recognizing multiple meanings, writing a news story

To start off this winning writing activity, tell students that news headlines are written and then sometimes used with more than one story at MMTV. Then divide students into pairs and assign each pair a headline from the list. Have the pair discuss the multiple meanings that the headline could have. Then have each partner choose one of those meanings. Have the students work independently to create a news, weather, or sports story for the headline. Remind each junior reporter that his story should include the five Ws of a news story: Who? What? Where? When? and Why? The network's ratings are sure to climb when these stories are aired!

We've Got Game
What the Lumberjacks Saw
The Most Fantastic Tip
One Last Lap
The Lead Floats
Bat Found on Plate
Diamond Destroyed
Endangered Fish Found in Local Bed
Ancient Mold Discovered at Museum
Boy Brings Home 15-Foot Pike
Sap Runs Early This Spring
Missing Ring Returns
Farmer's Ram Injures Neighbor
Draft Ends
Woman Inherits Cape
Four Cases of Measles Reported

Prices Take Nosedive

Back to the Drawing Board

Skill: Illustrating multiple meanings

Introduce your students to Miss Unda Standing, the famous artist host of MMTV's *Back to the Drawing Board*. Each week she is given the title for a painting to create, and every week she misinterprets the meaning of that title! (Take a look at her most recent work.) Provide students with drawing paper and colored pencils or markers. Direct each student to come up with a title that includes a word that has multiple meanings. Then have her follow Miss Standing's example by creating a work of art that matches (well, sort of) that title. Post all of the masterpieces on a bulletin board titled "The Gallery of Mixed-Up Meanings."

And Now a Word From Our Sponsor...

Skill: Listing multiple meanings of a word

It won't take much effort to sell students on this fun multiple-meaning activity! Announce to the class that all of the shows on MMTV are sponsored by multiple-meaning words. Then tell students that MMTV would like to hire each of them to create an ad for a word that has multiple meanings. Direct the student to treat the word as if it were an actual product. Encourage the student to get her audience interested in buying the product by mentioning all the ways it can be used. Give each student a sheet of art paper on which to illustrate the final version of her ad. Be sure to provide dictionaries so students can verify the multiple ways words can be used. Multiple-meaning words—you just gotta have 'em!

Announcing
New and Improved
RUN!
Get RUN today.
It gets you there fast!
It scores in baseball!
It creates holes in your stockings!
Get one today!
Comes in fast, faster, and super fast!

A proud sponsor of MMTV

Hey, MMTV viewers! Don't miss the cool ready-to-use reproducible on the next page!

Who Wants to Be a Multiple-Meaning Millionaire?

Welcome to the most popular game show on television, also an exclusive of MMTV (Multiple-Meaning Television)! You are our next lucky contestant. All you have to do is decide on the word that correctly fills the blanks in each sentence below.

Fill in all of the blanks correctly and you will become our newest multiple-meaning millionaire! Good luck! (The first one has been done for you.)

1. It will __*tire*__ you out to change that flat __*tire*__ all by yourself.

2. Mary Jane decided to _____ on the couch for the _____ of the day.

3. David likes to _____ his carrots in sour cream _____.

4. Because she started the _____, the _____ department had to _____ Ruthie.

5. Everyone who wants to march in the parade must _____ a line and fill out the appropriate _____.

6. We watched Willy _____ over the counter, enter the bank _____, and take the money.

7. Hope _____ her _____ shoe at school.

8. If you want to _____ the part of Laura in the _____, you must be able to _____ the flute.

9. Josh drove his remote control toy _____ into the tropical fish _____ and created a huge mess.

10. You'd have to use a very special _____ to find the weight of a single fish _____.

11. When Jon turned _____, he knew he was on the _____ road.

12. With only _____ of an old comb, Seth made a fairly straight _____ in his hair right before we had to _____.

13. Every time you hear the bell _____, you must pay a _____.

14. Even though the kitten had recently fallen into a _____, it seemed to feel _____.

15. I'm going to _____ off of the computer and put another _____ in the fireplace.

Bonus Box: Choose three of these words: *hard, long, tick, quarter, relish, field, hood, wake.* Write a sentence with each one like those above, using at least two different meanings of the word. Use a dictionary if you need help.

In "Purr-fect" Agreement

Activities to Teach Subject-Verb Agreement

Try the following grammar activities to help your students "purr-fect" the important skill of subject-verb agreement!

with ideas by Bonnie Baumgras, Kirk L. Adams Elementary, Las Vegas, NV

laugh

High-Flyin' Agreement

Skills: Subject-verb agreement, verb tenses

Send grammar skills sailing high with this learning-charged art activity! Briefly review subjects and predicates and past, present, and future verb tenses with students. Explain that the subject and verb in a sentence must agree in person (first, second, and third) and in number (singular or plural). After discussing agreement, read aloud the picture book *Kites Sail High: A Book About Verbs* by Ruth Heller. Copy several sentences from the book onto a transparency and point out the correct agreement. Then have each child use the materials and steps shown to create a kite that's decorated with examples of correct agreement. After students share their kites, hang the high-flyin' projects from a bulletin board or your classroom ceiling.

Materials for each child: 8" square of white construction paper, 2' length of yarn, 5 paper bows cut from pastel paper (see pattern), crayons or markers, pencil, access to stapler

Steps:
1. Turn the white paper square to look like a kite; then label it with an action verb of your choice.
2. Decorate the kite with different designs.
3. On scrap paper, write five sentences that include the following:
   a. the verb in present tense with a singular subject
   b. the verb in present tense with a plural subject
   c. the verb in past tense with a singular subject
   d. the verb in past tense with a plural subject
   e. the verb in future tense with a singular subject
4. Ask a classmate to help you proofread your sentences. Make any corrections.
5. Write each sentence on a bow cutout.
6. Staple one end of the yarn to the bottom of the kite. Then staple each bow onto the yarn.

Mary laughs at the kitten chasing the string.

My parents laugh at the weirdest things.

I laughed when I saw the movie.

Jack and Jill laughed when they saw me.

Ann will laugh when she sees her gift.

Pattern

Now "Ear" This!

Skills: Subject-verb agreement, listening

Your students will be happy to learn that their ears will usually tell them whether the subject and verb of a sentence agree. Give those ears plenty of practice with this simple listening activity. Before reading a story to students, use a pencil to lightly write in a few incorrect verbs to substitute for some of the correct ones. Slowly read the selection aloud, challenging students to listen for agreement mistakes. When students hear an error, direct them to tug one of their ears. Then ask one child to correct the mistake. Simple!

Indefinite Pronoun: a pronoun that doesn't name the word it replaces

Singular: another, anybody, anyone, anything, each, either, everybody, everyone, everything, much, neither, nobody, no one, nothing, one, somebody, someone, something
Plural: both, few, many, others, several
Either singular or plural: all, any, most, none, some (When these words refer to nouns or pronouns that can be counted, they are plural, as in "<u>All</u> of his <u>shirts were</u> in the laundry." When they refer to nouns or pronouns that can't be counted, they're singular, as in "<u>Most</u> of the <u>evening was</u> a total waste.")

Definite About Indefinite Pronouns
Skill: Subject-verb agreement with indefinite pronouns

Any, both, none—some subjects are definitely confusing when it comes to agreement! Help students learn how to write correct sentences using indefinite pronouns with this team game. In advance, write each of the listed pronouns on a separate index card. On the back of each card, write a number from 1 to 5. Then shuffle the cards and place them in a stack. Next, divide the class into several teams. Show the first person on Team 1 a card. If the student can use the pronoun correctly in a sentence, award his team the number of points on the back of the card. If the student cannot come up with a correct sentence, show the card to the first player on Team 2. Continue play in this manner until the cards are all used or time runs out. Declare the team with the highest score the winner.

somebody

4

Mistaken Messages
Skill: Reviewing subject-verb agreement

Review what students have learned about subject-verb agreement with this fun partner activity. Divide students into pairs. Give each pair a blank transparency, a wipe-off marker, and a die. Display a chart similar to the one shown. Have one student in each twosome roll the die to determine a subject and write a sentence that includes it. Direct his partner to repeat these steps. Then have each twosome rewrite one of its two sentences so that the agreement is incorrect. Finally, have the twosome copy their two sentences on a transparency in speech bubbles as shown.

Next, have each pair of students display its transparency and challenge the class to identify the mistaken message (the one that is incorrect). Also have the pair select a classmate to rewrite the incorrect sentence to correct its agreement. Continue until all student pairs have shared their sentences.

Roll a subject:
1 = the president of the United States
2 = a singer in a famous band
3 = your teacher
4 = your principal
5 = a well-known movie star
6 = a person you really admire

My cousin Lily and I am both great dancers.

Mrs. Adams was at the mall last night.

"Purr-fectly" Paired

Usually compound subjects are plural when they're joined by *and*. But some compound subjects are used together so often that they are considered one subject. When words like this are the sentence's subject, make the verb singular.

Example: Macaroni and cheese is my Dad's favorite meal.

Part 1: Circle the verb in each sentence. Write SQUEAK in the blank for every singular verb. Write MEOW in the blank for every plural verb.

1. _____ My shoes and socks (is, are) under the bed.
2. _____ Give and take (is, are) important in a friendship.
3. _____ Connie and Robert (was, were) the captains of the soccer team.
4. _____ The cats and dogs (is, are) chasing each other.
5. _____ Bacon and eggs (was, were) served at the club's breakfast.
6. _____ My computer and printer (is, are) turned off.
7. _____ Breaking and entering (is, are) a very serious crime.
8. _____ "Peace and quiet (is, are) all I want!" cried Mr. Greene.
9. _____ Art and math always (was, were) my two favorite subjects.
10. _____ Bread and butter (was, were) the only thing on her plate.

Each SQUEAK above is worth 7 points. Each MEOW is worth 10 points. Your total score should be 85 points.

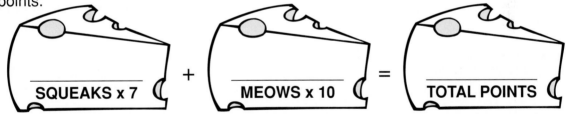

_____ SQUEAKS x 7   +   _____ MEOWS x 10   =   _____ TOTAL POINTS

When compound subjects are joined by *or,* the verb matches the subject that is closer to it.

Example: Either Millie or her brothers are putting up the groceries.

Part 2: Draw a cheese wedge ▷ around the correct verb.

1. Either she or her parents   **is**   **are**   calling us tonight.
2. Either Rachel or Robert   **is**   **are**   mowing our yard.
3. Either my brothers or my sister   **is**   **are**   responsible for the mess.
4. Either Stacey or the twins   **is**   **are**   working at the booth.
5. Either Kyle or the girls   **is**   **are**   painting the fence.

Bonus Box: On the back of this page or on another sheet of paper, write five sentences about events that have happened since the beginning of the school year. Use a compound subject in each sentence.

73

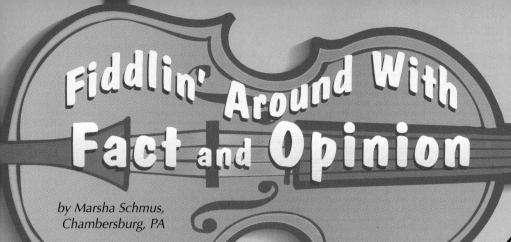

Fiddlin' Around With Fact and Opinion

by Marsha Schmus, Chambersburg, PA

Fast Facts (and Opinions)!
Skill: Writing facts and opinions

Encourage students to work cooperatively with this fast-thinking, beat-the-clock activity. Divide the class into two teams. Announce a topic such as school, vegetables, or outer space. Have one team brainstorm facts about the topic while the other team brainstorms opinions. Allow about five minutes for each team to collaborate and record its answers. At the end of the allotted time, have a volunteer from each team read aloud his team's list. Ask the other team to help you decide if each response is correct. Award one point for each correct fact or opinion. Then have the teams switch roles and play again with a different topic. The team with more points after four or five rounds is the winner. And that's a fact!

Personally, I think the TUNA FLAVOR is the best!

Truth in Advertising
Skill: Distinguishing between fact and opinion

Fact or opinion? With advertising, sometimes it's hard to tell! Share with students five or six packaged products or magazine advertisements about familiar items. Then divide the class into groups. Have each group read the text accompanying a product and then list the facts and opinions that group members can identify.

Next, have each student choose a favorite product that she uses regularly or has bought recently and design an ad for it. Allow the ad to be in the form of a TV commercial, a tape-recorded radio spot, or a magazine ad. Instruct the student to use facts taken directly from the product's packaging and include her own opinions based on personal experiences. Remind students that they should be cautious about accepting all statements on the package as facts, since the packaging is designed to sell as well as inform. Provide time for each student to present her ad to the class. During the presentation, have each classmate record at least one fact and one opinion that she recognizes in the ad. Invite volunteers to share their responses.

Fact-Finding Mission
Skill: Identifying facts in the news

Combine social studies and language arts with this current-events activity. Each day choose a student to share an event that she learned about from a newspaper or a news broadcast. Have the student begin by relating five facts about the event that include answers to the questions *who, what, where, when,* and *why.* Then have the student conclude by giving three personal opinions about the event. Invite other students to share their opinions about the event too. Within weeks, your students will recognize facts and opinions more readily—and be up on the news!

Leopards are the best fiddlers!

Fiddles are better than banjos!

THE TIMES
LEOPARD FIDDLERS CONVENTION TODAY

74

Yes, my ancestors can be traced back to ancient Egypt.

Getting to Know You
Skill: Writing facts and opinions

Invite students to get to know each other better while fine-tuning their fact-and-opinion skills. For a warm-up exercise, announce the name of a famous person. Have each student write eight to ten statements about that person. Then have the student classify each statement as either fact or opinion. Call on volunteers to share their statements.

Next, have each student write his name on a slip of paper, fold the slip, and put it in a bag. Draw pairs of names from the bag; then have the students in each pair meet. Direct each student to interview his partner and take notes. During the interview, each student must uncover five facts about his classmate and form five positive opinions. Have students check each other's lists to make sure the facts and opinions are classified correctly. Post the completed writings on a bulletin board titled "All About Us!"

The Facts of Life
Skills: Writing an autobiography, writing facts and opinions

You'll know your students a little better after this writing activity. And they'll know you better too! Instruct each student to write a short autobiography titled "My Elementary Years" that includes six facts and six opinions. Before students begin the assignment, discuss how opinions can be incorporated. (Examples: For me, broccoli is the best-tasting vegetable. My brother Samuel is the coolest guy.) To model the experience, write your autobiography telling about your elementary school years.

When finished, have each student underline the facts on her paper in red and the opinions in blue. Then invite her to share the most interesting fact and opinion about herself. (Share yours too!) Bind all of the stories into a booklet titled "Our Class: Up Close and Personal."

Absolutely the Very Best Vacation Spot on Earth!
Skills: Geography, creative writing

Sharpen both geography and writing skills with this creative project. First, invite students to bring to class a variety of travel brochures. Share the brochures, plus any of your own. Next, have each student design a brochure for a city, state, resort, park, or site that he has visited and knows well. Students should include the following factual information:

- name of the site, including its nickname or subtitle
- location
- how long it takes to travel to the site
- which forms of transportation are best to take
- interesting attractions
- climate of site's location

After including the facts, each student should embellish his brochure with several opinions. Opinions might describe breathtaking scenery, mouthwatering foods in award-winning restaurants, exciting amusement park rides, and other features of the site. To complete their brochures, have students add colorful illustrations that showcase their chosen attractions.

Hey! Let's go here! We can visit Uncle Albert!

NC ZOO
Asheboro, NC

Spicing Up the News

The news is supposed to be all facts, right? *The Daily Mews* wants to print opinions as well as facts. Read each news article below. Choose two of the articles to rewrite on another sheet of paper. Include at least five opinions in each article in addition to the given facts. Also include a different, more creative headline for each article.

(25¢) THE DAILY MEWS — "All the Facts!" March 30, 2002

FAD Parade

The FAD (Feline Appreciation Day) parade was held on Saturday morning at 10:00 A.M. The parade featured nine marching bands, five fire trucks, a Caterpillar tractor, dozens of clowns, and several floats honoring our town's distinguished cats.

The parade route traveled seven miles through the downtown area. Approximately 5,000 spectators lined the streets to join in the festivities.

Parent-Teacher Organization Bake Sale

The Catskills Elementary School PTO will host a bake sale and yard sale to raise money for the annual fourth-grade field trip to Katmandu. Parents will sell brownies, cakes, doughnuts, pies, and even homemade catsup!

The sale will take place Saturday from 9 A.M. to 5 P.M. in the school gymnasium. The PTO goal is to raise $2,000 to help students with their airline tickets.

Fire Levels Barn

More than 20 firefighters from three local departments fought a farm fire last night near Catawba. The fire began around 7:00 P.M. and totally destroyed a barn. The fire was brought completely under control by 11:00 P.M. All that remains is a pile of ashes.

A family of four cats is now without shelter. One eyewitness commented, "What a catastrophe!"

Fat Cats Win

The Fat Cats football team beat Crescent Valley last night 21–20. Leo Lee ran for 101 yards. He also scored two touchdowns. This is the Fat Cats' seventh straight win.

Next week, the team enters the playoffs with a perfect, unbeaten record. A crowd of 3,000 fans is expected at the game. Go, Cats!

Bonus Box: Choose one of the two articles that you didn't rewrite. Write the story using only opinions.

MATH UNITS

The TIMES

A Special Edition of Multiplication Ideas

Extra! Extra! Read all about it! Looking for some newsworthy ideas for teaching multiplication skills? Then check out the following creative activities, games, and reproducibles.

by Irving P. Crump

Four-Square Facts
Skill: Basic multiplication facts

Basic facts are in the headlines with this fun game! Divide students into groups of three or four and then provide each group with a deck of cards (all face cards are removed, ace equals one, and each number card equals its value). To begin, a dealer deals four cards in a 2 x 2 array to each player. He places the remaining cards in a stack and turns over the top card. He places this card beside the stack to begin a discard pile. The object of the game is to have the greatest product. To play:

1. Each player turns over any two of his four cards. The other two cards remain facedown.
2. Each player mentally multiplies the numbers on his two cards, as well as those on his opponents' cards.
3. The player to the dealer's left begins. If this player thinks he has the greatest product and no one can top it, he may "freeze." Each remaining player will then have one turn to try to beat that product. If the first player does not freeze, he draws the top card from either the deck or the discard pile. He then swaps one of his four cards with the one he drew. The card that is swapped is then placed faceup on the discard pile.
4. Play continues to the left. A player may freeze at any time when it's his turn if he thinks he has the greatest product.
5. After a player freezes and each of the other players has had one final turn, each player declares his product. A player may declare the product of the two cards showing, or he may choose any two of his cards and multiply them together. Thus, a player could pick up his two facedown cards, multiply them together, and possibly beat the current greatest product.
6. In case of a tie, players multiply their remaining two cards to see who has the greater product.

After a winner is determined, each player records his product (or products, if there's a tie) as his score for that round. Cards are then reshuffled to play another round.

Facts War
Skill: Basic multiplication facts

This fast-paced game is similar to the traditional card game War, but players compare products instead of single cards. Provide each pair of students with a deck of playing cards (ace equals one, number cards equal their values, and each face card equals ten). If needed, provide each pair of students with a multiplication table for checking. To play:

1. The dealer deals all of the cards facedown—half to her opponent and half to herself.
2. Each player turns over her first two cards, multiplies the two values, and announces the product.
3. The player with the higher product wins all four cards.
4. If the products are the same (8 x 5 = 4 x king), each player repeats Step 2. The winner keeps all eight cards.
5. If there's still a tie, then Step 2 is repeated. The player with the higher product keeps all of the cards that have been turned over.

Play continues until all of the cards have been used. The winner is the player who wins the most cards.

Multiples Are in the Cards!

Skills: Basic multiplication facts, multiples

Help students recognize multiples and practice basic facts with this card game. Provide each team of three or four students with a deck of playing cards (ace equals one, number cards equal their values, jack equals 11, queen equals 12, and king equals 13). Have a team captain shuffle the cards and stack them facedown. Next, write a digit from 2 to 9 on the board. Tell students that the object of the game is to make the first ten multiples of that digit. For example, if the digit is 8, then the multiples to make are 8, 16, 24,…80.

At a signal, the captain of each team turns over the first two cards. The students in that team multiply the two card values together, then decide whether the product is a multiple of the digit on the board. Have each captain call out the two numbers and their product. If the product is a multiple of the target digit, then the team earns that number of points. (Example: 2 x queen = 24; 24 is a multiple of 8.) Then have each team captain place the cards at the bottom of the stack. Continue play until all ten multiples of the target digit have been won.

Five-Factor Lotto

Skill: Recognizing factors of numbers

Factors are front-page news with this versatile grid game! Provide each student with a copy of the grid at the top of page 81. Direct each student to randomly fill in his grid with the numbers 2–10, writing each one four times. Also have each student make about 20 paper game chips. To play, call out a number that has factors in the grid, such as 30 (factors of 30: 1, 2, 3, 5, 6, 10, 15, 30). Direct each student to write 30 on a game chip and then place the chip on one of 30's factors, either 2, 3, 5, 6, or 10. Once a chip is placed, it can't be moved. Continue playing until a student has covered five factors in any row. To check, have the winner remove each game chip, announce its number, and name the factor under the chip.

Place Target

Skill: Multiplying by two-digit factors

Provide plenty of multiplication practice with this simple game! Have each student draw a 4 x 4 grid like the one shown. To the left of each row, have the student write a different digit from 2 to 9; at the top of each column, have the student write a different two-digit number. Each two-digit number should belong to a different tens family (10–19, 20–29, 30–39, etc.). When every student has finished, call out "Multiply!" At that signal, the student multiplies each single digit by each two-digit number and writes the products in the corresponding boxes. (See the example.)

After every student has completed all 16 problems, write a place target (a one-digit number) on the board. Tell students that each place target in the hundreds place of a product scores 20 points, each place target in the tens place scores ten points, and each place target in the ones place scores five points. Have each student find his total score.

Where's the Sign?

Skills: Multiplying by two-, three-, and four-digit factors; estimating

Go on a search for missing math signs with this nifty activity! Write on the chalkboard a multiplication sentence with all of the signs omitted. The sentence will look like a string of single digits (like the sample on the board at left). Share with students that these digits make a multiplication sentence but that the sentence needs signs inserted in the appropriate places. Tell students how many multiplication signs the sentence needs and that it must have an equal sign. (In the sample, one multiplication sign is needed to make 16 x 6 = 96.) Have students first estimate and then check their estimates by working out the problem on paper. Repeat with the other examples shown or problems from your math textbook.

Other examples:

1 3 7 7 9 5 9 *(one: 137 x 7 = 959)*   1 6 4 2 1 2 8 *(two: 16 x 4 x 2 = 128)*
4 5 3 1 3 5 *(one: 45 x 3 = 135)*   5 0 5 7 1 7 5 0 *(two: 50 x 5 x 7 = 1,750)*
2 5 6 6 0 *(two: 2 x 5 x 6 = 60)*

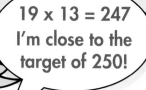

19 x 13 = 247
I'm close to the target of 250!

Hit the Product!

Skills: Using a calculator, estimating

Estimation and calculator skills are the newsworthy topics of this challenging activity. First, write the following prime numbers on the chalkboard so that every student can easily see them: 2, 3, 5, 7, 11, 13, 17, 19, 23, 29, 31, 37, 41, 43, 47, and 53. Each student will need a calculator, paper, and pencil.

To play, announce a target number (example: 250) and the number of factors each student may use (example: 2). The object of the game is for each student to choose two factors from the board whose product he estimates is close to the target number. First, have the student perform his multiplication with pencil and paper. Then have him check his work with the calculator. Award points to the student(s) who come closest to the announced target. Play additional rounds with different target numbers, as well as rounds in which students must use three or four factors to arrive at a target.

Short Takes

Skill: Shortcuts in multiplication

Provide each student with a copy of the shortcuts guide on the bottom of page 81. Review each shortcut with students; then give additional problems for them to solve by using the shortcuts. Remind students that some shortcuts are helpful when computing mentally or when only estimates are needed.

Five-Factor Lotto

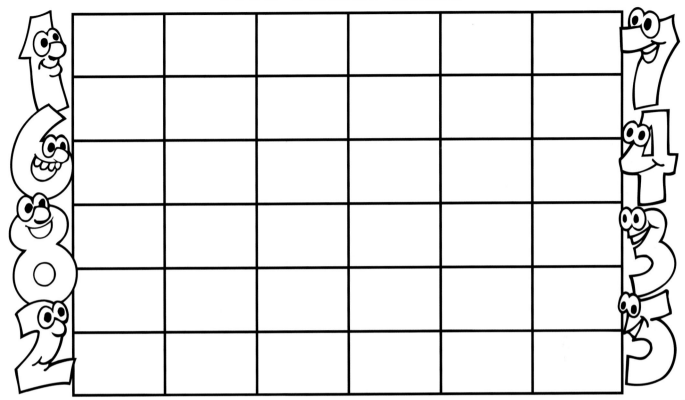

Note to the teacher: See "Five-Factor Lotto" on page 79 for information on playing this game.

Top 10 Shortcuts

1. **Multiply a whole number by 10:** Add a zero after the last digit of the number being multiplied.

    17 x 10 = 170   862 x 10 = 8,620

2. **Multiply a whole number by 100:** Add two zeros after the last digit of the number being multiplied.

    23 x 100 = 2,300   459 x 100 = 45,900

3. **Multiply a whole number by 1,000:** Add three zeros after the last digit of the number being multiplied.

    38 x 1,000 = 38,000   237 x 1,000 = 237,000

4. **Multiply a decimal number by 10:** Move the decimal point of the number being multiplied one place to the right.

    6.4 x 10 = 64.0   24.09 x 10 = 240.9

5. **Multiply a decimal number by 100:** Move the decimal point of the number being multiplied two places to the right.

    5.2 x 100 = 520.0   0.983 x 100 = 98.3

6. **Multiply a decimal number by 1,000:** Move the decimal point of the number being multiplied three places to the right.

    17.5 x 1,000 = 17,500.0   14.42 x 1,000 = 14,420.0

7. **Multiply a number by 5:** Multiply by 10; then divide the product by 2.

    47 x 5 = (47 x 10) ÷ 2 = 470 ÷ 2 = 235   148 x 5 = (148 x 10) ÷ 2 = 1,480 ÷ 2 = 740

8. **Multiply a number by 15:** Multiply by 10. Divide that product by 2. Add the two answers together.

    36 x 15   36 x 10 = 360   360 ÷ 2 = 180   360 + 180 = 540

9. **Multiply by 9:** Multiply by 10. Then subtract the number being multiplied from that product.

    23 x 9 = 23 x 10 − 23 = 230 − 23 = 207

10. **Multiply by 11:** Multiply by 10. Then add the number being multiplied to that product.

    75 x 11 = 75 x 10 + 75 = 750 + 75 = 825

First in America

What was the name of the first regularly published newspaper in the American colonies? To find out, follow the directions below. Remember these properties of multiplication:

Order property: The order in which numbers are multiplied does not change the product.
$$5 \times 8 = 8 \times 5$$

Grouping property: The way in which numbers are grouped does not change the product.
$$(4 \times 5) \times 6 = 4 \times (5 \times 6)$$

Property of one: The product of any number and 1 is that number.
$$24 \times 1 = 24$$

Zero property: The product of any number and 0 is 0.
$$12 \times 0 = 0$$

Part I: The capital letter in each number sentence below stands for a missing number. Find the value for each letter. The first one has been done for you.

1. $N \times 13 = 13 \times 7$
   $N = \underline{\ 7\ }$

2. $E \times 1 = 24$
   $E = \underline{\hspace{2em}}$

3. $(L \times 8) \times 3 = 9 \times (8 \times 3)$
   $L = \underline{\hspace{2em}}$

4. $17 \times W = 0$
   $W = \underline{\hspace{2em}}$

5. $B \times 20 = 20 \times 15$
   $B = \underline{\hspace{2em}}$

6. $8 \times (R \times 10) = (8 \times 3) \times 10$
   $R = \underline{\hspace{2em}}$

7. $5 \times 7 = 7 \times O$
   $O = \underline{\hspace{2em}}$

8. $54 \times T = 54$
   $T = \underline{\hspace{2em}}$

9. $(8 \times 7) \times T = 8 \times (7 \times 5)$
   $T = \underline{\hspace{2em}}$

10. $17 \times S = 15 \times 17$
    $S = \underline{\hspace{2em}}$

11. $(9 \times 5) \times 4 = E \times (5 \times 4)$
    $E = \underline{\hspace{2em}}$

12. $E \times 21 = 0$
    $E = \underline{\hspace{2em}}$

13. $37 \times 1 = H$
    $H = \underline{\hspace{2em}}$

14. $0 \times 72 = S$
    $S = \underline{\hspace{2em}}$

15. $6 \times (2 \times 15) = (6 \times T) \times 15$
    $T = \underline{\hspace{2em}}$

16. $16 \times 23 = O \times 16$
    $O = \underline{\hspace{2em}}$

17. $(10 \times 31) \times 5 = 10 \times (31 \times E)$
    $E = \underline{\hspace{2em}}$

18. $33 \times N = 0$
    $N = \underline{\hspace{2em}}$

19. $15 \times T = 51 \times 15$
    $T = \underline{\hspace{2em}}$

Part II: If a letter is used in a number sentence that shows the
- property of one, write it here: ___ ___ ___
- order property, write it here: <u>N</u> ___ ___ ___ ___ ___
- zero property, write it here: ___ ___ ___ ___
- grouping property, write it here: ___ ___ ___ ___ ___ ___

Part III: Now unscramble the letters in each group to discover the name of the newspaper:

___ ___ ___   ___ ___ ___ ___ ___ ___   ___ ___ ___ ___ ___ - ___ ___ ___ ___ ___ ___

Bonus Box: What year was this newspaper first published? Solve the following riddle to find out: The sum of the first two digits is twice as large as the last digit. The sum of all the digits is 12.

The TIMES Classifieds

🏠 For Rent	👥 Part-Time Jobs	☎ Services	💲 For Sale	💲 For Sale
3-bedroom tree house for rent Great view! $540 per month Call 887-5678.	Dairy Castle (Free shakes!) $4.75 per hour Call 888-9876.	Will baby-sit in your home. $5.50 per hour for 1 child, $7.50 per hour for 2 children, $8.50 per hour for 3 children. More than 3 children? Don't call. Call Cindi: 876-1245.	Kittens Cute, cuddly, adorable! 5 in all, $12 each Call 875-8531.	Used golf clubs (some slightly bent) $180 for set of 12 or $20 each Call Tiger at 873-1265.
2-bedroom camper for rent Small but neat $89 per week Call 886-6789.	Joe's Deli (Free subs!) $6.85 per hour Call Joe at 884-SUBS.	Will take care of your pet while you're away! Dogs & cats: $5.25 each per day. Birds: $6.25 each per day. Snakes: $50.00 each per day. All others: $8.50 each per day. Call Jon: 875-2356.	Puppies Must sell! 9 in all, $21 each Call 857-0923.	Used computer games $16 each or $200 for all 15 titles Call Jeri at 832-1221.

To Advertise Your Business or Service, Call 123-4567

Peppi's Pizza (Free pizza!) $4.95 per hour Call Peppi at 86-PIZZA.

Math tutoring Bring up your math grade! Maybe. Grs. 4–6: $28.00 per hour Call Addie: 873-2356.

Concert tickets Jon Bon Jovi—Oct. 5 4 tickets, $32 each Call Brandon at 823-9867.  ADMIT ONE

Place an Ad With Us TODAY!

Use the information in the ads above to solve the following problems. Show your work on another sheet of paper; then write your answers in the blanks provided.

1. How much would 7 golf clubs cost? _____
2. What is the cost of 6 hours of math tutoring? _____
3. How much would you earn in an 8-hour day working at Dairy Castle? _____
4. How much would it cost to rent the camper for 4 weeks? _____
5. How much would all 5 kittens cost? _____
6. How much would you make working at Peppi's for 5 hours? _____
7. How much would 3 concert tickets cost? _____
8. How much would 6 puppies cost? _____
9. Employees at Joe's Deli earn an average of $7.50 per hour in tips on weekend nights. About how much would you expect to earn if you worked 5 hours on Saturday night? _____
10. If Cindi baby-sat 1 child on Friday night for 4 hours and then 2 children on Saturday night for 5 hours, how much money did she earn? _____
11. If 3 housemates shared the tree house, how much rent would each one pay per month? _____ How much rent would each person pay for 12 months? _____
12. How much would Jon charge to look after your dog and ferret for 7 days? _____
13. How much money would you save by buying all 15 computer games instead of buying each one individually? _____
14. How much rent would you pay in 12 months if you rented the tree house? _____
15. How much would Jon charge to look after your cat, dog, and bird for 3 days? _____

Bonus Box: The regular price for the concert tickets is $85 per pair. How much money would you save if you bought the 4 Brandon is selling? _____

Activities for Teaching the Order of Operations

Getting dressed, following a recipe, packing a suitcase—knowing what to do first can determine if the outcome of these activities is terrific or a mess! The same is true with math operations. Use the following activities to bring order to your students' confusion over problems that involve multiple operations.

ideas by Peggy W. Hambright

Gotta Have Order!
Skill: Computation

Begin to help students understand the need for having an order of operations by asking the following questions: What would happen if you put on your shoes before your socks? Frosted a cake before baking it? Packed small suitcases in a car trunk before the big ones? Guide students to conclude that the order in which such tasks are done can definitely affect the outcome.

Next, guide students to discover that the same is true when it comes to performing calculations that involve different operations. Copy the first set of problems below (without the italicized solutions) onto the board for students to solve. Check the answers together. Repeat with the second set of problems, directing students to do the operations in parentheses first. Repeat again with the third set, this time having students do the computations in order from left to right. Afterward, ask students how the sets are alike and different *(all three sets contain the same numbers and operations, the answers to the first and second sets are the same, the answers to the third set are different and incorrect).* Explain that to avoid such confusion and to be consistent, mathematicians agreed to follow a certain order—the order of operations. To help students remember the order, display the poster shown along with the two reminders given.

Set 1
$5 \times 2 + 3 = 10 + 3 = 13$
$12 \div 2 + 4 = 6 + 4 = 10$
$7 \times 2 + 6 = 14 + 6 = 20$
$150 \div 5 + 5 = 30 + 5 = 35$

Set 2
$3 + (2 \times 5) = 3 + 10 = 13$
$4 + (12 \div 2) = 4 + 6 = 10$
$6 + (7 \times 2) = 6 + 14 = 20$
$5 + (150 \div 5) = 5 + 30 = 35$

Set 3
$3 + 2 \times 5 = 5 \times 5 = 25$
$4 + 12 \div 2 = 16 \div 2 = 8$
$6 + 7 \times 2 = 13 \times 2 = 26$
$5 + 150 \div 5 = 155 \div 5 = 31$

Order of Operations

1. Parentheses (do the work inside these first)
2. Exponents (if there are no exponents, skip this step)
3. Multiplication and division (whichever comes first left to right)
4. Addition and subtraction (whichever comes first left to right)

Helpful Reminders: Remember the sentence "<u>P</u>lease <u>e</u>xcuse <u>m</u>y <u>d</u>ear <u>A</u>unt <u>S</u>ally" or the word *PEMDAS* (p = parentheses, e = exponents, m = multiplication, d = division, a = addition, s = subtraction).

Problems	Answers
8 x 9 + 12	x, 84
7 x (4 + 9)	(+), 91
45 − 25 ÷ 5	÷, 40
(5 + 4) x (6 + 5)	(+), 99
86 − 7 x 2	x, 72
64 − 72 ÷ 9	÷, 56
300 ÷ (22 − 7)	(−), 20
18 − 12 ÷ 3	÷, 14
4 x 6 ÷ 8	x, 3
26 + 19 − 15	+, 30

Order Counts!

Skills: Recognizing which step to do first, solving problems

Put together an easy-to-make math center activity that will give pairs of students practice identifying which step to tackle first. Place a copy of the order of operations (see page 84) at the center as a helpful reminder. Next, program ten index cards with the problems listed on the right, writing a problem on the front of the card and its answer on the back. Direct the pair to stack the cards problem-side up in a pile between them. Have Student A take the top card and hold it so that the answer faces him and the problem faces Student B. Direct Student B to study the problem, identify which step to do first, and then solve the problem on paper. After Student A checks Student B's answer, have him put the card on the bottom of the pile. Then have Student B draw the top card and repeat the steps for his partner.

26 + 19 − 15

+, 30

1. 27 + 45 − 31 = 41
2. 889 − 200 x 4 = 89
3. 20 x 6 ÷ 3 + 43 + 27 + 53 = 163
4. 742 ÷ (7 x 2) + 7 = 60
5. 16 + (80 ÷ 4) + 6 x (8 + 7) = 126
6. 300 + 509 x 12 ÷ 12 − 19 = 790
7. 5 + 4 x 9 − 12 ÷ 6 − 1(6 + 3) = 30

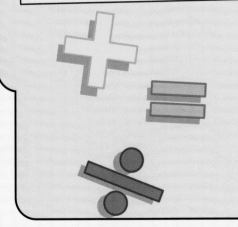

The Case of the Odds Versus the Evens

Skills: Order of operations, numeration

Cast students into the roles of lawyers to play a fun order of operations game. Divide the class into two teams, the Prosecutors and the Defenders. Write a problem without the solution (see the examples) on the chalkboard. Have two players from each team work together to use the order of operations to solve the problem. As soon as the pair has its answer, have the twosome call out "Order in the court!" Check the pair's answer. If correct, award the pair's team five points for an even-numbered answer or three points for an odd-numbered answer. If incorrect, give the opposing pair time to answer and earn points. If neither pair answers correctly, guide students to the correct solution but award no points. Continue in this manner until every student has had a turn.

To challenge students with another tough case, write four different numbers—such as 8, 3, 19, and 25—on the board. Have students use the numbers to write four problems that each have a different answer.

Ordering More Practice

Skills: Creating and solving problems using the order of operations

If you're looking for a ready-to-use activity to practice the order of operations, then you won't object to the reproducible on page 86! After each student completes a copy of this page, give him an index card. Challenge the student to label the front of the card with a problem similar to those on page 86. Have him write the answer to the problem on the back of the card. Collect the cards and check them for accuracy. Then use the cards as free-time fillers or as extra-credit problems on future math assignments.

Order, Please!

How well can you judge which operation to do first in a problem? Find out by following the directions below.

Directions: Use each number below four times and the order of operations to write a problem whose answer equals the number on the gavel. For example, if the number is 8 and the answer to reach is 152, you could write 88 + 8 x 8.

Order of Operations
1. Parentheses (do the work inside these first)
2. Exponents (if there are no exponents, skip this step)
3. Multiplication and division (whichever comes first left to right)
4. Addition and subtraction (whichever comes first left to right)

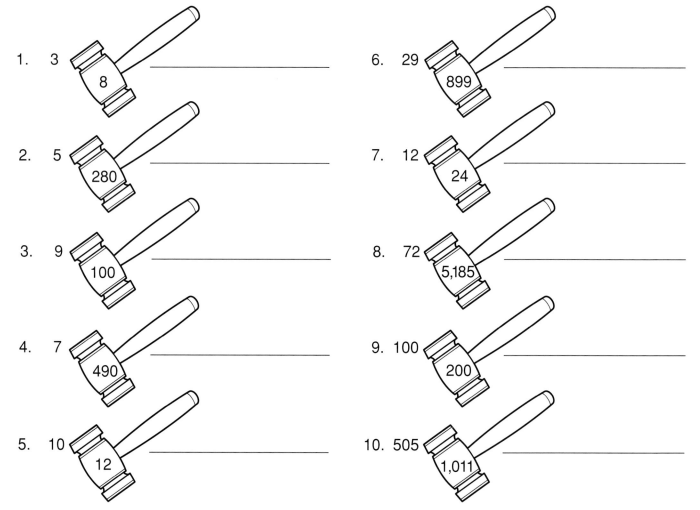

1.   3   8   _____

2.   5   280   _____

3.   9   100   _____

4.   7   490   _____

5.   10   12   _____

6.   29   899   _____

7.   12   24   _____

8.   72   5,185   _____

9.   100   200   _____

10.   505   1,011   _____

Bonus Box: Rewrite problem 1 so that the answer is 30. *Hint: Use parentheses, multiplication, the exponent 2, division, and addition.*

Investigating Integers

Just when students thought they had learned everything there was to learn about numbers, the number of numbers suddenly doubles! Guide your junior detectives as they investigate integers with the following creative activities and games.

by Irving P. Crump, Contributing Editor

Opening the Files

Skill: Introducing integers

To introduce this new set of numbers to your students, program eight 9" x 12" sheets of white construction paper with the following letter and number pairs. Write the letter on one side of a sheet and the number on the opposite side: G and 0, S and ⁺20, I and ⁻32, R and ⁺8, T and ⁻6, E and ⁺5, E and ⁻1, N and ⁻10. Distribute the sheets to eight students.

Next, ask the class the riddles shown below one at a time. After students determine each answer (listed in italics), have the student holding that number stand at the front of the classroom with his paper turned so that the number shows. After all eight students are standing, ask the rest of the class if the numbers are in correct least-to-greatest order. If not, have the class arrange the students correctly. Then ask the eight standing students to turn over their sheets to reveal the name of the new set of numbers they'll be studying: *INTEGERS!*

Questions:
1. What integer is neither positive nor negative? *(0)*
2. If a quarterback is sacked for a ten-yard loss, how would that be shown? *(⁻10)*
3. If you had $8 in your bank account and deposited $12 more, how much do you now have in the account? *($20 or ⁺20)*
4. If the temperature is ⁻2°F and drops four degrees, what is the temperature now? *(⁻6°F or ⁻6)*
5. What number is the opposite of 32? *(⁻32)*
6. An ocean is one mile deep. The distance from the bottom of the ocean to the top of a mountain is six miles. How tall is the mountain? *(5 miles or ⁺5)*
7. If you shoot a round of 44 at a par 36 miniature golf course, how much are you over par? *(⁺8)*
8. If ⁺1 represents gaining a pound, what represents losing a pound? *(⁻1)*

Who Has...?

Skill: Understanding and ordering integers

Help students gain a deeper understanding of integers with this fun game. Program 25 large index cards with the integers ⁻12 through ⁺12. (If necessary, adjust the number of cards so that each student will have one.) Distribute the cards randomly to students. Then ask the questions listed on the right one at a time. Have the student who holds the card with a correct answer to a question come to the front of the classroom. If more than one student has an answer (such as in the question "Who has a positive integer?"), have all of those students stand in correct order from least to greatest. After discussing each question and its answer, have students return to their seats. Follow up the game with questions that involve adding and subtracting.

Who has…
- the only integer that is neither positive or negative?
- a positive integer?
- a negative integer?
- an even integer?
- an odd integer?
- the integer that is the opposite of ⁺5?
- the integer that is the opposite of ⁻10?
- the integer that is the opposite of 0? (No one! 0 doesn't have an opposite.)
- an integer greater than ⁻1 but less than ⁺5?
- an integer less than 0 but greater than ⁻6?
- the integer halfway between ⁺2 and ⁺12?
- the largest negative integer?
- the smallest positive integer?
- an integer between ⁻5 and ⁺5?

Life-Size Adding and Subtracting

Skill: Adding and subtracting integers

Hand students some life-size problems that are big enough to help them remember how to add and subtract integers! Give half of the class 9" x 12" sheets of green construction paper and the other half red sheets. Tell students that each green sheet represents $^+1$ and each red sheet represents $^-1$. Then guide them through these steps:

1. Have a group of green students go to the front of the classroom and demonstrate $^+7 + ^+3$. (*$^+10$; Remind students that when two positive integers are added together, their sum is always positive.*)
2. Have a group of red students go to the front of the classroom and demonstrate $^-7 + ^-5$. (*$^-12$; Remind students that the sum of two negative integers is always negative.*)
3. Have four red students and nine green students demonstrate $^-4 + ^+9$. (*$^+5$; Review with students that each red represents $^-1$ and each green represents $^+1$. Since reds and greens are opposites, red + green = 0. To complete the addition, have students form pairs consisting of one green and one red. Then have those pairs sit down. Remaining are five greens or $^+5$.*)
4. Have ten reds go to the front of the room. Ask those students to demonstrate $^-10 - ^-6$. (*$^-4$; Six reds must sit down, or be subtracted from, the group of ten. That leaves four reds or $^-4$.*) Ask the same ten reds to return to the front of the room. Also have six greens join them. Ask this group to demonstrate $^-10 + ^+6$. (*$^-4$; Since each green represents $^+1$ and each red represents $^-1$, red + green = 0. Direct students to form pairs consisting of one green and one red. Then have those pairs sit down. Remaining are four reds or $^-4$. Remind students that subtracting a negative number is the same as adding its opposite.*)
5. Have nine reds go to the front of the class. Next, tell four greens to sit down. (That's impossible!) Since there are no greens standing, none can sit down. Challenge students to figure out how to demonstrate $^-9 - ^+4$. [*$^-13$; Since red + green = 0, have four green students and four more red students join the group. Ask the class to name the value of those students who joined the group (0; $^+4 + ^-4 = 0$). Now tell four greens to sit down, thus representing "subtract $^+4$." Remaining are 13 reds or $^-13$. Remind students again that subtracting $^+4$ is the same as adding $^-4$.*]

Hot on the Integer Trail!

Skill: Adding and subtracting integers

Challenge students in this game of strategy; then send them off to complete their own investigations! First, provide each pair of students with a copy of page 89. Also make a transparency of the page. Read and discuss the directions with the class; then challenge the class to play against you as a way to become familiar with the game's rules. To begin, roll a die, find the matching integer in the code, and write that integer in the first box of a trail on the transparency. Next, add that integer to 0 or subtract it from 0 and write the answer in the first blank. Roll the die again and announce the roll to the class. Have each pair find the matching integer in the

code and write it in a box on their copy of the sheet. Continue play until you and every pair of students have completed all four trails.

To score, determine by how much each target was missed. Remind students that these numbers will be positive integers. For example, if the final answer of the first trail is $^-2$, then the target was missed by 12. If the answer is 5, then the target was missed by 5. Use an integers number line to help students determine their scores. Then provide each pair of students with two clean copies of page 89 to play on their own.

Hot on the Integer Trail!

Challenge a classmate to track down these hot targets!

Target

 1. +10   0 ___ + ☐ = ___   + ☐ = ___   + ☐ = ___   + ☐ = ___

 2. −10   0 ___ − ☐ = ___   − ☐ = ___   − ☐ = ___   − ☐ = ___

 3. 0   0 ___ + ☐ = ___   + ☐ = ___   + ☐ = ___   + ☐ = ___

4. +5 or −5   0 ___ − ☐ = ___   + ☐ = ___   − ☐ = ___   + ☐ = ___

Scoring

I missed Target 1 by ___ . ___
I missed Target 2 by ___ . ___
I missed Target 3 by ___ . ___
I missed Target 4 by ___ . ___
         Total: ___ . ___

Materials: die, paper, pencil, 1 copy of this page per player

Objective: add and subtract integers to reach a target number

To play:

1. Roll the die to see who begins. The player with the higher roll is Player 1.
2. Player 1 rolls the die and finds the matching integer in the code.
3. Player 1 writes that integer in the first box of any trail 1–4. He then adds that value to 0 or subtracts it from 0 and writes the answer in the first blank.
4. Player 2 repeats Steps 2 and 3.
5. Player 1 takes another turn and writes his next integer in a box of any trail 1–4. Player 1 adds the box number to or subtracts it from the number in the blank on the left. The new sum or difference is written in the next blank. Boxes cannot be skipped.
6. Play continues left to right on each trail.
7. Continue play until each player reaches the end of all four trails.
8. Each player completes the scoring box, then adds his 4 numbers to find his total. The *lower* total is the winner.

code
1 = 0
2 = ⁻1
3 = ⁻2
4 = ⁺3
5 = ⁺2
6 = ⁺5

Conquering Transformations and Symmetry

Equip students to master transformations and symmetry with the following tasks—all guaranteed to help them succeed in their worthy quest!

Task 1: Slip-Sliding Away!
Skill: Translations

Focus your students on translating figures with this fun manipulative activity. Display a transparency of a sword drawn on a grid (see the illustration). Have each student copy the drawing anywhere on a sheet of ¹/₄-inch graph paper. Explain that a figure makes a *translation* when it slides up, down, right, or left. Then draw a second sword several squares northeast of the first one. Point out that the new drawing is the same size and shape as the first. Add an arrow to show the direction in which the figure moved. Next, have each student draw a simple knight (with one outstretched arm) anywhere on her grid. Then have the student draw at least five translations, moving the sword to different places before having it rest in the knight's hand. Remind students to include arrows so the sword's path can be easily traced.

Task 2: Acrobatic Reflections
Skill: Reflections

Make students flip over practicing reflections with this race-to-the-finish game! Explain to students that a figure makes a *reflection* (creates a mirror image of itself) when it flips over a line. Point out that the reflected image matches the original figure in size and shape. Display a transparency of a sheet of triangle grid paper (see the illustration). Explain that the shared sides between the triangles represent lines of reflection. Color one triangle with a wipe-off marker. Then cover that triangle with a green pattern block. Next, flip the pattern block over a line to cover its reflection. Remove the pattern block and color the triangle beneath it. Discuss how continuing the reflection process could make a path acrossthe grid.

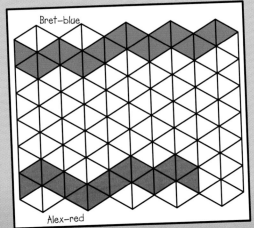

Next, give each pair of students a sheet of triangle grid paper, a green pattern block, a die, and two different-colored markers. Tell students that they are to simulate somersaulting acrobats. Direct each acrobat to use a different marker to color a triangle along one side of the grid. Then have the pair take turns rolling the die to determine the number of somersaults (times to flip the pattern block over a line) and coloring the corresponding number of triangles. Declare the first performer to reach the opposite side of the grid the faster acrobat!

Task 3: Making the Rounds With Rotations
Skill: Rotations

Pull up a chair at King Arthur's Round Table with this can't-be-beat activity on rotations! Label a circle transparency with the names shown. Also write each name on a slip of paper. Place the paper slips in a container. Display the circle, telling students that it represents King Arthur's legendary Round Table. Then explain that a figure makes a *rotation* when it turns around a point.

Next, divide students into two teams and assign each team a different color. Have a player from Team 1 draw a paper slip and then point a toothpick (Arthur's sword) from the center of the table to the knight whose name was drawn. Direct the same player to roll a die and turn the sword according to the directions in the box shown. This will determine which knight Arthur will dismiss. If the player turns the sword correctly, dismiss the knight by circling his name with that team's color. Then have a player from Team 2 take a turn. Watch the teams begin to strategize, anticipating the rolls that mean certain dismissal. After every knight has been dismissed (had his name circled), count each team's circled names; then dub the team with more names your Knights of Rotation!

Roll	Rotation
1	¹/₄ turn to the right
2	¹/₄ turn to the left
3	¹/₂ turn
4	your choice
5	³/₄ turn to the right
6	³/₄ turn to the left

Bye, Palomides! You're a quarter turn to the left!

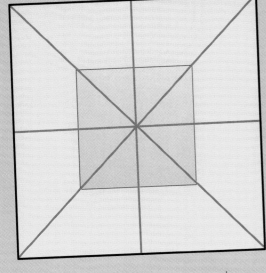

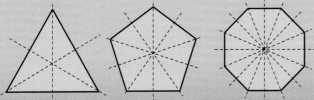

Task 4: Drawing the Line
Skill: Line symmetry in regular polygons

Use this activity to show students how to draw the line when it comes to line symmetry! Display a 12-inch paper square, telling students it represents a banner once carried by a knight. Explain that a figure has *line symmetry* if folding it in half creates two matching halves of the figure. Also point out that a figure can have more than one line of symmetry. Ask students to guess how many lines of symmetry the banner has. Then fold the paper in half once vertically and horizontally and twice diagonally (matching opposite corners). Unfold the paper and point out each fold line as a line of symmetry. Have a student identify the banner's shape *(a square, which is a regular polygon)* and compare its number of sides with its lines of symmetry *(four sides and four lines of symmetry)*.

Next, give each student a ruler, crayons, and three paper shapes: an equilateral triangle, a regular pentagon, and a regular octagon. Have the student draw each banner's lines of symmetry *(triangle, three; pentagon, five; octagon, eight)* and count the number of its sides. Help students conclude that the number of sides in a regular polygon equals the number of its lines of symmetry. Then invite students to decorate their banners.

A Message for King Arthur

An important message must be delivered to King Arthur, and time is of the essence! Follow the directions below to help you and a partner determine which knight—Galahad or Gawain—can deliver the message in a timelier way.

Directions:

1. Cut out the game pieces below (dotted lines only) and color both sides. Fold each game piece in half along the solid line and tape the sides together.
2. Place the game pieces on START. Player 1 is Galahad, and Player 2 is Gawain.
3. Take turns spinning a paper clip on the spinner. Move your game piece as directed by the spinner. Translate (slide), reflect (flip), or rotate (turn) from one square to another to reach King Arthur. Use tally marks to record the number of moves made.
4. Before reaching Arthur, each knight *must* land in the Face the Dragon! space and be turned facing the dragon.
5. The knight who reaches King Arthur in fewer moves is the winner.

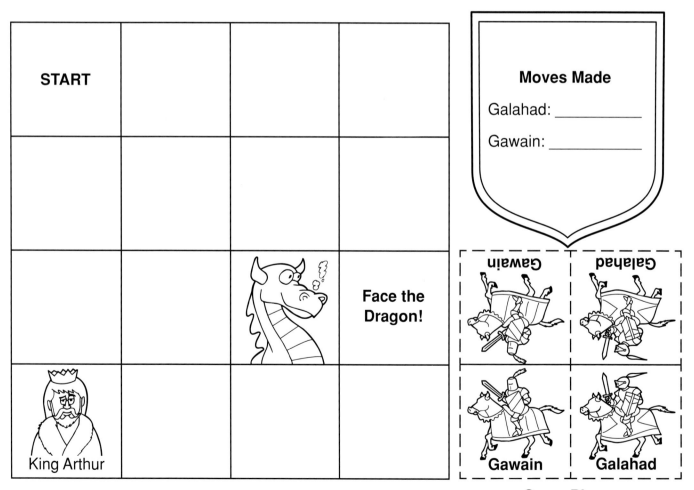

Game Pieces

Note to the teacher: Each pair of students will need scissors, crayons or markers, a paper clip, tape, and a pencil to complete this page.

Taking Note of Mixed Numbers
Noteworthy Ideas on Adding and Subtracting Mixed Numbers

A symphony of skills is needed to add and subtract mixed numbers: writing equivalent fractions, renaming whole numbers as fractions, reducing fractions, and—don't forget!—adding and subtracting. Help students better understand this challenging process with the following creative activities and reproducibles.

by Irving P. Crump, Contributing Editor

Noting Fraction Forms
Skills: Reviewing forms of fractions, simplifying fractions

Before students begin to add and subtract mixed numbers, use this game to review the different forms of fractions. Divide students into two teams; then draw the blank diagram on the chalkboard as shown. Have the first student on Team 1 roll a die three times and announce each number rolled as you write it in the diagram: the first number in the large whole-number box, the second number as the fraction's numerator, and the third number as the fraction's denominator. Then ask students to silently consider the following questions:

- Is this mixed number in its simplest form? (See Figure 1.)
- Does the fraction part need to be reduced? (See Figure 2.)
- Does the fraction part need to be changed to a whole number, then added to the existing whole number? (See Figure 3.)
- Does the fraction part need to be changed to a mixed number, then added to the existing whole number? (See Figure 4.)
- Does the fraction part need to be reduced, changed to a mixed number, then added to the existing whole number? (Or the fraction part can first be changed to a mixed number and then reduced; see Figure 5.)

Next, ask the student who rolled the die to evaluate the mixed number. If the mixed number is in its simplest form and the student correctly identifies it as such, award his team ten points. If the mixed number needs to be simplified and the student says so, award his team five points. If the student can then correctly simplify the mixed number, award his team a ten-point bonus. Then have the first player on Team 2 take a turn.

For more challenging rounds, have players roll two dice to determine each part of the mixed number.

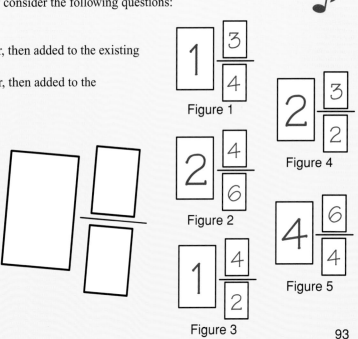

Figure 1

Figure 2

Figure 3

Figure 4

Figure 5

93

Mixed-Number Relay
Skill: Adding mixed numbers

Get students up and moving with this mixed-number relay! On each end of the chalkboard, draw a diagram like the one shown. Divide students into two teams, and have the first player from each team go to a diagram. Next, roll a die, announce the number, and tell each student at the board to write it in a box of his diagram. Repeat five more times so that each player writes two mixed-number addends, switching numbers if necessary to make sure that each fraction's numerator is less than its denominator. To play the game:

1. Player 1 of each team sits down, and the second player goes to the board. If the fractions in the mixed numbers have like denominators, Player 2 may solve the problem. If one fraction needs to be rewritten so that its denominator is like the other's, Player 2 rewrites it. (Example: If $\frac{1}{2}$ and $\frac{3}{4}$ are the fractions, $\frac{1}{2}$ needs to be rewritten as $\frac{2}{4}$.) If both fractions need to be rewritten with like denominators, Player 2 may rewrite *one* of them. (Example: $\frac{2}{3}$ and $\frac{3}{4}$ need to be rewritten as $\frac{8}{12}$ and $\frac{9}{12}$.) Player 2 then sits down.
2. If necessary, Player 3 goes to the board. He either solves the problem if the fractions have like denominators or, if necessary, rewrites the second fraction. Player 3 then sits down.
3. If necessary, Player 4 approaches the board. Both fractions should now have like denominators, so Player 4 solves the problem.

Award each team ten points for a correct sum. Award the team that finishes first with a five-point bonus if its sum is correct. Continue with additional rounds. For more advanced play, roll a pair of dice to determine the diagrams' numbers.

Red, White, and Blue Mixed Numbers
Skills: Measuring, adding mixed numbers

Give students lots of hands-on practice with measuring and adding mixed numbers with this partner activity. Provide each pair of students with four 9" x 12" sheets of construction paper (one red, one blue, two white), scissors, a ruler, and glue. Have each pair turn the red and blue sheets vertically and then measure and cut each into nine one-inch-wide strips. Next, write the following addition problems on the chalkboard:

$3\frac{1}{4}$ in. red + $4\frac{1}{2}$ in. blue
$5\frac{5}{8}$ in. red + $3\frac{7}{8}$ in. blue
$4\frac{3}{4}$ in. red + $2\frac{3}{8}$ in. blue
$6\frac{1}{8}$ in. red + $1\frac{1}{2}$ in. blue
$3\frac{3}{4}$ in. red + $4\frac{7}{8}$ in. blue

Have each student measure and then cut a $3\frac{1}{4}$-inch red paper strip and a $4\frac{1}{2}$-inch blue paper strip. Have the student label each strip with its measure, glue the two strips side by side as shown on a white sheet of construction paper, and then add the measures. Have the student repeat these steps with the other four problems.

When everyone has finished, have students exchange white sheets with their partners. Have each student measure his partner's combined red and blue strips to see whether their measures equal those written on the paper.

$$3\frac{1}{4} = 3\frac{1}{4}$$
$$+\ 4\frac{1}{2} = 4\frac{2}{4}$$
$$\overline{\ \ \ \ \ \ \ \ 7\frac{3}{4} \text{ in.}}$$

Pass It On!
Skills: Measuring, subtracting mixed numbers

Encourage accurate measuring and subtracting with this group activity. Divide students into rows of five students each. Provide each child with a ruler and scissors; give the first student in each row an 18" x 1" strip of light-colored construction paper. Direct the first student to measure and cut a $2\frac{1}{2}$-inch-long piece from his strip. Then have him pass the remainder of the strip to the next player. Have that child measure and cut a $3\frac{3}{4}$-inch-long piece from the strip and then pass the remainder of the strip to the next player. Continue with the remaining players measuring and cutting pieces of $2\frac{5}{8}$ inches, 3 inches, and $4\frac{1}{4}$ inches. Have the last student on each team write her name on the remainder of the strip and give it to you.

As you measure the teams' remaining strips, have the class subtract five times to determine how long each one should be: $18 - 2\frac{1}{2} - 3\frac{3}{4} - 2\frac{5}{8} - 3 - 4\frac{1}{4}$. *($1\frac{7}{8}$ inches)* Award 20 points to each team that has an exact measure, 15 points for a measure within $\frac{1}{8}$ inch, ten points for a measure within $\frac{1}{4}$ inch, and five points for a measure within $\frac{1}{2}$ inch.

Measure Twice, Cut Once!
Skills: Measuring, subtracting mixed numbers

Ask students why carpenters often say, "Measure twice, cut once." Then guide them through the following hands-on measuring and subtracting activity. Provide each pair of students with two 9" x 12" sheets of construction paper (one yellow and one green), scissors, a ruler, and glue. Have each pair turn the sheets of paper vertically and then measure and cut each into nine one-inch-wide strips. Next, write the following problems on the chalkboard:

1. $5^3/_8$ in. green – $3^1/_8$ in. yellow
2. $4^3/_4$ in. green – $2^5/_8$ in. yellow
3. $7^1/_2$ in. green – $3^5/_8$ in. yellow
4. $8^1/_8$ in. green – $4^1/_4$ in. yellow
5. $9^7/_8$ in. green – $5^3/_4$ in. yellow

Have each student cut a $5^3/_8$-inch green strip and a $3^1/_8$-inch yellow strip. Have the student write "1" on the yellow strip and then glue it onto the green one, making sure the ends are aligned. Have students repeat this process with problems 2–5. Next, invite volunteers to the board to solve the five problems as their classmates solve them at their desks. When everyone agrees that the answers are correct, have the students in each pair exchange paper strips with one another. Have each student measure only the green section of each strip, whose measure should match the difference shown on the board.

Picture a Problem
Skills: Drawing diagrams, adding and subtracting mixed numbers

Invite students to put their visual-thinking skills to the test with this problem-solving activity. Have students listen carefully as you read the following story:

Marie left her campsite and hiked $4^7/_8$ miles south to the river. She then hiked $3^1/_2$ miles west to a cave. Then she turned north and hiked $3^1/_4$ miles to a deserted cabin. After she rests awhile, Marie plans to hike east to pick up the first trail. When she leaves the cabin, how far does Marie have to hike to reach the campsite?

Have each student draw a diagram to help him solve the problem as you reread it. (Solution: The trail from the cabin to the first trail completes a rectangle, so it measures $3^1/_2$ miles. The distance from that point back to the tent is $1^5/_8$ miles: $4^7/_8$ miles – $3^1/_4$ miles. The distance from the cabin to the campsite is $5^1/_8$ miles: $3^1/_2$ miles + $1^5/_8$ miles.) Use the diagram to generate other questions that involve adding and subtracting mixed numbers. For example:

- How far will Marie hike all together?
- If Marie hiked to the river and then back to the campsite, how far would she hike?
- Marie hiked $2^3/_4$ miles toward the river and stopped to take a break. How much farther does she have to go before reaching the river?

Follow up by giving each student a large index card. On one side of the card, have the student write a story that includes at least three mixed numbers with a question to answer. Instruct him to draw a diagram that would help solve the problem on the opposite side. Have students exchange cards and solve each other's problems *without* looking at the diagrams.

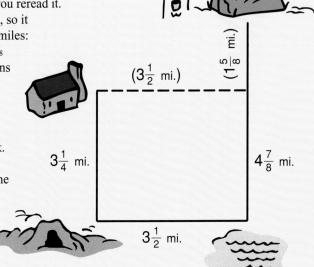

Do, Re, Mi: A Pattern I See!

Make sweet music when you complete these patterns! First, figure out the next two numbers that go in the notes of each pattern. Then describe the rule on the line that follows. The first one has been done for you.

1. $2\frac{1}{8}$ $2\frac{3}{4}$ $3\frac{3}{8}$ 4 $4\frac{5}{8}$ $5\frac{1}{4}$ $5\frac{7}{8}$ Rule: add $\frac{5}{8}$

2. $1\frac{1}{2}$ 3 $4\frac{1}{2}$ 6 $7\frac{1}{2}$ Rule:_____

3. $3\frac{1}{3}$ $5\frac{2}{3}$ 8 $10\frac{1}{3}$ $12\frac{2}{3}$ Rule:_____

4. $2\frac{1}{5}$ 4 $5\frac{4}{5}$ $7\frac{3}{5}$ $9\frac{2}{5}$ Rule:_____

5. $\frac{7}{8}$ $4\frac{1}{8}$ $7\frac{3}{8}$ $10\frac{5}{8}$ $13\frac{7}{8}$ Rule:_____

6. $3\frac{5}{6}$ $4\frac{5}{6}$ $6\frac{5}{6}$ $9\frac{5}{6}$ $13\frac{5}{6}$ Rule:_____

7. $1\frac{1}{2}$ 4 $2\frac{3}{4}$ $5\frac{1}{4}$ 4 Rule:_____

8. $7\frac{1}{2}$ 8 $9\frac{1}{2}$ 12 $15\frac{1}{2}$ Rule:_____

9. $3\frac{7}{10}$ $4\frac{9}{10}$ $6\frac{3}{10}$ $7\frac{9}{10}$ $9\frac{7}{10}$ Rule:_____

10. 9 $8\frac{1}{3}$ $10\frac{1}{6}$ $9\frac{1}{2}$ $11\frac{1}{3}$ Rule:_____

Bonus Box: You're a maestro if you can figure out the next term in this pattern: $1\frac{1}{8}$, $3\frac{3}{8}$, $6\frac{3}{4}$, $11\frac{1}{4}$, $16\frac{7}{8}$, _____.

Measure by Measure

Tune up your measuring know-how with the following activities! Use a customary ruler to make each measure. Show all of your adding and subtracting on another sheet of paper. Then write your answers in the blanks provided. In Part 5, EFI is a triangle; AHED is a quadrilateral.

Part 1 Measure each segment.	**Part 2** Measure and add.	**Part 3** Measure and subtract.	**Part 4** Find the distance.	**Part 5** Find the perimeter.
1. AB = _____	7. AB + EC = ___	12. AD – AH = ___	17. H to B to C to E = ____	21. EFI = ____
2. BC = _____	8. EI + EF = ___	13. EI – IF = ___	18. F to I to E to D = ____	22. EHB = ____
3. HE = _____	9. BF + EC = ___	14. EB – EF = ___	19. G to F to E to H = ____	23. AHED = ____
4. GF = _____	10. HE + HB = ___	15. HE – AH = ___	20. A to B to F to I = ____	24. HBFI = ____
5. EF = _____	11. EC + HB = ___	16. IF – FB = ___		25. DEFG = ____
6. AG = _____				

Bonus Box: Which route is shorter from A to C: A–G–I–E–C or A–B–E–C? By how much?

Graphing Activities That Hit the Spot!

Looking for ideas that will help students collect, organize, display, and interpret data? Then check out the following creative teaching activities and reproducibles. They're sure to hit the spot!

Graph SPOTS
Skill: Interpreting graphs

Information in our world is growing at an astounding rate, and a lot of it is often presented in graphs. Help students better understand the graphs they encounter with this evaluative activity. Collect graphs from a variety of sources, such as newspapers, magazines, advertisements, and food products. Glue the graphs onto 12" x 18" sheets of poster board, including many graphs of the same type (or a variety) on each sheet. Laminate the sheets; then distribute them to individual students, pairs, or small groups. Also provide each student with a copy of "Graph SPOTS" on page 101. Have the student choose one graph, read and interpret the information on it, and complete the reproducible. Post the students' evaluations and the graph posters on a bulletin board titled "Graphs We've Spotted!" *Lisa Groenendyk—Gr. 4, Pella Christian Grade School, Pella, IA*

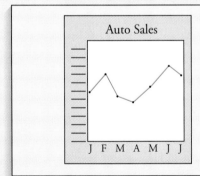
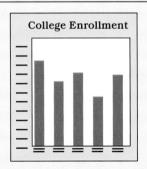

"Para-graphs"
Skill: Making bar and double-bar graphs

Challenge students to take a closer look at the words they read with this data-collecting activity! First, have each student bring to class a magazine or newspaper article. Instruct each student to read the first eight sentences in the article and count the number of words in each sentence. Then have students create bar graphs to display their data.

Next, discuss with students the vocabulary and the lengths of sentences they encounter in different types of reading material. Ask students how a paragraph in a newspaper article compares to one in a class novel. Then have each student choose a paragraph from each of three different types of reading materials, such as a novel, a magazine, a newspaper, an encyclopedia, a primary-level library book, etc. Have the student read the first five sentences in each selection and count the number of words and syllables in each sentence. Then instruct her to make a double-bar graph that compares the numbers of words and syllables in the three paragraphs chosen. To complete the activity, have each student share her conclusions in a brief paragraph. *adapted from an idea by Libby Latham-Davis—Gr. 4, Wateree Elementary, Lugoff, SC*

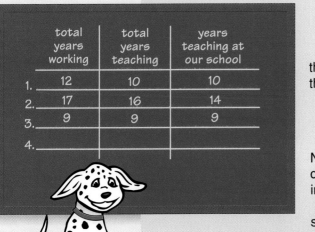

	total years working	total years teaching	years teaching at our school
1.	12	10	10
2.	17	16	14
3.	9	9	9
4.			

We Love Our Teachers!

Skill: Making a histogram

Students will learn more about the teachers in your school with this data-collecting activity! First, copy the following questions on the chalkboard.

- Including jobs in high school and college, how many total years have you been working?
- How many total years have you been teaching?
- How many years have you been teaching in our school?

Next, divide students into pairs. Instruct each twosome to copy the questions on a large index card. Then send one student pair to interview each teacher in your school.

When all data has been collected, draw a chart on the board similar to the one shown; then have each pair write its information in the chart. To complete the activity, divide the class into three groups. Assign one set of data—work years, teaching years, or years teaching in your school—to each group. Then have each student work independently to make a histogram that displays his group's assigned set of data.

It's in the Mail!

Skill: Making a circle graph

How much mail does the average family receive each week? Find out with this data-collecting activity! Brainstorm with students the different types of mail their families receive, such as bills, personal letters, magazines, advertising circulars, catalogs, credit card promotionals, and postcards. Next, have each student keep a tally of each piece of mail his family receives during a six-day period (Monday through Saturday), collecting his data in a frequency table. After the data has been collected, give each student a copy of the pattern on page 101. Then direct him to follow these steps:

1. Add to find the total pieces of mail.
2. Count the total pieces of mail in each category.
3. Find the percentage of the total pieces of mail that each category represents.
4. Multiply each percentage times 360 (the number of degrees in a circle) to determine the section size for each category.
5. Draw, label, and color each section of the circle.
6. Give the graph a title.

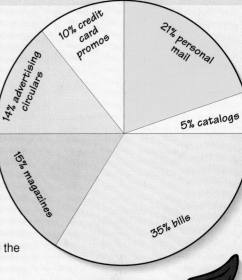

Family Mail

- 10% credit card promos
- 21% personal mail
- 14% advertising circulars
- 5% catalogs
- 15% magazines
- 35% bills

In the News

Skill: Making a line graph

There's more to a newspaper than just news, as students will find out with this line-graphing activity. Each day for a week, bring to class a local daily newspaper (including Saturday and Sunday editions). Ask students to donate their copies too. Next, divide students into groups of three. Assign each group one of the topics shown. Then have the group determine its data for each day and display it in a line graph. Remind students that a line graph shows change over a period of time, so they'll be graphing data from seven days' worth of newspapers. Have each trio glue its final graph on a 12" x 18" sheet of poster board. Display the graphs on a bulletin board backed with newspapers and titled "Line Graphs in the News!"

Topics:

- the number of pages in each edition
- the number of photographs in each edition
- the number of column inches devoted to the major front-page news story
- the daily high or low local temperatures listed in the newspapers
- the number of column inches devoted to advertising in one section
- the number of people whose photographs are featured in a particular section
- the number of different cities listed in the datelines of a particular section
- the number of games reported on in the sports section

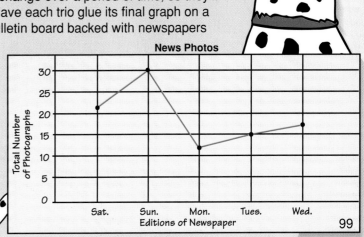

News Photos

Total Number of Photographs (vertical axis: 0, 5, 10, 15, 20, 25, 30)

Editions of Newspaper (horizontal axis: Sat., Sun., Mon., Tues., Wed.)

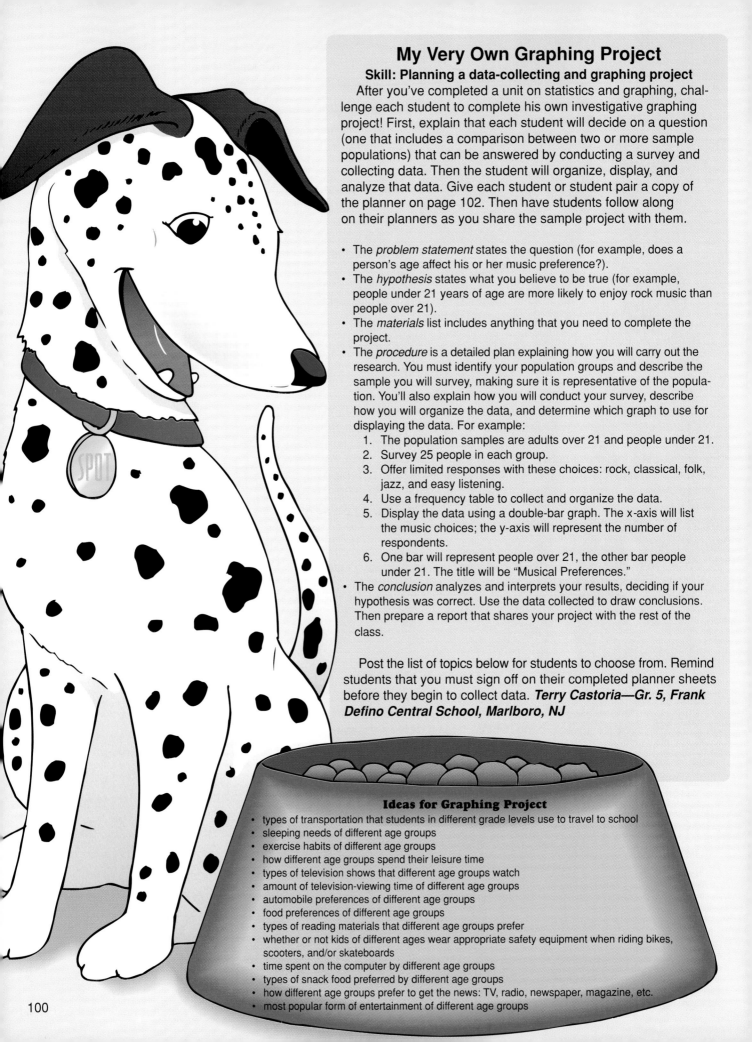

My Very Own Graphing Project

Skill: Planning a data-collecting and graphing project

After you've completed a unit on statistics and graphing, challenge each student to complete his own investigative graphing project! First, explain that each student will decide on a question (one that includes a comparison between two or more sample populations) that can be answered by conducting a survey and collecting data. Then the student will organize, display, and analyze that data. Give each student or student pair a copy of the planner on page 102. Then have students follow along on their planners as you share the sample project with them.

- The *problem statement* states the question (for example, does a person's age affect his or her music preference?).
- The *hypothesis* states what you believe to be true (for example, people under 21 years of age are more likely to enjoy rock music than people over 21).
- The *materials* list includes anything that you need to complete the project.
- The *procedure* is a detailed plan explaining how you will carry out the research. You must identify your population groups and describe the sample you will survey, making sure it is representative of the population. You'll also explain how you will conduct your survey, describe how you will organize the data, and determine which graph to use for displaying the data. For example:
  1. The population samples are adults over 21 and people under 21.
  2. Survey 25 people in each group.
  3. Offer limited responses with these choices: rock, classical, folk, jazz, and easy listening.
  4. Use a frequency table to collect and organize the data.
  5. Display the data using a double-bar graph. The x-axis will list the music choices; the y-axis will represent the number of respondents.
  6. One bar will represent people over 21, the other bar people under 21. The title will be "Musical Preferences."
- The *conclusion* analyzes and interprets your results, deciding if your hypothesis was correct. Use the data collected to draw conclusions. Then prepare a report that shares your project with the rest of the class.

Post the list of topics below for students to choose from. Remind students that you must sign off on their completed planner sheets before they begin to collect data. *Terry Castoria—Gr. 5, Frank Defino Central School, Marlboro, NJ*

Ideas for Graphing Project

- types of transportation that students in different grade levels use to travel to school
- sleeping needs of different age groups
- exercise habits of different age groups
- how different age groups spend their leisure time
- types of television shows that different age groups watch
- amount of television-viewing time of different age groups
- automobile preferences of different age groups
- food preferences of different age groups
- types of reading materials that different age groups prefer
- whether or not kids of different ages wear appropriate safety equipment when riding bikes, scooters, and/or skateboards
- time spent on the computer by different age groups
- types of snack food preferred by different age groups
- how different age groups prefer to get the news: TV, radio, newspaper, magazine, etc.
- most popular form of entertainment of different age groups

Circle Graph Pattern

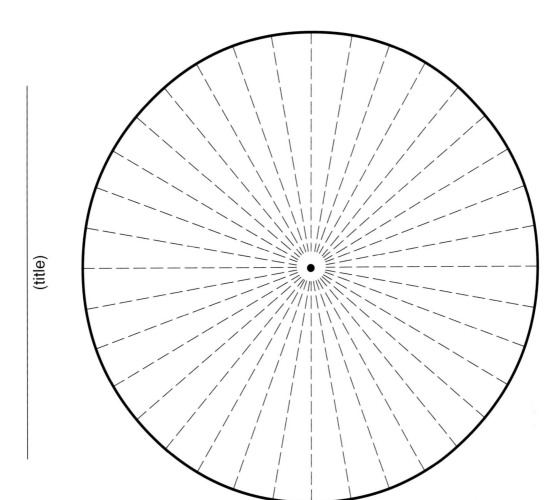

_____ _____
(title)

Note: Each section of the circle represents 10°.

Evaluating a graph

Graph SPOTS

Can you spot the following information on the graph that you're evaluating? After examining the graph, answer the following questions.

Source: Who or what organization created the graph? _____

What date is on the graph? _____

Is the information current? _____ Explain. _____
_____

Purpose: What does the graph communicate to us? _____
_____

Organization: What type of graph is it? _____

Title: What is the title of the graph? _____

Scale and/or symbols: What number scales are used in the graph? What symbols are used, and what do they represent? _____
_____
_____

Note to the teacher: Use the graph evaluation form with "Graph SPOTS" on page 98. Use the circle graph pattern with "It's in the Mail!" on page 99.

101

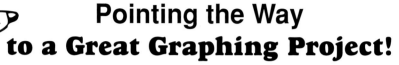

Pointing the Way
to a Great Graphing Project!

Ready to tackle a great graphing project? First, decide on a question you want to answer. Then complete the sections below. Staple additional sheets of paper to the back of this page if you need more space. Finally, ask your teacher and a parent/ guardian to sign the blanks at the bottom of the page.

Project Planner

Problem Statement: Write the question you want to answer. _____

_____

Hypothesis: What do you believe to be true? _____

_____

Materials: List any materials that you need.

_____   _____   _____

_____   _____   _____

Procedure: Explain how you will carry out your research.

1. Identify your population groups. _____

   _____

2. Describe the sample you will survey, making sure it is representative of the population.

   _____

3. Explain how you will conduct your survey. _____

   _____

4. Explain how you will organize the data you collect. _____

   _____

5. What kind of graph will you use to display your data? _____

6. How will you set up your graph? _____

   _____

   _____

Conclusion: Analyze and interpret your results. Was your hypothesis accurate? Use the data to draw conclusions. Then prepare a report about your project to share with the rest of the class.

Teacher: _____   Parent/guardian: _____

Spots and More Spots!

How many spots do 101 dalmatians have all together? Well, what about 23 dalmatians? Look at the doghouses below that show the number of spots on each dalmatian. Then follow the steps below to make a stem-and-leaf plot to organize and display the data. In a stem-and-leaf plot, the ones digits appear in rows as leaves. Tens (and larger) digits appear in a column as stems. The plot has been started for you.

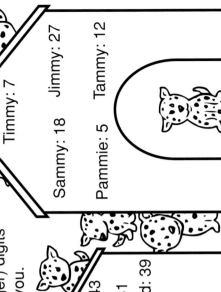

Bo: 20
Bib: 9
Bob: 38
Bub: 27
Spot: 12
Bear: 24
Brock: 27

Hal: 33
Al: 22
Kyle: 14
Sal: 15
Cal: 23

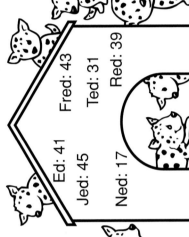

Ed: 41
Jed: 45
Ned: 17
Fred: 43
Ted: 31
Red: 39

Timmy: 7
Sammy: 18
Pammie: 5
Jimmy: 27
Tammy: 12

Step 1: List the number of spots on each dog. List the numbers from least to greatest.

_____

_____

Step 2: Complete the stem-and-leaf plot shown. Separate each number from Step 1 into stems (tens) and leaves (ones). List the numbers in order from least to greatest. Add a title to your plot.

_____
(title)

Stems	Leaves
0	5, 7
1	

Step 3: Use your stem-and-leaf plot to answer the following questions:

1. What is the range of the data? _____

2. What is the median of the data? _____

3. What is the mode of the data? _____

Bonus Box: Find the mean of the data listed on each doghouse. Round each answer to the nearest whole.

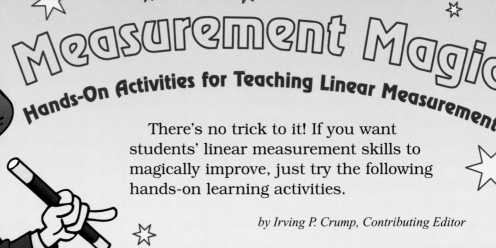

Measurement Magic

Hands-On Activities for Teaching Linear Measurement

There's no trick to it! If you want students' linear measurement skills to magically improve, just try the following hands-on learning activities.

by Irving P. Crump, Contributing Editor

Ready, Set, Review

Skill: Reviewing customary and metric units of measure

Introduce students to the magic of linear measurement by having them make measuring tapes to use with the activities in this unit. Give each student a copy of page 107, scissors, and glue. After each student makes a measuring tape as directed, point out that the tape represents one *meter*. Guide students to see that a meter is equivalent to 100 *centimeters,* and that each centimeter is divided into 10 *millimeters.* Ask students how many millimeters are in a meter. *(1,000)* Also share that a *decimeter* (10 centimeters) is another metric unit that is not used as often as meter, centimeter, and millimeter. Ask students to name the metric unit they'd most likely use to measure each of the following:

length of the classroom *(m)*	thickness of a slice of bread *(mm)*
width of camera film *(mm)*	length of a swimming pool *(m)*
height of a door *(m or cm)*	width of a sheet of paper *(cm)*
length of a basketball court *(m)*	perimeter of a calculator *(cm)*

Also review with students the customary units that are on the opposite edge of the tape. Have students note that the tape is nearly 40 *inches* long and that each inch is divided into halves, fourths, and eighths. Point out that one *foot* (12 inches), two feet (24 inches), and three feet (36 inches) are marked, and that a *yard* is equivalent to three feet, or 36 inches. Then have students use their tapes with the following measuring activities.

Body Facts

Skill: Measuring in customary and metric units

There's a bit of magic in some of our body's measurements! To discover it, divide students into pairs. Direct one student in each pair to use the metric edge of his measuring tape and the other student to use the customary edge. Then have students in each twosome take turns measuring each other and recording their measurements using these directions:

1. Have your partner hold out his arms to the side. Measure him fingertip to fingertip to find his arm span. Next, measure your partner's height. *(The length of a student's arm span is about the same as his height.)*
2. Measure the circumference of your partner's thumb by wrapping the tape around the base of the thumb. Then multiply that measurement by two. Next, measure your partner's wrist. *(The measurement of a student's wrist is about twice the measurement of his thumb.)*
3. Measure the circumference of your partner's neck. Multiply the measurement of your partner's wrist (see Step 2) by two. *(The measurement of a student's neck is about twice the measurement of his wrist.)*
4. Measure your partner's forearm from elbow to wrist. Then measure his foot from heel to toe. *(The length of a student's forearm is about the same as the length of his foot.)*

The Great 2,500-Millimeter Race
Skill: Measuring in metric units

1 = cm
2 = mm
3 = cm
4 = mm
5 = cm
6 = dm

We're going to race *how* far? After their initial shock subsides, show students that a 2,500-millimeter race is actually very short (the same as 2½ meters). Call on three students to demonstrate the distance with their measuring tapes. Then divide students into pairs. Give each pair a 2½-meter-long strip of paper. List on the chalkboard the information shown; then direct each twosome to write the numbers 0–9 on a sheet of paper. Each pair will also need a measuring tape. The object of the game is to see which pair can get closest to 2,500 millimeters without going over. To play:

1. Roll a die and announce the number showing.
2. Each pair notes the matching unit of measure for that roll. For example, if 5 is rolled, then the matching unit is centimeters.
3. Each pair chooses a number from its list (0–9) to use with that measure. For example, if 5 is rolled (centimeters), the pair could choose 7 to equal seven centimeters. After the pair chooses a number, it is marked through and cannot be used again. The pair then measures and marks that distance at one end of the paper strip. (In the example, the pair would measure seven centimeters and make a mark.)
4. Repeat Steps 1–3 nine more times. For each roll, each pair continues measuring from the previous mark.
5. Declare the pair whose line is closest to 2,500 millimeters (without going over) the winner.

If desired, run the race a second time. Have pairs turn over their paper strips and use the reverse side.

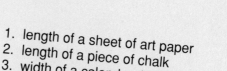

Measurement Hunt
Skill: Measuring to the nearest inch, half inch, and quarter inch

Use this fun activity to hunt down better measurement skills using customary units. First, remind students that measurements in the real world are always approximate. Discuss the factors that can affect the precision of measurements that they make: the measurement tool used and its scale, how they read the scale on the tool, and how accurate students think a measurement needs to be. Then send pairs of students on the following measurement scavenger hunt.

Number and label about 12 classroom objects for students to measure. (See the suggestions.) Provide each pair of students with an index card and a measuring tape. Direct each twosome to visit each of the 12 objects and measure it to the nearest inch. After recording the object's number and measurement, the pair moves on to another item. Have the twosomes circulate about the classroom until they have measured each object. Then discuss with the class their measurements. Ask why some measures may have varied and what factors came into play. Then repeat the activity by having students measure each object to the nearest half and then quarter inch.

1. length of a sheet of art paper
2. length of a piece of chalk
3. width of a calendar date box
4. height of a lunchbox
5. width of a TV or computer monitor screen
6. diameter of a clock face
7. height of a file cabinet
8. width of a window
9. length of a shoe
10. circumference of a plant pot
11. diameter of a doorknob
12. perimeter of a tabletop or desktop

Measurement Hunt 2
Skills: Estimating, measuring to the nearest centimeter

Send students off on another measurement hunt—but this time, with a little bit of a twist! First, copy the list of measurements shown on a chalkboard or transparency. Provide each pair of students with an index card on which to copy the list. Next, send each pair to search for an item in or near the classroom that students estimate would equal each measure listed. For example, a pair might estimate that the circumference of a pencil is about ten millimeters or that the height of a file cabinet is 1½ meters. Have each twosome jot down the item beside its corresponding measure. Remind students to estimate only—not to measure.

After every pair has written an item beside each measure, send the twosomes back to the items they selected—this time with a measuring tape. Direct each pair to measure each object to the nearest centimeter to see how close the actual measure is to the estimate.

10 mm	3 mm
1½ m	2 m
15 cm	3 dm
6 m	½ m
40 cm	65 cm

Steps 1–2

Step 3

Step 4

Step 5

Step 6

How Tall Is That Flagpole?
Skills: Estimating, measuring a tall object

Show students a neat trick for measuring tall objects with this outdoor activity. Point out to your class a tall object on your school grounds, such as a flagpole, large tree, water tower, or utility pole. Ask students to describe all the methods they could use to go about measuring such an object. Then take the class outside. (Take a pencil with you.) Have students offer their estimates on the height of the object; then measure it! Follow these steps:

1. Stand at a distance from the object and hold the pencil in a vertical position and out in front of you.
2. Move toward or away from the tall object until the pencil seems to extend from its top to its base. See the illustration.
3. Direct a student to stand at the base of the object.
4. Turn the pencil to the left or right so that it is aligned with the ground.
5. Tell the student at the object to start walking along the "path of the pencil" until he reaches the end of the pencil. Then tell him to stop and stay at that position.
6. Have two pairs of students use their measuring tapes to measure from the base of the object to where the student is standing. This measurement will equal the approximate height of the object.

The measurement should be fairly accurate. Identify other tall objects on your campus. Then have pairs of students work together to measure the heights of those objects.

Metric or Customary? Both!

Follow the directions below to make your own metric and customary measuring tape:
1. Carefully cut out the 5 sections.
2. Glue the sections to each other in the correct order.
3. Write your name on the back of the tape.

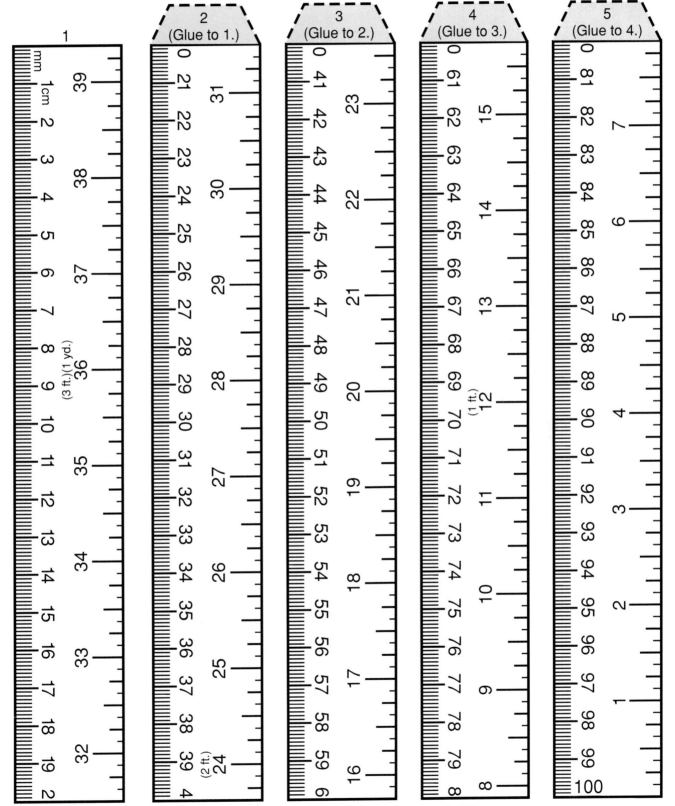

©The Education Center, Inc. • THE MAILBOX® • Intermediate • Feb/Mar 2002

Note to the teacher: Use with the activities on pages 104–106 and 109.

Masters of Magic

Part 1: He was an *illusionist,* a magician who performed large-scale tricks. One of his most amazing tricks was the "fantastic suitcase." He pulled birds, cages, hats, and pans from a thin suitcase. Then he ended the trick by lifting out his young son!

Who was this magician? To find out, read each letter and its measurement. Find that measurement on the ruler and write its letter above the arrow. The first one is done for you.

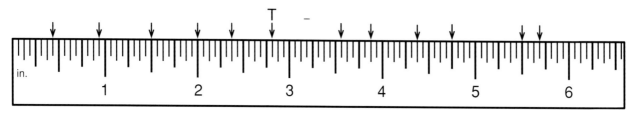

T = $2\frac{13}{16}$"   N = $5\frac{11}{16}$"   H = $3\frac{9}{16}$"   B = $1\frac{1}{2}$"   U = $4\frac{3}{8}$"   D = $4\frac{3}{4}$"

R = $2\frac{3}{8}$"   O = $\frac{15}{16}$"   I = $5\frac{1}{2}$"   E = 2"   R = $\frac{7}{16}$"   O = $3\frac{7}{8}$"

Part 2: He was one of the world's most famous escape artists. He could quickly free himself from leg irons, handcuffs, jail cells, and nailed crates. One of his most amazing tricks was escaping from an airtight tank that was filled with water!

Who was this magician? To find out, read each measurement marked with an arrow. Then write the letter at that arrow in the blank above its matching measurement. The first one is done for you.

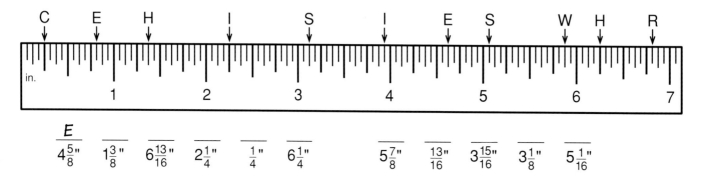

$\frac{E}{4\frac{5}{8}"}$ $\overline{1\frac{3}{8}"}$ $\overline{6\frac{13}{16}"}$ $\overline{2\frac{1}{4}"}$ $\overline{\frac{1}{4}"}$ $\overline{6\frac{1}{4}"}$ $\overline{5\frac{7}{8}"}$ $\overline{\frac{13}{16}"}$ $\overline{3\frac{15}{16}"}$ $\overline{3\frac{1}{8}"}$ $\overline{5\frac{1}{16}"}$

Part 3: The magician in Part 2 was born in Hungary. When he was a child, his family moved to Wisconsin. He took a new stage name when he began performing.

What was this magician's stage name? To find out, read each measurement below. Find the measurement on each of the 2 rulers above. Then write the letter that is closest to that measurement.

$1\frac{5}{16}$" = _____   1" = _____ $4\frac{1}{4}$" = _____ $4\frac{13}{16}$" = _____ $5\frac{7}{16}$" = _____ $5\frac{3}{4}$" = _____ $2\frac{3}{16}$" = _____

Bonus Box: In the first puzzle, what is the distance between the first and last letters of the magician's name?

Now You See It...Now You Don't!

Sleight of hand is one of the most common kinds of magic. It includes tricks that depend on the skillful use of the hands. Sleight-of-hand tricks are often performed with a deck of cards. One of the oldest sleight-of-hand routines was performed in ancient Egypt!

Complete the puzzle below to learn another name for sleight of hand. Use a metric ruler to measure each segment. Write the segment name in the blank with its matching measurement.

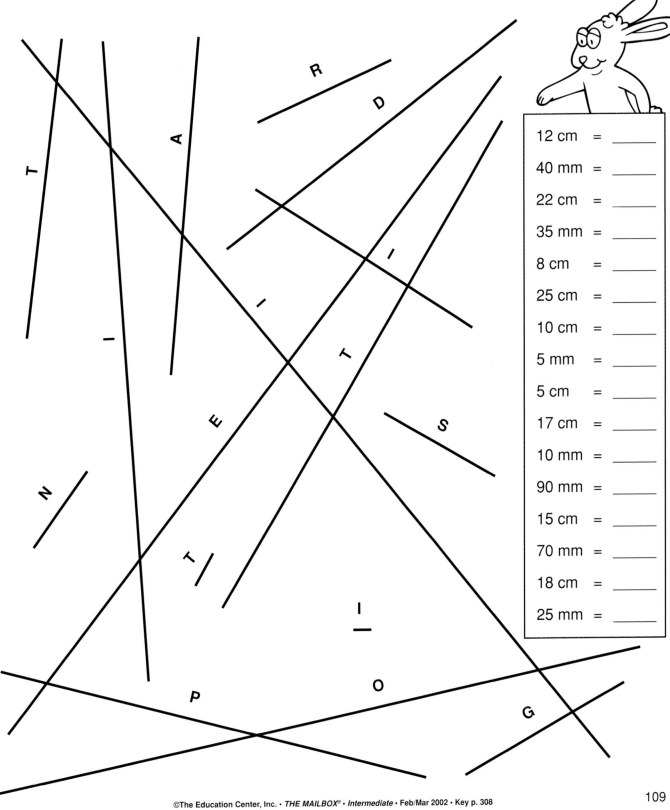

12 cm	=	_____
40 mm	=	_____
22 cm	=	_____
35 mm	=	_____
8 cm	=	_____
25 cm	=	_____
10 cm	=	_____
5 mm	=	_____
5 cm	=	_____
17 cm	=	_____
10 mm	=	_____
90 mm	=	_____
15 cm	=	_____
70 mm	=	_____
18 cm	=	_____
25 mm	=	_____

Chances Are...

Activities for Investigating Probability

Increase your students' chances of mastering probability with the following investigations!

Certain, Impossible, or Somewhere in Between?
Skill: Determining the likelihood of an event

What's the likelihood that students will love this activity? You can bet on it! Begin by briefly reviewing with the class the meanings of the following terms: *certain* (always happens), *likely* (could happen), *impossible* (could not happen). Next, have each student number a sheet of paper from 1 to 8. Then read aloud one statement at a time from the list shown. Have each student record whether he thinks that event's occurrence is certain, likely, or impossible. When students have responded to all of the statements, discuss the answers together. For more practice, challenge each student to write five similar statements of his own. Then have him trade with a classmate and check his partner's responses.

1. The clock will say six o'clock twice today unless it stops working. *(certain)*
2. You will grow nine feet today. *(impossible)*
3. I will eat a meat, a vegetable, a fruit, or bread today. *(likely)*
4. If you throw a paper airplane up into the air, it will come down unless something or someone interferes with it. *(certain)*
5. If I roll a die ten times, I will roll a five at least once. *(likely)*
6. The baby will take an afternoon nap. *(likely)*
7. I will sharpen my pencil today. *(likely)*
8. The girl walked 30 miles in just two hours. *(impossible)*

Smiley Probabilities
Skill: Representing the likelihood of an event with a number

Here's an easy-to-do probability activity that's sure to put a big :-) on everyone's face! Display the chart shown. Explain to students that the combinations of letters and symbols are called *smileys,* small pictures of faces (turned sideways) used to express different emotions. Ask, "If these 12 smileys are shown on cards, what is the likelihood of drawing a card that contains an exclamation point?" *(impossible)* Explain that this impossible event can be represented with the number 0. Ask, "What is the likelihood of drawing a card that does not contain the letter *S?"* *(certain)* Explain that this certain event can be represented with the number 1. Then ask, "What is the likelihood of drawing a card containing an asterisk?" *(2 of 12: kiss, hug and kiss)* Explain that this likelihood can be represented with the fraction $^2/_{12}$, which can be reduced to $^1/_6$. Finally, divide the class into pairs. Challenge each twosome to create three questions based on the chart: one to represent with a 0, one to represent with a 1, and one to represent with a fraction. Follow up by having each student complete a copy of "Odds Are…" on page 112 as directed.

:-)	Smile
:-(	Sad
:-D	Laugh
:'(	Cry
:-O	Shout
;-)	Wink
:-*	Kiss
{*}	Hug and kiss
:-&	Tongue-tied
:-()	Can't stop talking
%-(	Confused, unhappy
:-#	I wear braces.

Take a Spin!

Skills: Predicting the outcome of an event, testing predictions

Use this "spinner-ific" activity to help students learn more about predicting the outcome of events and testing their predictions. Pair students; then give each pair a sheet of unlined paper and two paper clips. Direct the pair to draw two spinners on its paper as shown. Next, display the questions shown on a chalkboard or transparency. Have each pair answer both sets of questions on another sheet of paper. Then have each twosome follow these steps to test its predictions:

1. Practice using the spinner with a paper clip and pencil as shown.
2. Copy the charts shown on another sheet of paper.
3. Spin each spinner 20 times and record the results in the appropriate chart.

Check students' results together.

TEST 1 Questions

If you spin Spinner A:

1. What is the probability of getting a 1? *(⁰⁄₆)*
2. What is the probability of getting an even number? *(⁶⁄₆ or 1)*
3. What is the probability of getting a number greater than 2? *(⁴⁄₆ or ²⁄₃)*
4. What is the probability of getting a 12? *(⁰⁄₆)*
5. What is the probability of getting a 2 or a 4? *(²⁄₆ or ¹⁄₃)*

TEST 2 Questions

If you spin Spinners A and B:

1. What is the probability of getting two 3s? *(⁰⁄₃₆)*
2. What is the probability of getting a sum of 7? *(⁴⁄₃₆ or ¹⁄₉)*
3. What is the probability of getting a sum of 10 or higher? *(²¹⁄₃₆ or ⁷⁄₁₂)*
4. What is the probability of getting a sum of 11? *(⁶⁄₃₆ or ¹⁄₆)*
5. What is the probability of getting a sum of 3? *(²⁄₃₆ or ¹⁄₁₈)*

TEST 1 Results for A		TEST 2 Results for A and B	
Spin	Result	Spin	Result
1		1	
2		2	
3		3	
4		4	
5		5	
6		6	
7		7	
8		8	
9		9	
10		10	
11		11	
12		12	
13		13	
14		14	
15		15	
16		16	
17		17	
18		18	
19		19	
20		20	

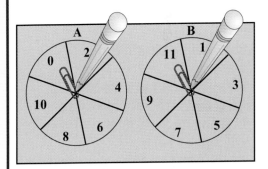

Fair and Square?

Skills: Determining the fairness of a game, identifying square numbers

Challenge students to predict a game's outcome before it's played with this nifty activity! Pair students; then give each twosome one die and six ½-inch round removable labels. Have each pair program the labels with the numbers 49, 32, 86, 64, 144, and 16 and affix them to the die. Explain that a *square number* is the product of a whole number multiplied by itself (for example, nine is the product of 3 x 3). Ask students whether they are more likely to roll a square number or a nonsquare number using the die *(square, because four of the six sides have square numbers)*. Then ask which type of number is less likely to be rolled *(nonsquare, because only two of the six sides have nonsquare numbers)*.

Next, display the game rules shown. Ask students which player they think will win the game *(the player assigned to the square numbers, since there are more square numbers on the die than nonsquare ones)*. Finally, have each pair play the game to see whether it is fair to both players *(no, because Player 1 has a greater chance to win than Player 2)*.

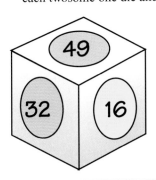

Rules for the game:

- Player 1 has the square numbers. Player 2 has the numbers that are not square.
- Each player takes turns rolling the die and recording the result of each roll in a frequency table for a total of 20 rolls.
- A player earns two points each time he or she rolls one of his or her assigned numbers.
- The winner is the player with more points after 20 rolls.

Number	Tally	Frequency
49		
32		
86		
64		
144		
16		

Name_____

Odds Are...

Is a giraffe likely to outlive a kangaroo? What are the chances of drawing a particular card from a deck? Find out for yourself by following the directions below!

Part 1: Study the chart of average animal life spans on the right. Use the words *likely* or *unlikely* to record the likelihood of each event below happening.

1. a giraffe outliving a kangaroo _____

2. a lobster outliving a polar bear _____

3. a gorilla living 15 years _____

4. a pig living 11 years _____

5. a mouse or a squirrel outliving _____
   a lion

6. an Asian elephant living 70 _____
   years

7. a Bactrian camel's life span _____
   being triple that of a kangaroo

8. a chipmunk's life span being _____
   half that of a cat

Animal	Average Life Span (in years)	Animal	Average Life Span (in years)
Box turtle	100	Cat (domestic)	12
Asian elephant	40	Dog (domestic)	12
Grizzly bear	25	Leopard	12
Horse	20	Giraffe	10
Gorilla	20	Pig	10
Polar bear	20	Squirrel	10
Rhinoceros (white)	20	Red fox	7
Black bear	18	Kangaroo	7
Lion	15	Chipmunk	6
Lobster	15	Rabbit	5
Rhesus monkey	15	Guinea pig	4
Rhinoceros (black)	15	Mouse	3
Bactrian Camel	12	Opossum	1

(Source: *The World Almanac for Kids 1998,* K-111 Reference Corporation)

Number	Symbol	Number	Symbol
1	I	20	XX
2	II	30	XXX
3	III	40	XL
4	IV	50	L
5	V	60	LX
6	VI	70	LXX
7	VII	80	LXXX
8	VIII	90	XC
9	IX	100	C
10	X	200	CC
11	XI	300	CCC
12	XII	400	CD
13	XIII	500	D
14	XIV	600	DC
15	XV	700	DCC
16	XVI	800	DCCC
17	XVII	900	CM
18	XVIII	1,000	M
19	XIX		

Part 2: Study the chart of Roman numerals on the left. Suppose that each number and its corresponding symbol is written on a different card. Use the code shown to represent the likelihood of each event below.

> **Code**
> 0 = impossible   1 = certain
> fraction between 0 and 1 = possible

What is the likelihood of drawing a Roman numeral...

9. containing an *I, V, X, L, C, D,* or *M?* _____

10. having both an *X* and a *V?* _____

11. not containing four of any letter? _____

12. having two *V*s? _____

13. that is a multiple of 10 and has an *X?* _____

14. having two *L*s? _____

15. that is a multiple of 3? _____

16. from 400 to 900 and having three *C*s? _____

Note to the teacher: Use with "Smiley Probabilities" on page 110.

SOCIAL STUDIES UNITS

Picturing Ancient Egypt

Use the following creative activities to help your students picture life in the historical hot spot of ancient Egypt!

ideas by Patricia Twohey

Scenes From Egyptian Life

Skills: Researching, summarizing, oral communication

What was life like for ancient Egyptians? Challenge students to answer that question on their own with this creative dramatics activity. First, divide the class into groups of three or four students each. Assign one of the research topics below to each group. When students have finished researching, have each group organize its notes into subtopics and write a one-page summary.

Next, announce that a famous movie director wants the class to produce a series of short films about ancient Egypt. Direct each group to use its summary to write a brief skit that will tell others about its topic. Allow three to six days for groups to write their skits, prepare simple props and costumes, and practice. Videotape each group's production; then replay the video and discuss the different aspects of Egyptian life that students have depicted.

If you'd rather students tackle a smaller project, try this variation. Instead of assigning skits, have each group create a still-life scene about its topic. Instruct one student to read aloud his group's summary while his group mates pose as Egyptians; then have each group member, in turn, explain his role in the scene.

Research Topics	
Marriage and Family Life	Language and Writing
Being a Kid in Ancient Egypt	Medicines and Magic
Egyptian Homes	Ancient Egyptian Transportation
Dining in Egypt	An Egyptian Classroom
Egyptian Fashions	Farming in Ancient Egypt
Artwork in Ancient Egypt	Death and Dying in Ancient Egypt

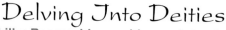

Delving Into Deities

Skills: Researching, writing an interview, oral communication

Ancient Egyptians believed in and worshipped a wide variety of gods and goddesses, who they believed influenced every aspect of nature and their daily lives. Introduce your students to these ancient Egyptian deities with a nifty research and oral communication activity. Write the name of each god or goddess listed below on a circle cut from gold paper; then place the circles in a basket. Announce that the ancient Egyptian gods placed special coins in a basket that was discovered floating in the Nile River. Then divide the class into pairs and have each pair select a coin.

Next, direct each twosome to research its god or goddess to learn about his or her importance to the Egyptians. Have the pair use the information to write an interview between the deity and a reporter for the *Egyptian Inquirer* newspaper. Instruct the pair to either tape-record its interview or perform it live for the class. For an art extension, have each twosome design a mask of its deity using a brown paper grocery bag and other art materials. Display the masks on a bulletin board.

Gods and goddesses: Amon, Anubis, Geb, Hathor, Horus, Isis, Nekhebet, Nut, Osiris, Re, Serapis, Seth, Shu, Tefnut, Thoth

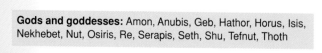

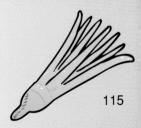

Pharaoh Info
Skills: Researching, summarizing, art

Throughout most of its history, ancient Egypt was ruled by a series of kings (and a few queens), called *pharaohs*. Introduce students to some of these rulers with this group research and art activity. Divide the class into groups of three students each. Have each group research to find out about the life, reign, and accomplishments of one of the rulers listed below.

When students have finished researching, explain that Egyptians were buried in colorfully decorated mummy cases. Show students pictures of cases from resource books. Then have each group trace an enlarged copy of the mummy case pattern on page 117 on a large sheet of butcher paper. Direct the group to cut out its shape and decorate it to resemble a mummy case for its ruler. Also, have the group summarize its research on a large index card. Provide time for each group to share its information and case with the class; then write each ruler's name and reigning time period on the board. Work with students to sequence the rulers in order, starting with the earliest pharaoh. Then hang the cutouts and cards chronologically on a classroom clothesline or in a hallway.

Rulers: Khufu, Amenemhet, Senusret I, Thutmose I, Hatshepsut, Thutmose III, Akhenaton, Tutankhamen, Ramses II, Seti I, Cleopatra, Ptolemy I, Nefertiti

Tutankhamen

Pyramid Building 101
Skills: Reading for specific information, following written directions

Ancient Egyptians were known for many outstanding accomplishments, but none more famous than the pyramids they built as tombs for their rulers. Give your students a chance to build their own pyramids with this fun activity. First, divide the class into four groups. Gather a collection of resource books about ancient Egypt. Then assign each group one of the following questions to research:

- What did ancient Egyptians believe about the afterlife?
- How did ancient Egyptians prepare bodies for burial?
- How were the pyramids built?
- What was the inside of a pyramid like?

After each group shares its information, give each student a copy of the directions on page 117 and the materials listed on it. If desired, display the finished pyramids in one or more large plastic containers filled with sand. Let students use art materials to create other items to add to the scene.

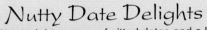

An Egyptian Treat
Measuring, following directions

Get a real taste of ancient Egypt by making a treat that was likely served along the Nile. Explain to students that dates grew wild and were harvested in August in the Nile Valley. Then have small groups of students make the easy recipe shown.

Nutty Date Delights

Place eight ounces of pitted dates and a little water in a blender. Blend to paste consistency. Remove to a bowl. Stir in one teaspoon cinnamon and one-half teaspoon cardamom. Add $3\frac{1}{2}$ ounces coarsely chopped walnuts. Shape mixture into small balls. Then roll each ball in honey and dip in finely ground almonds.

Name _____

Touring the Land of Pyramids and Pharaohs

Got your ticket handy? It's time to take a tour of ancient Egypt! Study the map shown. Then follow the directions below, using the labels in the box. Don't forget to bring your hat and sunblock!

Directions:

1. Color the two seas blue. Label each sea.
2. Trace the main river and its branches in blue. Label the river.
3. Note the two desert areas on the map. Label them. (Hint: The Western Desert is west of the Nile.)
4. Ancient Egypt was divided into the Lower Kingdom in the north and the Upper Kingdom in the south. Label the two kingdoms.
5. Three of ancient Egypt's past capitals are shown on the map. Underline them.
6. The Valley of the Kings was the burial place of many important pharaohs. It lies across the river from Karnak and Luxor. Label it.
7. Cut out the drawings below and glue them in the correct boxes.

Mediterranean Sea	Red Sea
Nile River	Western Desert
Eastern Desert	Lower Kingdom
Upper Kingdom	Valley of the Kings

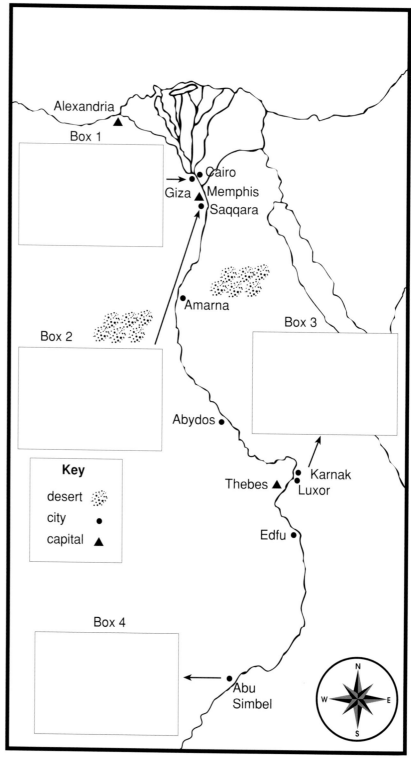

Monuments at Giza

Step Pyramid at Saqqara

Temples of Ramses II at Abu Simbel

Temples at Karnak

©The Education Center, Inc. • THE MAILBOX® • Intermediate • Aug/Sept 2001 • Key p. 308

116 **Note to the teacher:** Each student will need a blue marker or crayon, a pencil, scissors, and glue to complete this page.

Enlarge and use with "Pharaoh Info" on page 115.

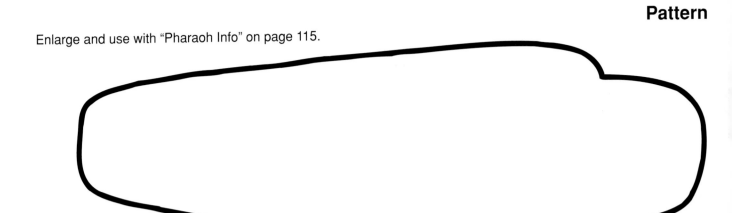

Name ————————————————————————————— Following written directions

Build Like an Egyptian!
Follow these directions to build a pyramid of your very own!

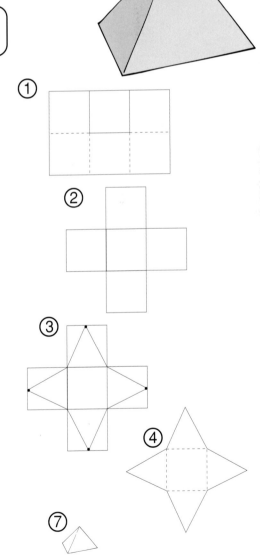

Materials for each student: scissors, tape, 12" x 18" sheet
of light brown or tan paper, ruler, pencil, gold or yellow paper

Steps:

1. Draw lines to divide the light-colored paper into six
   six-inch squares as shown.
2. Cut off two corner squares to make a T shape. Tape
   one of the cutout squares to the top of the T to make a
   cross shape as shown.
3. Measure three inches from the end of each of the four
   outer lines and draw a dot in the middle as shown. Draw
   lines from each dot to the corners of the middle square.
4. Cut on these lines to make four triangle shapes as
   shown.
5. On the center square, write a paragraph summarizing
   the facts you have learned from your group's research.
6. Ancient Egyptians were often buried with some of their
   possessions. They believed they could take these items
   with them into the afterlife. On each triangle, draw a picture of one of your personal treasures.
7. Trace the top two inches of the point of one of the triangles onto gold paper. Cut out the triangle and use it
   to trace three more triangles. Cut out the triangles. Then
   tape all four triangles together to make a mini pyramid.
8. Crease on the dotted lines in Figure 4 so that the pyramid
   walls fold up. Bring the walls up to a point; then place
   the smaller pyramid on top to hold the walls together.

Note to the teacher: Use with "Pyramid Building 101" on page 115.

Live From the American Landscape!

Investigating U.S. Landforms and Other Natural Features

Whether you're looking for spacious skies, amber waves of grain, purple mountain majesties, or fruited plains, America the beautiful seems to have them all. Investigate the landforms and other natural features that dot our country's landscape with the following activities.

with ideas by Simone Lepine—Gr. 5, Gillette Road Middle School, Cicero, NY

"Land-o"

Skill: Learning geographical terms

Make learning geography terms anything but boring with this variation of bingo. Give each student one of the terms below and a 12" x 18" sheet of art paper. Have the student make a poster that includes the word and its definition, an illustration, and one real-life example. After students share their work, display the posters on a bulletin board.

Next, make a class supply of the bingo card shown. Cover the display with a large piece of bulletin board paper; then display a transparency of the terms. Direct each student to randomly label each space on his card with one of the words. When the boards are ready, give each student a handful of markers. Read aloud a definition, checking off the term on your own copy of the list. Have each student who has the matching word on his card cover it with a marker. Continue until one child covers five words in a row in any direction and yells "Land-o!" If he has covered the correct words, award him a small prize. Then continue playing for several more rounds.

L	A	N	D-O
		FREE	

Terms

archipelago	divide	mountain
basin	dune	mountain range
bay	fjord	peak
butte	foothill	peninsula
canyon	glacier	plain
cape	gorge	plateau
cliff	hill	prairie
crevasse	isthmus	strait
delta	lake	valley
desert	mesa	volcano

Make a Model

Skill: Identifying landforms and other natural features

Who says play dough is just for little kids? Not in this game, which challenges students to build models of natural features. Let students help you create a batch of dough using the recipe shown. Then follow these steps:

1. Divide the class into teams of three or four.
2. Give each team a laminated sheet of construction paper or a plastic placemat and a large lump of dough.
3. Write a term from the list on this page on the board. Set a timer for one minute. Then challenge Team 1 to use the dough to construct a model of the natural feature on the team's mat.
4. When time is up, award Team 1 five points for a correct model and three additional points if the team can correctly define the term. If the model is incorrect, reset the timer and challenge Team 2 to construct the model.
5. Continue until time is up or all words are used. Declare the team with the most points at the end of the game the winner.

No-Cook Modeling Dough

Mix four cups flour, two cups salt, and one-fourth cup vegetable oil. Add water and food coloring until dough is desired consistency and color.

Carlsbad Caverns

_____

_____

_____

_____

_____

Time to Change
Skills: Researching, completing a chart

Once students learn about the variety of natural features found in the United States, they may ask, "But how did they get here?" Challenge them to answer that question themselves with this activity. First, explain that many of today's landforms were formed by the process of erosion. Erosion breaks rock and soil loose from the land at one place and moves it to another. Wind, ice, water, and temperature changes are just some of the agents of erosion. Further explain that some landforms were formed by forces related to the movement of the earth's tectonic plates, which can cause volcanoes and earthquakes.

After this discussion, divide the class into pairs. Have each twosome research one of the landforms shown to find out how it was formed. Next, have the pair decorate a large yellow or gray construction paper circle with an illustration of its landform (hand-drawn or cut from a magazine) and an explanation of how it was formed. Display the cutouts on a bulletin board titled "Time to Change."

Landforms

Appalachian Mountains	Great Lakes
Badlands	Great Sand Dunes
Bryce Canyon	Hawaiian Islands
Carlsbad Caverns	Mount Shasta
Cascade Range	Niagara Falls
Death Valley	Outer Banks
Everglades	Rocky Mountains
Grand Canyon	Teton Mountains

How Low (or High) Can You Go?
Skill: Understanding differences in elevation

Get students out of their seats and on their feet with this lively activity on elevation! Label ten 9" x 12" sheets of paper with the labels in the diagram below (one per sheet). Also give each student an enlarged copy of the diagram. Explain to students that the diagram—called a _cross section_—shows how the United States might look if cut across from east to west. The labels indicate the approximate locations and elevations of some prominent physical features.

After discussing the cross section, ask ten students to stand at the front of the classroom. Randomly give a poster to each child. Then challenge the seated classmates to direct the standing students so that they arrange themselves according to the cross section. After this is done successfully, have the two ocean students lie flat on the floor. Instruct the standing students to show their different elevations by changing their heights in some way. For example, the Rocky Mountains student might stand on a chair while the Great Basin child kneels. After the first group completes its cross section, have these students swap places with seated classmates. Then see whether the new students can arrange themselves without assistance.

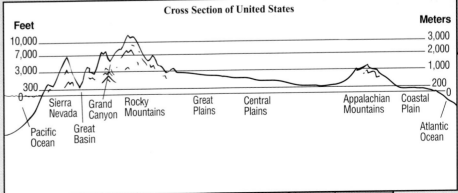

Cross Section of United States

Tops in Topography
Skills: Creating bar graphs, researching

Work a little math and research skills practice into your study of U.S. natural features! Post a transparency of the figures shown. Then have students use the figures to complete the following activities:

- For each set of data, create a bar graph that illustrates the differences between the five features.
- Label the features listed on a blank U.S. map (see page 122).
- Research any two of the features listed. Write a paragraph or design a poster that compares and contrasts the features.
- Research to find out the top five features in each category worldwide.
- Write a series of math word problems based on the data for your classmates to solve.

Highest U.S. Mountains	
Mt. McKinley, AK	20,320 ft.
Mt. Whitney, CA	14,494 ft.
Mt. Elbert, CO	14,433 ft.
Mt. Rainier, WA	14,410 ft.
Gannett Peak, WY	13,804 ft.

Great Lakes	
Lake Superior	31,820 sq. mi.
Lake Huron	23,010 sq. mi.
Lake Michigan	22,400 sq. mi.
Lake Erie	9,940 sq. mi.
Lake Ontario	7,540 sq. mi.

Longest U.S. Rivers	
Missouri	2,540 mi.
Mississippi	2,340 mi.
Yukon	1,979 mi.
Rio Grande	1,885 mi.
Arkansas	1,396 mi.

Hot, Cold, Wet, or Dry?
Skill: Understanding the relationship between land and climate

Help your students to understand how land features affect climate with the reproducibles on pages 121 and 122. Before students complete the pages, discuss these concepts:

- As air rises, it becomes colder and less able to hold much moisture. Therefore, when air that rises to go over a mountain becomes colder, it may lose much of its moisture. This means that a place located on a mountain will generally have a wetter, cooler climate than a place at a lower elevation.
- Mountains can affect the climate of nearby lowland areas. For example, the lowlands that lie west of the Cascades receive heavy precipitation from winds that blow in from the Pacific Ocean. But by the time these moisture-laden winds pass over the Cascades, they've lost most of their moisture. That leaves the area east of the Cascades dry.
- Areas nearer the equator receive more direct sun rays. They are therefore warmer than areas that aren't as close to the equator.

American Landscape Legends
Skills: Writing a legend, researching

Did you know that Niagara Falls was created by Paul Bunyan, who was only trying to give his messy daughter a much-needed shower? Many stories about this legendary hero attempt to explain how he created some of America's most famous natural features. Ask your media specialist to help you gather some books or stories about Paul Bunyan, including the titles below. Share the books with your class. Then have each student research one of the features listed below (and on page 119) and write a legend that explains how it came into existence. At the end of the story, have the student include a brief epilogue that cites real facts about the feature. Bind the stories, along with student-drawn illustrations, in a class book titled "American Landscape Legends."

Books About Paul Bunyan
- *The Bunyans* by Audrey Wood
- *Paul Bunyan* by Steven Kellogg
- *Paul Bunyan and the Winter of the Blue Snow* by Andy Gregg

Natural Features

Bonneville Salt Flats	Mississippi River
Crater Lake	Mojave Desert
Devils Tower	Monument Valley
Great Salt Lake	Mount McKinley
Great Smoky Mountains	Mount Saint Helens

This Just In!

The climate and natural features around the United States are as different as our country is big. More at 11:00! (But don't wait till then! Find out for yourself by completing the activities below.)

Part 1: Number your paper 1–10. Look at the map on page 32. Write the matching natural feature from the television beside each number.

Part 2: Below are five lists related to climate. Underline each city's name on the map with a crayon, marker, or colored pencil as directed. CAREFUL: A few cities will need to be underlined with two different colors.

Alaska Range
Appalachian Mountains
Atlantic Ocean
Cascade Range
Great Lakes

Gulf of Mexico
Mississippi River
Pacific Ocean
Rocky Mountains
Sierra Nevada

Top Five Driest U.S. Cities average yearly precipitation *(brown)*	Top Five Wettest U.S. Cities average yearly precipitation *(blue)*	Top Five Snowiest U.S. Cities average yearly snowfall *(orange)*
1. Yuma, AZ (2.65")	1. Quillayute, WA (105.18")	1. Blue Canyon, CA (240.8")
2. Las Vegas, NV (4.19")	2. Astoria, OR (66.40")	2. Marquette, MI (129.2")
3. Bishop, CA (5.61")	3. Tallahassee, FL (65.71")	3. Sault Ste. Marie, MI (116.1")
4. Bakersfield, CA (5.72")	4. Mobile, AL (63.96")	4. Syracuse, NY (114.0")
5. Phoenix, AZ (7.11")	5. Pensacola, FL (62.25")	5. Caribou, ME (110.0")

Top Five Hottest U.S. Cities average temperature *(red)*	Top Five Coldest U.S. Cities average temperature *(yellow)*
1. Key West, FL (77.7°F)	1. International Falls, MN (36.4°F)
2. Miami, FL (75.6°F)	2. Duluth, MN (38.2°F)
3. West Palm Beach, FL (74.6°F)	3. Caribou, ME (38.9°F)
4. Fort Myers, FL (73.9°F)	4. Marquette, MI (39.2°F)
5. Yuma, AZ (73.9°F)	5. Sault Ste. Marie, MI (39.7°F)

Part 3: Use the map and reference books to answer these questions on a separate sheet of paper.
1. How is it possible for California to have both very dry and very snowy cities?
2. How do mountains affect the climate in Las Vegas, Nevada?
3. What do all of the wettest cities have in common in terms of location?
4. What do the hottest cities have in common in terms of location? The coldest cities?

Note to the teacher: Use this page with "Hot, Cold, Wet, or Dry?" on page 120 and the reproducible on page 122. Provide students with access to encyclopedias or other references.

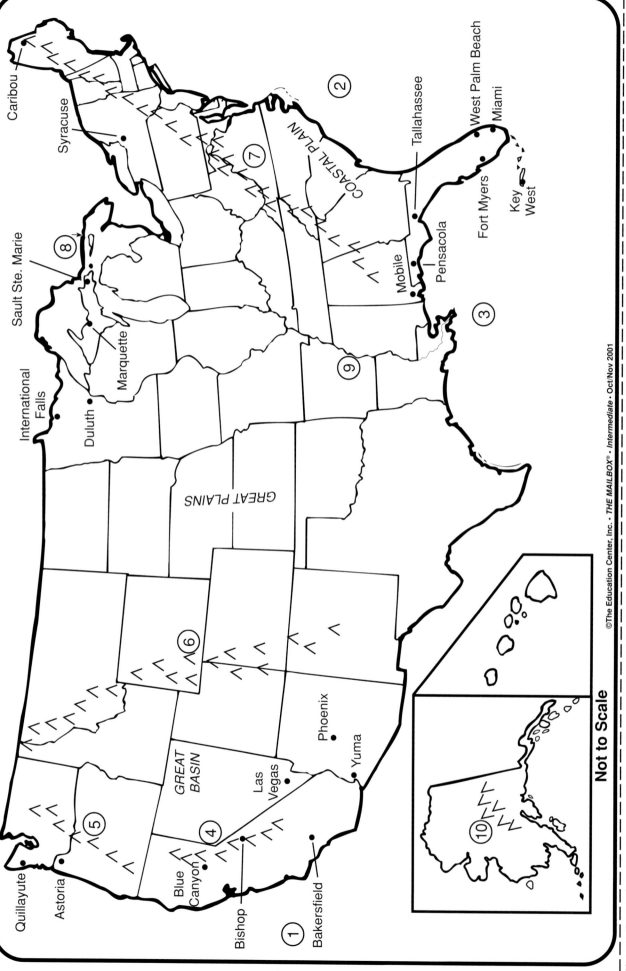

COASTAL PLAIN

GREAT PLAINS

GREAT BASIN

Not to Scale

Caribou
Syracuse
Sault Ste. Marie
International Falls
Marquette
Duluth
Astoria
Quillayute
Blue Canyon
Bishop
Bakersfield
Las Vegas
Phoenix
Yuma
Mobile
Pensacola
Fort Myers
Key West
Miami
West Palm Beach
Tallahassee

Note to the teacher: Use this page with "Tops in Topography" and "Hot, Cold, Wet, or Dry?" on page 121. To complete this map for "Hot, Cold, Wet, or Dry?" on page 120, each student will need a copy of page 121 and crayons, colored pencils, or fine-tipped markers in these colors: brown, blue, orange, yellow, red.

Stellar State History Activities

What can a stellar teacher like you find in this star-studded collection? Plenty of all-star activities that investigate your state's history!

with contributions by Dana Sanders, Cartersville, GA

This place called Virginia sounds pretty cool.

Scout It Out!

Skills: Understanding the influence of geography on a state, thinking critically

Make students aware of geography's role in the development of your state with this fun group activity. First, announce that the class is an official colonial scouting party that has been hired by a European monarchy to explore your state and report back on its suitability for colonization. Next, divide the class into three (or six) groups. Assign one of the following topics about your state to each group: physical features, climate, valuable resources. Give each group several sheets of chart paper and markers. Then instruct it to research its topic and write its findings on the chart paper.

On the day groups are to present their findings, play the role of a monarch by wearing a paper crown and a large, beach towel robe. Have each group present its findings to you and your court (the class). After the presentations, ask each student (or group) to write a letter to you giving his recommendations on the following:

• Should this area be colonized? Why or why not?
• What predictions can you make about life in this area?

What's in a Name?

Skill: Knowing the origins of important names of places in a state

There's a lot of history hidden in the names on your state's map. Bring that history out of hiding with this easy-to-do idea! First, help students brainstorm a list of simple songs with familiar tunes, such as "Row, Row, Row Your Boat" and "Jingle Bells." Write these song titles on the board. Next, display a large map of your state. Ask students to identify several cities, rivers, counties, and other places (monuments, tourist attractions, landforms, etc.) that your class has studied or read about. List these items on the board beside the previous list. Then divide the class into pairs and assign an item from this second list to each twosome. Instruct each pair to research its item to discover the origin of its name. Then challenge the duo to create a song—sung to a familiar tune from the first list—that can teach the class about the name's origin. Provide time for students to practice their songs before they present them to the class. If you have any extremely shy students, allow them to record their songs before class and play the recordings instead of performing live.

A Penny for Your Thoughts

Skills: Understanding major events in a state's history, writing a description

Raid your loose change jar for this "cents-ational" state history activity! Collect a penny for each student, trying to find a wide range of years. Give each student her penny. Then challenge the student to identify and research an important event in your state's history that occurred during the year that her penny was minted. Direct the student to take notes on her chosen event. Then have her write a description of the event on a large index card and tape her penny to a corner of the card. After each student shares her description with the class, have her glue the card on a large penny cutout as shown. Tape each cutout to a length of yarn. Then suspend the coins from your ceiling for a shower of state history facts!

Scrambled Skits

Skills: Understanding major events in a state's history, writing a skit

Use this creative group activity to set the stage for a better understanding of key events in your state's history. Divide the class into groups and assign one important event in your state's history to each group. Then challenge each group to write a short skit that tells about its event. The catch? The group must include at least five errors about the event in its skit. Provide one class period for writing the skits and another for practicing them. Make a copy of each group's completed skit, directing the group to highlight the errors on the copy for your reference.

As a group presents its skit, challenge each student in the audience to listen carefully and to make a list of any errors he catches. As students share their lists, have the performing group identify correct guesses. Not only will students learn more about your state's history, but they'll also add some shine to their listening skills!

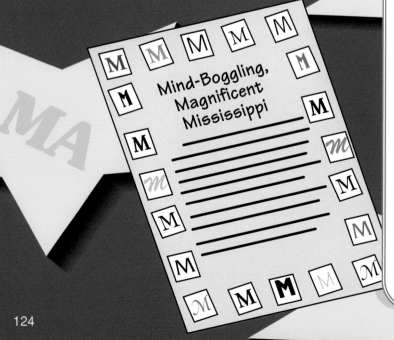

Operation Alliteration

Skill: Reviewing important people and events in your state's history

Review important facts about your state's history with this letter-perfect project. Begin by having each student list interesting facts about your state's history. Next, have the student use a dictionary to list words that begin with the same letter as your state. As the final step, have the student use both lists—the state history facts and the word list—to write an alliterative paragraph about your state's history. For a fun display idea, have students cut out samples of the letter they used from old magazines. Then have each child glue some of the letters around the edges of a sheet of construction paper. Finally, have the student copy or glue her paragraph inside the frame of letters. Display the projects on a bulletin board titled "Presenting Pertinent Paragraphs About Our State's Past."

State History Time Capsule

Skill: Evaluating the importance of major events in a state's history

Use the ready-to-go reproducible on page 127 to challenge your students to think critically about the major events in your state's history. Give each student a copy of page 127. After reading and discussing the introduction and steps as a class, have each student complete a copy of the page as directed. (If desired, let students complete Step 1 in pairs or small groups.) When students have finished the page, divide the class into small groups. Then have each student share his time capsule and letter with his group. If desired, have students cut out their time capsules to post with the letters on a bulletin board.

Historical Personalities Parade

Skill: Understanding how the ideas of significant people affected a state's history

Who were the people who put your state on the map? Find out with an activity that results in a super student-made display! First, make a list of important people associated with your state's history. Have each student choose a person to research. Direct the student to find out about the person's main contributions to your state and the nation, his or her personal characteristics, and other interesting or unusual facts. After the student has taken her notes, have her pretend to be her famous person and write a first-person description. Direct the student to proofread her description and make any corrections or changes. Then have her copy the description onto white paper.

Next, provide each student with the materials listed below and guide her through the steps. Display the finished figures and speech bubbles in a hallway to create a parade of famous folks from your state. For another activity on studying your state's famous people, see "Where Would We Be Without You?" on page 126. *Julia Alarie—Gr. 6, Essex Middle School, Essex, VT*

Materials: two to four 12" x 18" sheets of construction paper, pencil, ruler, scissors, glue, 9" x 12" sheet of white construction paper, crayons or markers

Steps:
1. Fold one larger sheet of construction paper in half lengthwise. Draw two straight lines on the folded paper as shown.
2. Cut along the lines, saving the scraps.
3. Unfold the upside-down V-shaped piece. This will be the torso and legs of your person.
4. Trim away the points of the two larger paper scraps as shown. Then glue them to the back of the torso for arms.
5. Cut out a paper circle for the head. Also cut out hands and feet and any objects you'd like the person to hold. Add details with crayons or markers to make the model look like your famous person. Then glue the features to the torso.
6. Fold the arms forward to create different positions.
7. Trim the excess paper around your description. Then glue the description onto the white construction paper. Cut the construction paper into the shape of a conversation bubble.

Where Would We Be Without You?

Thomas Edison, Martin Luther King Jr., Eleanor Roosevelt—where would our country be without the contributions of these ingenious and gifted Americans? In the same way, your state has been home to many talented people who have made great contributions to your state and our country.

Directions: Choose a famous person from your state. Write the person's name where indicated. Then research to find out how this person has impacted your state. In strip 1, draw a cartoon that illustrates how life in your state is different because of this person's contributions. In strip 2, draw a cartoon that illustrates how life in your state would be different if this person had never been born.

Famous person in my state: _____

★ ★ ★ ★ ★ ★ ★ ★ ★ ★ ★ ★ **Strip 1** ★ ★ ★ ★ ★ ★ ★ ★ ★ ★ ★ ★

★ ★ ★ ★ ★ ★ ★ ★ ★ ★ ★ ★ **Strip 2** ★ ★ ★ ★ ★ ★ ★ ★ ★ ★ ★ ★

State History Time Capsule

Can you do a favor for the head honcho in your state? The governor has decided to put together a time capsule for the citizens of a future century. You have been selected to choose appropriate artifacts to represent the history of your state. Follow the steps given to help out your governor.

Steps:

1. In the box, list at least seven important events in your state's history.
2. Think about how each event impacted the people of your state and the nation. Then underline the five events that you think are the most important.
3. For each underlined event, draw a picture in the time capsule of an artifact that represents the event.
4. On a sheet of notebook paper, write a letter to the governor describing the artifacts you have chosen. Tell why you have selected each event featured in this time capsule.
5. Staple your letter to the back of this page.

★ Important State History Events ★

_____
_____
_____
_____
_____
_____
_____
_____
_____
_____
_____
_____

★   ★

Bonus Box: Number the five items in your time capsule from 1 to 5, with 1 being the most important event. On the back of this page, write a few sentences explaining why your number one item deserves that ranking.

Celebrate Citizenship!

Activities on the Rights and Responsibilities of Citizenship

Salute citizenship—with all of its rights and responsibilities—using the following creative activities and reproducibles!

with ideas by Pat Twohey, Old County Road School, Smithfield, RI

Vocabulary Explosion
Concept: Terms related to citizenship

Create a dazzling fireworks display with this star-spangled vocabulary activity! After dividing the class into pairs, give each twosome a marker and a fireworks shape cut from red, white, or blue construction paper. Assign a term listed below to each pair; then have the twosome label the cutout with its word. Next, direct the partners to research the word and write its definition on the back of the cutout. After each pair shares its term, hang the fireworks from your ceiling with string. If desired, have each student record the terms and meanings in his own word journal. Have students make their journals using these steps:

1. Place eight sheets of white paper between two sheets of construction paper (one red, one blue).
2. Staple the white paper between the covers at the top.
3. Trim the journal to make a fireworks shape as shown.
4. Write each word and its definition in the journal, one word per page. Add an illustration that symbolizes or helps explain the word.
5. Label the journal "[Your name]'s Liberty Lexicon" and decorate the cover.

We, the Citizens
Concept: Meaning of citizenship

Encourage students to reflect on what it means to be a citizen with this poetry-writing activity. In advance, collect an empty coffee can (with the lid) for each student. List these questions on the board:

- What does it mean to be a citizen?
- What rights does a citizen enjoy?
- What responsibilities or duties does a citizen have?
- Why be a member of a nation instead of acting on your own?

Divide the class into groups to discuss the questions. Then have students share their ideas as you list them on chart paper. Guide students through the list shown below, pointing out that many rights have limits. For example, the freedom of speech doesn't allow a person to harm another person's reputation by telling lies.

Next, give each student a lidded coffee can. Have each student measure and cut a piece of white construction paper to fit around the can. Have the student write a poem on the paper about what citizenship means to her. After the student illustrates the poem, have her glue the paper around the can. Challenge each group formed earlier to come up with a unique way to display the decorated cans; then vote to select the class's favorite idea. Invite other classes to view your students' salute to citizenship.

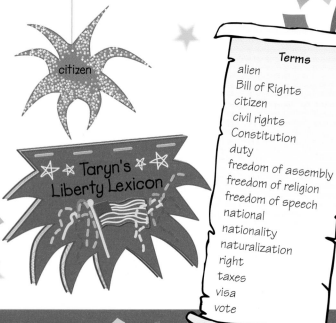

Terms
alien
Bill of Rights
citizen
civil rights
Constitution
duty
freedom of assembly
freedom of religion
freedom of speech
national
nationality
naturalization
right
taxes
visa
vote

Taryn's Liberty Lexicon

Celebrating Citizenship
by Shellie

Rights of U.S. citizens include the following:

- freedom of speech
- freedom of religion
- freedom of assembly
- right to vote
- right to run for political offices
- right to travel throughout the United States
- can't be forced to leave homeland
- can't lose citizenship except for serious actions

Name That Right!
Concept: Rights of citizenship

Use this nifty game to help students focus on the ways citizens exercise their rights every day. Divide the class into groups. Give each group three four-inch paper squares: one red, one white, and one blue. Write the following code on the board: red = freedom of speech, blue = freedom of religion, white = freedom of assembly. Have each group discuss these rights; then have it write on each card two situations during which a citizen would exercise that right (for example, a group might list "moving to a new town and deciding which church to attend" on the blue card). Give each group a folder in which to store its completed cards. Then play the following guessing game:

1. In turn, have one student from Group A read aloud a situation from one of his group's cards, keeping the card hidden in the folder.
2. Challenge Group B to identify the right that matches the situation.
3. Have Group A display the card that was read. If the guess is correct, award a red chip, plastic checker, or paper marker to Group B.
4. Repeat Steps 1–3 with Group B reading a situation to Group C. Continue until all situations on the cards have been read and discussed. Then declare the team with the most chips the winner.

Citizens Speak Out
Concept: The Bill of Rights

Introduce your class to the most famous Bill around. Bill Gates? No! The Bill of Rights, of course! Give each student a copy of page 131, a kid-friendly version of this famous document. Divide the class into pairs; then have each twosome read through the ten amendments and discuss what they think each one means and why it is important. Have the pair list on the back of the page three main ideas it gathered from reading the amendments. Then discuss the students' ideas as a class. Next, have each student complete the second part of page 131 as directed. Provide time for each child to give his speech to the class.

moving to a new town and deciding which church to attend

worshipping at a local synagogue

an environmentalist giving a speech on stopping pollution

a politician giving a campaign speech

holding a march to protest a new law

attending a meeting on a proposed park

by Brian

Serve on Juries

Pay Taxes

Do Your Duty, by George!
Concept: Responsibilities of citizenship

If George Washington—one of our country's most famous citizens—were alive today, he'd probably have plenty to say during this activity on the duties of citizenship. Point out that most nations require each citizen to pay taxes, defend his country, and obey laws. Many of those governments also require that certain citizens serve on juries. Discuss these duties, asking students to give reasons why citizens should (or should not) fulfill them. After the discussion, provide each student with a copy of page 132, a 9" x 12" sheet of gray construction paper, scissors, glue, and clear tape. Have each student complete his monument and share it with the class; then display the projects in the classroom or school library.

Unwritten Duties

Concept: Responsibilities of citizenship

Many people believe that citizens also have duties that are not demanded by the law. Challenge students to use this data collection activity to find out what others in the community think about these unwritten responsibilities. Give each student a form similar to the one shown. Instruct each child to poll a total of ten to 15 adults (family members, neighbors, and other adult friends) and fill out his form.

After students have finished their polls, divide the class into groups of four. Give each group a sheet of chart paper, a marker, and a ruler. Direct the students in each group to combine their data and create a bar graph to display their results for each question. Then instruct each group to analyze its graph and prepare an oral presentation to explain the findings. After each group gives its presentation, discuss these questions: What do the statistics tell us? How would you have answered the questions, and why?

Citizenship Poll

Do you agree that it is a citizen's duty to...	Yes	No
Vote	𝅫𝅫𝅫𝅫𝅫𝅫𝅫𝅫	||
Learn about public problems	𝅫𝅫𝅫𝅫𝅫𝅫	||||
Help other people in the community	𝅫𝅫𝅫𝅫𝅫𝅫𝅫𝅫	||

Reading About Citizenship

Concept: Making connections to citizenship

Help students make connections to the topic of citizenship with the aid of some outstanding children's books. Ask your librarian to help you gather copies of the titles listed. Display the questions shown below. Then read one of the books aloud and use the questions to guide a class discussion. After the talk, divide the class into groups. Give each group one or more books, a sheet of chart paper, and a marker. Have the group list its responses to the questions on the paper. Then have groups share their responses as a class.

Books:
- *Now Let Me Fly: The Story of a Slave Family* by Dolores Johnson
- *Who Belongs Here? An American Story* by Margy Burns Knight
- *The Garden of Happiness* by Erika Tamar
- *A Very Important Day* by Maggie Rugg Herold
- *The American Wei* by Marion Hess Pomeranc
- *Granddaddy's Gift* by Margaree King Mitchell

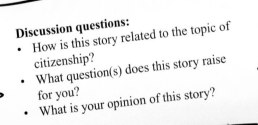

Discussion questions:
- How is this story related to the topic of citizenship?
- What question(s) does this story raise for you?
- What is your opinion of this story?

Speaking of Your Rights

What's the most famous Bill in the United States? The Bill of Rights, of course! This document states the first ten amendments to the U.S. Constitution. These amendments guarantee the basic freedoms that Americans—including you—enjoy today!

Part I: Read through the summary of the Bill of Rights below. Talk with your partner about what you think each amendment means and why it is important.

Amendment 1
You have freedoms of religion, speech, and the press. You also have the right to assemble peacefully and to let the government know if you disagree with its actions.

Amendment 3
Soldiers won't be kept in your home during peaceful times without your permission.

Amendment 5
You can't be held for a crime without an indictment from a grand jury (except in some military cases). You can't be tried twice for the same crime. You don't have to testify against yourself in court. You have the right to due process of the law. Your property cannot be taken for public use without payment.

Amendment 7
You have the right to a trial by jury.

Amendment 9
You have other rights that are not specifically listed in the Constitution.

Amendment 2
You have the right to own and bear arms (weapons).

Amendment 4
You or your property cannot be searched or taken without your permission or without a warrant based on a good reason.

Amendment 6
You have the right to a speedy and public trial by a fair jury. You have the right to know what you're accused of and to hear any witnesses against you. You have the right to find witnesses to support you and to have a lawyer defend you.

Amendment 8
You can't be charged excessive fines or bail or be punished in a cruel or unusual way.

Amendment 10
The federal government may have only the powers given to it by the Constitution. Any other powers belong to the states and to the people.

Part II: Choose one of the amendments above. On another sheet of paper, write a short speech giving your opinion of the amendment. Tell why you think it is or is not an important right for citizens to have and what life might be like without it. Practice your speech so you'll be ready to present it to the rest of the class.

©The Education Center, Inc. • THE MAILBOX® • Intermediate • Dec/Jan 2001–2

Do Your Duty, by George!

The Washington Monument in Washington, DC, honors one of our country's most famous citizens—George Washington. Make George proud by making your own mini monument about citizenship.

On each side of the pattern, list at least two reasons why citizens should carry out each duty. Then cut out the pattern and glue it to a sheet of construction paper. Cut out the pattern again and fold it on the dotted lines. Then tape the sides together to create your monument (see the illustration).

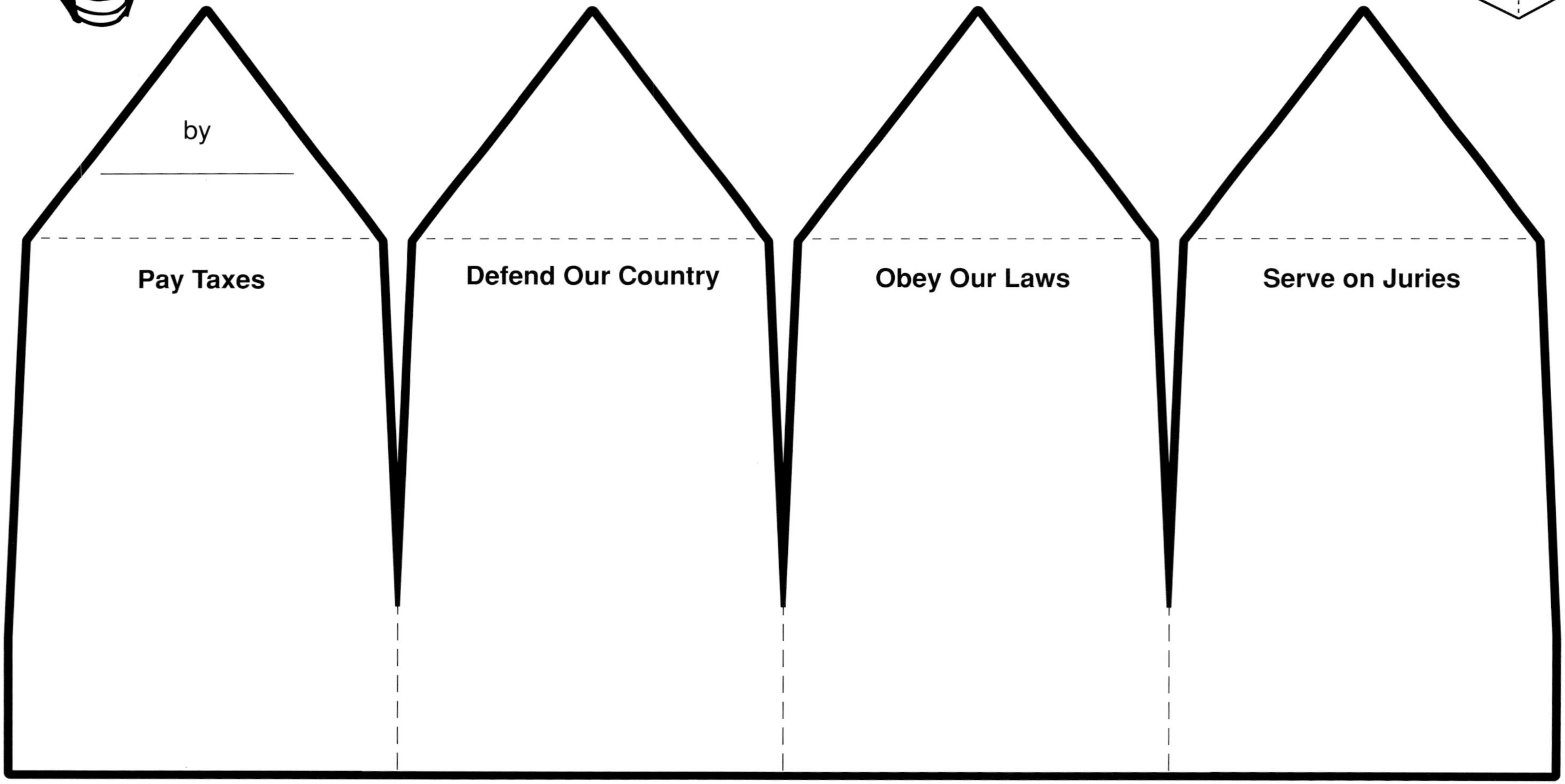

by _____

Pay Taxes

Defend Our Country

Obey Our Laws

Serve on Juries

©The Education Center, Inc. • *THE MAILBOX*® • *Intermediate* • Dec/Jan 2001–2

Note to the teacher: Use with "Do Your Duty, by George!" on page 129. Provide each student with scissors, glue, a 9" x 12" sheet of gray construction paper, and clear tape.

Colonial Kids
Growing Up in Colonial America

No televisions. No computers. Not even indoor plumbing. Life for the young people of colonial America was quite different from what today's children experience. Examine America's colonial period through the eyes of the kids who lived it using the following high-interest activities.

with contributions by Jennifer Roy, Saratoga Springs, NY

How Would You Feel?

Skills: Expressive writing, activating prior knowledge

How would you feel if you weren't able to bathe or shower for two whole months? Use attention-grabbing questions like this one, found on page 137, to generate interest in your colonial America unit. Just follow these steps:

1. Make one or two copies of page 137 (so that you have a card for each student).
2. Cut out the cards and place them in a paper bag.
3. Have each student draw a card from the bag and read it silently. Then have him write an answer to the question in his journal.
4. Ask each child to read his question and answer aloud. Invite other students to add their thoughts. Then share the background information for that question on page 309.

If desired, end the activity by posting a chart like the one shown. With students, fill in the first three columns. Have students complete the last section of the chart as they learn more about colonial America.

Colonial America			
What we already know	What we want to learn	How we'll locate information to answer the questions	What we've learned

What's in a Name?

Skills: Vocabulary, implied meanings, expressive writing

What's in a name? Plenty if you lived in colonial times. Colonial children were sometimes named for traits that the parents thought were important. That's why a roll call of children who were on the *Mayflower* includes such names as Resolved, Humility, and Desire.

After sharing the information about the naming of colonial children, challenge students to play the name game themselves! First, brainstorm with students a list of the difficulties colonists faced, such as lack of farming skills, harsh winters, sickness, etc. Next, display the list of colonial children's names shown and divide the class into groups of two or three students each. Have each group choose a name from the list and research its meaning using a dictionary. Then have the group write a diary entry from one of the child's parents explaining why that name was chosen and how the child might need to demonstrate the trait as a new settler. When the entries are finished, have each group use a black pen to copy its work onto a sheet of white paper. Then demonstrate for each group how to transform its paper into an authentic-looking document using the directions shown. Post the papers on a bulletin board labeled "My Name Is…"

Colonial Names
Humility
Remember
Resolved
Desire
Love
Patience
Charity
Constant
Unity
Experience
Waitstill
Preserved
Thanks
Unite
Supply

Preparing the paper:
Brew a cup of tea. Let the bag steep for five to ten minutes; then let the tea cool and remove the bag. Gently squeeze the tea bag and dab it on your paper. Let the paper dry completely. If desired, gently tear the edges to give the paper a weathered look.

Easy As A, B, C

Skills: Poetry, alliteration, penmanship

One of the items that helped the colonial child learn his letters and numbers was a folded card called a *battledore.* Battledores, which cost parents only a penny each, were printed with the alphabet, numbers, small pictures, and rhymes.

Use the reproducible activity on page 136 to help students make their own colonial battledores. Provide each child with a copy of page 136, scissors, and crayons or markers. Have the student complete the page as directed. Then discuss with students how learning to read and write with a battledore was different from how children learn in today's schools.

A Little Time for Fun

Skills: Mental math, addition

Life for colonial children may have been mostly work, but there was time to play. Smart colonial parents sneaked in a little math education using two games: ninepin and five alleys. Play your own versions of these fun games following the directions below.

- **Ninepin:** Collect nine empty Pringles potato chip cans and one small ball. Display a copy of the rules shown. Ask students if they recognize a pattern in the scoring rules (each successive goal after 39 is nine pins larger than the one before it). Then have students follow these rules:
1. Set up the cans in three rows of three or one long row of nine.
2. In turn, each player rolls the ball to knock over the pins. The player scores one point for each pin knocked down. He resets the pins after each roll.
3. The first player to score 31 points (with no leftover pins) is the winner.
4. If a player knocks down more than 31 pins, he must then try to get a score of 39.
5. If a player knocks down more than 39 pins, he must next try for a score of 48 (then 57, 66, and so on).
6. The first player to reach one of the goal numbers is the winner.
- **Five Alleys:** The Pilgrims made a wooden box that was divided into five alleys at one end, each labeled with a number. A child rolled a small ball from one end of the box into one of the alleys at the other end and added the number rolled to his running total. The player with the higher score at the end of ten rolls was the winner. To make the game, tape five small paper cups to one end of the bottom or lid of a large gift box; then write a different two- or three-digit number on each cup as shown. Slightly elevate the end of the box without the cups. Each player, in turn, rolls a marble or small ball from the elevated end of the box into one of the cups; then he writes that number on his paper. On his next turn, the player adds the number he rolls to the first number. The winner is the player with the higher score after ten rolls.

Colonial America on the Web
(current as of September 2001)
- **You Be the Historian**
http://americanhistory.si.edu/hohr/springer
Examine some real artifacts of one colonial American family, the Springers of New Castle, Delaware. Students are challenged to figure out what life was like 200 years ago for the colonial family by this site from the Smithsonian Institution's National Museum of American History.
- **Carol Hurst's Children's Literature Site**
http://www.carolhurst.com/subjects/ushistory/colonial.html
Visit this site for a list of activities and recommended children's literature on colonial America.

Attention, Colonial Mart Shoppers!

Skill: Researching a topic

In the early days of colonial America, there were no stores for colonists who wanted to shop till they dropped. But what if there had been? Invite your students to open the first ever Colonial Mart superstore with an activity that explores the daily life of colonial America. First, show students examples of ad circulars and catalogs from large stores like Wal-Mart or Target. Point out that the ads are often organized according to different departments, such as children's clothing, electronics, and toys. Let students examine the ad pieces in small groups.

Next, divide the class into the store departments shown. Provide each group with two sheets of art paper, crayons or markers, and reference materials about daily life in colonial America. Then instruct each group to create two (or more) pages for a catalog advertising the first superstore in colonial America, Colonial Mart. On its pages, have each group illustrate several colonial American items that might be sold in its department, including each item's name, price, and a description of how a colonist used it. Combine the group's pages between two covers to create your colonial catalog. For a variation that practices oral-presentation skills, challenge students to create commercials instead of catalog pages.

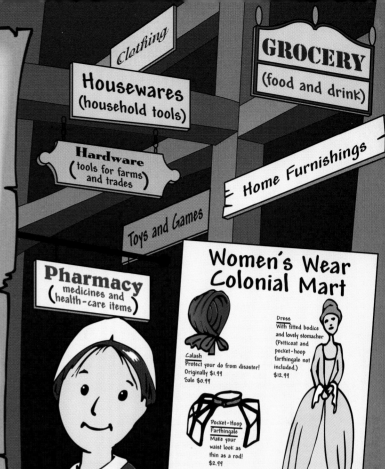

Home of the Free?

Skills: Critical thinking, making connections

Not all people who lived in colonial America would have called it the home of the free. African Americans and Native Americans were both adversely affected by colonization. Slaves knew oppression, while Native Americans saw their land being taken over by the growing population of colonists. Discuss these two groups with students. Then ask, "If you were a young slave or Native American in colonial America, what traits would you need to survive?" After students reflect on this question, divide the class into six teams. Provide each team with a large sheet of chart paper and a marker. Direct three teams to label the tops of their papers "African Americans" and three to label their papers "Native Americans." Then guide the teams through these steps:

1. Brainstorm a list of personality traits that children in your group would need to survive in colonial America. List these words across the top of your paper.
2. Draw three wheels below the word list as shown.
3. Choose three traits from the list and write each one in the center of a different wheel.
4. In the spaces between the spokes of each wheel, write five ways that kids today can demonstrate that trait.

When the charts are finished, pair each African American team with a Native American team. Then have teams share their charts, comparing and contrasting the difficulties faced by each group.

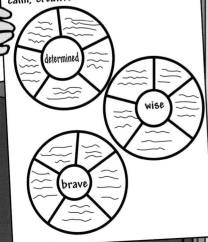

My Colonial Battledore

My Colonial Battledore

Name _____

Date _____

A B C D E F G H I J K L M N O P Q R
S T U V W X Y Z 1 2 3 4 5 6 7 8 9 0

A
B

A & B	*C & D*
E & F	*G & H*
I & J	*K & L*
M & N	*O & P*
Q & R	*S & T*
U & V	*W–Z*

Some colonial children learned to read and write using a small folded card called a *battledore*. A battledore included letters, numbers, small pictures, and rhymes. Use your best handwriting to make your own battledore. Follow these steps:

1. In box A, write a two-line rhyming verse that states a rule for everyday living.
   Example:
   Always listening, always kind,
   A better friend you'll never find.
2. Choose a letter of the alphabet. In box B, write an alliterative sentence made mostly of words that begin with that letter.
   Example:
   Betsy bought a blue blouse and a brown belt.
3. In each letter box, write a vocabulary word you would like to learn that begins with one of the box's letters. Look for words in the books you're reading, your textbooks, or the dictionary.
4. Cut out the battledore and fold it on the dotted lines.
5. Decorate the front of the folded battledore.

Note to the teacher: Use with "Easy As A, B, C" on page 134. If desired, have students add the vocabulary words to their weekly spelling list.

1. How would you feel if you had to say good-bye to all of your family and friends, knowing you'd never see them again?

2. How would you feel about working for someone for five to seven years without being paid?

3. How would you feel if you weren't able to bathe or shower for two whole months?

4. How would you feel if a strange-looking group of people suddenly appeared in your yard?

5. How would you feel if your house were blown down during a storm?

6. How would you feel about living with your entire family in a one-room house?

7. How would you feel if you weren't allowed to sit during meals?

8. How would you feel if your father announced that your family had just run out of food?

9. How would you feel if you only owned two or three outfits to wear?

10. How would you feel if you rarely saw your parents or any other grown-ups during the day?

11. How would you feel about being in a family with 12 brothers and sisters?

12. How would you feel if your mom and dad were your teachers?

13. How would you feel if you spent more time doing chores than you did being with friends, going to school, or playing?

14. How would you feel about never brushing your teeth?

15. How would you feel if you had to work on Christmas?

16. How would you feel if you were not allowed to learn to read or write?

17. How would you feel if your mother poured you a big glass of beer for breakfast?

18. How would you feel if your father wore a wig?

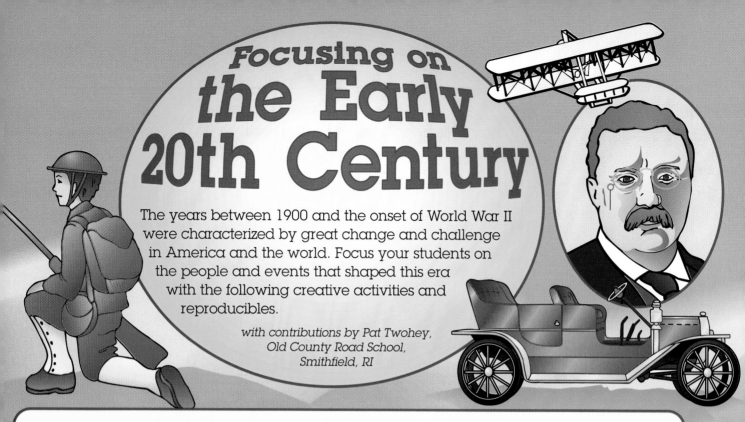

Focusing on the Early 20th Century

The years between 1900 and the onset of World War II were characterized by great change and challenge in America and the world. Focus your students on the people and events that shaped this era with the following creative activities and reproducibles.

with contributions by Pat Twohey, Old County Road School, Smithfield, RI

World War I: Causes and Results
Skills: Classifying, using context clues

Help your students understand the major causes and results of the Great War, or World War I (1914–1918), with this activity. Divide the class into groups of three or four students each. Give each group a copy of page 141, scissors, a glue stick, and a 12" x 18" sheet of construction paper. Inform students that they are going to be learning about World War I. Then challenge them to complete page 141 as directed, using context clues to help them arrange (but not glue) the strips on the construction paper. When students are finished, check and discuss their charts using the answer key on page 309. Allow a group to rearrange any incorrectly placed strips before it glues them to the paper. After students have studied World War I, have groups, pairs, or individual students repeat the activity on page 141 as a quick review or assessment.

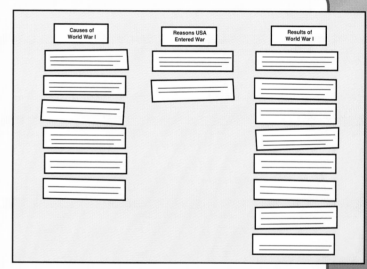

Causes of World War I

Reasons USA Entered War

Results of World War I

Headlines
- Jim Thorpe Loses Olympic Medals
- Lindbergh Flies Across Atlantic
- Peary Reaches North Pole
- Typhoid Mary Imprisoned
- Earthquake Devastates San Francisco
- President McKinley Shot
- Wright Brothers Make Powered Flight
- Queen Victoria of England Dies
- Marie Curie Wins Nobel Prize
- Prohibition Begins Today
- *Titanic* Sinks on Maiden Voyage
- King Tut's Tomb Found
- Henry Ford Unveils First Assembly Line
- *Lusitania* Sunk by Germans
- Tsar Nicholas Steps Down
- Pancho Villa Raids American Towns

Breaking News: Big Stories of the Era
Skills: Writing a news report, researching a topic

One thing's for sure—there was a lot of news to report during the early years of the 20th century! Introduce students to some of these news stories with this partner activity. Ask your school's librarian to provide your class with resources on early 20th-century America. Write each headline listed on a strip of paper; then place the strips in a bag. Next, divide the class into pairs. Have each twosome pull a strip from the bag, research the event, and write a brief television news report that answers who, what, where, when, why, and how. Each day during your unit, ask one or two twosomes to share their breaking news reports. For fun, decorate a bulletin board with a globe cutout and the title "World News Today." Position two student desks in front of the display; then have the reporting students don old suit jackets and ties and sit at the desks to give their report.

Women and the Vote
Skills: Expressive and persuasive writing

On an August day in 1920, a decades-long struggle ended when the 19th Amendment was signed into law. American women finally had the right to vote. To focus students on this historic event, announce that your school is holding an election to select a new mascot. Everyone will be allowed to vote except for students in your grade level. After your students protest (and they will!), ask each child to write a paragraph about how your announcement makes him feel. Let volunteers share their paragraphs.

Next, explain that the announcement was bogus. Point out that the frustration students felt is similar to that experienced by many American women in the early 20th century. Share the information shown above; then discuss the passage of the 19th Amendment. Conclude by having each student pretend to be a suffragist and write a letter to persuade his representative to vote in favor of the 19th Amendment. In the letter, have the student explain how women's suffrage will benefit the country and why voting for the 19th Amendment is the right thing to do. If desired, let students design posters that might have been seen at a suffrage rally before the 1920 vote. Display the letters and posters on a bulletin board titled "You Vote, Girl!"

The Great Depression
Skills: Sequencing, journal writing

Examine the causes of the depression and how it affected everyday folks with this activity. After discussing the depression, give each student a copy of page 142. Have each student complete Part 1 as directed. Then divide the class into small groups. Have group members compare their answers and decide together on a final sequence. Check the groups' answers as a class and discuss how the depression affected American life. Then have each student complete Part 2. For a sharing session, group students according to the person on page 142 they selected. Have students in each group read their journal entries to each other.

As a variation, have each student complete Part 2 on a six-inch paper square (leaving a margin along the left side). After the group sharing session, give each student the materials listed and display the steps shown. Place the completed booklets in your class library for students to read in their spare time.

Materials for each student: two 6" construction paper squares, crayons or markers, scissors, glue stick, stapler, three 6" notebook paper squares, pencil

Steps:
1. Color the portrait of your person on page 142.
2. Cut out the portrait and glue it to a construction paper square. Add a title such as "From the Diary of [name of person]."
3. Place the pieces of notebook paper behind your journal entry. Then staple the papers between the two covers to make a booklet.
4. After you study the New Deal, write another entry explaining how its programs have affected you and your life.

Who Will Make It Onto Mount Amerimore?

Americans to Research

1. Theodore Roosevelt
2. Woodrow Wilson
3. Herbert Hoover
4. Franklin Delano Roosevelt
5. Eleanor Roosevelt
6. Frank Lloyd Wright
7. Calvin Coolidge
8. Mary Pickford
9. Helen Keller
10. Walter Reed
11. George Gershwin
12. Henry Ford
13. Robert Peary
14. Babe Ruth
15. Jane Addams
16. Amelia Earhart
17. Nellie Tayloe Ross
18. Duke Ellington
19. Matthew Henson
20. Jim Thorpe
21. Charles Lindbergh
22. Langston Hughes
23. Carrie Chapman Catt
24. Robert Frost

Americans Who Made a Difference
Skills: Researching, writing and giving a speech

Early 20th-century America was filled with amazing Americans who did amazing things. Acquaint your students with just a few of these famous folks with this activity. Begin by displaying a picture of Mount Rushmore. Explain to students that the U.S. government has asked a famous sculptor to create a similar monument, called Mount Amerimore, to honor five Americans who made important contributions during the early 20th century. Assign a name from the list given to each student. Then have the student research his person and write a speech nominating him or her to be one of the honorees featured on Mount Amerimore. Remind students to include facts in their speeches that justify the person's nomination.

After each child gives his speech to the class, distribute a ballot that lists the nominees. Then have each student vote for the five people he believes most deserve to be honored. If desired, have each student with a winning nominee lead a different team of classmates in sketching a design for the monument.

Literature Links
Skills: Taking notes, writing a book review

If you want to integrate a study of early 20th-century America with your literature groups, then there are plenty of terrific books ready to be read! Ask your librarian to provide you with a collection of fiction and nonfiction titles related to this time period (1900–1940), such as those listed. Have each child select a book. Then give each student a sheet of duplicating paper. Have her fold the paper into thirds and label it as shown. As the student reads, direct her to note on the bookmark any events, people, places, or actions related to early 20th-century America. Each day ask a few students to share any notes they have recently made on their bookmarks.

When a student finishes her book, have her use the bookmark to write a review of the book. Instruct the student to end the review with a summary of what she learned about the early 20th century while reading.

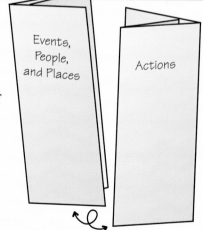

Events, People, and Places

Actions

Fiction:
- *Esperanza Rising* by Pam Muñoz Ryan
- *Theodore Roosevelt: Letters From a Young Coal Miner* (*Dear Mr. President* series) by Jennifer Armstrong
- *Dragonwings* by Laurence Yep
- *Good-Bye, Billy Radish* by Gloria Skurzynski
- *Over the Waves* by Marianne Olson
- *The Song of the Molimo* by Jane Cutler
- *Out of the Dust* by Karen Hesse
- *Brooklyn Doesn't Rhyme* by Joan W. Blos

Nonfiction:
- *Bully for You, Teddy Roosevelt!* by Jean Fritz
- *Earthquake! A Story of Old San Francisco* by Kathleen V. Kudlinski
- *Children of the Dust Bowl: The True Story of the School at Weedpatch Camp* by Jerry Stanley
- *Eleanor Roosevelt: A Life of Discovery* by Russell Freedman
- *Kids at Work: Lewis Hine and the Crusade Against Child Labor* by Russell Freedman

Focusing on World War I

Directions: Cut out the three boldfaced strips. Arrange them in three columns on your paper. Then cut out the other strips. Read each strip and place it in the correct column. (Hint: The numbers on the boldfaced strips tell you how many strips are in each column.)

Causes of World War I (6)	Reasons USA Entered War (2)	Results of World War I (8)
a. In Europe, people had strong feelings of pride in their own nation. Competition and angry feelings between countries grew. People in some countries wanted to rule themselves and be independent.	b. The U.S. government was angry that Germany tried to convince Mexico to go to war against the United States.	
c. Because the war cost countries so much money, nations had large debts after the war. This caused problems with the economies in these countries.	d. Because of the war, much land and property in Europe was destroyed.	
e. European nations began to compete for colonies in Africa and Asia. This created bad feelings between nations.	f. The U.S. government was angry that German submarines attacked U.S. ships.	
g. Many European countries began to build up their militaries because of greater tensions in Europe.	h. Because countries wanted to avoid another world war, a new international peacekeeping organization called the League of Nations was formed.	
i. Almost 10 million soldiers died. About 21 million more were wounded. Many other people died of disease, starvation, and other causes related to the war.	j. To keep Germany from starting another war, the size of its army and weapons supply was cut back. It was also not allowed to have submarines or aircraft.	
k. The future leader of Austria-Hungary, Archduke Francis Ferdinand, was assassinated in Bosnia-Herzegovina. Austria-Hungary then declared war on Serbia.	l. Because of the war, Germany lost some of its land to other countries.	
m. Because of the war, several old empires collapsed and new countries—such as Austria, Hungary, and Turkey—were created.	n. Because Germany was blamed for causing the war, it was punished most harshly under the Treaty of Versailles. This created some of the conditions that led to World War II about 20 years later.	
o. Alliances brought more countries into the war. For example, Russia decided to help Serbia fight Austria-Hungary. So Germany declared war on Russia. Then France (which was in an alliance with Russia) declared war on Germany.	p. Many European countries were afraid of war, so they formed alliances, or partnerships. If one country in an alliance was attacked, the other countries in the alliance agreed to help it. The Triple Entente was an alliance formed by France, Russia, and Great Britain. Germany, Austria-Hungary, and Italy formed the Triple Alliance.	

Note to the teacher: Use with "World War I: Causes and Results" on page 138.

Faces of the Great Depression

At the start of 1929, life in America looked pretty good. Unfortunately, the good times weren't to last for long. A combination of circumstances led to one of the most difficult periods in America's history. Complete the following activities about this era known as the Great Depression.

Part 1: Number these events in the order in which they occurred.

_____ People buy stock on credit to try to make more money.

_____ World War I ends.

_____ Factories increase production of goods.

_____ The Great Depression begins.

_____ Americans buy huge amounts of goods.

_____ President Franklin D. Roosevelt proposes New Deal programs to end the depression.

_____ Demand for products falls because people can't afford to keep purchasing them.

_____ Many banks and businesses fail. Many people lose their jobs.

_____ Warehouses and stores become full of products that go unsold.

_____ Stock prices drop drastically. Many investors lose all of their money.

Part 2: Pretend that it is 1932. Choose one of the people shown on this page. On another sheet of paper, write a journal entry as that person. Tell how the Great Depression has affected you. Write about your experiences, feelings, concerns, hopes, and ideas.

Edith Miller
Store Clerk

Maddie O'Brien
Factory Worker

Harry Newman
Schoolboy

E. M. Johnson
Banker

Josiah Bancroft
Farmer

Eli Warton
Store Owner

Mary Wallace
Farm Worker

Nicholas Costas
Railroad Worker

©The Education Center, Inc. • *THE MAILBOX*® • *Intermediate* • April/May 2002 • Key p. 309

142　**Note to the teacher:** Use with "The Great Depression" on page 139.

SCIENCE AND HEALTH UNITS

Shedding Light on Color

Light up your science curriculum with these bright ideas on investigating the relationship between light and color!

by Dr. Barbara B. Leonard, Winston-Salem, NC

Fascinating Facts About Light and Color

- Sir Isaac Newton discovered that white light forms when all the colors of the spectrum are mixed together.
- A *spectrum* is produced when white light is broken into a band of different colors: red, orange, yellow, green, blue, indigo (bluish purple), and violet.
- Water droplets, bubbles, and other curved or angled surfaces bend, or *refract,* white light, separating the white light into bands of colors.
- When an object absorbs all the colors in the spectrum, it reflects the light it absorbed and appears black.

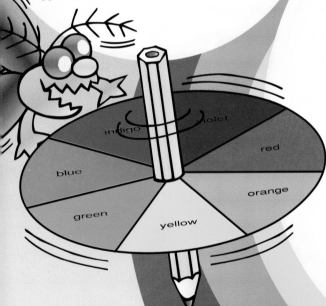

Spin Those Colors!

Concept: Blending colors to make white light

Put a new spin on your students' understanding of color with this hands-on activity. First, explain that Sir Isaac Newton discovered that sunlight is made of different colors: red, orange, yellow, green, blue, indigo (bluish purple), and violet. These colors form a band called a *spectrum.* To help students see how the colors of the spectrum create white light, give each child a copy of the color wheel pattern on page 147 and crayons or markers in the following colors: red, orange, yellow, green, blue, indigo, and violet. Have the student color the wheel's parts as labeled. Then have him spin the wheel using a method listed below and describe what happens. *(The colors blend into a creamy color because the human eye cannot detect different colors at this speed.)* Follow up by having students make more color wheels to see what happens when they spin a wheel that is half red and half yellow, half red and half blue, or half blue and half yellow.

Spinning Methods

- Poke a short, sharpened pencil (such as a golf pencil) through the center of the wheel. Spin the pencil like a top.
- Punch a hole in the center of the wheel; then place it on a record player's turntable. Play the record player at its highest speed.
- Remove one of the two beaters from a handheld electric mixer. Tape the wheel to the bottom of the remaining beater. With your teacher's help, operate the mixer at its highest speed.

To find out more about color, visit **www.crayola.com!** *(Current as of April 2001)*

Spotlighting Great Light and Color Books

Janice VanCleave's Physics for Every Kid: 101 Easy Experiments in Motion, Heat, Light, Machines, and Sound by Janice VanCleave

Light & Color by Frank Millson

The Optics Book: Fun Experiments With Light, Vision & Color by Shar Levine and Leslie Johnstone

Color Is in the Eye of the Beholder!

Concept: How cones in the human eye detect light

Open students' eyes to the workings of *cones,* the light-sensitive cells in the center of the retina. Explain to students that each of three kinds of cones responds most strongly to a different color: blue, green, or red. If overused, cones can get tired and stop working briefly. When this happens, other cones help out, producing an interesting effect called an *afterimage.* After this discussion, guide students through the steps below.

Materials for each student: blue, green, yellow, and black crayons or markers; scissors; sheet of white paper; copy of the heart, flag, and square patterns on page 147; stopwatch or clock with a second hand

Steps:

1. Cut out the patterns.
2. Color the heart pattern green and place it next to the white paper. Stare at the heart's black dot for 30 seconds while a partner times you. Then look directly at the white paper. *(After several seconds, a fuzzy red heart should appear on the white paper.)*
3. Color yellow the area on the flag that normally includes stars. Color green every other stripe on the flag, beginning with the first stripe and ending with the last. Color the remaining stripes black. Place the flag next to the white paper. Stare at the flag's black dot for 30 seconds; then look at the white paper. *(Old Glory should show its true colors of red, white, and blue.)*
4. Color the diamond in the small square yellow. Color the remaining area blue. Place the small square next to the white paper. Stare at the dot on the yellow diamond for 30 seconds. Then look at the white paper. *(The colors should be reversed, with the diamond being blue and the remaining area yellow.)*

Check out these interesting sites for more exciting activities and experiments with color! *(Current as of April 2001)*
www.exploratorium.edu/snacks/iconcolor.html
www.fi.edu/tfi/activity/physics/op-3.html

Your Order, Please

Concept: Food color and appetite

If your students could have blue, green, red, or yellow mashed potatoes, which would they pick and why? Turn your classroom into a cafeteria to find out! Ask parent volunteers to prepare bowls of instant mashed potatoes and elbow macaroni, each cooked in water heavily tinted with a different color of food coloring. Have other volunteers provide pitchers of different-colored juices or drink mixes, plus plasticware, paper plates, cups, and napkins. Arrange everything on a table; then have students go through cafeteria-style to choose what they want to eat. While students eat, have each child write a paragraph explaining why she chose the colors of foods that she did. Allow students to share their paragraphs. Then give each child a small bag of M&M's® candies and direct her to record the order in which she eats the candies. Is there a color connection? *(Color and food appeal are closely related. For example, blue is an appetite suppressant. Greens, browns, reds, and several other colors are generally thought to be more appealing in terms of appetite.)*

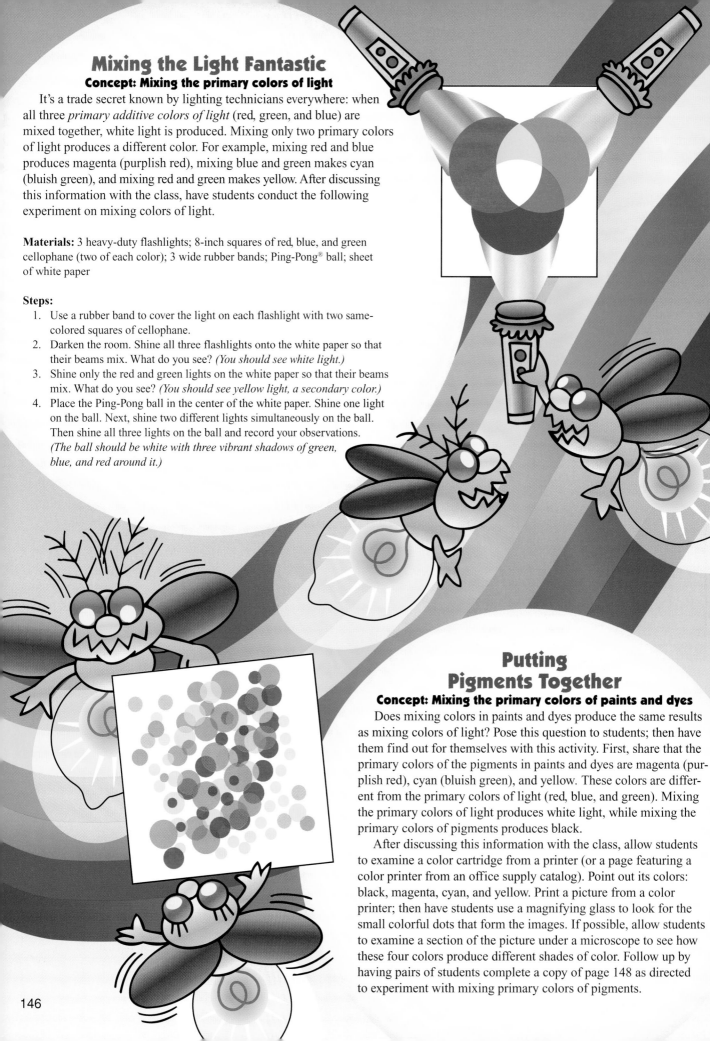

Mixing the Light Fantastic
Concept: Mixing the primary colors of light

It's a trade secret known by lighting technicians everywhere: when all three *primary additive colors of light* (red, green, and blue) are mixed together, white light is produced. Mixing only two primary colors of light produces a different color. For example, mixing red and blue produces magenta (purplish red), mixing blue and green makes cyan (bluish green), and mixing red and green makes yellow. After discussing this information with the class, have students conduct the following experiment on mixing colors of light.

Materials: 3 heavy-duty flashlights; 8-inch squares of red, blue, and green cellophane (two of each color); 3 wide rubber bands; Ping-Pong® ball; sheet of white paper

Steps:
1. Use a rubber band to cover the light on each flashlight with two same-colored squares of cellophane.
2. Darken the room. Shine all three flashlights onto the white paper so that their beams mix. What do you see? *(You should see white light.)*
3. Shine only the red and green lights on the white paper so that their beams mix. What do you see? *(You should see yellow light, a secondary color.)*
4. Place the Ping-Pong ball in the center of the white paper. Shine one light on the ball. Next, shine two different lights simultaneously on the ball. Then shine all three lights on the ball and record your observations. *(The ball should be white with three vibrant shadows of green, blue, and red around it.)*

Putting Pigments Together
Concept: Mixing the primary colors of paints and dyes

Does mixing colors in paints and dyes produce the same results as mixing colors of light? Pose this question to students; then have them find out for themselves with this activity. First, share that the primary colors of the pigments in paints and dyes are magenta (pur-plish red), cyan (bluish green), and yellow. These colors are differ-ent from the primary colors of light (red, blue, and green). Mixing the primary colors of light produces white light, while mixing the primary colors of pigments produces black.

After discussing this information with the class, allow students to examine a color cartridge from a printer (or a page featuring a color printer from an office supply catalog). Point out its colors: black, magenta, cyan, and yellow. Print a picture from a color printer; then have students use a magnifying glass to look for the small colorful dots that form the images. If possible, allow students to examine a section of the picture under a microscope to see how these four colors produce different shades of color. Follow up by having pairs of students complete a copy of page 148 as directed to experiment with mixing primary colors of pigments.

146

Looking Through Rose-Colored Glasses
Concept: The effect of color on emotions

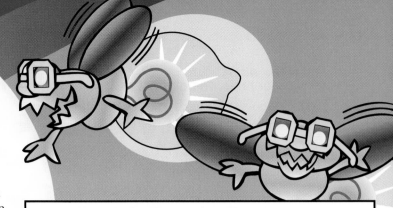

To investigate the psychology of color, cut a supply of 1¼-inch squares from different colors of cellophane (two same-colored squares per student). Give each student two cellophane squares, two 4" x 6" index cards, scissors, tape, and a copy of the glasses pattern below. Have each student trace the pattern on each card and cut out the tracings. Then have him tape the cutouts together at the nose piece and tape a cellophane square in place for each lens. Next, have the student put on his glasses, look at an object that matches his lens color, and record what he sees and how it makes him feel. Then direct him to look at other objects (both the same as and different from the color of his glasses) and record his observations. Afterward, have students trade glasses or change one lens to a different color and repeat the activity. Discuss students' observations; then share the chart shown. For an experiment with color, see "What's Hot to Wear?" on page 149.

Common Reactions to Different Colors		
Category	**Colors**	**Feelings Evoked**
warm	red, orange, yellow	excited, stimulated, energetic
cool	green, blue, violet	calm, peaceful
neutral	brown, gray	neither excited nor calm

Patterns
Use the flag, heart, and square patterns with "Color Is in the Eye of the Beholder!" on page 145.

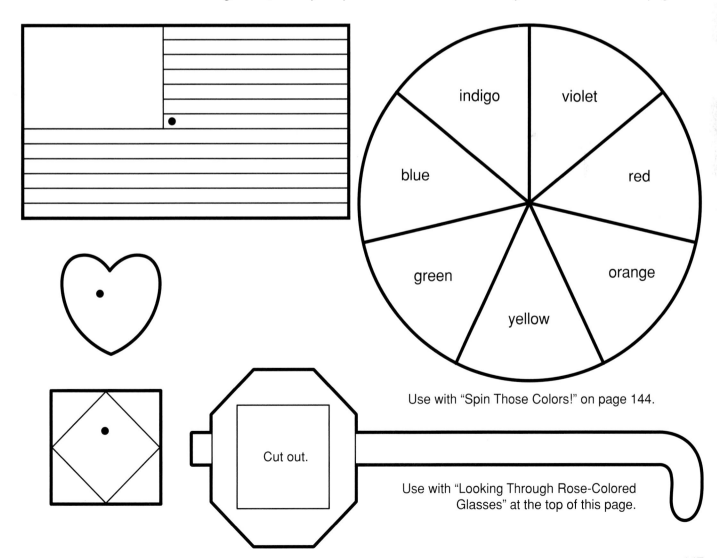

Cut out.

Use with "Spin Those Colors!" on page 144.

Use with "Looking Through Rose-Colored Glasses" at the top of this page.

Conjuring Up Colors!

If you mix together two colors of paint, will you get the same result if you mix the same two colors of markers? To find out, make a spot of color in each box below for each color or color combination in the chart. Then answer the questions.

Materials: paintbrush; water; paper towels; watercolors, tempera paints, water-based markers, crayons, and colored pencils, each in red, blue, and yellow

Color/Color Combinations

Medium	Red	Blue	Yellow	Red and blue	Red and yellow	Blue and yellow	Red, blue, and yellow
Watercolors							
Tempera paints							
Colored pencils							
Crayons							
Markers							

1. Which medium do you think is the easiest to use for mixing colors? _____
2. Which medium do you think produces the most intense colors? _____
3. Which medium do you think produces the faintest colors? _____
4. What color do you think would result if you mixed together all seven colors and color combinations in the chart? _____

©The Education Center, Inc. • *THE MAILBOX®* • *Intermediate* • Oct/Nov 2001 • Key p. 309

- -

Mixing It Up!

What colors do you get when you mix different colors of food coloring? Follow the steps below to find out!

Materials: 3 bottles of food coloring (red, blue, yellow), 3 bathroom-sized plastic cups, water, medicine dropper, spoon, bottom half of white Styrofoam® egg carton

Steps:
1. Half-fill each cup with water.
2. Add five drops of red food coloring to one cup, five drops of blue food coloring to the second cup, and five drops of yellow food coloring to the third cup. Stir each cup.
3. Place five drops of the red solution in one well of the egg carton. To the same well, add five more drops of the red solution. Stir. Place a drop of the resulting mixture in the corresponding spot on the art palette.
4. Repeat Step 3 for each remaining combination of colors listed.
5. Allow the drops to dry.

Colors Mixed	Resulting Color
Red and red	
Red and blue	
Red and yellow	
Blue and blue	
Blue and yellow	
Yellow and yellow	
Red, blue, and yellow	
All seven colors	

©The Education Center, Inc. • *THE MAILBOX®* • *Intermediate* • Oct/Nov 2001 • Key p. 309

Note to the teacher: Use with "Putting Pigments Together" on page 146.

What's Hot to Wear?

Does the color of your clothing affect how hot or cold you feel? Conduct the following experiment to find out!

Materials for each group: 3 different-colored items of clothing (light-colored, medium-colored, and dark-colored), 3 thermometers, sheet of paper, clock or watch

Whew!

Procedure:

1. Have each group member predict the color of clothing she thinks would make her feel warmer and another color that would make her feel cooler.
2. Place the thermometers in direct sunlight. Record the starting temperature of each thermometer in the chart (one per piece of clothing).
3. Position each thermometer inside one layer of a different item of clothing so that the top of the thermometer sticks out.
4. Wait ten minutes. Then record the ending temperature of each thermometer in the chart.
5. Subtract the starting and ending temperatures of each thermometer. Record each difference in the chart.
6. On the sheet of paper, make a graph that shows the change in temperature (use the numbers in the last column of the chart).

Color of Clothing	Starting Temperature	Ending Temperature	Difference in Temperature

Observations and conclusions:

1. Which color of clothing absorbed the most radiant energy (had the greatest increase in temperature)? _____

2. Which color of clothing absorbed the least radiant energy (had the smallest increase in temperature)? _____

3. Were you surprised by any of the results? If so, what surprised you? _____
_____

4. What variables other than color could have affected the temperature of each item of clothing?
_____
_____

5. What could be changed to make this experiment better? _____
_____
_____

Bonus Box: If you lived in the Arizona desert, what car color would keep you cooler? Why? If you lived in Maine during the winter months, what roof color would keep you warmer? Why?

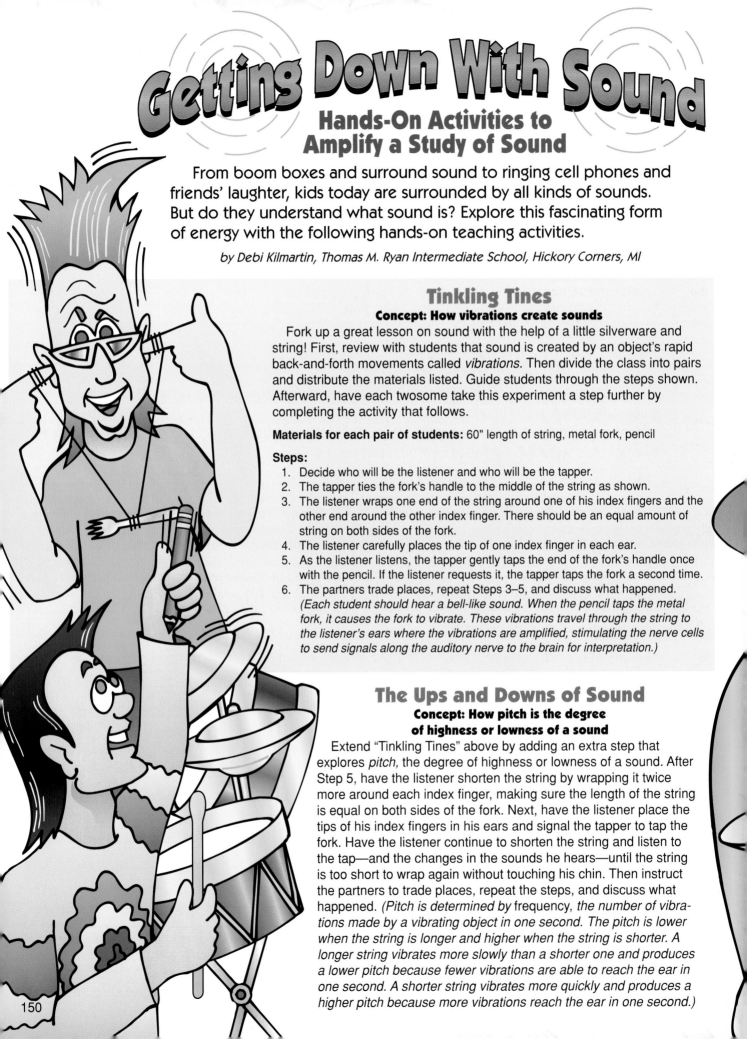

Getting Down With Sound

Hands-On Activities to Amplify a Study of Sound

From boom boxes and surround sound to ringing cell phones and friends' laughter, kids today are surrounded by all kinds of sounds. But do they understand what sound is? Explore this fascinating form of energy with the following hands-on teaching activities.

by Debi Kilmartin, Thomas M. Ryan Intermediate School, Hickory Corners, MI

Tinkling Tines

Concept: How vibrations create sounds

Fork up a great lesson on sound with the help of a little silverware and string! First, review with students that sound is created by an object's rapid back-and-forth movements called *vibrations.* Then divide the class into pairs and distribute the materials listed. Guide students through the steps shown. Afterward, have each twosome take this experiment a step further by completing the activity that follows.

Materials for each pair of students: 60" length of string, metal fork, pencil

Steps:
1. Decide who will be the listener and who will be the tapper.
2. The tapper ties the fork's handle to the middle of the string as shown.
3. The listener wraps one end of the string around one of his index fingers and the other end around the other index finger. There should be an equal amount of string on both sides of the fork.
4. The listener carefully places the tip of one index finger in each ear.
5. As the listener listens, the tapper gently taps the end of the fork's handle once with the pencil. If the listener requests it, the tapper taps the fork a second time.
6. The partners trade places, repeat Steps 3–5, and discuss what happened. (*Each student should hear a bell-like sound. When the pencil taps the metal fork, it causes the fork to vibrate. These vibrations travel through the string to the listener's ears where the vibrations are amplified, stimulating the nerve cells to send signals along the auditory nerve to the brain for interpretation.*)

The Ups and Downs of Sound

Concept: How pitch is the degree of highness or lowness of a sound

Extend "Tinkling Tines" above by adding an extra step that explores *pitch,* the degree of highness or lowness of a sound. After Step 5, have the listener shorten the string by wrapping it twice more around each index finger, making sure the length of the string is equal on both sides of the fork. Next, have the listener place the tips of his index fingers in his ears and signal the tapper to tap the fork. Have the listener continue to shorten the string and listen to the tap—and the changes in the sounds he hears—until the string is too short to wrap again without touching his chin. Then instruct the partners to trade places, repeat the steps, and discuss what happened. (*Pitch is determined by* frequency, *the number of vibrations made by a vibrating object in one second. The pitch is lower when the string is longer and higher when the string is shorter. A longer string vibrates more slowly than a shorter one and produces a lower pitch because fewer vibrations are able to reach the ear in one second. A shorter string vibrates more quickly and produces a higher pitch because more vibrations reach the ear in one second.*)

Gift Box Guitar
Concept: How pitch is related to how fast an object vibrates

Looking for a fun way to "strum" up an interest in sound? Then invite students to pluck on their own handmade guitars! First, ask students what makes sounds different from each other. After some discussion, pair students. Give each pair a copy of page 153 and the materials listed. Have each pair complete the page as directed to find out how different variables affect pitch. To extend the activity, have each pair place the rubber bands in its box and trade boxes and copies of page 153 with another twosome. Challenge each pair to arrange its new set of rubber bands from lowest to highest pitch and compare the arrangement with the other twosome's diagram. If results differ, help students conclude that it may be due to the overstretching of the bands or pitches that were too similar to differentiate.

Pam Crane

Listen to This!
Concept: How sound travels faster through solids and liquids than through air

Does sound travel faster through a solid than it does through air? Have students find out by doing this simple experiment!

Materials for each student: regular-sized rubber band, 8 oz. sturdy plastic cup

Directions:
1. Wrap the rubber band around the tip of your thumb and the third finger of one hand (see the illustration).
2. Stretch the rubber band between the two fingers as far apart as possible.
3. Pluck the rubber band with a finger of your other hand. Listen to the sound produced.
4. Wrap the same rubber band around the plastic cup from top to bottom. Make sure the rubber band is not twisted.
5. Hold the cup in one hand and pluck the rubber band with the other. Listen to the sound produced.
6. Hold the bottom of the cup next to your ear with one hand and pluck the rubber band with the other hand. Listen to the sound produced. How is it different from the sound produced in Step 3? *(Sound travels slowest through gases like air because its molecules are not close together. Therefore, the sound made when the rubber band is held between the fingers is low and soft because the band can only push a small amount of air. Holding the bottom of the cup next to the ear makes the sound easier to hear because the sound travels through a solid material—plastic. Sound travels fastest through solids because their molecules are close together.)*

Surrounded by Sound
Concept: Awareness of surrounding sounds

A field trip for a sound unit? Sure, and you don't even have to leave school to take it! Take students on a field trip around the school, challenging them to list all the sounds they hear in each location. Visit different spots on campus, such as the playground, cafeteria, and office. At each stop, have students record phrases that describe the sounds they hear. End the trip by returning to class to listen for sounds there. Then have each student use crayons or colored pencils, scissors, and her list of phrases to complete the poetry activity on a copy of page 154. Display the resulting sound poems on a bulletin board titled "Sounds Like Poetry!"

"Sound-sational" Sound Waves

Concept: How sound can be reflected

Help students discover that sound can be reflected with the following easy experiment.

Materials for each group of three students: 2 cardboard paper towel tubes, 4" x 12" piece of smooth cardboard, ruler

Steps:

1. Have one group member use one hand to hold the cardboard in an upright position on a desk or table. Have him use his other hand to angle the paper towel tubes, as shown, so that the front ends of the tubes are about an inch apart and an inch from the cardboard.
2. Have a second group member whisper a sentence into one tube while the third group member listens at the end of the other tube. (Tell the whisperer not to reveal the sentence beforehand.)
3. Have group members repeat the experiment two more times so that each student can perform all three roles. *(The listener can hear the whispered sentence even though the tubes are not connected. The whisper travels in a straight line through the paper towel tube, bounces off the piece of cardboard into the second tube, and continues in a straight line to the listener's ear. This happens because sound travels in a straight line through a medium of uniform density until it meets a surface [smooth, hard ones are best] and is reflected. For this reason, some concert halls are designed with suspended ceilings and angled boxes to help reflect sound from the stage to the audience and create the best possible sound.)*

Discriminating Sounds

Concept: How the human brain can interpret and distinguish different sounds

Demonstrate the brain's ability to make sense of sound with this fun "eggs-periment"! Gather 16 same-colored, plastic, snap-together eggs. Also gather eight pairs of objects small enough to fit inside the eggs, such as pieces of macaroni, grains of rice, dice, marbles, cotton balls, beans, safety pins, and thumbtacks. List the eight objects on a sheet of paper. Then place one object in each egg and put the eggs in a box or basket. Place the container at your science center along with the list of objects and a copy of the directions below.

Directions (for two players):

1. The players remove the eggs from the container and arrange them in rows.
2. Player 1 picks up any two eggs, shakes one egg at a time, and listens to the sound (or lack of sound) it makes.
3. If Player 1 thinks the sounds match, he looks at the list of objects and guesses which item is in that pair of eggs. Then he opens the eggs to see if he is correct. If he's correct, he keeps the eggs and takes another turn. If the objects don't match or he identified the wrong object, he returns the eggs to their original positions and Player 2 takes a turn.
4. The players continue taking turns until all the eggs are matched.
5. The winner is the player with more pairs of eggs.

Twang It High, Twang It Low

What makes sounds different from each other? Construct a box guitar to find out!

Materials: small, sturdy gift box (4" x 5" x $1\frac{1}{2}$" or slightly larger); rubber bands of different lengths, widths, and colors; crayons or markers

Steps:

1. Choose five to six different rubber bands. Make sure each one is a different length and width.
2. Remove the box's lid. Then stretch each rubber band around the box bottom. Arrange the rubber bands with an equal amount of space between them. Make sure they're not twisted.
3. Pluck one rubber band at a time and listen to see if it makes a high or a low sound.
4. Rearrange the rubber bands on the box so they're in order from lowest to highest pitch.
5. Show how the rubber bands are arranged on your box by drawing wide and narrow bands of color on the diagram at the right.
6. Answer the questions below in complete sentences.

Questions:

1. How are your rubber bands different from each other? _____
   _____
2. Does the length of the rubber bands make a difference in the sounds they make? Explain.
   _____
3. Does the width of the rubber bands make a difference in the sounds they make? Explain.
   _____
4. Does the color of the rubber bands make a difference in the sounds they make? Explain.
   _____
5. Do some rubber bands fit more tightly around the box than others? If so, do they make a different sound than those that fit more loosely? Explain. _____
   _____
   _____
6. Based on your arrangement of rubber bands, which strings on an acoustic guitar would play higher notes? _____
   Lower notes? _____

Bonus Box: Which would have a lower pitch: a long, wide rubber band or a short, wide rubber band? Write your answer on the back of this page.

Note to the teacher: Use with "Gift Box Guitar" on page 151.   153

Name _____

Sounds Like Poetry!

Clocks tick, water drips, pencils fall to the floor, phones ring, horns honk, radios blare, people talk—sounds are all around us! Capture some of these sounds in a poem by following the directions below.

Directions: Read the sample poems below. Choose the type of poem you'd like to write. Then write your poem on another sheet of paper. Include as many descriptive phrases collected from your sound field trip as possible. After editing your poem, copy it neatly inside the frame. Then color and cut out the frame.

RAT-A-TAT!

Acrostic: a poem whose lines begin with letters that spell a word vertically

<u>B</u>aton tapping on the director's stand
<u>A</u> flute trilling a high note
<u>N</u>umerous feet tapping the beat
<u>D</u>rums beating a fast rhythm

Free Verse: a poem that doesn't follow a specific form and doesn't have to rhyme

Lunchtime

I walk into the cafeteria.
I hear…
Milk slurping through straws,
Paper bags rustling,
Containers popping open and
    snapping shut,
Clinking silverware,
Chairs scraping against the
    floor,
Trays dragging along a rail, and
Trash dropping into cans—
The sounds of lunchtime.

Definition Poem: a poem that defines a word or an idea in a creative way

Basketball

What is basketball?
bouncing leather balls
shrieking referees' whistles
squeaking shoes on a gym floor
the swish of a free throw
voices yelling, "We won!"
That's basketball!

List Poem: a poem made from a list; the title often names the list

Things That Are Loud!

Booming bass drums
Teachers' whistles
Pans clanging in the cafeteria
Kids' voices in the hallway
The slamming of locker doors
Voices leaving at the end of the day

Note to the teacher: Use with "Surrounded by Sound" on page 151.

Taking a Look at Vertebrates

Amphibians, birds, fish, mammals, and reptiles…just how much do your students know about vertebrates? Sneak a peek at this fascinating group of animals with these exciting and fun-to-do activities!

ideas by Kimberly A. Minafo, Pomona, NY

Just a Drop in the Bucket

Concept: Size of vertebrate population

Begin your study of vertebrates by asking students to do a little population calculation! Prepare a 10 x 10 grid for each child. Also color four squares on an additional grid and mount it on construction paper as shown. On the back of the paper, write "Only about 4 percent of the animals on Earth are vertebrates."

After reviewing the five classes of vertebrates (fish, mammals, birds, reptiles, and amphibians), challenge the class to name 100 animals as you list them on the board. Have a reference book handy in case students get stuck. Place a check mark beside each vertebrate in the list. Have each student count the vertebrates listed. Then ask students to think about this question: Is this number greater than, less than, or equal to the percentage of animals in the world that actually are vertebrates? Give each child a blank grid; then direct him to color in squares on the grid to show what he thinks is the correct percentage. When students are finished, have them hold up their grids. Then display your mounted grid. Ask, "What could the four colored squares on this grid mean?" Then flip the paper to reveal the statement on the back. After students ooh and aah at this amazing statistic, invite them to speculate on why there are fewer vertebrates than invertebrates. Conclude by discussing how important vertebrates are to the food chain.

Only about 4 percent of the animals on Earth are vertebrates.

The Evidence Is In!

Concept: Characteristics of vertebrates

Turn students into "bone-a-fide" vertebrate experts with this reading and research activity. In advance, label resealable plastic bags with categories such as size, speed, feeding habits, adaptations, and parenting; then hang the bags on a bulletin board. Also cut out a large supply of construction paper bones and place them in a separate bag on the board. After a student reads an interesting fact about vertebrates, have her write it on a bone cutout (the fact on one side, the reference on the other side) and place it in the appropriate bag.

At the end of the unit, divide students into groups. Give each group a different bag of bones, glue, markers, and several sheets of construction paper. Challenge the group to sort its bones into subgroups and then display the resulting information as shown. Conclude by having each child summarize what she learned about her group's category on a large bone cutout. Provide time for students to share their bones with the class.

Animals' Activity Levels

Lions lie around for up to 21 hours a day!

Koalas sleep more than 14 hours a day!

Sea turtles have swimming frenzies for the first 24 to 48 hours of their lives!

Vampire bats can fly, run, jump, and hop!

155

Just Look at Those Legs!

Concept: Diversity of vertebrates

Help students understand the diversity within a class of vertebrates with this activity. Discuss with students that animal legs come in a variety of shapes and sizes and that the feet attached to those legs are even more diverse. Next, have each student research the legs and feet of any two different birds, reptiles, amphibians, or mammals. Then give students the materials listed and guide them through the steps below. When the projects have been completed (see the example), have each student write a paragraph comparing and contrasting the leg and foot structures of her two animals. Afterward, display students' projects side by side on the chalk tray or a table. Then take students on a virtual nature walk by having them share their information strips or summarize their paragraphs for the class.

Materials for each student: tissue paper roll, $4\frac{1}{2}$" x 6" strip of white paper, $2\frac{1}{2}$" square of white paper, markers, scissors, clear tape, six 1" x 9" paper strips (three each of two different colors)

Steps:

1. From the white square, cut a circle slightly larger than the tissue roll's opening. Notch the circle's edges and mold them around one end of the tissue roll. Tape the edges to the roll.
2. Wrap the white strip around the tissue roll and tape it in place.
3. Hold the tissue roll so that its covered end faces down. Then, on opposite sides of the roll, draw and label the leg and foot of each vertebrate researched.
4. On each set of colored strips, record three reasons why the leg and foot structures of each vertebrate are important to it.
5. Fold the labeled strips and place them inside the tissue roll.

My legs are very strong.

My sharp talons dig into my prey so I don't drop it.

The lower part of my legs is bare.

Bald Eagle

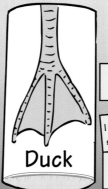

My feet help me swim well.

I waddle because my legs are set on the side and toward the rear of my body.

My feet are webbed.

Duck

Are You Qualified?

Concept: Characteristics and adaptations of vertebrates

Focus students' attention on the special abilities of vertebrates with this nifty research and writing project. First, gather facts about a vertebrate of interest to your students, such as the American alligator. Demonstrate for students how to use the facts to complete a resumé, such as the one shown. Afterward, have each student research a vertebrate of his choice, focusing on its special abilities and unique adaptations. Then have the student write a resumé for the vertebrate and share it with the class. For a fun extension, see "Vertebrates for Hire" on page 157.

RESUMÉ

Name: Albert E. Alligator

Nickname: Gator Breath

Class: Reptilia

Year of birth: 1985

Age: 16

Address: Rivers, ponds, lakes, and other wetland areas of the southeastern United States

Personal description: I am a male alligator, about 11 feet long and weighing 447 pounds. I have four short legs and am shaped like a large lizard. I have a powerful tail that you'd better watch out for! My skin is rough and scaly. I am a protected animal that eats fish, turtles, mammals, birds, and snakes. Sometimes, I even eat one of my own kind!

Job goal: I am looking for a job as a private investigator. I would be great at the job because with my dark, uniform color, I can lurk in murky waters and spy on suspected criminals. When confronted, I could use my large sweeping tail to knock my attacker down. Then I could either use my tail to keep him from getting away or threaten to bite him with my 80 teeth!

Vertebrates for Hire

Concept: Characteristics and adaptations of vertebrates

Follow up "Are You Qualified?" on page 156 with this creative-thinking activity. Arrange students' resumés around the perimeter of a bulletin board titled "Vertebrates for Hire!" Next, give each student an index card to label with a job for which his vertebrate might be suited (see the examples listed). After collecting the cards, use them to create a ballot that lists the different job titles as shown. Place a class supply of ballots in a plastic bag labeled "Blank Ballots" and attach it to the bulletin board along with another bag labeled "Completed Ballots." Also mount the job cards on the board. During free time, have students read the job titles, review the resumés, and complete the ballots. After each student has had a chance to vote, have groups of students tally the ballots. Discuss the results of the vote as a class.

Official Ballot

Directions: Write in the name of the vertebrate you think is most qualified for each job listed below. Explain why you voted for this vertebrate in the space provided.

Job	Most Qualified Vertebrate	Why I Voted for This Vertebrate
Treetop Duster	giraffe	It's tall enough to reach treetops.
Stone Overturner	African elephant	Its trunk can lift heavy objects.
College Mascot	American alligator	The alligator lives in Florida and is a mascot for a Florida college.
Flyswatter		
Mail Carrier Chaser		

The Carnivore Café and Steak House
The Place Where Meat Eaters Meet!

If you're a meat-eating predator, you've come to the right place! Chef Bearclaw, himself a carnivore, has been with us for 11 years. We offer generous servings of our menu items because we know some of our carnivorous customers like big meals. For your convenience, you can even catch your own favorite animal right out back on our two-acre ranch and have Chef Bearclaw prepare it to your liking. If you're on the run, ask for one of our special take-out meals.

We allow all carnivores (even weasels) to eat at our establishment. But don't plan on having a long, leisurely dining experience. You see, some of our guests are so hungry they can't wait for their meals to be prepared. They just might [have] you for dinner!

Hours: 1 P.M. to 3 A.M.
Dine at your own risk!

Grilled Gazelle
Marinated in Sahara sweet sauce and ready to eat in seconds so you don't have to wait! We take care of the horns and bones for you! Enough for a pride of lions to share! $237.99

Salmon à la Riverbed
Four salmon on a bed of river algae, sprinkled with extra crispy pieces of trout. Not too small, too hot, or too expensive. $49.99

Roadkill Delight
Our "Dead Deal of the Day" especially for hyenas! Ask your server for details. $9.99 or less

Mini Munchers
A bowl of bird, rabbit, and squirrel pieces, perfect for eagles and other carnivores! Free refills for just $5.99 more. $26.99

What's for Dinner?

Concept: Feeding habits of vertebrates

Investigate the feeding habits of vertebrates with this deliciously fun activity. Ask your media specialist to help you gather resources containing pictures of *carnivores* (meat-eating animals), *herbivores* (plant-eating animals), and *omnivores* (animals that eat both plants and meat). Also divide chart paper into three sections (carnivores, herbivores, and omnivores).

Next, divide students into three groups (one per section on the chart) and give each group its corresponding set of books. Direct each group to look through its books and call out names of vertebrates for you to list under each heading. Then challenge each group to research the eating habits of its assigned animal group. After the research has been completed, give each student markers and a 12" x 18" sheet of paper. Have him follow the directions below to create a menu that could tempt the palates of his assigned vertebrates. For fun, serve animal crackers for students to munch on as they share the meritorious menus!

Steps:
1. Fold the paper in half to make a menu.
2. On the front cover, write the name of your restaurant. Add a paragraph that introduces diners to the restaurant and explains the eating habits of vertebrates who might patronize the restaurant.
3. On the inside, list four to six different menu items with imaginative titles. List each item's main ingredients. Also mention which diners might enjoy the selections the most.

157

The Chordata Academy

It takes a backbone to be a student at the prestigious Chordata Academy! The school's board hires only the finest teachers. Also, headmaster Lionel Kingofbeasts takes great care in preparing class rosters so that students and teachers are perfectly matched. Help Lionel get this year's rosters ready by completing the list of student qualifications under each teacher's name (some may be used more than once).

The Chordata Academy
We welcome all vertebrates!

Qualifications:

warm-blooded
feed young with milk
breathe with lungs
have feathers
cold-blooded

most have hair or fur
live part of life in water,
   part on land
live in water
hatch from eggs

have scales
breathe with gills or lungs
most bear live young
have a beak or bill
breathe mainly with gills

Instructor Aves Birdy's Class

- vertebrate _____
- _____
- _____
- _____
- _____
- _____

Lionel Kingofbeasts
Headmaster

Professor Reptilia's Class

- vertebrate _____
- _____
- _____
- _____
- _____

Mr. Mammalia's Class

- vertebrate _____
- _____
- _____
- _____
- _____
- _____

Dr. Amphibia's Class

- vertebrate _____
- _____
- _____
- _____
- _____

Ms. Four-Fish's Class

- vertebrate _____
- _____
- _____
- _____
- _____

Bonus Box: Design a school flag for Chordata Academy.

Note to the teacher: To complete this page, students will need access to science books, encyclopedias, or other reference materials.

THE GENES SCENE
Groovy Activities on Genes and Heredity

Looking for activities to help students understand the basic concepts of heredity? Then try the following custom-made activities on for size. They're sure to be a perfect fit!

by Dr. Barbara B. Leonard, Winston-Salem, NC

Sports Star or Couch Potato?
Topic: Inherited versus acquired characteristics

Start your study with an activity that helps students think about the difference between inherited and acquired traits. First, explain that *heredity* is the passing on of biological attributes from one generation to the next. Then share the scenarios shown with students. Ask, "Which traits do you think Burt inherited from his parents? Which ones has he acquired because of his environment?" Repeat the discussion with Jeanie's scenario. Help students understand that as powerful as genes are, they don't completely control who we are. For example, a person may have inherited the potential to play the piano. But if he never takes lessons or practices, that potential may not be realized. After the discussion, ask each student to meet with a partner to talk about these questions:

- What are some traits you think you inherited from your parents?
- What traits do you think you have acquired from your environment?

Scenarios
- Burt Kromosome has a muscular build like his dad, a former professional football player. Burt roughhouses with his dad and can beat him at hand wrestling. But he'd rather sit on the couch watching TV and munching on potato chips. Burt could stand to lose some weight, but he says he'll never be out of shape.
- Jeanie Gene's mother teaches French and Spanish. Jeanie makes top grades in both languages, but she has trouble with math. Her parents hired a tutor, and now she makes the honor roll at school.

I'm tall like my dad, but I have my mom's hair and eyes!

A Jumble of Genes
Topic: What makes us unique

Encourage students to consider what makes them unique with this thought-provoking activity. Bring in photos of your family. Have students examine the photos for physical traits that might have been passed down from parent to child, such as hair color, facial features, and height. Explain to students that, like you, they have inherited certain traits from their parents and grandparents. If you have siblings in the photos, have students compare your physical characteristics with theirs. Ask, "If siblings have the same parents, why don't they always look exactly alike?" Why? Because each person's mixture of about 50,000 genes differs slightly from everyone else's. Go over the definitions of *gene* and *chromosome* shown. Then conclude the activity by having each student list ways she is like and different from each of her parents.

gene: a section of a chromosome that is often associated with a certain characteristic or group of characteristics, such as hair color

chromosome: the structure on which genes are located, found in cells of all organisms

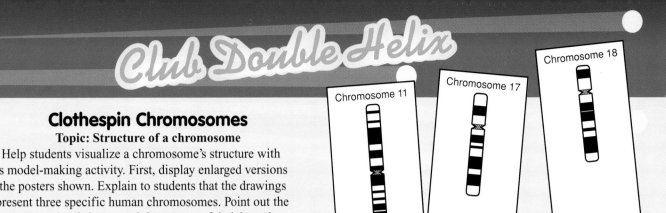

Club Double Helix

Clothespin Chromosomes
Topic: Structure of a chromosome

Help students visualize a chromosome's structure with this model-making activity. First, display enlarged versions of the posters shown. Explain to students that the drawings represent three specific human chromosomes. Point out the chromosomes' rod shapes and the pattern of dark bars that resemble bar codes. Then explain that the bands represent the genes that influence physical traits.

Next, provide each student with a spring-loaded wooden clothespin and a marker. Direct each student to mark both sides of the clothespin with the bands of one chromosome, adding the corresponding number (see the illustration). Have students clip their completed models to the matching posters or keep them as reminders of a chromosome's structure. For diagrams of other chromosomes, check out the Genome Database at http://www.gdb.org *(current as of January 2002).*

X for Girls, Y for Boys
Topic: Determining a baby's sex

What are the chances that a baby will be a boy? 50%, 80%, 30%? Answer that puzzling question with an experiment students will flip over! First, review with students that humans have 23 pairs of chromosomes. One chromosome in each pair comes from the mother and the other from the father. The 23rd pair determines a baby's sex. How? A mother will always pass along an X chromosome. But a father can pass along either an X chromosome (producing a girl) or a Y chromosome (producing a boy). Because males produce an equal number of X and Y chromosomes, the chances that a baby will be a boy is 50%.

After this introduction, divide the class into pairs. Display tables similar to the ones shown. Have each twosome copy the tables on paper. Then give each pair a penny to use in conducting the probability test on the right. Conclude by helping students average their data to see if the percentage of tossing tails is close to 50%.

	Predicted %	Actual %
Boys		
Girls		

Chromosome From Mother	Chromosome From Father	Girl (XX) or Boy (XY)
X		
X		
X		
X		
X		
X		
X		
X		
X		
X		

Probability Test:

Heads represents the X chromosome (a girl), and tails represents the Y chromosome (a boy).

1. Predict the percentage of ten coin flips that could be heads (girls). Record your prediction.
2. Predict the percentage of ten coin flips that could be tails (boys). Record your prediction. If necessary, adjust your predictions so that the total percentage for heads and tails equals 100%.
3. Take turns flipping the coin five times each. Record the outcome of each flip (X or Y) in the father's column of the chart.
4. Record the baby's sex (XX or XY) in the girl/boy column to show how the chromosomes from the mother and father combine.
5. Find the actual percentage of boys. To do this, divide the total number of Ys in the father's column by ten (the total number of flips) and multiply the quotient by 100. Record your answer in the chart.
6. To find the actual percentage of girls, divide the total number of Xs in the father's column by ten and multiply the quotient by 100. Record your answer.

What Genes Are You Wearing?

Topic: Dominant and recessive genes

Tackle the topic of dominant and recessive genes with this fun-to-do partner activity. First, share with students that if each parent carries two different factors for a trait, then one is *dominant* and the other *recessive*. Provide each student with a copy of the checklist shown that leaves out the italicized words. Discuss with students the physical expression of each trait (see the illustrations). Then pair students. Have each student complete a checklist by circling the expressions his partner exhibits. When the twosomes are finished, combine the class's results by making tally marks in a chart you've drawn on the board. Have students guess the dominant and recessive traits. Then share the answers. Explain that only one dominant gene has to be inherited for that trait to have the potential of being expressed. If no dominant gene is inherited, then the recessive gene is expressed. For example, if T = tongue roller and t = nonroller, a person who *can* roll his tongue has either TT or Tt genes. If the person *cannot* roll his tongue, he has tt genes. Encourage students to take home extra copies of the checklist to complete with other family members.

Checklist for _____

Expressed Trait	Physical Expression of Trait
Earlobe Shape	Free *(dominant)* or Attached *(recessive)*
Forehead Hairline	Widow's Peak *(dominant)* or Straight *(recessive)*
Tongue Rolling	Roller *(dominant)* or Nonroller *(recessive)*
Middigit Finger Hair	Hair *(dominant)* or No Hair *(recessive)*
Thumb	Straight *(dominant)* or Hitchhiker *(recessive)*
Dimples in Cheek	Dimples *(dominant)* or No Dimples *(recessive)*

Mendel's Genes

Topic: Dominant and recessive genes

For another nifty experiment on dominant and recessive genes, place on a table five containers, each labeled with one of the following: flower color, pod color, seed color, seed shape, or plant height. Give each group of five students one copy of the gene cards at the top of page 162. Have group members cut the cards apart, color them, and place them in the appropriate containers. Next, give each student a copy of page 163 to complete as directed. Afterward, have each group share its drawings with the class and note whether any plants exhibited some of the same traits or gene combinations.

Genetic Disease Detectives

Topic: Genetic diseases

Challenge students to investigate inherited genetic diseases with this research activity. Give each student a copy of the case sheet at the bottom of page 162 to help him research one of the topics below. Have the student search science books, encyclopedias, and Web sites such as those listed. Then schedule time for students to present their findings to the class.

Genetic Diseases: cystic fibrosis, sickle cell anemia, muscular dystrophy, hemophilia A, Huntington disease, Tay-Sachs disease, hemochromatosis, Gaucher's disease

Web Sites *(current as of January 2002)*:
Cystic Fibrosis Foundation: www.cff.org
The American Sickle Cell Anemia Association: www.ascaa.org
Muscular Dystrophy Association: www.mdausa.org
Taryn's World (a Web site for children with genetic diseases): www.tarynsworld.org/taryn/index.htm

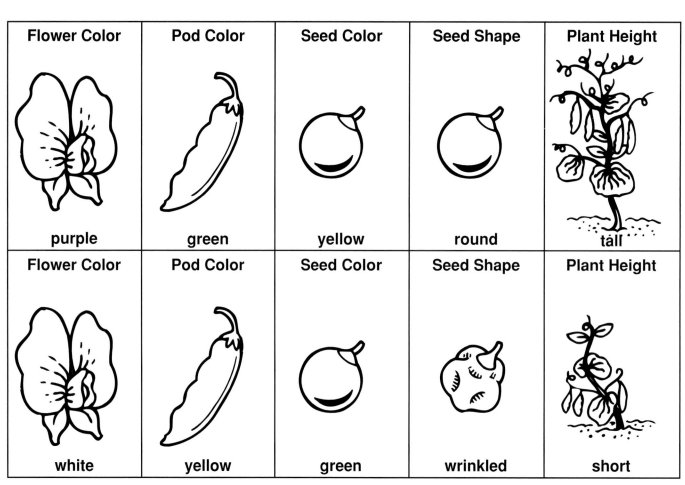

Flower Color	Pod Color	Seed Color	Seed Shape	Plant Height
purple	green	yellow	round	tall

Flower Color	Pod Color	Seed Color	Seed Shape	Plant Height
white	yellow	green	wrinkled	short

Name _____

Genetic Disease Case Sheet

Research

Name of disease: _____

What are the symptoms of the disease? _____

Who gets the disease? _____

When was the disease first identified? _____

Where (on what chromosome) is the defective gene located? _____

How does the disease affect the person who has it? _____

Source(s) of information for report: _____

Note to the teacher: Use the gene cards at the top of the page with "Mendel's Genes" on page 161. Use the case sheet with "Genetic Disease Detectives" on page 161.

Mendel's Genes

Gregor Mendel, an Austrian monk born in 1822, helped explain how heredity works. He studied pea plants that he grew in a monastery garden. By doing this, he was able to identify several plant traits and trace how they were passed from parent plants to their offspring. Follow the directions below to "grow" your own pea plant!

Directions:

1. Choose a trait: flower color, pod color, seed color, seed shape, or plant height. Choose a trait that is different from those selected by others in your group.
2. Draw two gene cards from the container labeled with your trait.
3. Check the table of pea traits to see if the characteristics on your cards represent dominant or recessive genes. Record each characteristic in the chart below, using a capital letter to represent a dominant gene and a lowercase letter for a recessive gene.
4. Gather data about the remaining traits from your group and record it in the chart below.
5. Determine the physical traits that your plant will express. (Remember: If at least one of the genes is dominant, that is the trait that will be expressed. If neither gene is dominant, the recessive trait will be expressed.) Compare answers with your group mates to see if they match.
6. Draw a picture of your plant. Make sure it expresses all of the physical traits listed in the chart.

Pea Traits

Trait	Dominant Characteristic	Recessive Characteristic
Flower color	purple (P)	white (p)
Pod color	green (G)	yellow (g)
Seed color	yellow (Y)	green (y)
Seed shape	round (R)	wrinkled (r)
Plant height	tall (T)	short (t)

Trait	Gene for Plant 1	Gene for Plant 2	Expressed Physical Trait
Flower color			
Pod color			
Seed color			
Seed shape			
Plant height			

Plant Drawing

Shuttling Through

3, 2, 1...liftoff! Launch your amateur astronauts on a tour of the solar system using these out-of-this-world activities!

Dr. Barbara B. Leonard, Winston-Salem, NC

Earth's Nearest Star

The sun is a yellow star. Its innermost region is the *core,* where nuclear reactions occur. As hydrogen changes into helium, the energy produced moves outward through the remaining layers and leaves the sun. The largest layer is the *radiative layer.* Above the radiative layer is the *convection layer.* Then comes the *photosphere,* or surface, where sunspots are visible. The photosphere is the innermost layer of the sun's atmosphere. The middle region of the sun's atmosphere is the *chromosphere.* It is made of hot gas that moves violently. Above the chromosphere is the *corona.* The gases of the corona are constantly expanding outward into space. A *solar prominence,* a cloud or sheet of gas, can rise up above the chromosphere and extend into the corona.

Schedule shuttle stops at these great Web sites! (current as of September 2001)

- Genesis mission Web site, part of NASA's program to study the sun: www.genesismission.org
- StarChild Web site sponsored by NASA's Goddard Space Flight Center (click on Level 2 links): starchild.gsfc.nasa.gov/docs/StarChild/StarChild.html

A Sun of Your Own

Concept: The sun's structure

Send students on a "sun-sational" tour of everyone's favorite star with this model-making activity. Share the facts above about the sun's structure. Also, invite shuttlers interested in learning more about the sun and the solar system to browse the suggested Web sites above. Then distribute the materials and guide students through the steps that follow.

Materials: 9" x 12" sheet of yellow (or orange) construction paper, 12" square of waxed paper, scissors, ruler, black fine-tipped marker, 2 paper clips, glue, pattern on page 166

Steps:

1. Cut a 3" x 9" strip from the construction paper to make a nine-inch square. Set the strip aside.
2. Fold the nine-inch square in half and in half again to make a 4$\frac{1}{2}$-inch square.
3. Cut out the pattern on page 166 and clip it to the 4$\frac{1}{2}$-inch paper square. Cut along the dashed lines. Remove the clips and pattern and unfold the circle.
4. Fold the waxed paper square in half twice. Trim the paper's outer edge into a curve similar to that on the pattern. Fringe the edge of the folded waxed paper. Then unfold the circle.

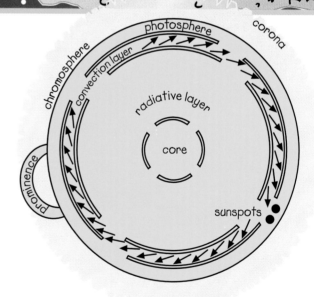

5. Glue the yellow circle to the middle of the waxed paper circle.
6. Label the sun's layers as shown. Add curved arrows to the convection layer to represent the movement of energy to the photosphere. Draw two to three dots on the photosphere to represent sunspots.
7. Cut a prominence from the 3" x 9" paper strip. Glue it to the edge of the chromosphere so that it extends into the corona.

the Solar System

Swinging Into Orbit

Concept: A planet's orbit around the sun

Take a closer look at how planets orbit the sun with this hands-on investigation. Review with students that an *orbit* is the path a planet travels to make one trip around the sun. Then give each student a ten-centimeter length of plastic straw, one meter of string, a ruler, and two small washers. Direct the student to thread the string through the straw and tie a washer to each end of the string.

Next, have the student hold the straw (representing the sun) upright in her right hand with about 15 centimeters of string dangling from the top. Have her hold the bottom of the string in her left hand. Direct the student to stand a safe distance from her classmates and whirl the top washer counterclockwise (the direction planets would revolve if viewed from above the sun's north pole). Have her gradually release more string as she whirls it until she has demonstrated a range of orbits with different diameters. Conclude by asking students to estimate and then measure the string's length when it was orbiting the fastest *(about 15 cm)* and slowest *(about 80 cm)*. Then have them predict which planet orbits the sun the fastest *(Mercury)* and slowest *(Pluto or Neptune)*. For a "space-tacular" follow-up activity, see "O, What a Trip!" below.

O, What a Trip!

Concept: The elliptical orbit of planets

Help students visualize the oval-shaped path of a planet's orbit with this eye-opening investigation.

Materials: 2 pushpins, 9" x 12" sheet of cardboard, 8½" x 11" sheet of white paper, metric ruler, 22 cm length of string, colored pencils (red, blue, and black), tape

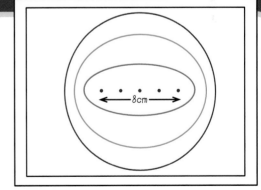

Steps:

1. Tape the white paper atop the cardboard.
2. Insert the pins into the center of the paper so they are eight centimeters apart (see the illustration). One pin is a *focus*, or fixed point, and represents the sun.
3. Tie both ends of the string together to form a loop. Wrap the loop around the pins as shown.
4. Place the red pencil inside the loop, extending it until the string is tight. Keeping the string taut, carefully move the pencil around the paper to make a complete revolution. The resulting oval shape is called an *ellipse.* The path of a planet as it revolves around the sun is an ellipse.

5. Move the pins so they are four centimeters apart. Repeat Step 4 using the blue pencil. Explain how the blue path differs from the red *(bigger and more like a circle).*
6. Move one pin two centimeters closer to the other. Remove the other pin. Repeat Step 4 using the black pencil. Explain how the black path differs from the others *(forms a circle).*

At the end of the activity, point out to students that the orbits of the planets are elliptical, with the sun always at one of the foci (Kepler's first law of planetary motion).

Relatively Speaking...

Concept: Relative size and distance of planets

Help students grasp the size of the planets and how far apart they are with this hands-on activity. Divide students into teams of four: pilot (team leader), mission specialist I (recorder), mission specialist II (materials manager), and copilot (encourager). Distribute a copy of page 167 and the materials listed to each team. Remind students that *scale* is the ratio between measurements on a map or model and the actual measurements (as in a scale of one inch equals one kilometer). Discuss page 167 with students, calculating the first answer on each chart together, if necessary. Then have the teams complete the page as directed.

When students have completed all three assignments, tape each planet model (see the materials list on page 167) to a different index card and label it. Head outside with the class, taking along the models, a 50-meter measuring tape, and a basketball to represent the sun. Use the basketball to anchor the front end of the measuring tape on the ground. Select one student to stand at the 40-meter mark; then have nine other students position the planet models on the tape using the scale of one meter equals one astronomical unit. Mission accomplished!

Meteorites Away!

Concept: How craters are formed

Invite your amateur astronauts to create a meteor shower of sorts with this data-collecting activity. Gather the materials listed on page 168 and divide students into groups of four or five. Then give each group the materials and a copy of page 168 to complete as directed. Afterward, have students compare the craters created by the marble and grape or the Ping-Pong ball and golf ball. Then have students discuss whether meteorites of similar size but different mass create similar craters (*those with greater mass create deeper craters*).

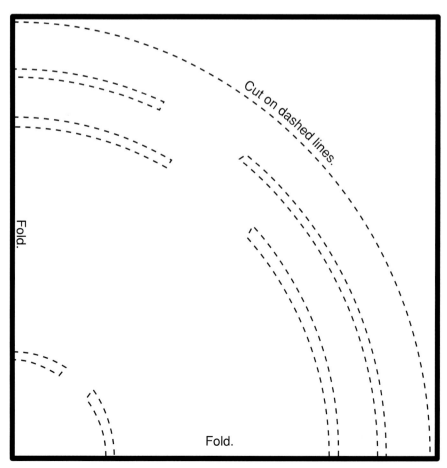

Ping-Pong ball | Marble

Golf ball

Tennis ball | Grape

Pattern

Use with "A Sun of Your Own" on page 164.

Cut on dashed lines.

Fold.

Fold.

Mission Prep 101

Welcome, junior astronauts! You've been recruited to conduct a special study of the solar system aboard the next shuttle. To prepare for this mission, your team must complete three important assignments. Good luck!

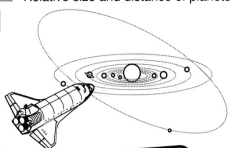

Materials for each team: calculator, metric ruler, 40 cm strip of paper or adding machine tape, 9 planet models (3 poppy seeds, 1 medium grape, 2 mustard seeds, 2 peppercorns, 1 piece of M&M's or Skittles candy)

Assignment I: Notice that the distances in the chart below are in millions of kilometers. Simplify these numbers by converting them to *astronomical units* (AU). One AU is equal to the average distance between the earth and the sun (149.6 million km). To calculate astronomical units, use a calculator to divide each planet's distance from the sun by the earth's distance from the sun. Round each answer to the nearest tenth and record it in the chart.

	Mercury	Venus	Earth	Mars	Jupiter	Saturn	Uranus	Neptune	Pluto
Distance from sun (millions of kilometers)	57.9	108.2	149.6	227.9	778.3	1,427	2,871	4,497	5,914
AU			1						

Assignment II: Draw a line segment 40 cm long on the strip of paper. Mark each centimeter. Label the beginning point "Sun." Using the scale one centimeter equals one AU, plot and label points along the line segment to show each planet's relative distance from the sun. Use the millimeter marks on your ruler to plot tenths of units.

Assignment III: Study the chart below. Notice that the scale of each planet's diameter has been changed from kilometers to millimeters. Measure the diameter of each of the planet model items in millimeters. Select the model that best represents the diameter of each planet and record it in the chart. Then place each model on its corresponding point on the distance line created in Assignment II.

Diameter	Mercury	Venus	Earth	Mars	Jupiter	Saturn	Uranus	Neptune	Pluto
Actual (km)	4,880	12,100	12,756	6,794	143,200	120,000	51,800	49,528	~2,330
Scaled (mm)	0.49	1.21	1.28	0.68	14.32	12.0	5.18	4.95	0.23
Model									

Note to the teacher: Use with "Relatively Speaking…" on page 166.

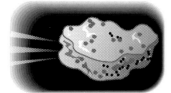
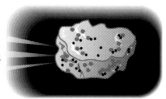

Meteorites Away!

Create a shower of meteorites and see the kinds of crater creators they become!

Materials for each group: 5 lb. bag of flour, 9¼" x 11¾" aluminum pan, brown tempera paint, meterstick, ruler, newspaper, balance scale, tweezers, toothpicks, pencil, paper strips, objects to represent meteorites: grape, marble, Ping-Pong ball, golf ball, tennis ball

Steps:

1. Place the pan on the newspaper. Fill the pan with flour to a depth of three inches. Sprinkle tempera paint over the flour's surface.

2. Record the name of each meteorite object in the chart at the right.

3. Weigh each meteorite object and record its mass in the chart.

4. Select a meteorite object and hold it above the pan at a height of 20 centimeters. Drop the object. Then carefully remove it from the resulting *impact crater,* or bowl-shaped hollow. Use tweezers to remove the smaller objects. Label the crater with a paper strip.

Meteorite Object	Mass	Crater	Height of Drop			
			20 cm	60 cm	1 m	2 m
		Width				
		Depth				
		Width				
		Depth				
		Width				
		Depth				
		Width				
		Depth				
		Width				
		Depth				

5. Measure the crater's width and depth and record the measurements in the chart. To measure small craters, mark the measurements on a toothpick with a pencil. Then use a ruler to measure from the tip of the toothpick to each mark.

6. Repeat Steps 4–5 with each remaining meteorite object.

7. Repeat Steps 4–6, dropping each meteorite object from a height of 60 centimeters, then 1 meter, and finally 2 meters.

8. Label the following parts on the crater drawing on the left: floor, wall, rim, *ejecta* (material thrown out of the crater), *rays* (the streaks extending outward from the rim).

Bonus Box: Predict the crater depth of each meteorite object above if it were dropped from a height of 80 meters. Write your predictions on the back of this page.

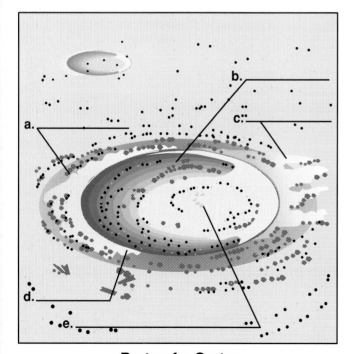

Parts of a Crater

LITERATURE UNITS

Frindle

by Andrew Clements

The pen may be mightier than the sword, but the frindle is mightier yet! At least that's what Nick Allen thinks when he makes up the word *frindle* to replace *pen*, much to the dismay of his fifth-grade language arts teacher, dictionary devotee Mrs. Granger. The furor that follows makes for a story that students and teachers alike will cheer.

with ideas by Tina Cassidy

After Chapter 2

Skill: Learning new vocabulary

Mrs. Granger, a lover of the English language, introduces a "Word for the Day" every morning to teach her students new vocabulary. Follow Mrs. Granger's lead with the following vocabulary-building activity. Provide each student with a small, inexpensive notepad (or one made from scrap paper). Have each student label the front of his notebook as shown. Then challenge each child to locate one new word each morning in a dictionary, library book, textbook, or other resource, such as one of the Web sites listed. Have the student write the word and a definition in his notebook. Then challenge him to use that word at least once during the day. Each time the student uses the word, have him jot the quote in his notebook. At the end of the week, have each child copy his favorite quote onto a large index card and highlight the new word. Display the cards on your classroom door or a bulletin board with the title "Quotable Quotes."

Word Web Sites
(current as of February 2001)
- www.LearningKingdom.com (click on "Cool Word of the Day")
- www.wordcentral.com/index.html (click on "Daily Buzzword!")

Word Master — Ian

After Chapter 3 and at the End of the Book

Skills: Writing a diary entry, analyzing a character

Nick's first day in Mrs. Granger's class doesn't go at all like he expects! Give your class a chance to walk in Nick's shoes with this character analysis activity. Challenge each student to pretend that she is in Nick's class on that first day of fifth grade. Have the student write a diary entry giving her impressions of the class and Mrs. Granger. What will a year in Mrs. Granger's class be like? After everyone finishes writing, let student volunteers share their entries. Then collect the papers.

At the end of the book, redistribute the papers and have students reread their entries. Then have each child write another entry describing her last day in Mrs. Granger's class. Ask students to answer this question in the entry: What do you think of Mrs. Granger now? Provide time for students to share these final entries.

After Chapter 4

Skills: Using a dictionary, vocabulary development

Poor Nick! He's stuck inside looking up words in a dictionary instead of playing ball with his friends. Do your students also complain when you make vocabulary assignments? Change their groans to cheers with this activity. Begin by posting this riddle on the board: Would you be insulted or pleased if someone said you were very statuesque? Students will quickly realize that looking the word up in a dictionary will help them answer the question. Post a different riddle on the board for the next couple of mornings (see the examples). Then challenge students to submit their own riddles for you to post each day.

Would you wear a miter or drive it?

Which would be easier to pack in a suitcase: a redingote or a lummox?

After Chapter 6

Skill: Identifying causes and effects

In chapter 6, a series of events leads to Nick's idea for his new word. Use these events to give students practice identifying causes and effects. First, help the class create a timeline of the events leading to Nick's idea as shown. Guide students to see the causes and effects in the timeline. Then tell students that their lives are also full of causes and effects. To prove this point, have each student think about the previous day and list at least five events that happened to him. Then have the student draw a timeline of his day on a large sheet of paper. Below the timeline, have the student write five cause-and-effect statements about the timeline, such as "Because I brought money, I was able to buy lunch." Provide time for students to share their timelines and statements.

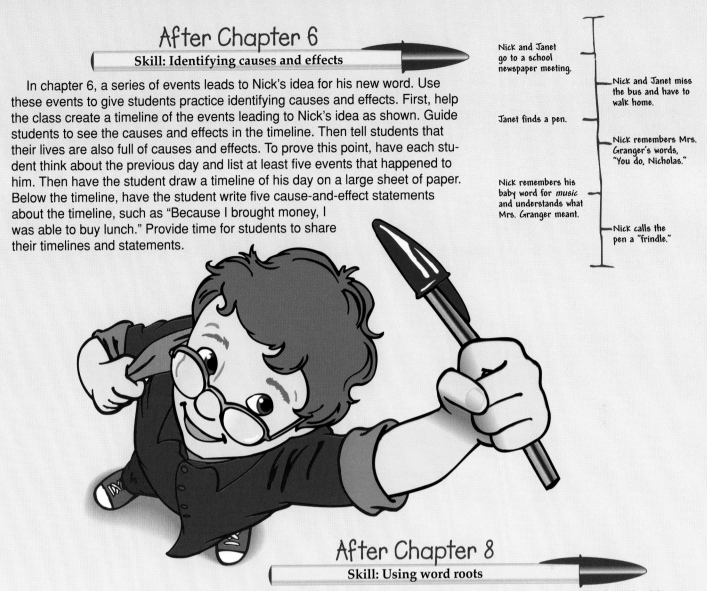

Nick and Janet go to a school newspaper meeting.

Nick and Janet miss the bus and have to walk home.

Janet finds a pen.

Nick remembers Mrs. Granger's words, "You do, Nicholas."

Nick remembers his baby word for *music* and understands what Mrs. Granger meant.

Nick calls the pen a "frindle."

After Chapter 8

Skill: Using word roots

In chapter 8, Mrs. Granger tells Nick that the word *pen* has a long history to it. Explore the history behind other words with a group activity on roots. To prepare, label a small sheet of chart paper for each of the word roots and meanings (in parentheses) shown. Tape the charts around the classroom.

Materials for each group: 12 small index cards, markers, sheet of paper, pencil, dictionary

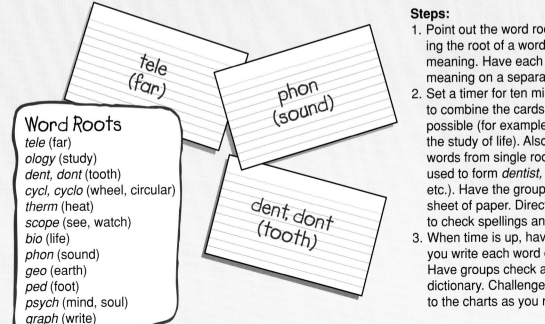

tele
(far)

phon
(sound)

dent, dont
(tooth)

Word Roots
tele (far)
ology (study)
dent, dont (tooth)
cycl, cyclo (wheel, circular)
therm (heat)
scope (see, watch)
bio (life)
phon (sound)
geo (earth)
ped (foot)
psych (mind, soul)
graph (write)

Steps:
1. Point out the word root charts. Explain that knowing the root of a word will help students learn its meaning. Have each group write each root and its meaning on a separate index card.
2. Set a timer for ten minutes. Challenge each team to combine the cards to make as many words as possible (for example, *bio* and *ology* form *biology*, the study of life). Also encourage students to form words from single roots (for example, *dent* can be used to form *dentist, dental, denture, dentistry,* etc.). Have the group's recorder list the words on a sheet of paper. Direct groups to use the dictionary to check spellings and meanings.
3. When time is up, have each group share its list as you write each word on the appropriate chart. Have groups check any questionable words in a dictionary. Challenge students to add more words to the charts as you read *Frindle*.

After Chapter 12

Nick's word causes quite an uproar in his school and hometown. Each character sees the word a little differently. To help students understand the different perspectives of the characters, divide the class into groups of four. Assign each student in a group a different character: Nick, Mrs. Granger, Mrs. Allen, Mr. Allen, the students at Lincoln Elementary, Mrs. Chatham, Judy Morgan, or Bud Lawrence. Then give each child a copy of the glasses pattern on page 174 and have him follow these steps.

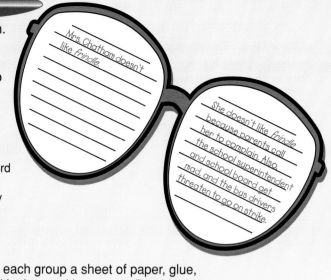

Mrs. Chatham doesn't like frindle

She doesn't like frindle because parents call her to complain. Also, the school superintendent and school board get mad, and the bus drivers threaten to go on strike.

1. On the left lens, write about your character's point of view of the word *frindle*.
2. On the right lens, explain why you think the character feels that way about *frindle*.
3. Color the glasses frame with your favorite color.
4. Cut out the glasses.

After each group meets to discuss the different viewpoints, give each group a sheet of paper, glue, and markers. Have each group glue its glasses on the paper and title the resulting poster. Provide time for each group to present its point of view poster to the rest of the class.

At the End of the Book

Celebrate the end of *Frindle* by challenging the class to create its own unique pop-up dictionary.

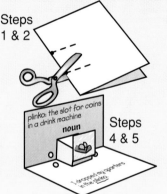

Look it up!

Steps 1 & 2

plinko: the slot for coins in a drink machine
noun
I dropped my quarters in the plinko.

Steps 4 & 5

Materials for each student: sheet of duplicating paper, 2½"-square piece of white paper, glue, scissors, markers, ruler
Steps:
1. Fold the duplicating paper in half. Measure three inches from the top and bottom edges of the folded paper as shown and mark both spots.
2. Cut a two-inch slit at the marks as shown.
3. Unfold the paper. Then pull the resulting flap toward you and crease it at the fold.
4. Turn the paper as shown. At the top of the paper, write your new word, its definition, and its part of speech. Below the flap, write a sentence using the word.
5. On the small paper square, draw and color a picture to illustrate your sentence. Pull out the flap; then glue the picture to the front of the flap as shown.

Gather the finished pages together in alphabetical order between two decorated covers. Then punch a hole on each side of the flaps (see the illustration) and tie the pages together with yarn.

During Reading

Encourage students to pick up their pens—rather, their frindles—and write about the following prompts as they read this captivating tale.

Before reading: How would you describe a troublemaker? How does a troublemaker act?
Ch. 1: Now that you've read the first chapter, does Nick fit your description of a troublemaker? Why or why not?
Ch. 3: Nick's plan to trick Mrs. Granger doesn't work as he had planned. Describe a time when something you planned didn't go quite like you had expected.
Ch. 6: In this chapter, Nick gets a big idea. Describe a big idea you once had. What caused you to think up this idea? Did you go through with your idea? Why or why not?
Ch. 8: What do you think is in Mrs. Granger's letter? Explain your answer.
Ch. 9: Do you think Nick should quit using his new word in school? Why or why not?
Ch. 12: Nick is suddenly getting a lot of attention nationwide. How would you feel if you were in Nick's shoes? Why?
Ch. 15: How do you think Nick's life would have turned out if he had never thought of *frindle*?

Dictionary Dilemma

Use the dictionary!

Mrs. Granger gave the students the words in the word box to look up for homework. To be nice, she also gave them the guide words to help them locate each word. **Directions:** Help the students complete their assignment by following these steps. The first one is done for you.

1. Write each word in the matching blank.
2. Look at the number beside the blank. Circle that letter in the answer.
3. Write the circled letter in the numbered blank below to answer the riddle.

Word Box

haul	carbon	signify	sheer
candle	catastrophe	heat	music
silver	moonstruck	cappuccino	mosaic
hail	cease	siege	hash
motto	musty	hemisphere	shirt

1. hatch—hawk: h(a)u l (2)

2. hackle—hake: _____ (2)

3. heartache—heavy: _____ (4)

4. hello—hen: _____ (2)

5. harmonica—hassle: _____ (2)

6. museum—mussel: _____ (4)

7. mortise—motion: _____ (6)

8. motive—mourning: _____ (3)

9. monumental—morass: _____ (10)

10. mustang—mute: _____ (3)

11. sheep—shield: _____ (3)

12. sideboard—sieve: _____ (5)

13. silhouette—simper: _____ (5)

14. sight—silent: _____ (6)

15. shipshape—shiver: _____ (4)

16. caramel—careless: _____ (5)

17. cause—ceiling: _____ (2)

18. candid—cannon: _____ (5)

19. cast—cattle: _____ (9)

20. canvas—capsule: _____ (6)

Why did the student eat his vocabulary test?

Because his teacher told him the __ __ __ __   was __
                                    3 11 10 8   5

__ __ __ __   __ __ __ __ __   __ __   __ __ __ __ __ !
15 17 2 18   19 6 4 20 12   16 14   7 1 9 13

Bonus Box: Choose a set of guide words above. Think of at least one more word that would be found on that page. Write the guide words and word(s) on the back of this page.

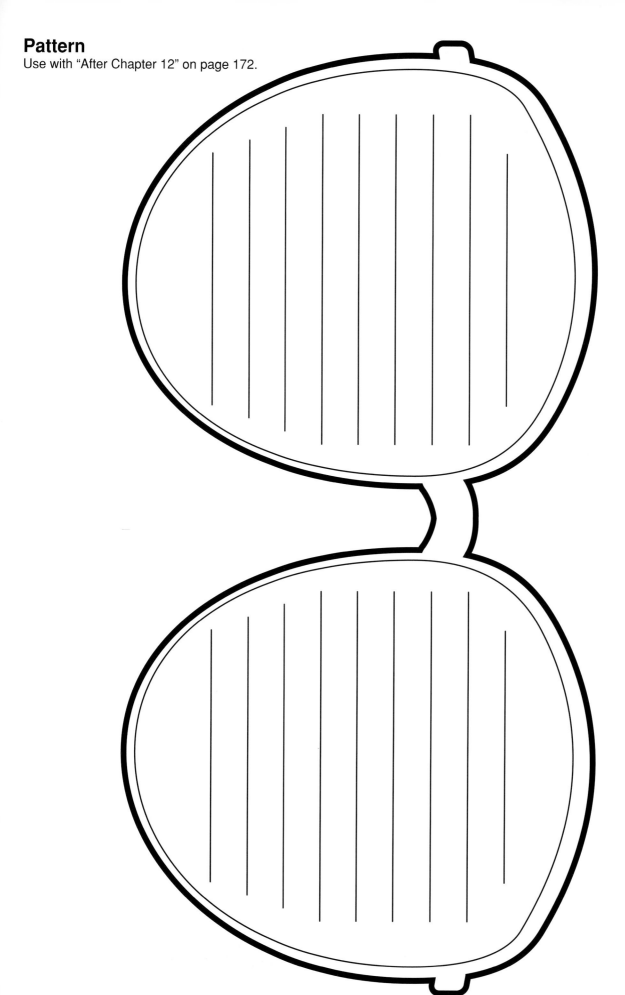

Bud's Frindle Shop

Bud Lawrence knows an opportunity when he sees one! He has opened Bud's Frindle Shop and is making lots of money for himself and Nick.

Directions: Use the prices listed to help Bud solve the problems below. Show your work on another sheet of paper. Write the answers in the blanks.

Price List		
Frindle T-Shirts $7.00	Frindle Flags $2.25	Frindle Notebook $1.00
Frindles gross: $5.40 each: $.25	Deluxe Dictionary $8.75	Frindle Baseball Caps $10.00
Frindle Posters $2.50	Frindle Sunglasses $7.75	Frindle Erasers $.50

1. Which is the better buy: a gross of frindles or 36 individual frindles? _____
   How do you know? _____

2. Nick wants to get a pair of sunglasses for each of his 20 classmates. How much money will he need? _____

3. Bud Lawrence made $1,360 in his first week; $2,775 his second week; and $5,730 his third week. How much money did he make in his first three weeks? _____

4. Mrs. Granger wants to buy a new dictionary for each of her 50 students. How much money will she need? _____

5. Janet Fisk has $20 to spend at Bud's shop. She wants a T-shirt, a poster, and a pair of sunglasses. Does she have enough money? _____ How do you know? _____

6. Bud made $100,000 on frindle products in his first year. He has to give Nick 30 percent. How much money will Nick get? _____

7. Nick's baseball team wants to wear frindle baseball caps and T-shirts to every game. Bud will give them a 10 percent discount on the total cost. If there are ten kids on the team, how much will they have to pay all together? _____

8. Figure out two different ways to spend $25 at Bud's Frindle Shop. Write your answers on your own paper.

Bonus Box: Add two items to the price list above. Then write two story problems that include those items. Give the problems to a friend to solve.

Lily's Crossing

A Newbery Honor Book
by Patricia Reilly Giff

It's the summer of 1944, and Lily's annual vacation at Rockaway Beach isn't going as planned. A terrible war is raging, her best friend has left the beach, and now her father is being sent overseas. Left with only Gram, Lily is painfully lonely until a refugee from Hungary moves next door, changing her life forever. For an unforgettable reading experience, share this touching story about friendship and sacrifice with your students.

with ideas by Jan Brennan, Avon, CT

Before Reading

Skills: Identifying characters and settings, making predictions

Introduce students to this story with an activity that sets the stage for a great end-of-book review. First, read aloud the summary of the story found on the book's back cover. On chart paper, write the following headings as shown: Main Characters, Setting (Where and When), and Potential Problems. Invite your students to help you fill in the main characters and setting of the book in the appropriate spaces on the chart. Then ask them to predict potential problems that might occur. Refer to the chart at the end of the book to compare students' predictions with the actual problems the characters encountered.

Main Characters	Setting (Where and When)	Potential Problems

While Reading

Skill: Responding to a prompt

As students read *Lily's Crossing,* challenge them to respond to the following thought-provoking prompts:

Ch. 4: Lily describes the house at Rockaway Beach. Describe a room in your house in detail. Remember, you want the reader to see the room just as you do.

Ch. 7: Lily's four main problems are telling lies, daydreaming, lack of friends, and Gram. List four problems that you have. Explain why they are problems; then write one possible solution to each problem.

Ch. 10: When Lily and Albert team up to save the cat, they are drawn closer together. Write about a drama that you were part of and how it changed your relationship with someone.

Ch. 12: How did you feel about Lily and Albert sneaking into the movie theater? If Lily had asked you to go, what would you have done?

Ch. 16: Albert's Nagymamma secretly gave him money to use for something important. If you had some secret "important money," how would you spend it?

Ch. 17: Gram tells Lily that she can do anything if she really works at it. Do you agree? Explain your answer.

Ch. 20: Lily is surprised to find out that Gram had sent a letter to Margaret. When was the last time you were surprised by something someone did? Why were you surprised?

Ch. 24: Gram tells Lily and Albert that people go to war to keep their loved ones safe. How do you feel about war? How would you feel if one of your family members left to go to war?

Ch. 28: Sister Benedicta tells Lily that all writers daydream and that what is important is knowing the difference between lies and daydreams. What do you think is the difference?

After Chapter 3
Skill: Expressive writing

When Lily and Margaret sample Eddie's candy, Lily reminisces about her friend's big brother. Use this event as the springboard to an expressive-writing activity. First, explain to students that expressive writing uses sensory detail and emotions to share experiences and insights about people, ideas, places, and things. Then give each child a copy of page 179. Direct each student to choose a favorite person in her life (other than a classmate) and use the reproducible organizer to take notes on the friend. After the student completes the organizer, have her use her notes to write a memoir about her encounter with the person. To display the memoirs, have the student trace her story's paper in the middle of a slightly larger sheet of white art paper. Direct the student to decorate the resulting frame and then glue the memoir in the center as shown. Post these projects on a bulletin board titled "Picturing Our Favorite People."

After Chapter 8, End of Book
Skill: Making inferences

Lily forms a first impression of Albert when she spies on him. When Albert catches Lily spying on him, he forms an impression of her. Have students think about these first impressions and how they changed with this activity. After reading chapters 4–8, divide the class into two groups. Instruct each student in Group 1 to write about Lily's first impression of Albert. Have each child in Group 2 write about Albert's first impression of Lily. Provide time for students to share their responses.

At the end of the book, have students discuss these questions: Is Lily's first impression of Albert a lasting one? What about Albert's first impression of Lily? How do you know? What might have changed those first impressions? Are first impressions important? As a writing extension, have each student write about an experience he had meeting someone for the first time. Did his first impression change after he got to know the person, or was it accurate?

After Chapter 15
Skill: Identifying character traits

When Lily and Gram go to church to pray for Eddie, Lily sees a banner honoring those serving in the war. Challenge students to use the materials and steps listed to create their own special banners that compare their personality traits with those of Lily or Albert.

Materials for each student: large sheet of white art paper; scrap paper; glue; scissors; different-sized star templates; yellow, gray, and blue construction paper; markers, crayons, or colored pencils; coat hanger; tape

Steps:
1. Choose Lily or Albert. On scrap paper, list at least five positive personality traits that the character possesses. Then list five positive traits that you have.
2. Cut the white paper, as shown, to make a banner shape.
3. On scrap paper, design a banner that compares your traits with the character's. Leave the banner's tabs blank.
4. Once your design is ready, make the banner using the materials.
5. Tape the tabs of the banner over the bottom of a coat hanger.

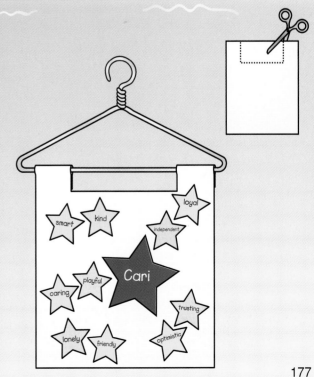

After Chapter 24
Skills: Critical thinking, writing a friendly letter

In chapters 15, 20, and 22, Lily reads letters from her father in which he repeatedly encourages his daughter to read several books. At the end of chapter 24, Lily finally realizes that the books—all set in France—are clues to secretly let her know Poppy is in that country. Challenge your students to develop their own mysterious messages with this thinking and writing activity. First, review with the class how to write a friendly letter. Then instruct each student to follow the steps below:

1. Secretly choose a country or setting your class has studied or read about.
2. Write a letter to a friend telling him about a make-believe vacation you are enjoying in that area. Do not name the place in your letter; instead include clues (like Poppy did) that will give the reader hints about the location's identity.

Provide time for each student to read his letter aloud; then challenge the class to identify the mystery location.

Sheila Krill

Culminating Activity
Skills: Recognizing historical fiction, reading comprehension

Explore with your students some of the key elements of good historical fiction with this culminating activity. Begin by displaying a chart or transparency labeled with the following information:

A good historical fiction book
- tells an interesting story that blends fact with fiction
- includes details that are accurate, including the setting and the historical events
- reflects the values and spirit of the times instead of being written from today's point of view

Lead a class discussion about these three points; then divide the class into small groups. Direct each group to look back through the book to find at least two or three examples that support each of the three requirements above. Discuss the groups' findings as a class.

Want to Read More?

If your students are eager to read other historical fiction books set during World War II, suggest the following excellent books:

- *Stepping on the Cracks* by Mary Downing Hahn
- *Molly's Fire* by Janet Lee Carey
- *My Secret War: The World War II Diary of Madeline Beck* (Dear America series) by Mary Pope Osborne
- *Number the Stars* by Lois Lowry
- *Waiting for Anya* by Michael Morpurgo
- *Twenty and Ten* by Claire Huchet Bishop
- *Keep Smiling Through* by Ann Rinaldi

Picturing _____

As they sit eating candy in the attic, Margaret and Lily wonder about Eddie's life as a soldier. Lily begins to think about how Eddie looked, what she liked best about him, and how he used to play along when she told one of her wild tales.

Part 1: On the line above, write the name of a favorite person in your life (other than someone in your class). Fill in the spaces below with information about this person. Provide lots of details, including your feelings about your special friend. Use the back if you need more space.

What this person looks like:
_____
_____
_____
_____
_____
_____
_____
_____

What I like best about this person:
_____
_____
_____
_____
_____
_____
_____
_____
_____

A favorite experience I had with this person:
_____
_____
_____
_____
_____
_____
_____
_____
_____

Part 2: A *memoir* is a written record of the writer's own experience. On another sheet of paper, use the details in the picture frames to write a memoir about the experiences you had with your favorite person. Start your memoir with an introduction telling who the person is. End it with a conclusion.

Note to the teacher: Use this page with "After Chapter 3" on page 177.

Name_____

Analyzing plot, predicting outcomes

Big Lies

One of Lily's main problems is telling lies. As the story progresses, Lily begins to understand that there are consequences to telling lies and that she must stop. Reread the chapters indicated below. Write the lie Lily told in each star. Then predict two possible outcomes that could happen because of that lie.

Lie 1
Chapter 3

Lie 2
Chapter 3

Lie 3
Chapter 3

Possible outcome: _____
_____
_____
_____
Possible outcome: _____
_____
_____
_____

Possible outcome: _____
_____
_____
_____
Possible outcome: _____
_____
_____
_____

Possible outcome: _____
_____
_____
_____
Possible outcome: _____
_____
_____
_____

Lie 4
Chapter 9

Lie 5
Chapter 9

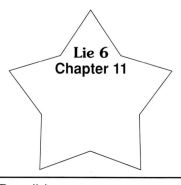

Lie 6
Chapter 11

Possible outcome: _____
_____
_____
_____
Possible outcome: _____
_____
_____
_____

Possible outcome: _____
_____
_____
_____
Possible outcome: _____
_____
_____
_____

Possible outcome: _____
_____
_____
_____
Possible outcome: _____
_____
_____
_____

Bonus Box: On the back of this page or another sheet of paper, write an explanation you would give a four-year-old about why lying is wrong.

©The Education Center, Inc. • THE MAILBOX® • Intermediate • Oct/Nov 2001 • Key p. 310

Is That a Fact?

Facts are different from opinions. A *fact* is a statement that can be proven true. An *opinion* is what someone thinks is true. For example:

Fact: The Mollahans took the piano to the beach.
Opinion: Paprika, the kitten, is the best pet in the world.

Directions: Below are statements that Lily might have made during the story.

If the statement is a fact, turn the circle into a musical note.

If the statement is Lily's opinion, turn the circle into a kitten.

1. A boat is patrolling the waters.

2. All anybody ever talks about is the war.

3. *The Three Musketeers* is better than *Madeline.*

4. American soldiers are fighting in Europe.

5. I got a letter from Poppy today.

6. The war will last forever.

7. Albert's belt makes him look ridiculous.

8. A silver star stands for a missing soldier.

9. We listened to the radio to hear about the war.

10. Gram would never understand why I need money.

11. I tell lies.

12. Paprika is getting bigger and stronger.

13. Being a writer is the hardest job in the world.

14. Eddie was the best big brother in the world.

15. Poppy came home from the war today.

16. Daydreaming is a worthless activity.

Bonus Box: On the back of this page, write an opinion about your bedroom. Then write a fact about it.

©The Education Center, Inc. • *THE MAILBOX®* • *Intermediate* • Oct/Nov 2001 • Key p. 310

Note to the teacher: Use this page after students have finished reading the book.

A Wrinkle in Time

A Classic Newbery Winner by Madeleine L'Engle

It is a dark and stormy night when Meg, Charles Wallace, and their mother are surprised by a mysterious visitor. Things become even more astonishing when the caller leads the children on a travel through time to rescue Meg's missing father. Will the Murry kids and their friend Calvin triumph over the forces of evil that oppose them? Find out by sharing this timeless adventure and the activities that follow with your students.

with ideas by Terry Healy, Eugene Field Elementary, Manhattan, KS

During Reading

Skill: Responding to a prompt

Encourage students to respond to each chapter in *A Wrinkle in Time* with these thought-provoking prompts.

Ch. 1: Meg has a hard time appreciating her strengths. List ten things that you do well both in and out of school.

Ch. 2: Without hearing a word from Meg, Charles Wallace knows that she has had a bad day at school. Describe how someone can tell if you've had a good or bad day at school when you haven't said a word.

Ch. 3: When he is with the Murry family, Calvin says that he no longer feels alone. Write about a person in your life who makes you feel like Calvin feels with the Murrys.

Ch. 4: Mrs. Which states that the only way to cope with something deadly serious is with a sense of humor. Do you agree that a sense of humor is important when you're faced with a big problem or challenge? Explain your answer.

Ch. 5: The children suggest several famous people who could be considered "fighters" against the Powers of Darkness. Name someone you view as a hero. Explain why you admire this person.

Ch. 6: What would it be like to live in a world where everything is exactly alike?

Ch. 7: How would you feel about having someone else make all of your decisions for you?

Ch. 8: Meg doesn't like being different, but she doesn't want to be like everybody else either. Tell about a time in your life when it was good to be different.

Ch. 9: What do you think Meg means when she says that *like* and *equal* are not the same thing?

Ch. 10: Why do you think Meg is so angry with her father? Would you have been angry with him too if you were Meg? Why or why not?

Ch. 11: Aunt Beast encourages Meg to describe who Mrs. Whatsit, Mrs. Who, and Mrs. Which *are,* not what they look like. Write a description of yourself that tells about who you are, not about how you look.

Ch. 12: Meg goes to rescue Charles Wallace even though she is very afraid. Write about a time when you were afraid to do something, but you did it anyway.

After Chapter 1

Skills: Reading for details, critical thinking

Challenge students to dig into the details of chapter 1 with this simple activity. Divide the class into small groups and give each group a copy of the statements shown. Direct students within each group to discuss whether they agree or disagree with each statement. Require students to give at least two pieces of supporting evidence from the book to support each of their opinions. Use this easy-to-adapt activity with any chapter or book your class is reading.

Statements

- Meg should feel better about herself.
- Charles Wallace is very unusual.
- Meg and her mother aren't alike at all.
- Mr. Murry hasn't been gone for a very long time.
- Mrs. Whatsit isn't a human being.

After Chapter 3

Skill: Analyzing a character

Get better acquainted with the real Meg Murry—who Meg has a hard time seeing herself—with this character analysis activity. Review the part in chapter 1 when Meg frowns at her reflection in the mirror. Ask students, "Does Meg see who she really is when she looks in a mirror?" After students reflect silently for several minutes, divide the class into pairs. Give each twosome the materials listed. Then guide students through the steps that follow. When everyone is finished, divide the class into groups of three twosomes each. Have students compare their portraits to see if they saw Meg in the same light.

Materials for each student pair: 9" x 12" sheet of white construction paper, ruler, pencil, colored pencils or markers, crayons, sheet of notebook paper, tape

Steps:

1. Draw a one-inch-wide frame on the construction paper as shown.
2. Skim chapters 1–3 to find descriptions of Meg's physical appearance. In the center section of your paper, draw and color a picture of Meg based on the descriptions.
3. Use a pencil to write characteristics of Meg's personality in the frame. Trace over the words with a colored pencil or marker. Then lightly color the frame with a crayon.
4. On the notebook paper, write two evidences from the book that support each characteristic on the frame.
5. Tape the list you completed in Step 4 to the back of your picture.

After Chapter 4

Skill: Recognizing descriptive language

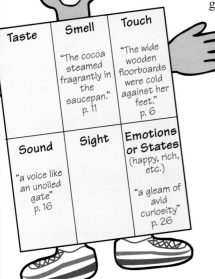

Help students recognize Madeleine L'Engle's use of descriptive language with this activity. First, explain to students that a good author uses specific details and sensory words and phrases to paint a picture for the reader. Point out some examples from chapter 4 (see those listed on the illustration). Next, have each child divide a sheet of paper into six labeled sections as shown. Instruct him to list descriptive language from chapters 1–4 for each category, including page numbers. Provide time for students to share their lists. Then give each student a sheet of white construction paper, scissors, and glue. Have the student cut out hands, feet, and a head and color them to resemble himself or a character from the book. Then have him glue the cutouts to his paper as shown.

After Chapter 6

Skills: Recognizing theme, writing a paragraph

Mrs. Whatsit gives the children special "gifts" based on their own unique selves. The importance of appreciating one's uniqueness versus the desire for conformity is one of the major themes of *A Wrinkle in Time*. To investigate this theme, give each child an 8" x 10" piece of wrapping paper and a same-sized piece of oaktag, glue, and a gift bow. Direct the student to glue the wrapping paper onto the oaktag. After the glue dries, have the student fold the paper as shown. On the inside of the folded project, have the student list five traits or abilities he possesses. Below the list, have him write a paragraph telling how he might use these gifts now and in the future. Finally, have the student attach the bow to the package as shown. After students share their paragraphs, discuss what life would be like if everyone were the same (like in Camazotz) rather than unique.

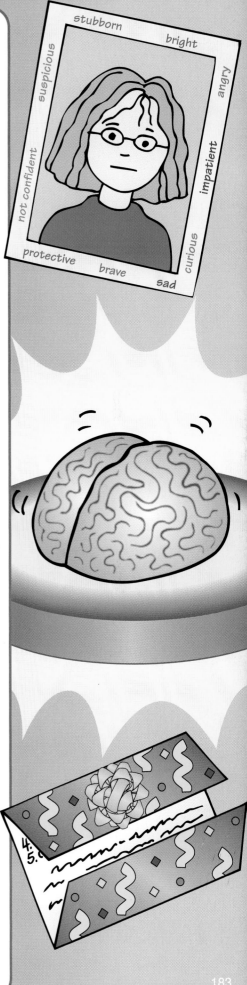

After Chapter 8
Skill: Identifying settings

By the time they find Mr. Murry, the children have traveled to several different places. Help students recall and describe those settings with this activity. Write each setting below on a slip of paper and place it in a bag. Divide the class into groups; then give each group a sheet of chart paper and a marker. Have one student from each group draw a setting from the bag. Caution groups to keep their settings secret. Then have each group skim chapters 1–8 to locate descriptions of its setting. Have the group list on the chart paper words and phrases that describe the setting.

When students are finished, have one group at a time read its list aloud. Challenge the other groups to identify the setting that was described. To extend, post a large sheet of butcher paper. Then have the groups illustrate their settings to create a mural chronicling the children's journey so far.

Settings
- Meg's attic bedroom
- Murry home
- haunted house
- Uriel
- in Orion's Belt
- Camazotz
- CENTRAL Central Intelligence building

After Chapter 12
Skills: Identifying themes, point of view

Spotlight the themes explored in *A Wrinkle in Time* with this activity. Have students brainstorm the major themes, focusing them on these five ideas:
- good versus evil
- appreciating one's unique individuality
- courage
- the inadequacy of words
- the triumph of love

After discussing events from the story that illustrate each theme, tell students to pretend that they are reporters for *Science News Monthly* magazine. Divide the class into pairs. Then have each twosome write an interview with Meg, Charles Wallace, or Calvin to find out what the character learned from the rescue mission. Encourage students to include in the interview the character's thoughts on one or more of the story's themes. Let each pair of students read the interview aloud, with one partner pretending to be the character and the other the reporter.

At the End of the Book
Skill: Summarizing story details

Wrap up the reading of this suspenseful story by having students make their own Wrinkle in Time capsules. In advance, have each student bring a coffee or Pringles can (with a lid) to school. Have the student measure and cut a piece of paper to fit around the can. After the student decorates the paper with the book's title and author and illustrations, have him glue it around the can. Then have him fill the can with items that he thinks represent the five most critical points in the story. Allow the student to include actual items or use art materials to make small cutouts. Provide time for each child to empty the contents of his capsule and explain to the class why he chose each item.

Seeing Conflict Clearly

One thing that *A Wrinkle in Time* has plenty of is conflict. In fiction, a conflict is usually one of four kinds:

- **Man vs. Man:** one person has a problem with another person
- **Man vs. Nature:** one person struggles against a force of nature
- **Man vs. Society:** a person has a problem with society, such as school, tradition, or law
- **Man vs. Self:** a person struggles with himself or herself, trying to decide how to solve a problem

CODE

Yellow = Man vs. Man
Green = Man vs. Nature
Blue = Man vs. Society
Red = Man vs. Self

Part 1: Can you see the conflicts in *A Wrinkle in Time* clearly? Color the glasses according to the code. On the last two pairs, list two other conflicts found in chapters 1–3.

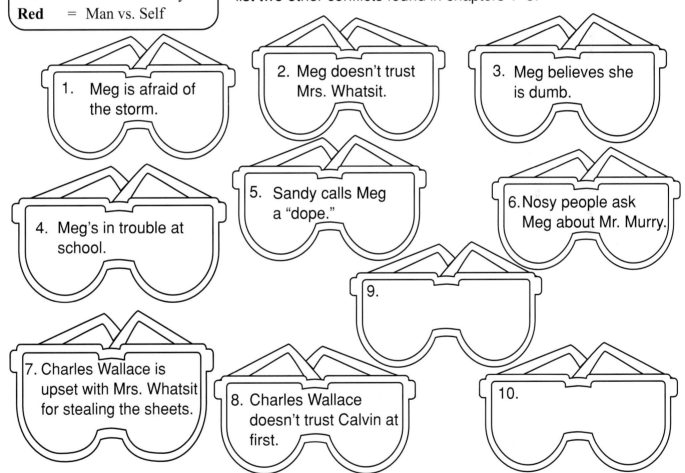

1. Meg is afraid of the storm.
2. Meg doesn't trust Mrs. Whatsit.
3. Meg believes she is dumb.
4. Meg's in trouble at school.
5. Sandy calls Meg a "dope."
6. Nosy people ask Meg about Mr. Murry.
7. Charles Wallace is upset with Mrs. Whatsit for stealing the sheets.
8. Charles Wallace doesn't trust Calvin at first.
9.
10.

Part 2: On another sheet of paper, sketch a large pair of glasses. In the left lens, write about a recent conflict you have experienced. In the right lens, write the kind of conflict your problem represents.

Bonus Box: On the back of this page, describe a conflict you have seen on a recent television program. How was it resolved?

Note to the teacher: Use after students have read chapter 3.

A New World of Words

Explore a new world of words as you travel through *A Wrinkle in Time.* Use a dictionary or thesaurus to find two synonyms for each word on a planet. Write the synonyms in the blanks. When you're finished, color the planet of the word you will try to use at least once today, either in speaking or writing.

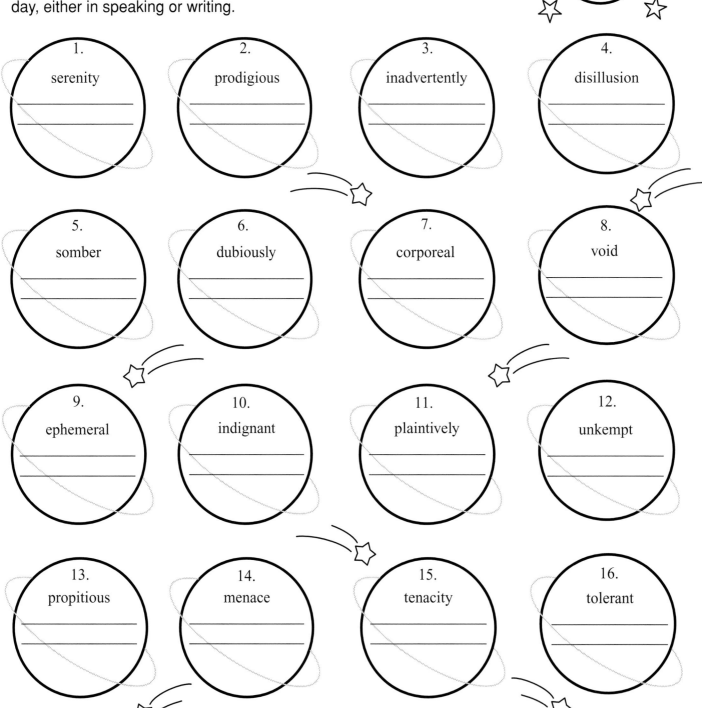

1.
serenity
_____
_____

2.
prodigious
_____
_____

3.
inadvertently
_____
_____

4.
disillusion
_____
_____

5.
somber
_____
_____

6.
dubiously
_____
_____

7.
corporeal
_____
_____

8.
void
_____
_____

9.
ephemeral
_____
_____

10.
indignant
_____
_____

11.
plaintively
_____
_____

12.
unkempt
_____
_____

13.
propitious
_____
_____

14.
menace
_____
_____

15.
tenacity
_____
_____

16.
tolerant
_____
_____

Bonus Box: On the back of this page or another sheet of paper, list the new vocabulary words above in backward alphabetical order (Z to A).

Meg's World

Part 1: Meg's world in *A Wrinkle in Time* is filled with many interesting and different characters. Choose five of the characters listed in the box. Write each name in a star. Then fill in the blanks with facts about that character. Only one fact can be about the character's physical appearance.

Characters

Mrs. Murry	Mrs. Which
Charles Wallace	The Happy Medium
Calvin O'Keefe	Aunt Beast
Mrs. Whatsit	Mr. Murry
Mrs. Who	The Man With Red Eyes
	IT

Part 2: Choose one of the activities below to complete on another sheet of paper.

 If you could become any character in the book, whom would you choose and why? Write your answer in a letter to Madeleine L'Engle.

 Pretend that you are Meg, Calvin, or Charles Wallace. Write a short speech that reveals the most important thing that happened to you on your journey to free Mr. Murry.

 What quote from the book would you put on your bedroom wall? Design a poster that includes the quote and the character who said it. On the back of the poster, write a paragraph telling why you chose this quote.

©The Education Center, Inc. • *THE MAILBOX*® • *Intermediate* • Dec/Jan 2001–2

Note to the teacher: Use this activity at the end of the book.

187

Shiloh Season

A Heartwarming Novel by Phyllis Reynolds Naylor

In this sequel to the Newbery Medal winner *Shiloh*, author Phyllis Reynolds Naylor picks right up where she left off. Marty Preston now owns Shiloh, the abused beagle he saved from Judd Travers. But that doesn't mean Judd has forgotten or forgiven Marty for taking his dog. Though Marty and Shiloh are in danger, it is Judd who will ultimately need to be saved. Invite students to join Marty and Shiloh's adventure by completing the following creative activities and reproducibles.

with ideas by Simone Lepine, Gillette Road Middle School, Cicero, NY

Before Reading
Skills: Making connections, comparing and contrasting

Most kids can relate to Marty's devotion to his dog, especially if they also have pets. Several days before introducing the story, ask each student who owns a pet to bring a photograph of his animal to school. Then, to begin the activity, give each child a sheet of art paper. Ask each student who owns a pet to use his photo to create a poster about his pet. Invite each child who doesn't own a pet to design a poster about an animal he'd like to call his own. Display the finished posters on a bulletin board titled "Our Pet Pals." Next, have students label paper strips with steps for taking good care of their animal friends, such as "clean its cage" or "keep its water dish filled." Staple these strips around the border of the bulletin board.

If desired, use these posters to introduce an end-of-the-book activity. Have each child create a second poster that features a favorite person in his life. Mount these posters on a second bulletin board. Around this display's border, have students staple paper strips that they've labeled with ways they take care of their loved ones, such as "talk with him every day" or "help her do her chores." Have students compare and contrast the two displays. Then discuss Marty's kind actions toward the injured Judd and why both animals and people need to be treated with kindness to be kind themselves.

During Reading
Skill: Responding in writing to literature

Encourage students to respond to *Shiloh Season* with these thought-provoking prompts.

Ch. 1: Do you agree with Marty that "a promise is a promise, even if I shouldn't have made it in the first place"? Give at least two reasons for your answer.

Ch. 3: Marty has a hard time sleeping because he's worried about Shiloh. How do you act when you are worried? Describe one thing that worries you now or worried you recently.

Ch. 4: Pretend that you are Marty trying to talk David out of spying on Judd. What do you say?

Ch. 5: Marty says that spying on Judd is "one of the stupidest things" he's ever done. Describe a time when you did something that you later realized was pretty foolish.

Ch. 6: Marty wonders what kind of kid Judd Travers was when he was growing up. Describe what you think Judd was like as a child.

Ch. 7: Since Marty has lied once about Shiloh, Marty's dad has a hard time trusting him. What do you think Marty will need to do in order to regain his father's trust?

Ch. 8: Marty wishes he'd been born into a family of nine boys. What would be the advantages of having lots of brothers and sisters? The disadvantages?

Ch. 10: The vet says that a dog will act mean when it's scared. Do you think people are like dogs in this way? Explain your answer.

Ch. 12: Do you think Marty is right not to tell his dad about Judd shooting at him and Shiloh? Explain your answer.

Ch. 13: What is the hardest decision you ever had to make? Why was it so hard to decide what to do?

Ch. 15: Why do you think Marty decides to tell his dad everything he's been keeping from him? Would you have done the same thing? Why or why not?

Ch. 16: What do you think will happen next between Judd, Marty, and Shiloh?

After Chapter 1
Skills: Drawing inferences, analyzing a character

As the book begins, Marty's mom tries to explain to her son why Judd might be drinking more. She tells him that perhaps Judd "looks in the mirror and don't like what he sees." Discuss with students what Mrs. Preston might mean and whether it's easy to see yourself as clearly as others see you. After the discussion, give each pair of students a copy of the reproducible on page 191. Challenge each twosome to list on the mirror words and phrases that describe what Judd may see when he looks in the mirror. Beside each word or phrase, have the students list a supporting detail (and its page number) from the book. When students are finished, discuss their lists. Then have each student pair decorate its mirror's frame with markers and cut it out. Post the mirrors on a bulletin board titled "Mirror, Mirror." For another way to use the mirror reproducible, see "Note to the teacher" at the bottom of page 191.

Essay Organizer

1. How I felt about the kindness project before I started it:	2. My favorite act of kindness and why it was my favorite OR the hardest act of kindness and why it was difficult:
3. How I feel about the kindness experiment and what I learned from it:	4. Words that describe me and my feelings:

After Chapter 4
Skill: Expressive writing

When Marty asks Doc Murphy if there is a way to make a mean dog nice, the doctor responds, "My own guess is that a little kindness will fix almost anything wrong with man or beast…." Discuss this comment with your students. Then challenge them to test Doc's theory with this activity. To begin, give each student a copy of page 192. Read the directions as a class; then have each student complete the page as directed.

After students have completed the experiment, set aside time for them to talk about their experiences, using the questions at the bottom of page 192 to generate discussion. Then display a transparency of an essay organizer similar to the one shown. Have each child copy the organizer on his paper and record information about the kindness experiment in each box. Then have the student use the organizer to write an expressive essay that describes her experience. Encourage students to use sensory details and emotions to share their insights about the kindness experiment. Bind the completed essays in a class book.

After Chapter 7
Skill: Recognizing and exploring theme

In this chapter, Marty's dad lets his son know that his trust in him has been shaken by his lies about Shiloh. Trust is an important theme in *Shiloh Season*. Discuss with students the definition of *trust* and its importance in relationships. Then give each child a sheet of white unlined paper. Direct each student to use a pencil to write the word *LIE* in big letters on her paper. Next, tell everyone to erase the word as thoroughly as possible. When students have finished erasing, ask them if they can still see the word on their papers. Most will likely answer that it is still faintly visible. Then discuss these questions:

- How is your paper like the emotion of trust?
- What happens to trust when someone lies?
- How can someone regain a person's trust once he or she has betrayed it?
- How can you tell that Shiloh trusts Marty? (Provide evidence from the story.)
- How can you tell that Shiloh doesn't trust Judd? (Provide evidence from the story.)

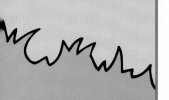

After Chapter 9
Skills: Making predictions, exploring plot

When Becky disappears during a game of hide-and-seek, the family worries that Judd may have shot her while hunting in their woods. Marty feels he'll be responsible if Becky is hurt by one of Judd's stray bullets. He starts to wonder if he made the right decision when he agreed not to report Judd's illegal shooting of the doe in exchange for Shiloh. Briefly discuss with students how the story would be different if Marty had reported Judd to the game warden in the author's first book, *Shiloh*. Then divide the class into pairs. Challenge each pair to pretend to be Marty, who has decided earlier to report Judd. Direct the twosome to write a diary entry describing what happened after Marty talked to the game warden. Have the students answer these questions in their entries:

- What happens to Shiloh and Marty?
- What happens to Judd?
- What happens to the relationship between the Preston family and Judd?

As an extension, have each twosome write a paragraph describing a plot for the sequel that Naylor might have written (instead of *Shiloh Season*) based on the events described in the diary entry.

After Chapter 12
Skill: Comparing and contrasting

News about Judd's dogs attacking Dara Lynn travels fast. By the next day, the story has grown beyond the facts, with tales of Judd's dogs stealing babies and tearing off arms! Marty's teacher uses the situation to talk with the class about the differences between truth and gossip. For a great compare-and-contrast activity, divide the class into groups. Give each group a large sheet of bulletin board paper and a marker. Instruct each group to draw a large Venn diagram on the paper, as shown, and complete it by listing the similarities and differences between truth and gossip. After each group shares its diagram, discuss these questions with students:

- How could the gossip about Judd's dogs have hurt Judd? The community?
- What consequences does gossip have for the people who spread it? The people who hear it? A person who is the topic of gossip?
- Can there be a little truth in gossip? Why or why not?
- Can changing or altering the truth—even just a little—be harmful? Why or why not?

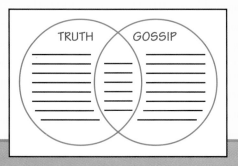

At the End of the Book
Skill: Exploring plot

If you're looking for action, *Shiloh Season* doesn't disappoint. But which events are the most important ones in the book? Get students thinking about this packed plot with the following culminating activity. First, ask students to pretend that Phyllis Reynolds Naylor has decided she'd like a new cover for her book. She's hired your class to submit several proposals for the design. Divide the class into groups of three or four students. Give each group a large piece of butcher paper. Then instruct the students in each group to decide together on three events from the book that they think are the most critical to the plot. Have them illustrate the events on the paper, adding the title and author of the book to complete the cover design. When each group shares its finished cover, have its members give at least two reasons why they think each event is critical enough to feature on the cover.

If your students are eager to read more about Marty and Shiloh, suggest that they read the first and third books in the Shiloh trilogy, Shiloh and Saving Shiloh.

Mirror, Mirror on the Wall

Note to the teacher: Use with "After Chapter 1" on page 189. Provide each student with markers and scissors. As a variation, write each student's name on a separate copy of this page. Discuss with students positive words they could use to describe each other. Then distribute the copies, making sure that no student gets his own. Have each child label the mirror with a positive word or phrase to describe the classmate listed at the top. Then signal students to swap papers and repeat the activity. Continue until each child has labeled every classmate's mirror. Collect the mirrors and add your own comments. Then give each student his mirror so he can read the kudos from his classmates.

191

Try a Little Tenderness

In *Shiloh Season,* Marty asks Doc if there is a way to make a mean dog nice. Doc responds, "My own guess is that a little kindness will fix almost anything wrong with man or beast...."

Directions: Find out how kindness affects you and others with this experiment. In the next several days, try to do as many of the acts of kindness listed below as you can. Write a ✔ in the box of each act that you complete. In the empty boxes, note any acts of kindness you did that aren't already listed. When you are finished, write the answers to the questions below on another sheet of paper.

Due date: _____

	Give a sincere compliment to a family member.		Help a classmate study for a test.
	Draw a picture to give to someone as a gift.		Make a family member's bed for him or her in the morning.
	Tell a joke to make someone laugh.		Help the teacher clean the classroom at the end of the day.
	Say "thank you" to someone who helps you.		Say "good morning" to an adult you see in the morning at school.
	Tell a friend that he or she does something well.		Do something extra to help someone out at home.
	Hold the door open for another person.		Leave a thank-you note on the desk of your school's secretary.
	Send a nice note to a former teacher or another adult (besides a parent).		
	Help a classmate clean out his or her desk.		
	Surprise a parent or other family member with a big hug or thank-you card.		

1. How did people react or respond to your acts of kindness?
2. How did you feel when you were doing an act of kindness?
3. Did anyone do an act of kindness for you? If so, how did it make you feel?
4. Which kind act did you enjoy doing the most? Why?
5. Which kind act was hardest for you to do? Why do you think it was so difficult?
6. Do you agree with Doc's opinion about kindness? Why or why not?

Special Delivery Vocabulary

In *Shiloh Season,* Marty's dad delivers mail—rain or shine. This book also delivers some vocabulary words that you might not know.

Directions: As you read *Shiloh Season,* be on the lookout for the vocabulary words listed below. Write the page number and the part of speech that shows how each word is used in the sentence. Read the meanings in the last column. Inside each envelope write the number that matches the word's meaning.

Parts of Speech
Noun (n) names a person, place, thing, animal, or idea
Verb (v) shows action or a state of being
Adjective (adj) describes a noun
Adverb (adv) describes a verb, adjective, or another adverb

	Word	Page #	Part of Speech	Match the Meaning	Meanings
Ch. 1–4	a. anxious	____	____		1. ill will toward someone
	b. poacher	____	____		2. feeling of deep resentment
	c. spite	____	____		3. one who kills wild animals illegally
	d. grudge	____	____		4. worried
	e. ford	____	____		5. shallow part of a body of water
Ch. 5–8	f. misery	____	____		1. put out of place
	g. sly	____	____		2. great unhappiness and suffering
	h. miserly	____	____		3. tempt
	i. lure	____	____		4. stingy
	j. dislocate	____	____		5. tricky
Ch. 9–12	k. peaceably	____	____		1. indirectly
	l. rabies	____	____		2. fight or object
	m. protest	____	____		3. disease of warm-blooded animals
	n. secondhand	____	____		4. keeping apart from others
	o. solitary	____	____		5. in a calm manner
Ch. 13–16	p. brewery	____	____		1. factory where malt liquor is produced
	q. unconscious	____	____		2. near the inside of the body
	r. amble	____	____		3. move by digging
	s. internal	____	____		4. walk or stroll
	t. burrowing	____	____		5. not aware

Bonus Box: Choose three of the words above to add to your spelling list for the week. On the back of this page, plan two ways you will study the words.

Bud, Not Buddy

A Newbery Winner by Christopher Paul Curtis

Times are tough in 1936, particularly for ten-year-old Bud Caldwell. Motherless and on the run, Bud—not Buddy—is convinced that the meager contents of an old suitcase hold the key to finding his father. Journey with Bud in his search—a quest with laugh-out-loud moments and unforgettable characters—using the following creative activities and reproducibles.

with ideas by Simone Lepine, Gillette Road Middle School, Cicero, NY

After Chapter 2
Skills: Making evaluations, analyzing a character

How does Bud survive being an orphan at ten and on his own during the depression? One thing he uses is "Bud Caldwell's Rules and Things for Having a Funner Life and Making a Better Liar Out of Yourself." Use this list of survival strategies as the basis for a skill-packed bulletin board activity. Cover a board with white paper and add the title "Noteworthy Life Rules." Draw two musical staffs on the paper as shown. Then label two index cards with the rules mentioned in chapter 2. Glue each card to a black paper circle mounted on the top staff, adding a stem with a black marker. Next, have each student label a small index card with a lesson she has learned in her life. After students share their lessons, have each child glue her card on a black paper circle, mount it on the bottom staff, and add a stem. Challenge students to compare and contrast their rules with Bud's. Point out that many of Bud's rules (shared later in the book) imply that adults can't be trusted. Ask, "Why do you think Bud feels this way? Do you agree with him? Why or why not?" As students continue reading, have them add to the top staff Bud's other rules mentioned in subsequent chapters.

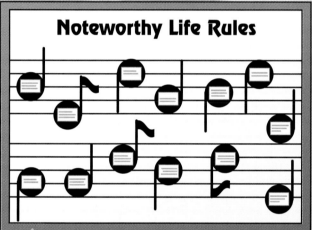

After Chapter 4
Skills: Making connections to literature, critical thinking

All Bud owns in the world fits inside a battered suitcase tied shut with twine. Not only do these few items have sentimental value for Bud, but they also hold clues to his father's identity. Before reading this chapter, ask each child to bring in an empty food box (such as those used to package rice, crackers, macaroni and cheese, etc.). After reading, have each student color and cut out two copies of the pattern on page 197 and glue them on opposites sides of his box as shown. Then have students take their suitcases home and pack them with a few items that are important to them. (Allow students to draw pictures of items they aren't comfortable bringing to school or that are too large to fit inside the box.) Each day ask a few students to share the contents of their suitcases with the class. If possible, store the suitcases in your room until the conclusion of the book to use with the "After Chapter 19" activity on page 196.

This suitcase belongs to
Shelly .

After Chapter 5
Skills: Sequencing, analyzing causes and effects

Even though he has every reason to despair, Bud holds to what his mother always told him: "…when one door closes, don't worry, because another door opens." Use this activity to open the door to the cause-and-effect relationships found in this novel. Give each student five to seven copies of page 198. Direct the student to cut out and stack the patterns and staple them along the left side to make a booklet. Then have him label the first page as shown. As he reads, have the student label the top half of each page with a major story event and the bottom half with the effects of that event (writing on the back of the door if he needs more space). Periodically discuss students' work on their booklets, either as a large group or in pairs.

After Chapter 9
Skills: Reading a map, using a scale of miles

In chapter 7, a librarian shows Bud how to determine the amount of time it would take to walk from Flint, Michigan, to Chicago, Illinois. After deciding the trek would be too long, Bud decides (in chapter 9) to walk to Grand Rapids to find his father instead. He plans his trip carefully, including the journey's distance, travel time, and route.

Challenge your students to sharpen their map-reading skills by planning a walking trip similar to Bud's. Divide the class into four groups. Assign a cardinal direction—north, south, east, west—to each group. Then direct each group to plan a walking trip of approximately 120 miles from your hometown to a destination located in the direction assigned. Instruct the group to include the following information in its plan:

- destination
- towns through which you will travel
- roads you will need to take
- potential challenges on the route and a plan for overcoming them

Provide time for each group to present its plan to the rest of the class.

After Chapter 10
Skill: Analyzing a character

There seem to be two sides to Bud's character. On the one hand, he's a brave young boy who faces very real problems in an optimistic, rational way. On the other hand, Bud is a wildly imaginative little boy who often lets unrealistic fears get the best of him. To help students examine Bud's personality, divide the class into pairs. Have one student in each pair look through the book through chapter 10 to find examples of Bud's bravery. Direct her partner to find examples of his fearfulness. Have partners share their examples with each other and discuss the following questions:

- In what ways is Bud brave?
- How does a positive attitude help Bud overcome problems?
- In what ways is Bud fearful? Of what is he afraid? Why do you think he's afraid of these things?
- How are you like Bud? How are you unlike him?

After Chapter 17
Skill: Recognizing and using figurative language

When Bud hears Herman E. Calloway's jazz band for the first time, he describes it using the rich figurative language of similes, metaphors, and personification. Review these three figures of speech with students. Then read aloud this portion of chapter 17. Have students work with you to identify the examples of similes, metaphors, and personification in the section. Then discuss how these figures of speech helped them "hear" the music Bud describes. If possible, ask your school's music teacher to provide you with recordings of jazz greats, such as Duke Ellington, Lionel Hampton, or Benny Goodman. Then instruct each student to think of an everyday object. Direct the student to write a description of the object—without mentioning its name—using at least three similes. Have each child share his similes with the group and challenge classmates to guess the mystery object.

After Chapter 19
Skill: Writing a personal narrative

After the truth comes out about his relationship to Herman E. Calloway, Bud unpacks his bag for the last time. He also gives away some of his prized possessions, having learned that he no longer needs them to keep memories of his mother alive. Ask students to think of people in their lives for whom they have fond memories. Then instruct each student to choose one person and create a web, as shown, to record memories about him or her. After she finishes her web, direct the student to use it to write a personal narrative about her person. Provide time for students to share their narratives. If desired, have each child roll up her story and tie it with a length of ribbon. Then have her place the scroll inside the suitcase created in the "After Chapter 4" activity on page 194 before taking it home to unpack.

fishing together at the family reunion

my eighth birthday

Aunt Mary

Christmas Eve story

terrific zoo trip last spring

At the End of the Book
Skill: Reviewing story elements, creative thinking

For a closing activity that reviews the story elements in *Bud, Not Buddy,* give each student a copy of page 199 and the materials listed on it. Have each student follow the directions on the page to complete a flyer that reviews the setting, characters, and plot of this award-winning book. Display the projects on a bulletin board titled "All About <u>Bud, Not Buddy</u>."

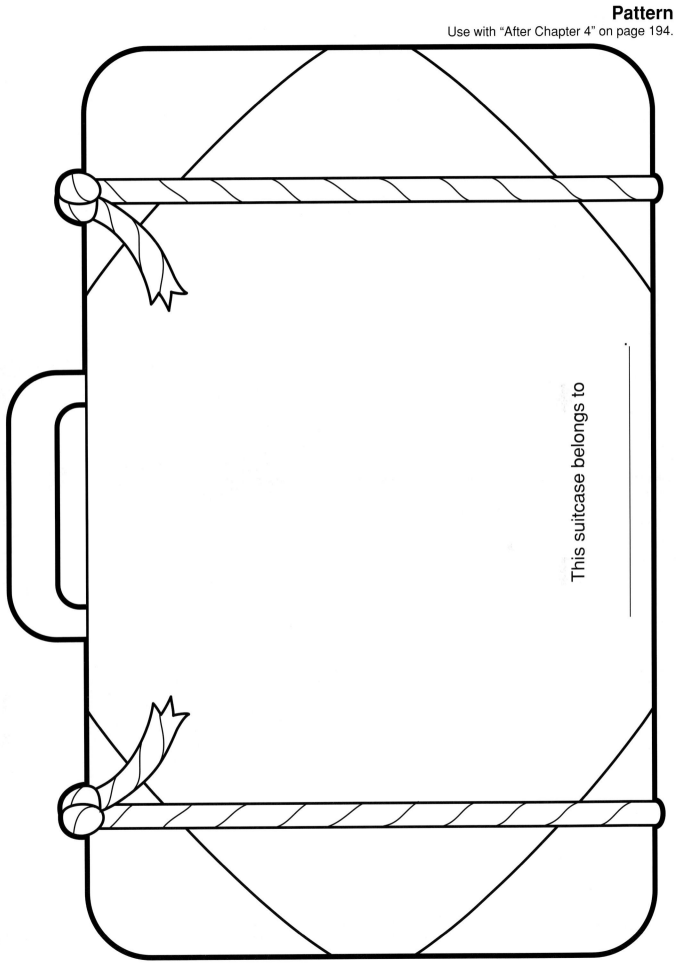

This suitcase belongs to

Patterns
Use with "After Chapter 5" on page 195.

Have I Got a Book for You!

Now that you've finished reading *Bud, Not Buddy*, it's time to let the rest of the reading world find out about this book. How? By completing Parts 1–3 below!

Part 2: Draw a picture of your favorite part of the book. Add a descriptive caption at the bottom of the illustration.

Materials: crayons or colored pencils, sheet of light blue paper, glue

Part 1: In each rock below, write a word or phrase that describes Bud. Be as descriptive as you can.

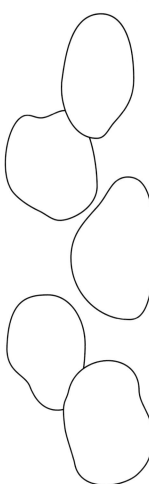

Part 3: Fold a sheet of paper into thirds, as shown, to make a flyer. On the front, create an advertisement for *Bud, Not Buddy.* Include inside the flyer information and pictures about the book's setting, main characters, and plot. On the back, write a paragraph giving your opinion of the book. Then glue your folded flyer in the space below.

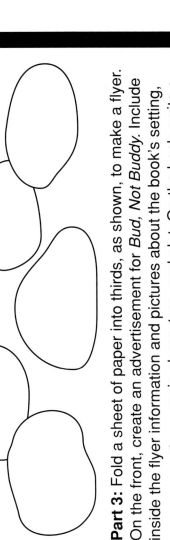

GLUE FOLDED FLYER HERE.

Note to the teacher: Use with "At the End of the Book" on page 196.

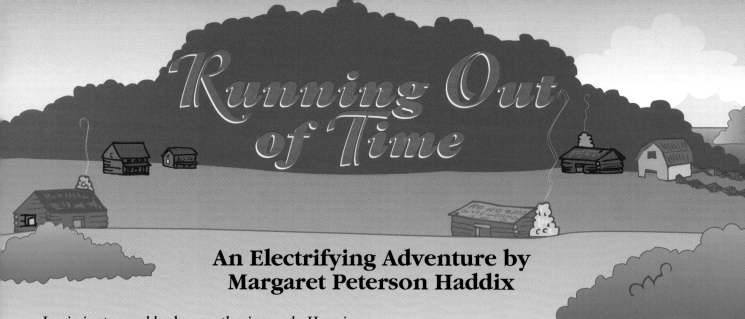

Running Out of Time

An Electrifying Adventure by Margaret Peterson Haddix

Jessie is stunned by her mother's words. How is it possible that it's not 1840, but 1996? How can it be that her home of Clifton isn't a 19th-century village, but a reconstructed town that serves as a tourist attraction? And why are Clifton's residents forbidden to leave, even to get medicine for the children who are dying of diphtheria? Jessie wants answers—but first she must escape Clifton and get help before it's too late. For a book no one will want to put down, introduce students to this suspenseful tale and the following activities.

with ideas by Chris Christensen, Las Vegas, NV

Before, During, and After Reading

Skills: Character analysis, making predictions

Jessie will need bravery and much more to complete her dangerous mission. Focus on this character's development from the story's beginning to its end with these three related activities:

- **Before reading:** Write on the board the qualities shown below. Ask students to discuss the list and provide examples from their own lives. Explain that this book features a character who will need these qualities to survive a very dangerous situation. Show students the book's cover and ask them to predict what that situation might involve.
- **During reading:** Label six sheets of chart paper as shown. Post the charts in the classroom. After reading each chapter, ask students to suggest situations during which Jessie displays one of the characteristics on a chart. List students' suggestions on the appropriate chart.
  - **At the end of the book:** Analyze the charts to identify the characteristic Jessie displays most frequently. Discuss with students how the story would have been different if Jessie had not possessed this trait.

Determination
Problem-Solving Skills
Courage
Clearheadedness
Love for Family
Will to Live

During Reading

Skill: Responding in writing to literature

Encourage students to respond to *Running Out of Time* with these thought-provoking prompts.

Ch. 1: Most people in Clifton don't like going to Dr. Fister when they are sick. What qualities does a good doctor possess?

Ch. 3: Using *okay* in Clifton isn't allowed because it is a word from the "future." List five modern words you use that Jessie would not have known. Write a brief definition for each word.

Ch. 5: Mrs. Keyser doesn't have time to tell Jessie everything about the outside world. What ten things about modern life should she have explained to Jessie? Give a reason for including each item in your list.

Ch. 7: Jessie's clothing helps her blend in with the visitors. Do you think style was as important to young people in the 1800s as it is today? Why or why not?

Ch. 9: It is strange for Jessie to watch her family and friends from the Clifton visitors center. Write a diary entry Jessie might have written about this experience.

Ch. 11: Jessie has to find a way to get past the fence. Describe a tricky problem you recently solved.

Ch. 14: Using the telephone is a new experience for Jessie. Select a modern machine or gadget. Write instructions telling Jessie how to use it.

Ch. 17: Mr. Neeley doesn't ask Jessie to describe herself over the phone. List possible reasons why he doesn't.

Ch. 20: When Jessie phones the state health department, the woman who answers thinks it's a prank call. What would you have said to get this adult's help?

Ch. 23: Mr. Lyle explains the purpose of the Clifton experiment on a television program. Write what you would have said to Mr. Lyle if you had been a caller to that program.

Ch. 25: Jessie is frightened about all the changes that are about to happen. Pretend you are Jessie. Write a letter to your reporter friend, Bob, describing your fears.

After Chapter 3

Skill: Making comparisons

Jessie is shocked to hear the truth about Clifton. A second shock awaits her when she enters a world that's vastly different from the only one she's ever known. To help students understand this challenge, refer them to chapter 1 when Caleb Benton was sent to fetch Mrs. Keyser. Ask, "If you became very sick in the middle of the night, what might your parents do?" Compare the Bentons' actions with your students' responses. Then explain that students will make booklets that compare life in Clifton with their lives. Distribute the materials listed and discuss the steps shown. When students finish their booklets, divide them into small groups to share and compare their work. Then place the booklets in a basket for free-time reading.

Materials for each student: notebook paper, pencil, three 5¹/₂" x 8¹/₂" strips of white paper, 5¹/₂" x 8¹/₂" strip of construction paper, access to a stapler, crayons or markers

Steps:
1. Skim chapters 1–3. List ways that life in Clifton differs from your life.
2. Stack the white strips atop the construction paper strip. Fold the four strips in half and staple at the fold to make a booklet.
3. Open the booklet as shown. Label the left-hand page "Then" and the right-hand page "Now." On the "Then" page, illustrate an aspect of life in Clifton. On the "Now" page, illustrate how your life differs from Jessie's.
4. Below each picture, write a sentence explaining the illustration.
5. Repeat Steps 3–4 four more times to complete the remaining pages.
6. Decorate the booklet's cover. Include a title and your name.

Then

Now

Jessie hung her dress on a nail.

I hang my clothes on hangers in a closet.

After Chapter 9

Skill: Expressive writing

Fighting her emotions, Jessie watches her loved ones from the visitors center. How would your students feel if they were being watched like the folks in Clifton? Find out with this thought-provoking writing activity. If you don't already have a mirror in your classroom, bring a small one from home (or tape a sheet of aluminum foil on the wall to simulate a mirror). Ask students to pretend that the mirror is actually a telescopic mirror similar to those used by tourists to view Clifton. Explain that tourists have been watching your class for months. After some discussion, have each student write a letter to the director of the experiment's visitors center. In her letter, have the student answer these questions:
- How do you feel about being watched?
- Should students have been told about the experiment? Why or why not?
- Should the experiment be continued? Why or why not?

After a sharing session, display the letters on a bulletin board titled "Want to Be Watched?"

After Chapter 15

Skill: Cause and effect

Give students practice identifying causes and effects with this easy-to-do activity. Divide the class into six groups. Give each group a 12" x 18" sheet of white paper, a marker, five to seven index cards, and five to seven paper clips. Assign a different chapter from 10 to 15 to each group. Then guide students through these steps:

1. Draw a T chart, as shown, on the paper.
2. Scan your chapter and list examples of causes on the chart.
3. Write a matching effect for each cause on a separate index card. Shuffle the cards.
4. Slip a paper clip on the effect side of the chart across from each cause.
5. Create an answer key that gives the correct matches. Write your group's chapter number at the top of the key.

Next, pair the groups and have them swap charts, cards, and keys. Instruct each group to scan the chart's chapter, clip each effect card beside its matching cause, and check with the answer key. Repeat the activity until each group has worked with every T chart.

Chapter 13	
Causes	Effects

After Chapter 17

Skills: Reading a map, writing directions

Against all odds, Jessie successfully manages to travel within 15 miles of Indianapolis despite her mother's vague directions. Pose this question to students: How prepared would you be to tell someone how to get to the state capital from your hometown? After students have pondered this question, divide the class into groups and give each group a state map. Challenge each group to use the map to plan a route from your hometown to the state capital (or another city in your state). Direct the group to write its directions in a series of numbered steps. If desired, also have students use the map scale to determine the mileage. When groups are done, have students compare and contrast their routes.

At the End of the Book

Skills: Exploring genres, making evaluations

For a culminating activity that's packed with learning, run right for this idea! Display the information shown below and discuss the genres listed. Then tell students that a new bookstore is opening nearby. The owner—who heard that your class had read *Running Out of Time*—asked you to identify the book's genre for her. Ask, "Which genre on the chart would you choose?" Then divide the class into groups. Give each group a sheet of art paper and crayons or markers. Have the group discuss which genre best describes *Running Out of Time*. Once the group reaches a consensus, have the members write a letter to the bookstore owner identifying the genre and giving reasons why it was selected. Then have the group design a poster to persuade customers to buy the book. After each group shares its letter and poster, celebrate with warm slices of homemade bread—just like the kind Jessie took with her into the real world!

Fiction: a narrative piece with content produced by the author's imagination and not necessarily based on fact

Mystery: a fiction piece that involves solving a crime or unraveling secrets

Realistic fiction: a story that can actually happen and is true to life

Science fiction: a story that explores the impact of actual, imagined, or potential science, usually set on other planets or in the future

Take a Look in Your Book

Chapter: _____   **Pages:** _____

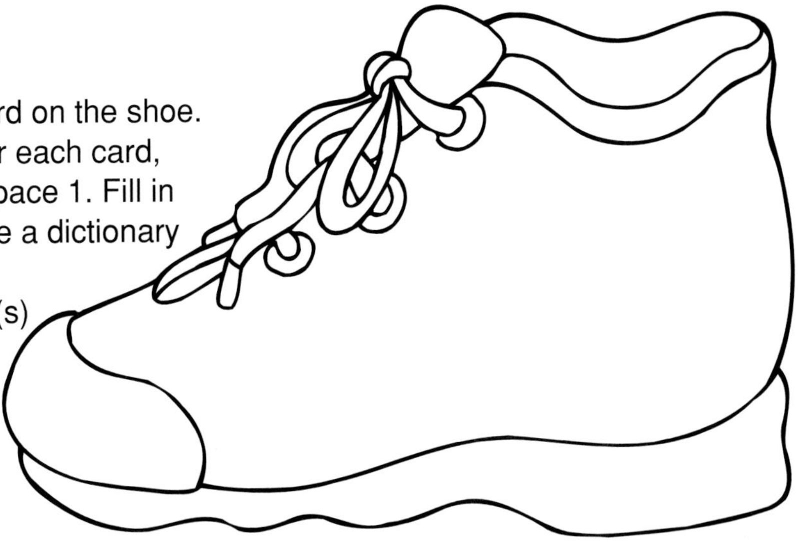

Running Into New Words

You will need one index card for each word on the shoe.
Draw the design shown on each card. For each card,
write one of the words from the shoe in space 1. Fill in
the other sections as indicated below. Use a dictionary
and thesaurus to help you.

   2: word's pronunciation and definition(s)
   3: antonym for the word
   4: synonym for the word
   5: sentence using the word

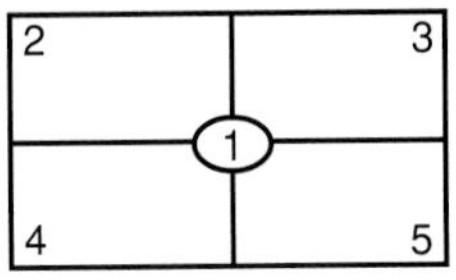

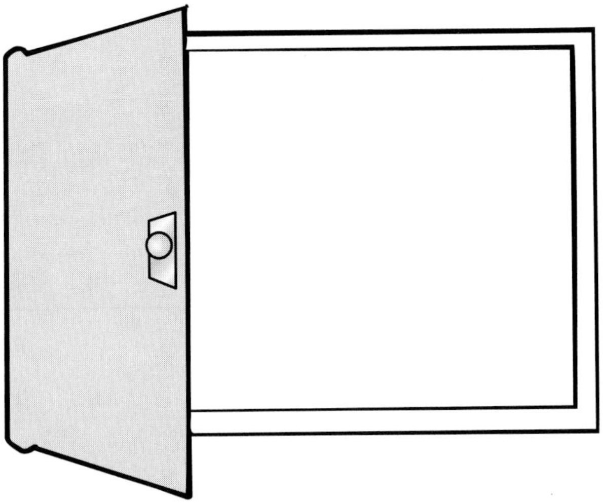

Out of Chapter _____

Answer the question(s) in the box on the lines below. Use the back of this page if you need more
space.

_____

_____

_____

_____

_____

_____

_____

_____

Time for Your Thoughts

Staple a sheet of notebook paper to the back of this page. On the paper,
write a response to the prompt below.

Note to the teacher: Use with "During Reading" on page 200. Before making copies, label the blanks at the top and fill the shoe with new words
from the chapter. Write a question(s) in the middle box and a journal prompt (see "During Reading" on page 200) in the bottom one. Then make
student copies. Each student will need an index card for each vocabulary word and access to a dictionary, thesaurus, and stapler. If desired, have
each student store his cards in a small resealable bag. Periodically have students swap cards with partners and drill each other on the words.   203

What If?

Many events in *Running Out of Time* are important to the story. What if some of them were changed? For example, what if Jessie's father were Clifton's doctor instead of its blacksmith? What if Jessie had not believed her mom's story about the true nature of Clifton?

Directions: Read each situation below. On the blanks, write how you think the story would have been different if that event had happened.

What If...

1. Pa had found out about Mrs. Keyser's plan to send Jessie for help? _____

   _____

2. Jessie hadn't had the courage to escape? _____

   _____

3. Mrs. Spurning had recognized Jessie as a student from the Clifton schoolhouse? _____

   _____

4. Jessie hadn't been able to get past the guard at the gate? _____

   _____

5. Jessie hadn't been able to reach Mr. Neeley by telephone? _____

   _____

6. There were no way of escaping Mr. Neeley's apartment? _____

   _____

7. No one had shown up for the press conference? _____

   _____

8. Hannah had not tripped Mr. Seward? _____

   _____

9. Mr. Lyle and Mr. Clifton had not been arrested? _____

   _____

10. Jessie and her siblings were not returned to their parents? _____

    _____

Bonus Box: Pretend that Margaret Peterson Haddix, author of *Running Out of Time,* has asked you to change one event in the story. On the back of this page or on another sheet of paper, identify the event you'd change. Then explain how and why you would change it.

©The Education Center, Inc. • *THE MAILBOX*® • *Intermediate* • Apr/May 2002

204   **Note to the teacher:** Use this page after students have read the book.

OTHER CURRICULUM HELPERS

What Can't You Do With an Envelope or Two?

Learning Activities Using Canceled Envelopes

Let the simple tips below show you how to use canceled envelopes to teach basic skills across the curriculum. Bet they'll earn your stamp of approval!

ideas by Kimberly A. Minafo, Carmel, NY

How to get started: Spread the word among friends and co-workers that you are collecting used envelopes (ones that bear both a return and a main address). Collect several dozen envelopes. Then have students use them in the ways suggested below and on page 207.

Language Arts

• Write about the object pictured on the stamp using two different forms of writing. For example, a dog stamp could lend itself to writing an informative piece about being a responsible pet owner and a persuasive piece in which you urge a parent to let you get a pet. A flower stamp could lead to a description of a flower garden or a haiku poem.

• Examine an envelope with a magnifying glass. Then write a detailed paragraph describing the envelope. Include in your observations such things as the fibers in the paper, details in the stamp's image, watermarks, etc.

Social Studies

• On a blank map, locate and label all the cities, states, and countries in the addresses on a stack of envelopes.

• Research the history of the person or object pictured on the stamp. Then write a paragraph or short report to share your findings.

• Group together all the envelopes that have a state capital in either the main or return address. Then group the envelopes according to U.S. region.

Critical Thinking

- Use two Hula-Hoop® toys to create a giant Venn diagram. Then sort a stack of envelopes to show how they are alike and different.

- Sort the envelopes into two piles. Then challenge a classmate to guess the category of each pile.

Math

- Find the average of the street (or post office box) numbers listed in the main and return addresses on three envelopes.

- Find the mean, median, mode, and range of the zip code numbers on a stack of five envelopes.

- Record all the numerals shown on a group of envelopes. Then arrange the numerals in least to greatest (or greatest to least) order.

- Using a map and its scale of miles, estimate the distance between the cities of the sender and receiver on an envelope.

- Stuff five different-sized envelopes with varying amounts of folded paper. Weigh each envelope on a scale. Then use a current postage chart to determine the postage needed to mail each envelope. Add to find the total cost of mailing the five envelopes.

- Determine the frequency of specific data on envelopes. For example, use tally marks to determine how often a particular city's name occurs in the addresses on a stack of envelopes. Or find the most commonly used letter in peoples' last names, the number of numerals in the street or post office box numbers, the months most frequently stamped on the postmarks, etc.

- Evaluate the handwriting used on each of five envelopes in terms of legibility and neatness. Use a rating scale of 1 to 5, with 5 being the highest quality. Average the scores. Then display the envelopes with their scores.

- Use the information on an envelope to create word problems. For example, "If the zip codes of the recipient and sender were each multiplied by 40, which product would be greater?"

Journal Gems

Bright Ideas for Using Journals Across the Curriculum

Add sparkle to writing skills no matter what subject you're teaching with these "gem-dandy" journal ideas.

Our Class Journal

Shelly's Reading Journal

My Math Journal

What is the world's largest reptile?

Do reptiles hibernate?

Class Queries

Class Queries Journal

Improve reading comprehension skills and tie careers into your curriculum with this journaling idea. Whenever possible, contact a local expert whose job relates to a topic your class is studying. Cover a composition notebook with construction paper or self-adhesive covering. Label the notebook "Class Queries." After each lesson, brainstorm with students a list of follow-up questions they would like to ask the expert. Choose one or two of the questions; then have a student write them in the notebook (leaving space for an answer). At the end of the unit, help students review the questions and eliminate any that have already been answered in class. Then share the journal with your expert and ask her to write her answers to the questions in the journal. When the journal is returned, have a few students read the responses to the class. Use the journal periodically to review concepts taught earlier.

Kimberly A. Minafo, Pomona, NY

Here's How I Do It!

After teaching a concept that involves a new skill, such as long division or plural spellings, try this journal idea to determine whether students have grasped the concept. Announce that your students have been given the job of explaining the concept to children in the grade directly below yours. Have each student record his explanation of the concept in his journal. Then pair each child with a partner and have them compare their entries. Emphasize that the explanations do not have to be identical, just clear. Not only can this journaling idea help students think and write sequentially, but it's also easy to adapt to any skill.

Terry Warner
Brookview Elementary, Jacksonville, FL

Journals as Testing Tools

Use your students' journal entries as pre- and posttests. For example, before beginning a math unit, ask students to respond to a question such as "What is a decimal?" At the end of the unit, repeat the question to see if students have mastered the concept. To evaluate whether students can apply what they've learned, also ask each child to write a word problem that includes the concept in his math journal. Journals as assessment tools—what a concept!

Picture Journals

If a picture is worth a thousand words, then this journal idea is priceless! Collect a supply of old magazines and newspapers. Also let students bring in appropriate pictures from home. Have each student cut out favorite pictures and glue them inside his journal. Encourage students to include pictures of people they admire, quotes that inspire or motivate them, and pictures of things that make them feel a certain emotion, such as happiness, sadness, or wonder. Students will appreciate the chance to express themselves in this unique way. Plus, you can use the pictures as prompts for a variety of writing and vocabulary activities.

Kelly Haugh
Mother Seton School
Union City, NJ

Grandma

Ms. Seals

Literature Workshop Journals

Reading comprehension skills are sure to shine with this idea on using journals in your independent reading program. Twice weekly, have each student read silently a book of his choosing for 30 minutes. At the end of the reading period, have him write a letter in his journal telling you about what he read. Collect the journals; then respond to each child's letter with a short comment and one or two questions about his book. During the next literature workshop, have the student start his letter by answering your questions from the previous entry. Then have him finish the letter by telling you what he read that day in his book.

Dorothy Vaughn—Gr. 4
Oakwood Elementary, Oakwood, GA

Class Journal

Make journaling a class venture with this easy-to-manage activity. Purchase a sturdy binder notebook to use as the class journal. Begin the journal by writing an introduction to the class. Then send it home each night with a different student. Have that child write in the journal, either responding to what others have written, adding a story or poem of her own, or commenting on what was studied in class that day. Don't forget to take the journal home frequently so you can add your two cents' worth!

Irene Taylor, Fort Ann, NY

Twosome Talk

It's a rare kid who doesn't get a thrill from passing a note to a classmate. Make that offense perfectly legal in your classroom with this journaling idea. Divide the class into pairs and give each twosome a journal. Then invite the partners to take turns writing to each other about the subjects the class is currently studying. You can bet students will love showing off what they know!

Kimberly A. Minafo, Pomona , NY

A Nose for Newsletters

Ideas for Creating and Using Class Newsletters

Create a class newsletter that's a must-read—and work on important skills at the same time—with these hot-off-the-press ideas from our readers!

Fabulous Photo Newsletters

If a picture is worth a thousand words, then why not include one or two in your class newsletter? At the beginning of the year, use a word-processing program to create a newsletter template that has sections such as the following:

- Newsletter's title, the date, and a place for a photo or clip art
- In Class This Week (an overview of units being studied and dates of scheduled tests)
- FYI (miscellaneous information and dates of field trips or other special events)

Each time your class does something especially interesting, capture that moment with your school's digital camera. Save all of the photos on a disk. Each Friday, download a current photo into the template and update the weekly information; then print the newsletter and make photocopies. In just a matter of minutes, your fab photo newsletter is ready for students to take home. Be sure to hand a copy to your principal to keep her updated about what's going on in your classroom, too.

Debra Wilham—Gr. 4, Mt. Pulaski Elementary, Mt. Pulaski, IL

Student-Written Newsletters

Give your students a real-life purpose for writing by having them take responsibility for producing your class newsletters. Each month, have each student use a word-processing program to write a paragraph about a class activity she enjoyed during the month. Have her edit her writing and enhance it with appropriate clip art. Then help students compile the paragraphs into a class newsletter. If desired, include a special section of your own suggesting ways parents can strengthen skills at home with their children. Students are more apt to share newsletters with their parents when they've authored them!

Kim Bostick—LD Resource
Old Town Elementary
Winston-Salem, NC

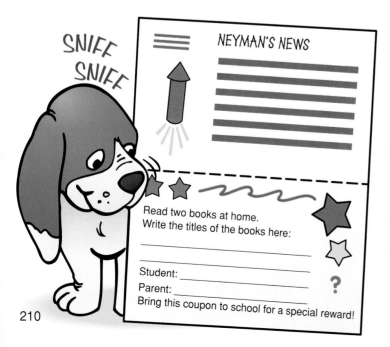

Newsletter Reading Incentive

How can you know if the newsletters you send home are being read? Find out with this nifty idea! At the bottom of each newsletter, include a special coupon, such as the one shown, that can be cut out and redeemed at school if it has been filled out and signed by a parent. Be sure to make each reward so appealing that students who do not participate one week will want to do so the next!

Julie Granchelli
Lockport, NY

#58—November 20
If your food could talk, what would you say to it? Create a conversation you could have with your meal at dinnertime.

Journal-Prompt Newsletters

Create a class newsletter that's anything but ordinary with the help of your daily journal prompts. Assign a number to each day's prompt as shown. Have students include that number along with the date and their name when they respond to the prompt in their journals. Then, as you prepare each newsletter, have each child submit to you the number and date of a journal entry from that week or any other time during the year. Pull the appropriate journal and add that child's entry into your class newsletter. The result is a newsletter that both parents and students will find hard to put down!

Melissa Wood—Gr. 4, Memorial Day School, Savannah, GA

Math Newsletters

Make math concepts taught at school crystal clear to parents by creating hot-off-the-press math newsletters just for them! Each time you begin to teach a new math concept, send home a newsletter that explains each objective and the recommended teaching procedure. Also include sample problems, games, and hands-on activities that parents can use to reinforce the concept at home. Parents will appreciate your efforts and students will get the same instruction from parents that they get at school!

Julie Granchelli, Lockport, NY

Book-Talk Newsletters

Recommend books for independent reading with a newsletter that's written by the best children's literature critics around—your students! After a student reads a book, have her summarize it briefly and give it a rating of one, two, or three stars. Then compile the book reviews each month, including several of your own, into a newsletter to send home. Remember to give your librarian a copy to display in the media center!

Julie Granchelli

School News

Turn your students into investigative reporters with a newsletter activity that sharpens interviewing and writing skills. Every week or so, have a different team of students select an interesting school-related topic to research, such as what the school principal does during an average morning or the number of school lunches served each day. Have the team create a list of questions and interview the appropriate person(s). If desired, allow team members to photograph the interviewee with a digital camera. Then direct the reporters to use a word-processing program to turn their notes into an investigative news report for your class newsletter.

Kathleen Kopp—Gr. 4, Lecanto Primary School, Hernando, FL

FOR THE RECORD

Ideas for Using Books About Records

What's the most popular book in your classroom? More than likely, it's *Guinness® World Records 2001* or a similar title that features amazing records. Check out the following ideas that will turn your students' fascination with records into meaningful—and fun!—learning experiences.

ideas by Daniel Kriesberg, Bayville, NY

Helpful Tips

● Obtain multiple copies of a records book. They're usually inexpensive and available from several book clubs. Also ask students to donate their old copies. (Don't worry if all of the copies don't have the same copyright date.)

● Make a transparency or create a reproducible of instructions for students to follow when completing an activity.

● Have students share books and work in pairs or groups of three.

Math

● When learning to read numbers up to the millions and billions places, have students locate examples of records that include these large numbers. Have students write the numbers and related facts on their papers; then have them take turns reading the numbers to their partners.

● Have students find and read decimal numbers that are included in some of the records. Then have them write the decimal numbers in the correct order.

● After reading aloud some examples of records, have students determine whether the numbers are estimates or exact numbers. Make a chart of their responses. Then have students find five examples of each in the book. Based on their findings, discuss with students when it makes sense to estimate a number and when an exact number is possible and necessary.

● Have students make up story problems to solve based on records in the book.

● Create a place-value scavenger hunt for students. Include items such as the following:
  — Find a record that has a 7 in the hundreds place.
  — Find a record that is close to 15.4.
  — Find a number that is less than 1 million but greater than 500,000.

● To help students gain a better understanding of the numbers they come across, have them measure some of the records they encounter. For example, have students measure the distance equal to the height of the world's tallest man.

● Have students use the information from a book's chart or graph to make a different type of graph. For example, if the information in the book is in a bar graph, have students present the same data in a circle graph. Then have students create questions about the information in the graph.

Language Arts

● If a student needs an idea for a story, direct him to a records book. Every record has a story behind it. Challenge students to create stories about the people who set the records. Why did an individual seek to set a record? How many attempts did he or she make? What happened next? What is that individual doing now?

● Create a set of questions that students must answer with the help of the record book's index. For example, ask where one can find information about the Beatles, the largest jet in the world, and the most intelligent robot ever made.

Creative Thinking

● Have students look through a records book and find a record for the class to challenge. Then divide students into groups. Have each group write a letter to the book's publisher to find out the criteria for setting a record and how records in the book are verified. Even if students can't challenge a record, they can plan how they would do it and how they would solve any problems they encounter.

● Have students write their own class version of a records book. In groups, have students list the records they want to feature in the book. They might include items such as the following:
   — using the same pencil for the most number of days
   — the longest string of days without an absence
   — the longest, biggest, heaviest, and smallest of a variety of items
Then have students write entries about their records and draw illustrations to accompany them.

Social Studies and Science

● Display a world or U.S. map. Have students use pushpins to locate cities in which records have been set. Or have students locate places that are mentioned in records, such as the highest mountain on Earth, the deepest place in an ocean, or the site of the hottest temperature ever recorded.

● When studying weather and climate, have students research weather extremes listed in the book.

● Have students find the latest population figures and display them in a graph or chart.

HEY, IT'S STUFFED ANIMAL DAY!

You're just a Beanie Baby toy away from some powerful skills practice when you celebrate Stuffed Animal Day!

with ideas from Diane Coffman, Deland, FL

Getting Ready: A week in advance, announce that the class will celebrate Stuffed Animal Day the following week. On this day, each student may bring a favorite stuffed animal to class. Send a note to parents explaining the celebration and the types of activities students will complete (see suggestions below). Ask that each student attach a nametag to his animal before bringing it to school. Have a few extra toys on hand for students who may need them.

WRITING

- Have each student write a descriptive paragraph about his toy without identifying it. Collect the paragraphs. Then have each student place his animal on a table at the front of the room. Redistribute the papers and challenge each student to identify the animal described in the paragraph he was given.
- Challenge each student to write a first-person account about Stuffed Animal Day, written from his toy's perspective. Or have each student write a conversation between himself and his stuffed friend.

SCIENCE

Explain that *scientific classification* is a method scientists use to categorize the world's organisms into related groups. If possible, display an example of an animal classification chart. Point out that the groupings get more specific as you move from the first group (kingdom) to the last (species).

Next, have students place their animals on a table at the front of the room. Display the chart shown (with no labels except for the top box). Ask students to suggest ways the animals could be divided into two groups based on similar characteristics. Choose one method and label the second row of boxes. Then divide the animals on the table into the two groups. Ask, "How can we further divide each of these two groups?" Have students suggest ideas. Then list one method in the third row of boxes (see the sample). Continue until the class has completed the chart. If desired, divide the class into groups and have each group complete a new chart using different groupings.

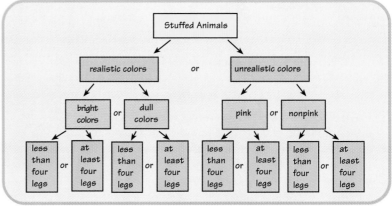

MATH

- As a follow-up to the science activity above, have students in each group write fractions, decimals, or percentages to describe the number of stuffed animals in specific groups. For example, what fraction of animals has wings? What percentage?
- Have students create different types of graphs to represent data about the animals (for example, a bar graph to show the numbers of mammals, birds, reptiles, amphibians, and fish).

MATH MATTERS

Math Matters

Show students that math matters and can be loads of fun with the following easy-to-do activities!

Nifty Numeration Systems

Skills: Numeration, computation

Strengthen students' numeration know-how with a creative activity that also boosts computation skills. Share the Egyptian and Roman numeral systems with students. Then challenge each student to invent a brand-new system. Give each child 17 index cards and a plastic resealable bag. On one card, have the student name her numeration system and write the symbols that represent the digits 0–9. Next, direct the student to write a different problem that can be solved with her system on each of eight cards. Have her label the remaining eight cards with the answers to the problems. Provide time for each child to explain her numeral system to the class; then have her store all her cards in her plastic bag.

To provide more numeration and computation practice, divide the class into pairs. Have each twosome play a game of Concentration with one player's cards; then have the partners play a second round using the other player's cards. *adapted from an idea by Mary Christensen—Gr. 4, Emmott Elementary, Houston, TX*

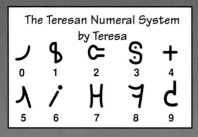

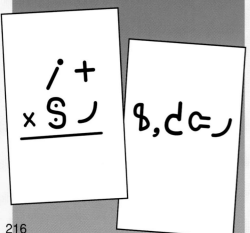

Picture-Perfect Geometry

Skill: Understanding geometric terms

Put life into learning ho-hum geometry terms with this picture-perfect idea! Grab a Polaroid® camera and head outdoors with your class. Have the students stretch out on the ground in poses that illustrate or represent different geometric terms. Then snap a photo of each pose. After the pictures are developed, label each photo with a black marker (see example). The next time you introduce or review one of the pictured terms, pull out the appropriate photo and pass it around. You'll put a whole new angle on geometry! *Roberta E. Haertlein—Grs. 5–6, Baptist Temple Christian Academy, Holbrook, MA*

A right angle measures 90°.

Transparent Place-Value Strips

Skill: Place value

Show students how simple it can be to read difficult numbers by supplying them with easy-to-make place-value charts. From clear transparency sheets, cut out and label a 2¼" x 5¾" chart with a quarter-inch grid at the bottom for each student as shown. Give each child a chart and a sheet of quarter-inch graph paper. To use the charts, call out a number or write it on the board. Have each child write the standard form of the number on the graph paper, writing each digit in a separate square and the decimal point on a line as shown. After recording the number, the student places his see-through chart over the number so that the decimal point on his chart is aligned with the number's decimal point. Then have the student read the number from left to right, using the chart's headings for help. Simple! *Carla Brauer—Gr. 6, Central Elementary, Sidney, NE*

Two thousand six hundred eighty-nine and two hundred forty thousandths

Sundae Solutions

Skills: Parts of a whole, reducing fractions

Give students the scoop on fractions with this cool activity! Provide each student with a 9" x 12" sheet of white construction paper, scissors, crayons, glue, and a pattern for a scoopful of ice cream, such as the one shown. Direct each child to cut a bowl shape and six ice-cream scoop shapes from the paper. Have him color the scoop shapes to represent his favorite ice-cream flavors. Next, instruct the student to label the front of his bowl with his name and a question such as the one shown. Have him write the answer to his question—in lowest terms—on the back of the bowl. Then have him glue the scoop shapes in place. Provide time for students to rotate around the room and answer each other's sundae questions. Yummy practice! *Sarah Bigbie—Gr. 4, Butts Road Intermediate, Chesapeake, VA*

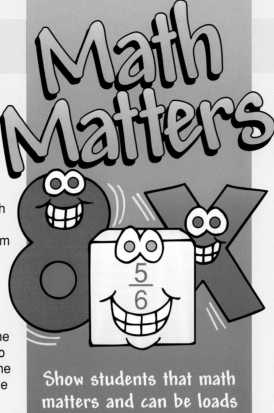

Math Matters

Show students that math matters and can be loads of fun with the following easy-to-do activities!

Measurement Bowling

Skill: Converting units of liquid measurement

Challenge students to bowl their way to better measurement skills with this fun game! Have students bring in containers that represent different liquid capacities. Label each container accordingly: gallon, half gallon, quart, pint, or cup. Then arrange the containers as pins at one end of the classroom. To play, have one student at a time roll a playground ball at the pins, trying to knock down as many pins as possible. Then ask the bowler how many gallons (or quarts, etc.) her knocked-down pins represent. Award points for correct answers. Don't be surprised if your students want to keep playing long after it's time to stop! *Sue Hadden—Gr. 5, Hylen Souders Elementary, Galena, OH*

Symmetry City

Skill: Symmetry

Reinforce the concept of symmetry with a kid-pleasin' construction project that becomes an attention-getting display. Give each student a 9" x 12" piece of poster board, scissors, and colored pencils or markers. Explain to students that they will be making symmetrical figures for an imaginary town called Symmetry City. Have each student fold his poster board in half lengthwise and draw half of a character, plant, animal, or building on the fold as shown. Next, direct him to cut out the drawing—without cutting along the fold—and use colored pencils or markers to draw the matching half and add details. Display the completed cutouts on a tabletop with the title "Welcome to Symmetry City!" *Julie Alarie and Betsy Conlon—Gr. 6, Essex Middle School, Essex, VT*

What part of my sundae is chocolate?

Trevor

gallon

pint

Making Connections to Multiples

Skill: Identifying common multiples

Two student volunteers are all you need to make identifying common multiples an easy concept to grasp. Call two students to the front of the room and write their names on the board. Have the class name characteristics of one student and then the other as you list them on the board. Then have the volunteers sit down. Direct the class to look at the lists on the board and identify the common characteristics of the two students. Circle the characteristics as they are named and connect them with a line. Next, have students name multiples of 2 and 4 as you list them on the board. Direct the class to identify the common multiples in each list as you circle and connect them with a line. So simple! *Tara DiNuzzo and Meredith Nicholls—Gr. 4, E. G. Hewitt Intermediate School, Ringwood, NJ*

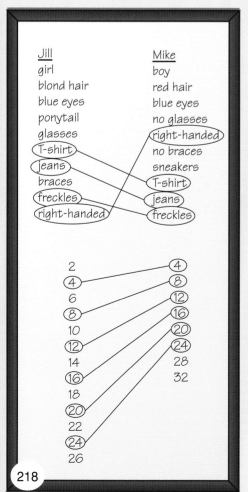

Math Matters

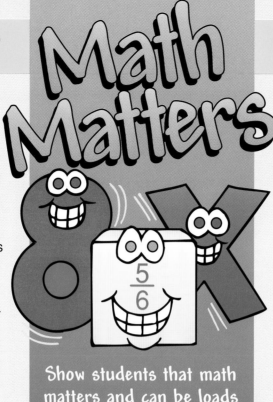

Show students that math matters and can be loads of fun with the following easy-to-do activities!

Gingerbread Geometry

Skill: Representing geometry terms

Sweeten students' knowledge of geometry terms with this fun-to-do activity! List geometry terms that are appropriate for your grade level on the board (such as *rhombus, parallelogram, acute angle,* etc.). Then give each student colored pencils or crayons and a simple house pattern such as the one shown. Instruct each student to create a gingerbread house picture by drawing, coloring, and labeling examples of the geometry terms you listed on the board. As a special treat, allow students to snack on slices of gingerbread or gingersnaps as they work! *Kiersten Sasaki, Copiague Middle School, Copiague, NY*

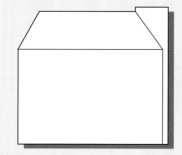

Percentage Pictures

Skills: Writing fractions, converting fractions to percents

To practice writing fractions and changing them to percents, provide each student with a 10 x 10 grid and crayons in five different colors. Instruct the student to draw and color a simple picture on the grid, using all 100 squares and coloring each square only one color. When he has finished coloring, have the student count and record the number of squares of each color. Then have him write each number as a fraction whose denominator is 100. Next, have the student add all the fractions together to get $^{100}/_{100}$, or one whole. Explain that a fraction whose denominator is 100 is a *percent,* which means hundredths. Then direct students to write their fractions as percents. Post students' calculations with their pictures. Then, as students' skills strengthen, repeat the activity using grids of 200—or 500—squares! Make the activity more challenging by having students reduce fractions to lowest terms, divide the numerators by the denominators to find the decimals the fractions represent, and multiply the decimals by 100 to change them to percents. *Julie Eick Granchelli, Lockport, NY*

Color	Number	Fraction	Percent
Red	35	$^{35}/_{100}$	35%
Green	22	$^{22}/_{100}$	22%
Brown	16	$^{16}/_{100}$	16%
Silver	2	$^{2}/_{100}$	2%
Yellow	25	$^{25}/_{100}$	25%
Total		$^{100}/_{100}$	100%

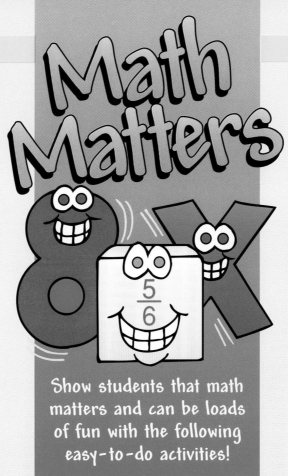

Show students that math matters and can be loads of fun with the following easy-to-do activities!

Decimal Spin

Skill: Writing and reading decimals

Put a new spin on math practice with this easy activity on writing decimals! Have each student trace two circles side by side on his paper and divide each into eight equal parts. Then have him place a large decimal point between the circles as shown. Direct the student to label each part of the left circle with a different whole number and each part of the right circle with a different decimal value (see the example). Finally, give each student a paper clip to use with a pencil to make a spinner.

To practice, each student spins a whole number and then a decimal. He combines them and writes the resulting number in standard form. To play, the student spins and records 20 such numbers. Then he reads the numbers aloud to a partner. If desired, have students round their numbers to a specific decimal place. Or have each child spin numbers to create addition, subtraction, and multiplication problems for a partner to solve. *Domenick C. Renzi—Gr. 5, Bells Elementary, Turnersville, NJ*

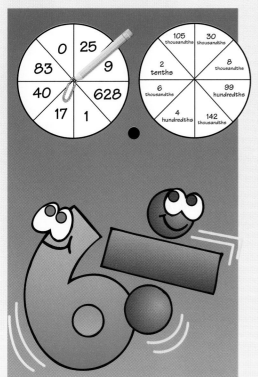

A Cookie's Cost

Skills: Finding the unit price, making a bar graph

How much does one cookie cost? Pose this question to introduce a yummy group activity on finding unit prices. Have parents provide six different bags of cookies, including each bag's cost. Write the cost on a separate index card and tape it to each bag. Then display the bags in the front of the room and divide students into six groups. Have each group predict which bag of cookies is the best buy. Then give a different bag of cookies to each group. Challenge the group to find the cost of a single cookie and report it to the class. If students need help, guide them to conclude that they should divide the cookies' cost by the number of cookies in the bag (see the nutrition label for the approximate number). Record the groups' findings (rounded to the nearest cent) on the board. Then allow students to munch on the cookies while they make bar graphs that illustrate the data! *Melany Reeves—Gr. 5, Albert Harris Intermediate School, Martinsville, VA*

Fraction of a Heart

Skills: Fractional part of a whole, reducing fractions

Challenge students to get to the heart of fractions with this sweet activity! Have each student sort a half cup of small candy hearts by color on a half sheet of black construction paper. Direct the student to count the number of each color, plus the total number of candies, and record the amounts on an index card as shown. Next, have him arrange the candies (like colors together) in a heart shape on the black paper and glue them into place. On his index card, have the student write a fraction in simplest terms—using the number of a color as the numerator and the total number of candies as the denominator—to show the part of the candies represented by each color. Finally, have him glue the index card as a key to the back of his paper. *Donna K. Brooks—Gr. 4, West View Elementary, Spartanburg, SC*

	Number	Fraction
Purple candies	23	$^1/_4$
Pink candies	18	$^9/_{46}$
Green candies	17	$^{17}/_{92}$
Yellow candies	12	$^3/_{23}$
Orange candies	22	$^{11}/_{46}$
Total candies	92	

219

Skill: Reviewing NCTM standards

Looking for a way to review important math standards and make sure your students are prepared when it's testing time? Each week create two review sheets, each divided into five sections of problems representing the skills you want students to review (see the sample). On Monday, give each student a copy of the two sheets. Have him work on the problems throughout the week during his free time. Check the sheets together on Friday. This ongoing review will familiarize students with the lingo of the new math standards *and* help parents become aware of what their children need to know. ***Kim Dempsey and Lisa M. Mellon—Gr. 4, Southwest Elementary, Waterford, CT***

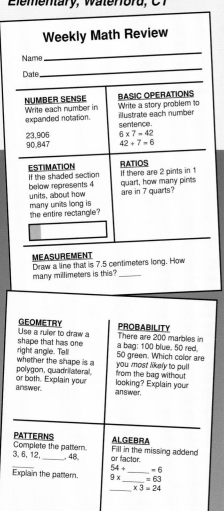

Weekly Math Review

Name _____

Date _____

NUMBER SENSE
Write each number in expanded notation.

23,906
90,847

BASIC OPERATIONS
Write a story problem to illustrate each number sentence.

6 x 7 = 42
42 ÷ 7 = 6

ESTIMATION
If the shaded section below represents 4 units, about how many units long is the entire rectangle?

RATIOS
If there are 2 pints in 1 quart, how many pints are in 7 quarts?

MEASUREMENT
Draw a line that is 7.5 centimeters long. How many millimeters is this? _____

GEOMETRY
Use a ruler to draw a shape that has one right angle. Tell whether the shape is a polygon, quadrilateral, or both. Explain your answer.

PROBABILITY
There are 200 marbles in a bag: 100 blue, 50 red, 50 green. Which color are you *most likely* to pull from the bag without looking? Explain your answer.

PATTERNS
Complete the pattern.
3, 6, 12, _____, 48, _____
Explain the pattern.

ALGEBRA
Fill in the missing addend or factor.
54 ÷ _____ = 6
9 x _____ = 63
_____ x 3 = 24

COMMUNICATION
How are these two shapes alike?

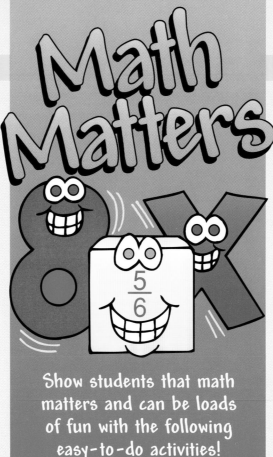

Math Matters

8X

5/6

Show students that math matters and can be loads of fun with the following easy-to-do activities!

The Greatest Remainder Game

Skill: Dividing by two-digit divisors

Provide painless division practice and strengthen students' number-sense skills with this fun group game! Divide students into groups of two to five players. Give each group a deck of playing cards with all tens and face cards removed. Direct each player to draw a division diagram, as shown on the right, on her paper. Announce that the object of the game is to have the greatest remainder. Next, have one player at a time draw a card and reveal its number to her group. Direct each group member to record the card's number in any space on her diagram. Make it clear that once a number has been recorded, it cannot be moved. When all the blanks have been filled, have each player work the problem she created and record its remainder as her score for that round. Declare the winner to be the first player reaching a specific number of points or the one having the greatest score at the end of a set time or number of rounds. To vary the game, change the number of spaces in the division blank or play Less Is Best, with the winner being the player with the lowest total score. ***Julia Alarie—Gr. 6, Essex Middle School, Essex, VT***

Skill: Geometric turns

This activity will have your students literally jumping to demonstrate geometric turns! Begin by having students practice the different turns (quarter, half, three-quarter, full). First, direct students to stand facing the front of the room. Call out, "Quarter turn," and have students jump in place and land facing the adjacent wall on their right. (Checking's easy because all students should be facing the same direction!) Instruct students to return to the original position facing the front of the room. Then, in turn, have students practice making a half turn, a three-quarter turn, and a full turn—each time to the right or left—returning to the original position after each jump. Next, call out the turns in a different order, *without* having students return to the original position. Finally, really challenge the jumpers by indicating right or left before calling out the turns. They'll love it! ***Domenick C. Renzi—Gr. 5, Bells Elementary, Turnersville, NJ***

6 R 24

1 2) 4 5 6
    − 4 3 2
        2 4

My score
24

ENGLISH MADE EASY

English Made Easy

Who Am I?
Skill: Common and proper nouns

Combine grammar and social studies with a neat writing activity that focuses on nouns. Assign each student a famous person to research. On the top half of a sheet of paper, have the student write a brief paragraph about his assigned person, circling all of the proper nouns. On the bottom half, have the student rewrite the paragraph, omitting the proper nouns and replacing them with common nouns (and phrases, if necessary).

When everyone is finished, have a volunteer read his common nouns paragraph to the class. Challenge the class to guess the identity of the famous person based on the common noun clues only. If students cannot guess the person, then have the volunteer read his proper nouns paragraph—omitting the name of the famous person—and challenge classmates to guess the mystery person. Adapt this idea to use during a study of a country, U.S. regions, an individual state, or a historical event.

Jeanene Skoch, Kaohsiung American School, Kaohsiung, Taiwan

Proofreading Posters
Skill: Editing

Do your students always seem to lose the photocopies of proofreading symbols that you distribute at the beginning of the year? Eliminate this problem—and also make editing easier for visually impaired students or those who have difficulty concentrating on fine print—with this simple solution. First, decide on the proofreading symbols that you and your students most often use. Gather three sets of construction paper sheets—each set a different size and color. Then follow these steps:
1. Write each proofreading symbol on a 6" x 9" sheet of construction paper.
2. Write each symbol's definition on a 9" x 12" sheet of construction paper.
3. On a 12" x 18" sheet of paper, write a sample sentence that illustrates the use of each symbol.

Laminate each poster and back it with magnetic tape. Then display one or more sets of the posters on your board. Encourage students to refer to the posters when they're editing their own or a classmate's writing.

Kimberly Vaughn—Gr. 6, Handy Elementary, Foothill Ranch, CA

Roll and Write
Skills: Parts of speech, vocabulary

Build parts-of-speech power with this cool game die! First, fill a large paper grocery bag with crumpled newspaper, leaving some space at the top. Fold over the top of the bag and tape it securely to seal in the newspaper. Now you have a giant die! Label its six faces "verb," "adjective," "noun," "adverb," "proper noun," and "conjunction"—one label on each face.

Next, divide students into four or five teams, and have each team choose a recorder. To play, roll the die and announce the category showing. Set a timer for one minute; then challenge each team to list as many words as possible that fit that category. After one minute, call time and have each recorder read her team's answers. For every correct response, award that team one point. Use the giant die for other types of games as well by simply relabeling the faces.

Heather Graley, Columbus, OH

English Made Easy

Picturing Nouns
Skill: Types of nouns

To wrap up a unit on nouns, try this picture-perfect idea! First, decide on the types of nouns that you want students to focus on, such as singular, plural, common, proper, singular and plural possessive, abstract, concrete, collective, or compound. Next, provide students with construction paper, scissors, glue, a pen or fine-tipped marker, and an assortment of old magazines. For each type of noun, have the student cut a picture from the magazine and glue it on his construction paper. Then have him label the picture correctly as shown. Some pictures may fit in more than one category, so caution students to be careful in writing their labels. What a fun, creative way to assess students' noun know-how!

Megan Strickler—Gr. 5, Steekee Elementary, Loudon, TN

singular noun: clock

plural possessive noun: Bears' home

singular possessive noun: girl's dog

plural noun: shoes

Spotlight on Sentences
Skill: Identifying and writing different kinds of sentences

Did you see that mouse?

I really don't care for mice that much.

Oh my gosh, it's a mouse!

Jon, go tell Mr. Smith we have a mouse.

Without a doubt, students will remember the four kinds of sentences after they dramatize them! Act out a brief, four-line skit that consists of one each of the four kinds of sentences: declarative, imperative, interrogative, and exclamatory. After your presentation, ask students to classify each line of dialogue. Next, divide students into groups of four and have each group write an original skit comprised of one of each kind of sentence. Invite each group to present its skit to the class, with each group member reciting one sentence. Challenge the audience to listen carefully and classify each line of dialogue according to the kind of sentence.

Michael Pudney—Grs. 4–5, Germantown Central School, Germantown, NY

Silver Screen Sentences
Skill: Writing sentences

Looking for a way to jump-start students' sentence-writing skills? Show the class about ten to 15 minutes of a children's video. Then turn off the video and have each student write ten sentences about what she saw. If you're studying a particular grammar concept, have students incorporate that skill into their writing. With this simple technique, students will have a fresh, easy topic to write about instead of struggling for an idea. No more "I don't know what to write about!"

Rebecca Shavel—Gr. 4, Rostraver Elementary, Belle Vernon, PA

English Made Easy

Newsworthy Verbs
Skill: Identifying verbs and verb tenses

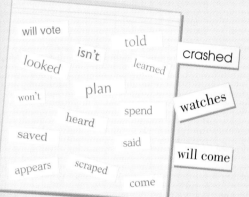

Here's a hot-off-the-press way to practice identifying verbs and their tenses! Divide the class into groups of two or three. Give each group a resealable plastic bag, and give each student a newspaper page and scissors. Direct each student to cut out the VIVs—very important verbs—from his page and add them to his group's bag. Then have each group sort its words into present, past, and future tense verbs. Instruct the students to glue their verb categories onto colorful construction paper: green for present, red for past, and blue for future. Display the mini collages in three separate sections of a bulletin board titled "Hot-off-the-Press Verbs."

Caroline Roux—Gr. 4, Henry Wilson Elementary, Manchester, NH

Find Your Match!
Skill: Reviewing grammar and vocabulary concepts

Review important grammar and vocabulary concepts in a snap with this versatile game. Label each of nine 9" x 12" sheets of construction paper with the following categories: compound words, contractions, consonant blends, consonant digraphs, homonyms, synonyms, antonyms, prefixes, and suffixes. Next, program index cards with words that match the categories (at least four cards per category). Arrange the category sheets along the chalk tray and give each student an equal number of word cards. Have four students at a time place their word cards behind the correct category sheets. When all cards have been placed, select a student to read aloud the cards behind the first category. Have the other students raise their hands if they hear a mismatch; then discuss where the misplaced word belongs. Check the remaining categories in the same way. To repeat the activity later, add more categories, use more difficult words, or change the categories to parts of speech.

Donna Doyle—Gr. 5, Greenwich Catholic School, Greenwich, CT

"Hand-y" Review
Skills: Reviewing verb, participial, gerund, and infinitive phrases

Have a ball reviewing different kinds of phrases with this "hand-y" activity! Use a permanent marker to label a beach ball with action verbs. Draw a large hand on the board and label it as shown. Then divide students into two teams. Have students toss the ball from one team to the other. After a few tosses, call out "Pinky," "Ring," "Middle," "Pointer," or "Thumb." Have the ball's catcher look at the word closest to the right-hand finger that was called. Then have him say a sentence using that verb in a phrase as directed. Award two points for a correct response. Declare the team with the higher score at the end of the game the winner.

Colleen Dabney—Gr. 6, Williamsburg–JCC Public Schools, Williamsburg, VA

English Made Easy

What's in the Bag?
Skill: Using adjectives

Bag better parts-of-speech skills with this touchy-feely activity! Place a different object in each of five or six lunch-sized paper bags. Divide students into groups and give each group a bag. Have the students in each group take turns closing their eyes and reaching inside the bag to feel its contents. Next, direct group members to list on chart paper at least five specific adjectives that describe the object. In turn, have each group share its adjectives with the class. Award a point to the first group to identify each described object correctly.

Joyce Hovanec—Gr. 4, Glassport Elementary, Glassport, PA

Our object feels heavy, solid, smooth, oblong, and cold.

Is it a river rock?

Quotation Dictation
Skill: Using quotation marks

All you need to liven up your students' next practice with quotation marks is your handy, dandy tape recorder! Invite one student at a time to record a sentence with a tape recorder. Immediately replay the sentence; then have each student write the sentence in the form of a direct quotation as shown. Challenge students to punctuate the sentence correctly and identify the speaker without using a tired, overused verb. As soon as students hear their voices, they'll be hooked and pleased to practice!

Cheryl Fowler—Gr. 5, Scotts Branch Elementary, Baltimore, MD

I can't wait until recess!

Sue exclaimed, "I can't wait until recess!"

Lonely Adverbs
Skill: Identifying adverbs

Keep students from overlooking adverbs that don't end in *ly* with this activity. Title a bulletin board "Making Lonely Adverbs Feel Loved." Surround the title with heart cutouts labeled with common adverbs that do not end in *ly* (see the illustration). Next, review with students that some adverbs are not easy to spot because they do not end in *ly*. Challenge students to make these overlooked adverbs feel less lonely by finding them in sentences in their current reading materials. Have students copy sample sentences onto sentence strips, draw heart shapes around the lonely adverbs, and display the strips on the board. With all the attention these adverbs will be getting, their loneliness will soon disappear!

adapted from an idea by Carolyn Berger—Grs. 6–8
Holy Name of Jesus School, Valhalla, NY

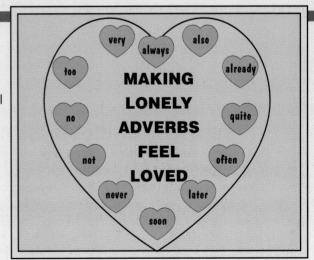

very   always   also   too   already   no   quite   not   often   never   later   soon

MAKING LONELY ADVERBS FEEL LOVED

very

Everyone at the game got very wet when the unexpected rain started to fall.

English Made Easy

Eager Editors

Skill: Editing for specific purposes

What intermediate-age student wouldn't relish the prospect of correcting a younger child's paper? Extend that opportunity to your class with this high-interest activity. Ask a co-worker who teaches a second-grade class to provide you with writing samples written by her students. Without identifying the second grader, write a part of one sample on the board. Direct each student to copy the sample on his paper. Then have him edit the piece for punctuation and other writing mechanics. After students have edited the sample, have each child (or the entire class) revise the piece by combining sentences and adding details, such as adjectives, adverbs, and descriptive phrases. Before you know it, students will apply the same type of careful editing to their own writing assignments!

Amy Evans—Gr. 4, Grace Christian School, Blacklick, OH

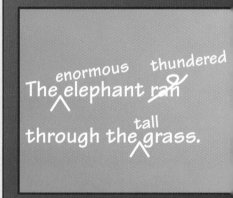

Soda Pop Survey

Skill: Writing direct and divided quotations

Quench your thirst for better punctuation skills with this kid-pleasing activity on using quotation marks! To begin, share the following scenario with students:

You recently invented a brand-new soda pop. It's only been on the market for about one month, so you'd like to do a little research to find out what the public thinks of your invention. You have just conducted a phone survey during which you interviewed ten people who have tried your soda pop. Write the responses of these ten people as direct or divided quotations.

Encourage students to create comments that tell a little about the personality of the respondent as well as give his or her specific opinions about the drink (see the examples). Have each student write her ten sentences on her paper and share them with the class or a small group.

Dorothy

"I wouldn't drink another bottle of Happy Snappy if I were dying of thirst!" complained a bitter Mr. Jeremy Moon.

"That Happy Snappy soda pop," sighed a polite Beulah Smalls, "is the best thing since ice cubes!"

Sentence Stretcher Game

Skill: Expanding sentences

Stretch students' sentence-writing skills with this cool partner game. Divide the class into pairs. Give each twosome a die, ten slips of paper, and a paper cup. Have each pair copy each sentence shown on a separate slip and place the slips in the cup. To play, Partner A draws a sentence and rolls the die. Then she looks at the key and "stretches" the sentence, writing the new version on her paper and having her partner check it. If the student is successful, she adds the number rolled to her score. Then she returns the slip to the cup and Partner B takes a turn. The first player to reach 20 points is the winner.

Shelley Pearsall—Gr. 5, Center Elementary, Strongsville, OH

Key

1 = Lose a point!
2 = Add a prepositional phrase.
3 = Add three adjectives.
4 = Add an adverb.
5 = Add words to make the subject or predicate compound.
6 = Add a simile or metaphor.

Sentences

1. I lifted the hat from the table.
2. The librarian read the book.
3. Waves hit the shore.
4. The dancer moved across the floor.
5. Karen walked to school.
6. The turtle sat on the log.
7. The dragon waited near the castle.
8. The cook mixed the ingredients.
9. The family ate dinner.
10. Flowers grow in the garden.

READING ROUNDUP

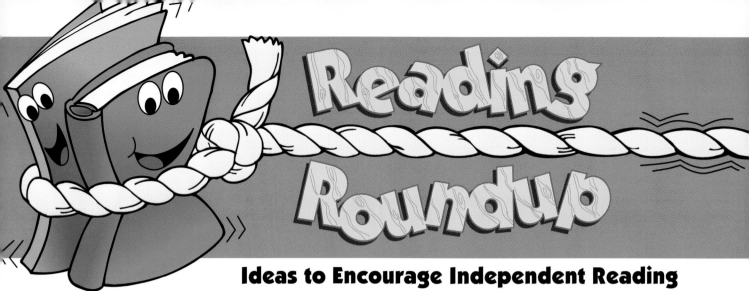

Reading Roundup

Ideas to Encourage Independent Reading

Home-Reading Folders

Skills: At-home reading, sharing about books

Track at-home reading in a flash while helping students learn to share about books. First, create a reading log and a book-sharing checklist such as those shown. Staple the forms to opposite sides of an opened folder for each child. Send the folders home, directing each child to read independently for 15 minutes every weeknight and 30 minutes on weekends. Ask students to have their parents sign the logs on Sunday nights to verify that the reading was done. On Monday, check the folders for signatures. Then have pairs of students meet and use the folder's checklist to guide them through a book chat.

Melissa Theroux—Gr. 4, Sterling Memorial School, Oneco, CT

Reading Award Winners

Skill: Completing a book report

Turn students on to reading Newbery books with a project that can coincide with television's broadcast of the Academy Awards. After each student reads a Newbery book, have him design a movie poster that includes the book's title and author, a short retelling, and a picture of a major scene. For authenticity, have the student advertise real actors as the main characters, describing each one on the poster with at least two adjectives. Also have the student include a movie review with quotes from classmates who have read the book. Conclude with a Newbery Awards Day on which students present their posters. Vote on awards for best writer, best casting, best artistic performance, and best overall design. Then mount photos of the winning students on cutout Oscar Awards and attach them to the posters. Display the projects on a bulletin board titled "Our [current year] Newbery Awards Show."

Becky Davis—Gr. 5, Daniel Wright Elementary Columbus, OH

The ABC Project

Skill: Reporting on a biography or autobiography

Motivate students to read biographies and autobiographies with a letter-perfect bookmaking project! First, gather biographies at appropriate reading levels and ask each child to choose one. After approving each child's selection, explain that each student will create an ABC book on her biography's subject. Direct each student to keep an ABC list as she reads. For each letter, have the student record an important accomplishment or quality of the featured person. (For *x* and *z,* allow students to use words that contain those letters.) Encourage students to use sticky notes to mark pages or paragraphs that feature important events they might want to include in their books.

When the biographies have been read and the lists completed, give each child crayons or colored pencils and a small prebound book of 26 blank pages. Have the student label each page in order with a letter. Then have her add a picture and at least two sentences about that letter's topic. After decorating the covers, have students meet in small groups to share their alphabet books with each other.

*Lori Jensen—Gr. 4
Hilton Elementary , Brighton, MI*

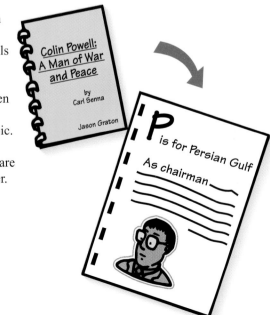

Book-in-a-Box
Skill: Reporting on a book

Bring out students' creativity with a unique book report that you can use with any genre! In advance, ask students to bring to class small gift boxes with lids, such as those used for jewelry. Provide each student with one box, scissors, glue, crayons or markers, and a long strip of white paper. Then have students follow these steps:

1. Trace the bottom of the box on one end of the paper strip.
2. Make nine more side-by-side tracings so that you'll have a long strip with ten sections.
3. Cut out this paper strip.
4. Leave the first section of the strip blank. Write the title and author of your book on the second section.
5. In sections 3–9, illustrate seven important events from your book in order. Leave the last section blank.
6. On the opposite side of each illustration, write a sentence or two describing the event you illustrated.
7. Accordion-fold the strip. (Trim the strip a little, if necessary, to make sure that it will fit in the box.)
8. Write the title and author of your book on the box lid. Decorate the box.
9. Glue the first section of the paper strip to the inside of the box lid. Glue the last section to the bottom of the box.
10. Hold the lid above the box. Slowly refold the paper strip until it is entirely inside the box. Then cover the box with its lid.

Evelyn Sanders—Gr. 5
K. D. Malone Elementary
Rockaway Township, NJ

And the Award Goes To...
Skill: Examining characters

After they have read novels, invite students to try this creative approach for presenting book reports. First, have each student write a first-person account of her book from a favorite character's viewpoint. Have the student describe herself, her actions in the story, and how other characters in the book respond to her. On the day they present their reports, encourage students to dress up as their characters. Then follow up by hosting an awards show. Have students vote for winners in such categories as the best major male and female characters, best minor male and female characters, and best animal character. Award the winners with foil-covered trophies cut from poster board.

Kris Ramsey—Gr. 5
Neil A. Armstrong Elementary
Mooresville, IN

Reado
Skill: Reading a variety of literature

Motivate students to read a variety of literature with this yearlong independent reading program. Provide each student with a copy of card 1 on page 230 to use during the first half of the year. (Use card 2 for the second half.) Instruct each student to keep a reading log on which he records the date, the title and author of the book or magazine he read, and the number of pages. Then have the student color the box for that selection on his Reado card. When a student colors five boxes in a row, reward him with a small treat. When he completes his entire card, reward the student with an inexpensive book from a book club. Adapt the cards to fit the reading levels, needs, and interests of your students.

Crystal Jefferson, Ephesus Road Elementary, Chapel Hill, NC

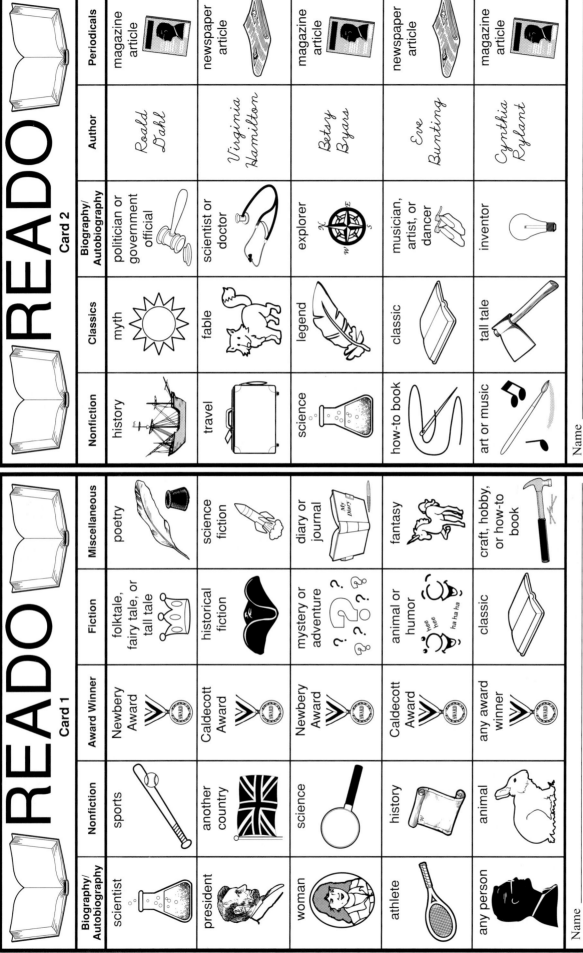

READO

Card 2

Nonfiction	Classics	Biography/ Autobiography	Author	Periodicals
history	myth	politician or government official	Roald Dahl	magazine article
travel	fable	scientist or doctor	Virginia Hamilton	newspaper article
science	legend	explorer	Betsy Byars	magazine article
how-to book	classic	musician, artist, or dancer	Eve Bunting	newspaper article
art or music	tall tale	inventor	Cynthia Rylant	magazine article

Name _____
Date began _____ Date completed _____
Color the box of each type of literature that you read.

©2002 The Education Center, Inc. · THE MAILBOX® · Intermediate · April/May 2002

READO

Card 1

Biography/ Autobiography	Nonfiction	Award Winner	Fiction	Miscellaneous
scientist	sports	Newbery Award	folktale, fairy tale, or tall tale	poetry
president	another country	Caldecott Award	historical fiction	science fiction
woman	science	Newbery Award	mystery or adventure	diary or journal
athlete	history	Caldecott Award	animal or humor	fantasy
any person	animal	any award winner	classic	craft, hobby, or how-to book

Name _____
Date began _____ Date completed _____
Color the box of each type of literature that you read.

©2002 The Education Center, Inc.

Note to the teacher: Use with "Reado" on page 229.

Lifesavers...
Management Tips
for Teachers

LIFESAVERS...
management tips for teachers

Grading Notebook

At night when you're ready to grade papers, do you have all of the supplies you need? Here's a great organizer! Buy a three-ring binder, plus several pocket folders and a pencil bag that fit in the binder. Next, put the items that you need for grading (red pens, liquid paper, stickers, etc.) in the pencil bag. In one pocket folder, store a copy of your grading scale and a list of praise words to write on students' papers. At the end of the day, put the sets of papers that you plan to grade in the other pocket folders, and you're ready to go! This binder is also a great organizer to give to an assistant who grades papers for you.

Amy Evans—Gr. 4
Grace Christian School
Blacklick, OH

Great Groupings

Spice up your methods of forming student groups with these clever suggestions:
- Have each student choose a playing card. Form groups according to the value or suit of the cards.
- Distribute play money, and then form groups of the different denominations. Refer to groups by their values: the 5s, the 10s, the 20s, etc.
- Dividing students into two equal teams? Use checkers!

Marsha Schmus—Grs. 3–5 Gifted and Talented
Chambersburg, PA

Ready in a Minute

Use an hourglass timer to motivate your students to settle down before or after recess, during subject transitions, or when they're too talkative. Just turn over the timer and let the sand start flowing! When your students are settled, tip the timer back to its original position. If all of the sand slips away, inform students that they've lost their recess or another privilege. Having such a visible way of measuring success really helps students use their time wisely.

Kim Droge and Frank V. Bergman—Gr. 5, Manhattan, KS

Take-Home Totes

Do you have a collection of fabric tote bags that you've gathered from various conferences and promotions? Hang several of these bags on an extra coat hook in your classroom. When a student is absent, gather his missed assignments and books and put them in a bag. Then ask a classmate who lives nearby or a family member in another grade to take the tote bag to the absent child. Sending assignments home in a special tote helps make sure the work travels safely between home and school.

Linda Budelman—Gr. 4
Washington School
Hawthorne, NJ

W.T.B.D. Files

To help prevent students' work from getting lost in that black hole known as the student desk, try this idea! Laminate a large, light-colored sheet of construction paper for each child. Fold the sheet in half, leaving a one-inch margin at the top, and then staple it along each side. Give these files to students on the first day of school. Have each student write her name in the margin at the top of the file and then decorate it using permanent markers. Tape the completed file to the student's desk using strong transparent tape.

When a student has incomplete work, have her place it in her W.T.B.D. ("work to be done") file and work on it when she has extra time. At the end of the day, have the student transfer any incomplete work from her file to her homework folder and take that work home to finish. No more lost papers!

Tammy Trouchon—Gr. 6, Rawhide Elementary, Gillette, WY

Have I Copied That Yet?

If you've ever forgotten whether you already made copies of a test or worksheet, this tip's for you! Note the items that need to be reproduced in your planbook; then use a yellow marker to make a dot beside each note as shown. After you make the copies, just put a red check in the appropriate dot. It's "dot" simple!

Lisa Anderson—Grs. 5–6, Sacred Heart Elementary
Osage, IA

SUBJECT	MONDAY _1/14_ Date	TUESDAY _1/15_ Date	WEDNESDAY _1/16_ Date
Math	Subtracting Mixed Numbers page 252 ✓ WS 74	Chapter 7 Review	Chapter 7 Test
LA			

Estimation Contests

Here's just the ticket for motivating students to monitor their behavior! Purchase an inexpensive roll of tickets. At the start of each month, announce an estimation contest that is related to the season or a topic you're studying (see the suggestions). Each time you catch a child exhibiting exemplary work habits or behavior, reward him with a ticket. Have the student write his name and an estimate on the back of the ticket. Then have him deposit the ticket in a large jar. At the end of the month, check the tickets to determine the winning estimate. Students will quickly realize that the better their behavior, the more entries they earn in the contest. To keep motivation high, start a new contest each month.

Lisa Carlson—Gr. 4
Bear Path Elementary
Hamden, CT

Robert
1,000
paper clips

Estimation Contest Ideas
August: number of miles on the principal's car odometer
September: number of paper clips needed to make a chain equal to the length of the longest wall in the classroom
October: weight of a large pumpkin
November: pounds of turkey cooked by the cafeteria staff
December: number of mini candy canes in a jar
January: inches of snowfall in your community (or another cold-weather area)
February: length of the entire class's valentines, lined up end to end
March: number of peanuts in a large jar of roasted peanuts
April: number of books in your school's library
May: number of items in the school's lost-and-found box

Homework Rubric

Are you less than satisfied with the quality of homework your students are turning in? Make your expectations crystal clear with this idea. Have each student tape a copy of the rubric shown inside her homework folder. When a student completes her homework and places it in the folder, she can glance at the rubric to check that she's met all of the requirements.

Christine Hooper
Gr. 5
Weston School
Manchester, NH

Homework Rubric	CHECK PLUS ✔+	CHECK ✔	CHECK MINUS ✔−
HEADING	• First name • Last name • Date • Assignment	• Lacks one part of the heading	• Lacks more than one part of the heading
NEATNESS	• Legible • Written in pencil	• Legible • Not written in pencil	• Illegible • Not written in pencil
COMPLETENESS	• Homework is complete.	• Homework is more than two-thirds complete.	• Homework is less than two-thirds complete.

Desktop Planning Calendar

Keep important plans, dates, and reminders handy with the help of a blank bulletin board calendar. Laminate the calendar and place it on your desktop. Each month use a wipe-off marker to program the calendar with important reminders and notes. At the end of the month, just wipe the calendar clean so you can reprogram it for the next month.

Lisa Stephens—Gr. 5, Centerville Elementary, Anderson, SC

Coloring Bags

Stop spending precious minutes distributing and collecting individual coloring supplies each time your students need them. Instead, collect a zippered plastic bag for each student. Then fill each bag with a set of eight different-colored crayons, markers, or map pencils. (Collect leftovers at the end of the year to use in the bags.) Store the bags in a basket or box. Then distribute and collect them as needed.

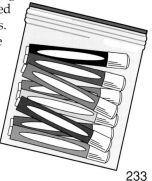

Judy O'Dell—Gr. 6
Caddo Middle Magnet School
Shreveport, LA

Proud Papers

Encourage parents and students alike to review each week's schoolwork with this easy-to-do idea. Instruct each student to label one pocket of a pocket folder "Work to Take Home" and the other pocket "Proud Paper to Return." Every Friday, distribute the papers that are to go home along with a copy of the form below. Direct each student to select the paper she is most proud of and complete the top half of the form. Then have her staple the form to her paper, put it in the proud-paper pocket, and place the remaining papers in the take-home pocket. Instruct parents to complete the bottom half of the form at home as they review the papers. On Monday, collect the proud papers and the forms. Then, at the end of each grading period, return them to each child to compile into her own proud-paper book.

Tammy Trouchon—Gr. 6
Rawhide Elementary
Gillette, WY

Proud-Paper Reflections

Proud paper for the week of _____
I am proud of this paper because _____
_____

Student's signature

I am proud of my child's work because _____

Parent's signature

Inexpensive Incentive Charts

Keep your students well supplied with seasonal incentive charts for a fraction of the usual cost! Cut 9" x 12" sheets of colorful construction paper into fourths. Using a marker, label each quarter sheet with a different child's name and several rows of Xs. To reward a student, simply affix a sticker atop an X. If desired, coordinate the charts with your bulletin board by gluing a section of seasonal bulletin board border to the top of each one. What a small investment for such cool charts!

Jean Juvancic—Gr. 4
St. Louise deMarillac School
LaGrange Park, IL

Abby

Congratulations!

Saving Class Notes

Help absent students catch up on class notes they've missed with this easy tip! During class discussions, record your notes on a transparency. List the names of students who are absent at the top of the transparency. After school, make copies of the notes for yourself and the absentees. When the absent students return, give them copies of the notes they missed. Also, use the copies to put an end to the "We didn't talk about that!" syndrome when tests are returned. Just show your copies of the notes as proof!

Julie Adams—Grs. 5–8 Science
St. Mary's Catholic School
Elgin, IL

Personal Work Files

Improve the way students keep track of their assignments with this organizational idea. Have each child purchase a 9- to 12-pocket expanding plastic file. Print a class supply of computer labels (see the illustration) for students to affix to their files' tabs, making sure that all students place their labels in the same order. Suggest that they use any extra pockets to hold paperback books. Periodically check to see that students are placing their work in the proper pockets. Have students take the files home at night and keep them atop their desks while at school. With one glance, you'll be able to tell if a file has been left at home!

Mary Twining—Gr. 4
McGregor School
Toledo, OH

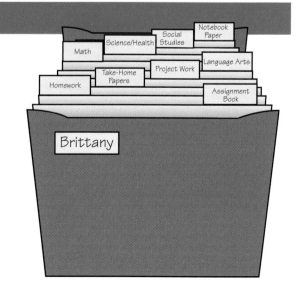

Class Homework Motivator

Motivate students to be more consistent about turning in homework with an incentive that makes everyone a winner! Each time every student turns in an assignment on time, have one child record the assignment and date on a chart. (If a student is absent, give the class credit if he turns in the assignment the day he returns.) When the class has listed ten assignments, celebrate by letting students choose a special activity to enjoy later in the week.

Krystal Boxeth
Academia Cotopaxi
Quito, Ecuador

Make Homework Count!	
Assignment	Date
1. Math, p. 78	Feb. 5
2.	
3.	
4.	

Ten Free Answers

Reward students who consistently turn in homework by giving them a much deserved break. Create a sheet similar to the one shown that features a cute cartoon or clip-art character. At the end of each grading period, present a copy of the sheet to each student who completed every assignment during that period. When a student wants to skip a question on an assignment, have him bring his reward sheet and assignment to you. Write "OK" next to the question on his assignment; then mark out one numbered box on the student's reward sheet. Specify that a student not skip more than two questions on any one assignment. Also reserve the right to refuse the use of the sheet on questions you want all students to answer. In time, more and more students will scramble to turn in all of their work and earn a sheet of free answers!

Name _____
Congratulations!
Because you have worked hard, you will be given free answers (or "Bufords") to ten homework questions of your choice!

BUFORD

Directions: When you wish to receive a free answer, give this paper to your teacher. She will mark your paper and subtract one Buford box below. You may use no more than two Bufords on an assignment. Use them wisely! When they're gone, they're gone!

1	2	3	4	5	6	7	8	9	10

Sharon Vance—Gr. 5
Nash Intermediate School, Kaufman, TX

"Day-o-meter" Monitor

Use a simple visual reminder to motivate students to stay on task and be on their best behavior. Just write the numbers 1 to 10 vertically on a magnetic board, with 10 at the top. Place a fun magnet next to the number that indicates the class's behavior (10 being tops). Then move the magnet up or down throughout the day to let students know at a glance how their behavior rates.

Leighton Rudd—Gr. 4
Bucklin Grade School
Bucklin, KS

"Day-o-meter"
10
9
8 ☺
7
6
5
4
3
2
1

Getting an Upgrade

Offer students a chance to up their grades with this cool incentive. Each time a student's grade falls below 70 percent, allow him to correct his paper. Recheck the paper using a different-colored pen so the student can see the results of his second effort. If the new grade is at least 70 percent, add five points to the original grade. Soon students will see that it pays to correct their graded work!

Nancy Burns—Gr. 5
Virginia E. George
   Elementary
Albany, MO

~~68~~ (73)

Math Test   Jeff

1. $\frac{6}{8} = \frac{3}{4}$
X 2. $\frac{1}{2} = \frac{4}{10}$ ($\frac{5}{10}$)
X 3. $\frac{7}{8} = \frac{20}{24}$ ($\frac{21}{24}$)
X 4. $\frac{5}{8} = \frac{20}{40}$ ($\frac{25}{40}$)
5. $\frac{2}{3} = \frac{6}{9}$
6. $\frac{4}{5} = \frac{8}{10}$

Conference-Time Photo Album

Make the most of the limited time you have for parent-teacher conferences with this picture-perfect timesaver. Beginning on the first day of school, photograph your students engaged in different activities in every subject you teach. Arrange the photos in an attractive album, complete with captions that explain each pictured activity. Since the album answers many questions parents have about what students do during the school day, you can use your limited time to discuss the important issues concerning their children.

Dawn M. Carroll—Gr. 6
Our Lady of the Sacred Heart
Orchard Park, NY

Popsicle Stick Partners

Make pairing students random and fun with this idea! Gather a craft stick for each student. Place a different chart-sized sticker on one end of half of the sticks. Then place a matching sticker on one end of the remaining sticks. Put the sticks in a jar sticker end down. When it is time for partner work, have each student draw a stick and find his partner with the matching sticker. If you have an odd number of students, leave one stick blank and let that student join a twosome of his choice. What a simple way to organize partners!

Connie Ericson—Gr. 4
Mable Woolsey Elementary
Knoxville, IL

June Jump Start

Get a jump start on next school year's preparations with this timesaving idea. Spend a few extra minutes each day in June copying materials you will use during the first few weeks of school. When school begins next year, just pull out those papers and wave to colleagues waiting in line for the copier!

Kelly Gray, Epping Middle School, Epping, NH

Homework Appeal

Motivate students to consistently turn in their homework with this incentive. Write the word *HOMEWORK* on the board. Each day that all students turn in their homework, erase a letter. When the entire word is erased, reward the class with a night of no homework! Students will quickly see that being responsible leads to great rewards.

Kristin Mosura—Gr. 4, Riverside Elementary, Shreveport, LA

Roll-a-Site Organizer

Keep your favorite Internet sites organized with this "in-site-ful" tip! Purchase an inexpensive Rolodex file. Write the Web address and a brief description of each site on a different card. Then arrange the cards alphabetically in the file as shown. To organize the cards even more, turn the tabbed alphabetical dividers over and label them with specific subjects or topics. Surfin' the Web was never simpler!

Vicki Good—Gr. 4
Loda Grade School
Loda, IL

Parent Replies

During the hectic morning, it's often difficult to reply to every note from parents. Respond quickly and easily to those messages with this tip. At the beginning of the year, program a note informing parents that you have received their message (see the example). Duplicate the note to keep a supply handy during the school year. As parent messages come in, simply fill in the parent's name and send the note home with the student. Parents will appreciate the acknowledgement of their message, and you can get back to them at your convenience.

Kathleen Lynch—Gr. 5
Carl W. Goetz Middle School
Jackson, NJ

Date: _____

Dear _____,

I have received your note/phone message and will reply as soon as possible. Thank you for your patience.

Sincerely,
Ms. Lynch

WRITE ON!

Write On!

Ideas and Tips for Teaching Students to Write

An Unwanted Mess

My brother has two gerbils. The gerbils' cage sits on a table in his room. Mom was cleaning his room one day and accidentally knocked over the gerbils' food. It had been left too near the edge of the shelf. It made a big mess. Boy, was Mom mad!

"Did It" Dots

Skill: Editing for a specific purpose

This peer-editing activity is one that students will love *and* stick to doing! Each time a student edits a classmate's writing for a specific purpose, such as using plural possessives, give her a supply of colorful sticky dots. Have her edit her partner's work to see if she met the requirement for that assignment. Then, each time she finds a plural possessive in that student's writing, have her mark it by placing a "did it" dot in the margin near the example. Not only does this idea help ensure that students include specific essentials in their papers, but it also helps refine everyone's editing skills.

Jill R. Bluth, Draper, UT

Drawing by Direction

Skill: Using spatial signal words

Up, down, around, below… Use this cool activity to help students hone in on using specific spatial signal words like these in their writing. Display a poster of spatial signal words, such as those shown. Explain that such words answer the question "Where?" Next, give each student three plain index cards and red, blue, black, and yellow crayons. On the first card, have the student draw and color a simple set of five shapes (see the example). Collect the cards and redistribute them so that no student gets his own card. Then direct each child to write a paragraph on another card using spatial signal words to describe in detail what is pictured on his shapes card. Finally, have the student trade his description with a partner. Challenge each child to illustrate his partner's description on his remaining card exactly as it's written. Afterward, have the partners compare their drawings with the originals to see if they match. If they don't, have the pairs discuss how to revise the descriptions to make them more specific. Do this again as a warm-up activity the next time students write expository, how-to, or descriptive paragraphs.

Shelley Pearsall—Gr. 5, Center Elementary, Strongsville, OH

Spatial Signal Words

opposite	next to	toward
under	right	in
over	left	on
above	middle	out
below	between	by
around	north	beside
near	south	behind
far	east	in front of
across	west	alongside

The yellow triangle is in the middle of the card. Above the yellow triangle is a small blue circle. Next to the yellow triangle on the right side is a red square with black diagonal stripes. Next to the triangle on the left side is a skinny blue triangle. In the upper right corner of the card is a red diamond.

Characters

giant named Glufus
family member
detective
neighbor
scientist
tiny elf

Settings

forest
castle
schoolroom
neighborhood
cave
village

Problems

being bashful
an argument
forgetting something important
losing some money
nosy neighbors
mischievous little brother

Rx for Writer's Block

Skill: Narrative writing

Cure even the worst case of writer's block with this simple remedy. Cover a shoebox so that it resembles a brick, or paint a Styrofoam® block red. Glue a different set of story elements—characters, settings, problems, themes, etc.—to the sides of the block and place it at your writing center. Change the listings periodically. Then, whenever a student says he can't think of anything to write about, send him to the writer's block for relief!

Cheryl Davis, Oceanair Elementary, Norfolk, VA

Write On!

Ideas and Tips for Teaching Students to Write

Convince Me!

Skills: Persuasive writing, letter writing

Cover two important writing skills at once with this letter-perfect activity! First, review persuasive writing techniques and the basics of letter writing with students. Next, brainstorm with them a list of things they'd like to persuade you to do or change in the classroom (see the sample list). Then have each student write a letter to convince you to make one of the changes. Remind students to make their requests respectfully and to include specific reasons for them. Suggest that they even play the devil's advocate and present both sides to make their arguments even more effective. After you've read the completed letters, share whether any convinced you to make a change. Also give pointers about how students could have made their letters even more persuasive.

Irene Taylor, Fort Ann, NY

Things to persuade Ms. Taylor to do or let us do:

- rearrange the desks every two weeks
- have a snack break every morning
- not give homework on Fridays
- chew gum in class
- have extra computer time after lunch

Chain-of-Events Books

Skill: Cause and effect

Help students learn to recognize and write cause-and-effect sequences with this fun book-making activity. Begin by reading to the class *There Was an Old Lady Who Swallowed a Fly* by Simms Taback. Afterward, read *I Know an Old Lady Who Swallowed a Pie* by Alison Jackson. Have students compare and contrast the two books. Then challenge each student to create and illustrate his own book that follows the format of the ones you read aloud. Require only that the book's main character have a reason for what he or she swallows. For example, a character who wants to write a book might swallow a journal of ideas, a pencil, a notepad, a folder, and a desk! A character who wants to become a champion golfer might swallow a Tiger Woods video, a set of golf clubs, a golf cart, and a box of tees. Allow students to share their stories with the class; then place the books in your class library. Every time students read the books, they'll remember that one event can lead to another and another and…

Donna Hackney—Gr. 4, Stevens Park Elementary, Dallas, TX

I'm a Rock Star!
by Cheri

CD Stories

Skill: Narrative writing

Turn those junk mail CDs that offer free Internet hours into fun writing prompts! Ask parents and co-workers to help you collect a class supply of these unsolicited disks. Give each child a disk and tell her to pretend it is a CD that she's just recorded. Then list the information in the box shown on the board. Have each student use the list to help her write a story about her just-released CD. After students share their completed stories with the class, have each child tape the tale to her CD as shown and hang it from the ceiling.

Teresa Chowansky, Roosevelt Elementary
Ridgefield Park, NJ

- the type of music you sing
- how and when your singing career got started
- the title of the most popular song on your CD and what it is about
- how you'll spend the money earned from this CD
- plans for future CDs
- how your popularity has affected you

Write On!

Ideas and Tips for Teaching Students to Write

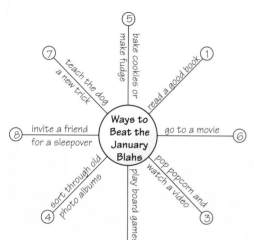

The spidergram shows a circle labeled "Ways to Beat the January Blahs" with eight legs:
1. read a good book
2. play board games
3. pop popcorn and watch a video
4. sort through old photo albums
5. bake cookies or make fudge
6. go to a movie
7. teach the dog a new trick
8. invite a friend for a sleepover

"Spidergram" Prewriting
Skills: Planning and writing a well-organized paragraph

Reinforce prewriting skills with a "spider-rific" graphic organizer! Have each student draw a large circle with eight "legs" on his paper as shown. Direct the student to label the circle with his topic. Then have him fill in each leg with a specific idea or detail about the topic. After all legs are filled in, have the student number each detail in order of importance. As the student writes one sentence for each detail, have him check off that spider leg. The result is a paragraph that's specific, sequenced, and sensational!

Patricia Dancho—Gr. 6, Apollo-Ridge Middle School, Spring Church, PA

Banning Blah Beginnings
Skill: Writing an introduction

Help your students write outstanding introductions for their essays and stories with the following activities:

- On the board, write a list of "boring beginnings" that you've collected from students' work, such as "One day…," "My name is…," and "Once upon a time…" Have the class hum the tune "Taps" as you erase each phrase, symbolizing that students are henceforth banned from using these blah beginnings in their written work.
- Have students search in their library books and textbooks to find paragraphs that begin with a question or an exclamation. List these introductions on the chalkboard. Point out that this type of introduction ensures that action begins in the first sentence, grabbing a reader's interest right from the start.
- Divide the class into groups of four. Give each group a copy of a dull introductory paragraph (see the example shown). Set a timer for five minutes; then challenge students to use a thesaurus and their imaginations to rewrite the paragraph so that it is more interesting. Provide time for each group to share the dull paragraph and the revised version. Students are sure to hear the difference!

> Hi. My name is Miller. I am a nine-year-old boy who loves baseball. Today was an exciting day for me. Let me tell you why.

Michelle Bauml—Gr. 5, Polk Elementary, Lake Jackson, TX

Summarizing With Picture Books
Skills: Writing a summary, sequencing

All you need to teach students how to write a super summary is your favorite picture book. After reading the book to students, divide the class into groups of three. Give each group a copy of a three- to five-page section of the book. Then have the group decide on the section's main idea and write it on a sentence strip. Have each group share its main idea sentence strip and tape it on the board. Then point out that students can form a summary of the story by simply sequencing and combining the groups' main ideas. With students' help, organize the strips in order on the board. Finally, work together to write introductory and concluding sentences for the summary. That about sums it up!

Gayle Lamers—Gr. 4, Jackie Carden Elementary
Fort Worth, TX

PETE'S A PIZZA
WILLIAM STEIG

Pete's dad decides to cheer him up by making him into a pizza.

Pete's dad pretends to add toppings to the pizza, which is really Pete.

Write On!

Ideas and Tips for Teaching Students to Write

A Fly on the Wall

Skill: Writing a historical fiction story

Boost narrative-writing skills with an activity that asks students to retell a historical event from an unusual perspective. Instruct each student to pretend that he is a fly on the wall of a room where an important historical event is taking place. For example, if you are studying the Civil War, he might be in the house at Appomattox Court House, Virginia, where General Robert E. Lee signed surrender papers. Instruct each student to write a historical fiction story describing the event from the perspective of a fly on the wall. Go over the guidelines shown, directing students to use information from their social studies texts and other sources to help them. Have students share their finished stories in small groups. Then bind the tales in a class book titled "All Abuzz About [the historical event]!"

Judy Reid Sholtis—Gr. 5, Christ the King Catholic School, Daphne, AL

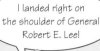

Guidelines
- Write in first person.
- Identify the setting of the story.
- Include information about how you got into the building, who you heard, and what you saw.
- Include at least three facts about the event.
- Use names of specific people and places.
- Be entertaining as well as informative.

I landed right on the shoulder of General Robert E. Lee!

A Bad Case of...

Skill: Narrative writing

For an activity that's guaranteed to engage even your most reluctant writers, grab a copy of the delightful picture book *A Bad Case of Stripes* by David Shannon. In this story, a follow-the-crowd kind of girl suddenly finds herself covered from head to toe with stripes. Her bad case of stripes only worsens until a little old lady provides an unusual cure. Read this book aloud to your class and discuss what it has to say about being different and the pressure to conform. Then ask each student to imagine that he has just contracted a bad case of a one-of-a-kind sickness, like Camilla in the story. Have the student illustrate a self-portrait of himself with the special condition (see the example). Then have him write a story that explains how he contracted the disease and how he was eventually cured.

Melody B. Adent—Gr. 6, Drayton Hall Middle School, Charleston, SC

A Bad Case of Buttons

Better Beginnings

Skill: Varying sentence beginnings

Variety is the spice of life, but students often forget that adage where sentence beginnings are concerned. Help them learn to vary their sentence beginnings with this eye-opening activity. After everyone has written the first draft of a writing assignment, have each student swap papers with a partner. Direct students to circle the first word of each sentence with a marker or colored pencil. Then have each child list the circled words at the bottom of the paper before returning it to her partner. Students will be amazed at how many times *I* or *The* is listed on their papers. Next, display and discuss the chart shown. As a class, have students use the chart to revise several of their sentences. Then have each child revise her own work so that no two sentences begin alike. If you don't plan on keeping the chart up in your classroom, have each student copy it on a large index card to keep in her writing folder.

Transition Words	Subordinate Conjunctions	
after	after	so
before	although	that
next	as if	though
finally	because	unless
first	before	until
therefore	if	when
then	in order that	where
when	since	while

Patricia E. Dancho—Gr. 6
Apollo-Ridge Middle School
Spring Church, PA

Write On!

Ideas and Tips for Teaching Students to Write

Mystery Animals
Skill: Descriptive writing

With the help of a few summer yard sales, you can bag a great descriptive-writing activity! Collect a class supply of small stuffed animals. Place each toy in a numbered paper bag and staple the bag shut. Then distribute one bag to each student and have her complete these steps:

1. Find a quiet spot to secretly open your bag and view its contents. (Do not take the animal out of the bag.) Then close the bag securely.
2. Take notes on the stuffed animal's physical characteristics.
3. Write a one-paragraph description about the animal without mentioning its species.

After students have completed their paragraphs, give each child a large sheet of drawing paper. Then have students read their descriptions aloud in numerical order. As a child reads her paragraph, have each of her classmates draw a picture of the animal he thinks she is describing. At the end of the sharing time, have students empty the bags and check their guesses. Then discuss the paragraphs that resulted in the most correct guesses.

Terry Warner—Gr. 4, Brookview Elementary, Jacksonville, FL

Wall of Inspiration
Skill: Brainstorming ideas for writing

Here's an easy way to inspire students who think they have nothing to write about. Completely cover a large bulletin board or wall space with a variety of items that will stimulate your students' creative juices, such as old gameboards, humorous ads, magazine covers, book jackets, ticket stubs, cereal boxes, photographs, brochures, candy wrappers, posters, and articles of clothing. Encourage students to use the Wall of Inspiration when they need a writing idea. At the end of the month, change the display. If desired, assign the wall to a small group of students each month. Make the group responsible for collecting and displaying new items as well as taking down the display at the end of the assigned month.

Marla Taviano—Grs. 5–6 Gifted and Talented
Laketon Elementary, Laketon, IN

Theme Park Fun
Skill: Writing a newspaper article

Summer's here, and that means the gates of amusement parks everywhere are swinging open. Take advantage of theme park fever with this motivating activity. Announce that each student has been hired to design a new kid-friendly amusement park for your town. Brainstorm with students a list of items to consider in planning their parks, such as a catchy name and theme, admission fees, rides, food vendors, and other entertainment features. After each student has made notes about his design, have him use them to write a newspaper article about the park's opening. Remind students that each article should include a headline, a byline, a lead, and a body that answers questions about the park for the reader. If desired, share with students an example of a theme park brochure that includes a map of the facilities. Discuss the items shown on the map, such as park rides, eating establishments, and rest rooms. Then have each student create a labeled map of his park.

Jennifer Dziak—Gr. 5, 43 Academy, Buffalo, NY

Deep-Sea Adventure World Opens Today

Red-Hot Reading Comprehension

Red-Hot Reading Comprehension

Spice up your language arts program with red-hot reading comprehension activities from our readers!

Main Idea Web
Skill: Identifying main ideas

Teach your students this easy-to-do strategy for identifying main ideas. After students have read a story or piece of informational text, direct each child to draw a circle with five spokes on his paper as shown. Have the student write an event or important detail from the selection on each spoke. Then instruct him to reread the five details, determine what they have in common, and write this main idea in the circle. End the activity by letting students share their webs and identify the main idea together. Not only does this idea work well with guided reading groups, but it also helps ESL students strengthen their comprehension skills. *Diana Springfield—Gr. 5, Benjamin Franklin Elementary, Glendale, CA*

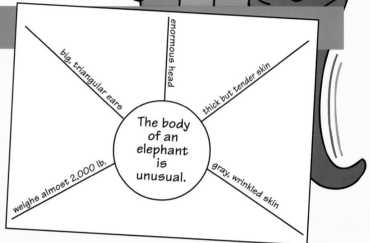

big, triangular ears

enormous head

thick but tender skin

The body of an elephant is unusual.

gray, wrinkled skin

weighs almost 2,000 lb.

pp. 17–22 ③

1. I once lost a dog like Zach did. I cried in the bathroom too!
2. Will Zach and his family find Tina before Christmas Day?
3. I predict that Tina will come home the next day because she has a built-in compass!

"Comp" Cards
Skills: Making connections, predicting

Better comprehension skills are in the cards with this silent reading activity! At the end of the silent reading period, have each student label an index card with at least three sentences about what she read. If desired, require that students write about each of the following:

- a personal connection I made with what I read
- a question about what I read
- a prediction about what I think will happen next

Have the student number the card and store it in her own card file box. The next day, have the student review the previous day's card before she begins reading again. By the end of the book, the student will have a handy collection of reminders to help her review the book or prepare a book report project. *adapted from an idea by Karen DiGuglielmo, Overbrook School for the Blind, Philadelphia, PA*

How Ya Feelin'?
Skills: Analyzing characters, making connections

Use this activity to help your students learn to analyze the characters they encounter. Before a particularly emotional moment in the book students are reading, list six to eight emotions on the board. Make sure that a few of the feelings are ones displayed by the character(s) in the day's reading selection. Discuss the words with students. Then direct each child to read the day's selection and identify the emotions felt by the character. Have the student write a short paragraph that explains his choice and gives supporting evidence from the text.

After students share their paragraphs, discuss how a good author shows emotion not only through a character's words but also through his actions. As an extension, have each student choose an emotion from the board and write about a personal experience he has had that evoked that feeling. *Adam Fassanella—Gr. 4, Hinsdale School, Winsted, CT*

That basketball game reminds me of the color orange because a basketball is orange.

Colorful Summaries
Skills: Retelling, sequencing, summarizing

Help your students increase their comprehension of story events with this colorful strategy. Cut out an assortment of colorful construction paper squares. Give each student several squares. Then challenge him to read the passage silently and associate ideas from the story with specific colors. For example, a student may associate a boat ride with the color blue because it reminds him of water. Another child may associate a dog in the story with the color brown because her puppy is brown. When a student connects a color with a story event, have him place the appropriate square in the middle of his desktop. As he continues reading, have him stack the colored squares in order behind the first square chosen. After the student has finished reading, have him use the sequenced cards to help him retell or summarize the story in his own words (either verbally to a partner or in writing). *Glenna Allen—Gr. 5, Joe Lawrence Elementary, Mesquite, TX*

Vocabulary Pictures
Skill: Developing vocabulary

Use the power of a picture to help your students learn and recall the meanings of unfamiliar words. List the new words from a reading selection on the board. Read over the words with the class to make sure students know their pronunciations. Then assign one word to each student (or student pair). Direct each child to use context clues and a dictionary to determine the word's meaning. Then have the student label a sheet of art paper with the word and draw a picture that illustrates its meaning (see the example). Have students share their word pictures with the class. With a picture to visualize, students are sure to remember new vocabulary more easily. *Colleen Dabney, Williamsburg–JCC Public Schools, Williamsburg, VA*

generous

Here, it's ALL yours!

WOW!

$

AGREE

I agree that James should have crawled into the giant peach.

Go to Your Corner!
Skills: Making evaluations, thinking critically

Throw a little comprehension practice into your read-aloud time with this idea. Write "AGREE" on a sheet of paper, "DISAGREE" on a second sheet, and "NOT SURE" on a third sheet. Tape each sign in a different corner of your classroom. As you read aloud to students, periodically stop at a critical point in the story. Then ask whether students agree or disagree with a character's actions. At your signal, have each child leave her desk and stand in the corner that signifies her answer. Call on a few students to explain their choices. Then have each child return to her desk and continue listening to the story.

Use the signs with content-area reading selections too. Before students read a passage, announce a statement about the topic, such as "Endangered animals should be protected at any cost." Have students respond as described above. After students read the selection, repeat the statement and have each child choose a corner. Discuss whether anyone changed her opinion based on what she read. *adapted from an idea by Jennifer Anderson—Gr. 4, Wedgwood Elementary, Florissant, MO*

Red-Hot Reading Comprehension

Spice up your language arts lesson plans with red-hot reading comprehension activities from our readers!

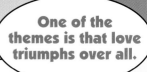

Thinking About Theme
Skills: Identifying, comparing, and contrasting themes

Do your students often confuse a story's theme with its plot? To help them learn to identify themes, label a sheet of chart paper as shown. Discuss the three examples of common themes in literature. Ask students to suggest stories or books they've read that feature one or more of these themes. Then, as you and the students read and discuss other stories or books, list new themes featured in them on the chart. Before long, students will be able to identify a story's theme with little or no assistance.

For more reading comprehension practice, list on the board two stories or books the class has recently read. Decide as a class which themes from the chart are featured in each tale. Then have each student write a paragraph that compares and contrasts the themes found in the two stories. *Colleen Dabney, Toano Middle School, Williamsburg, VA*

One of the themes is that love triumphs over all.

Common Themes in Literature
- Good friends are hard to find.
- If you work hard enough, you can achieve your dreams.
- It's okay to be different.

It's a letter from Marty Preston!

Character Letters
Skill: Understanding characters

Wrap up the reading of a small-group or class novel with this letter-writing activity. After students have read a book, have each child write a letter to a character of his choice. In the letter, have the student describe what he likes about the character. Also have him ask two or three questions about something the character does (or doesn't do) in the story. Collect the finished letters; then distribute them to students, making sure no one receives his own letter. Direct each student to respond to the letter he receives as if he were the character. Then have him deliver the letter and his response to the appropriate classmate. Provide time for students to share their letters and the responses penned by their classmates. *Amanda Wilkins—Gr. 4, Starside Elementary, De Soto, KS*

Vocabulary Skits
Skill: Developing vocabulary

Raise the curtain on better vocabulary skills with this creative group activity! At the end of a story, chapter, or book, divide the class into groups of four or five. Give each student an index card labeled with a vocabulary word from the selection. Direct her to look up the word in a dictionary, find its meaning (according to its context in the selection), and share the definition with her group. Then give each group ten to 15 minutes to create a skit that includes each word and gives clues to its meaning. Challenge groups to quickly find or make simple props to use in their performances. After each skit is presented, discuss the meanings of the new words. Use this idea to introduce or review new vocabulary in social studies or science units too. *Laurie Johansen—Gr. 5 Gifted, T. J. Lee Elementary, Irving, TX*

Sequencing in Circles
Skills: Sequencing, summarizing

If sequencing has your students going around in circles, stop the spinning with this graphic organizer! After students have read a story or book, give each child a wire coat hanger, six to ten index cards, and six to ten spring-type clothespins. Then have each student follow these steps:

1. Bend the coat hanger in a circle shape as shown.
2. Write each main event from the story on a separate index card.
3. Clip the cards in order around the coat hanger.
4. Share your organizer with a partner. Make corrections by removing or rearranging the cards as needed.
5. Number the cards in order.
6. Use the sequenced cards to write a summary of the story.

Reuse the hangers any time you want students to practice sequencing and summarizing story events. Also use the organizers to help students sequence steps in a nonfiction how-to selection.
Simone Lepine—Gr. 5, Gillette Road Middle School, Cicero, NY

Inference Bag
Skill: Making inferences

Better reading skills are easy to bag with this nifty activity on making inferences. After students have finished reading a book together, fill a canvas tote bag or paper grocery sack with several small items that could be associated with the book's characters. Tell students that the bag contains objects that belong to the characters. Then pull each item out of the bag one at a time and ask students to infer which character might own it. Require students to give evidence from the story to support their answers. Continue in this manner until the bag has been emptied. *Colleen Dabney, Toano Middle School, Williamsburg, VA*

Zippy Summarizing
Skill: Summarizing

Add some zip to your reading lesson plans with this summarizing activity. First, label a separate file folder for each child. Give each student a plastic zippered bag and a stack of small index cards. Have the student label one card with her name and the book's title and author. Then have her place this card in the bag. As the student reads, have her summarize each chapter on a separate index card and place it in the bag behind the title card. After the book is finished, hold a conference with the child to discuss it. Then staple the cards together in order and place them in the child's folder. After the student has read several books, help her evaluate her summarizing and writing progress by examining the collection of cards in her folder.
Kimberly A. Minafo, Pomona, NY

Chapter 6
David and Marty talk about seeing Judd shoot the squirrel. Marty tries to tell Judd the truth about spying on him, but Judd just yells at him. When Marty talks to his dad about Judd, he finds out that his dad told Judd to stay off their land.

Red-Hot Reading Comprehension

best friends + argument = two blue buddies

Examples:
toddler + kitten = _____
clean car + mud puddle = _____
homework assignment – paper = _____
restaurant – good service = _____
soccer team – coach = _____
best friends + argument = _____
four puppies + one food bowl = _____

Prediction Equations
Skill: Making predictions

Use this simple daily activity to demonstrate how readers can use details in written selections to predict a future action. Each morning write an equation, such as the ones shown, on the board. Then challenge each student to put the details together and predict a logical outcome. For example, if the equation is "dog – water = ____," a student might predict an outcome of "a thirsty dog" or "a dog that can't have a bath." Encourage students to be creative and come up with as many logical outcomes as possible.

Diana Boykin—Gr. 4, DeZavala Elementary, Midland, TX

Tell Me What You See
Skills: Visualizing, retelling

Students who struggle to comprehend narrative text often have trouble visualizing what's being read. To help students sharpen this skill, try this quick activity. As you read a story aloud, periodically stop reading and ask one or more students to explain what they visualize at this point in the story. As a variation, distribute sheets of art paper and ask each student to draw a picture of what he visualizes. At a glance, you'll be able to see if students are comprehending what is being read. This activity works equally well if students are reading silently or if you're working with an individual child or a small group of readers.

Lea Iverson—Gr. 6, Lincoln Elementary, Elk River, MN

I see James on his hands and knees trying really hard to pick up the green things.

T Take turns. ☆
A Attend to everyone. ☆
L Link ideas. ☆
K Keep on the subject. ☆
T Take time to discuss topics in depth. ☆
I Interrupt no one. ☆
P Put no one on the spot. ☆
S Share the time equally. ☆

Talk Tips
Skill: Participating in a literature circle

If your students participate in literature circles, try this idea to help them make the most of their discussion time. Display the poster shown and discuss the tips with students. During literature circle meetings, encourage students to use the poster to praise classmates who use specific tips or identify areas that aren't being addressed. Also use the tips to help students assess their literature discussions after they're over. Ask each student in a circle to do three things: grade the group's success on following the guidelines, specify a tip the group used well, and describe one area that needs improvement.

Lori Ann Hayman—Gr. 4, Sandymount Elementary, Finksburg, MD

GAME PLANS

High-Scoring Hoops

Don't be surprised to see your students playing this math game at recess!

Skill: Review of basic multiplication facts

To prepare: Take your students, along with two basketballs, to an outdoor basketball court. (Or play indoors using a trash can and two Nerf® balls.)

To play:
1. Divide students into two teams. Have the teams line up side by side behind the foul line facing the basket.
2. Give the first player on each team a basketball.
3. Tell students that the first game will include the 2s multiplication table.
4. Call out "times 4" or any digit. At that signal, the first two players shoot and try to score a basket.
5. The first player to make a basket answers the math fact 2 x 4. If she is correct, her team earns points equal to that product *(8)*. If she is incorrect, her opponent gets a chance to answer and earn points. If both players are incorrect, no points are scored.
6. Each player gives her ball to the next teammate and goes to the end of her team's line.
7. Continue play until every student has had a chance to shoot. After calling out all of the facts for the 2s table, begin another multiplication table.

—Marsha Schmus—Grs. 3–5 Gifted and Talented, Chambersburg, PA

If desired, make a copy of the two games. Then cut out each idea and glue it on a 4" x 6" index card. File the cards for ready reference whenever you need a game idea.

Silent Outburst

Motivate students with this fun vocabulary builder when you begin a new unit of study or review skills already learned.

Skills: Introduce or review any topic of study, build vocabulary

To prepare: List ten words or concepts related to a unit you plan to study. Don't share your list with the class.

precipitation
humidity
barometer
climate
forecast

To play:
1. Divide the class into teams of four to six students each.
2. Tell students the topic. Then have each child, independently and silently, list as many words as he can think of that are related to the topic.
3. Allow about two minutes; then call time.
4. Appoint a scorekeeper for each team.
5. Read a word from your list. Tell every student who has that word on his list to raise his hand.
6. If everyone on a team has the word, the team earns 3 points. And if only one student on the team has the word on his list, the team scores 5 points. Tell every student who has that word on his list to raise his hand. If two or more (but not all) of the players have the word, the team scores 1 point.
7. Continue play with the other words on your list. When finished, discuss the words that students wrote that were not on your list or include them on your word wall.

—Lynne Kizpolski—Gr. 5, Clara Barton School, Cherry Hill, NJ

Game Plans

"Spinography"

Send your students on a trip across the USA with this "map-nificent" map skills game!

Skills: Reviewing cardinal directions, identifying U.S. states

To prepare: Divide students into groups. Provide each group with an unlabeled political map of the United States, a paper spinner labeled as shown, crayons, a pencil, and a paper clip.

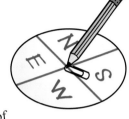

To play:

1. Have the first student in each group choose a state in the middle of the country, label it "1," and color it.
2. Spin the spinner and announce the direction to the class. This is the border that each group will try to reach: either Canada (N), Pacific Ocean (W), Atlantic Ocean (E), or Mexico (S).
3. Have the second student in each group spin the spinner. That student moves in the direction spun to a state bordering the first one. He labels the second state "2" and colors it.
4. If a student moves to a state that has already been colored, he spins again.
5. The game continues until a group reaches and colors a state bordering the goal determined in Step 2. The winning group then shares its route by calling out, in order, the numbers and their corresponding states.
6. For an extension, have each group identify the capital of each state colored.

—Kimberly A. Minafo, Pomona, NY

If desired, make a copy of the two games. Then cut out each idea and glue it on a 4" x 6" index card. File the cards for ready reference whenever you need a game idea.

Hang It Up!

Watch students' spelling skills soar with this cooperative game!

Skill: Spelling

To prepare: For each group, label colorful pants and shirt cutouts with one letter each. Make sure you have enough letters for the words students will spell. Divide students into groups. Provide each group with a set of lettered clothing cutouts, several spring-type clothespins, and a length of string.

To play:

1. Call out a spelling word.
2. Have the students in each group work together to spell the word, using the pants and shirt cutouts.
3. Direct each group to "hang its wash" by pinning the letters on the string to spell the word.
4. The first group to hold up its clothesline with the correct spelling earns two points. Other teams that spell the word correctly earn one point each.
5. Declare the team with the most points at the end of the game the winner.

—Sara Gabel—Gr. 6, Governor Mifflin Intermediate School, Wyomissing, PA

Game Plans

Classroom Feud

Students will love this review game based on a popular TV game show!

Skill: Review of any skill or unit of study

To prepare: Provide each student with an index card. On the card, have the student write a question that relates to the skill or unit you've just covered and then sign his name. Collect the completed cards. Place a desk at the front of the classroom. Put a chalkboard eraser in the middle of the desktop.

To play:
1. Divide students into two teams. Invite the first player from each team to go to the desk at the front of the room. Have these players stand on opposite sides of the desk, facing each other with their hands flat on the desktop.
2. Read a question from an index card.
3. If a player thinks he knows the answer, he grabs the eraser and gives his answer. If correct, his team earns a point.
4. If the player is incorrect, his opponent then gets the opportunity to answer the question. The opponent may consult his teammates. If his answer is correct, his team earns a point.
5. If both the first player and the opposing team are incorrect, then the first player may try again—this time with his team's help. If correct, the team earns a point. If not, share the correct answer with the class.
6. Continue play until all the questions have been answered. The winning team is the one with more points.

—Cari Lott, Roosevelt-Lincoln Middle School, Salina, KS

Which Confederate general surrendered to Grant at Appomattox?

Matt

Can It!

Review any topic or skill with this challenging cooperative game!

Skill: Review of any skill or unit of study

To prepare: Number and then cut apart a list of review questions. Number the lids of a set of empty film canisters. Put each numbered question in its corresponding canister. Then place all the film canisters at the front of the classroom.

To play:
1. Divide students into teams and assign a recorder for each team. The recorder needs a pencil and a sheet of paper.
2. At a signal, have a student from each group get a film canister from the front of the room and take it to his group.
3. Have the recorder in each group write the number from the top of the canister and then remove the question. After the group discusses the question and reaches a consensus about an answer, the recorder writes the answer on his team's sheet.
4. The recorder returns the question to its canister and another student takes the canister back to the front of the classroom. He then picks up a different canister and takes it to his group.
5. Continue play until a team answers all of the questions. Reward each team with a point for each correct answer. Award bonus points to the team that finished first.

—Barbara Bergner—Gr. 5, Hillcrest Elementary, Delphi, IN

If desired, make a copy of the two games. Then cut out each idea and glue it onto a 4" x 6" index card. File the cards for ready reference whenever you need a game idea.

Game Plans

Leapfrog

Leap into a review of any topic or skill with this challenging cooperative game!

Skill: Reviewing any skill or unit of study

To prepare: Make 30–40 copies of the frog pattern on page 35. Program the frogs with point values of 5–50 in increments of five. Program five frogs with the word *LEAPFROG*.

To play:
1. Shuffle the frogs and stack them facedown.
2. Divide students into five to six teams and have each team decide on a name. Also have each team choose a captain.
3. List the team names horizontally across the chalkboard for scorekeeping.
4. To begin, pose a review question to the first team. Allow the team about a minute to discuss the question. Then call on the team captain for the answer.
5. If the answer is correct, the captain draws the first frog from the stack. Award his team the number of points shown on the frog. Record the score on the board. If a Leapfrog card is chosen, no points are earned.
6. If the team cannot answer the question or the answer is incorrect, the team does not choose a frog. Pose the same question to the next team.
7. Whenever a team draws a Leapfrog card, all of that team's accumulated points "leapfrog" over the team listed immediately on its right. The points are then added to the next team's total.
8. Continue play for a predetermined number of rounds. The team with the most points at the end of the game is the winner.

—*Jeffrey J. Kuntz—Gr. 5, West End Elementary, Punxsutawney, PA*

State That State!

Review U.S. geography with this fun group game.

Skill: Identifying U.S. state names and locations

To prepare: Number the states (1–50) on a blank political map of the United States. Make a copy of the map for each team.

United States

To play:
1. Divide students into four or more teams and provide each team with a map.
2. To begin, a player from Team 1 calls out a number on the map and names the corresponding state.
3. If the player is correct, his team earns a point. Every team then crosses out that state on its map. If the player is incorrect, no points are earned and the state is not marked out.
4. A player on Team 2 then takes a turn.
5. Play continues until all of the states have been correctly identified.

As a variation, have students name only the state capitals or both the state and its capital.

—*Joyce Hovanec—Gr. 4, Glassport Elementary, Glassport, PA*

If desired, make a copy of the two games. Then cut out each idea and glue it on a 4" x 6" index card. File the cards for ready reference whenever you need a game idea.

Game Plans

Capacity War

It's a friendly war when students compute and compare units of capacity!

Skill: Comparing customary units of capacity

To prepare: Provide each pair of students with a deck of playing cards. Have each twosome remove the face cards and jokers from the deck.

2 gallons > 6 quarts

To play:
1. In Capacity War, clubs are cups, diamonds are pints, hearts are quarts, and spades are gallons. Aces are equal to 1. For example: A 7 of hearts represents 7 quarts.
2. A player deals all of the cards facedown to his opponent and to himself.
3. Each player turns over his top card.
4. Players determine who has the card with a greater capacity. For example: A 4 of hearts (4 quarts) is greater than a 6 of hearts (6 quarts).
5. The player whose card has the greater capacity. However, a 2 of spades (2 gallons) is greater than a 2 of diamonds (2 pints). However, a 2 of spades (2 gallons) is greater than a 2 of diamonds (2 pints). The player whose card has the greater capacity wins both cards.
6. If the values of the two cards are equal (4 of hearts = ace of spades), a war begins. Each player draws the next two cards from his deck, stacks them facedown, and then draws and turns up a third card. The player whose card has the greater capacity wins all eight cards.
7. Players compare their upturned cards. The player whose card has the greater capacity wins all eight cards.
8. Play continues until all cards have been won. The player who has more cards is the winner.

—Jean Russell—Grs. 4–5, Whispering Meadows Elementary, Ft. Wayne, IN

©The Education Center, Inc. • THE MAILBOX® • Intermediate • June/July 2002

If desired, make a copy of the two games. Then cut out each idea and glue it onto a 4" x 6" index card. File the cards for ready reference whenever you need a game idea.

High Five!

Point values can grow and grow and grow some more in this fun, anytime review game!

Skill: Review of any skill or unit of study

To prepare: Divide students into two teams.

For 30 points, reduce $\frac{18}{24}$ to lowest terms.

To play:
1. Ask the first player on Team 1 a review question.
2. If that player answers correctly, she earns five points for her team. If she is incorrect, ask the first player on Team 2 the same question. If that player answers correctly, award his team ten points.
3. If the Team 2 player also answers incorrectly, ask the second student on Team 1 the same question. Increase the value of the question to 15 points.
4. Continue alternating play in the same manner. Each time a question is answered incorrectly, increase its value by five points and give the next player on the opposing team a chance to answer it.
5. Play for a set amount of time or until students have answered all review questions.

For 15 points, name and spell the capital city of Canada.

—Julie Kaiser—Gr. 4, Pine View Elementary, New Albany, IN

©The Education Center, Inc. • THE MAILBOX® • Intermediate • June/July 2002

SEASONAL IDEAS & REPRODUCIBLES

Celebrate the Season

Holiday and Seasonal Activities for the Classroom

Back-to-School

First-Day Puzzles

Introduce yourself to your new class—and your students to one another—with an activity that's big on **writing.** In advance, write a brief paragraph about yourself on the bottom half of a sheet of paper. Underline 15 or more key words in the paragraph. Above the paragraph, create a word-search puzzle that includes the underlined words. Make a copy of the page for each student. On the first day of school, give each student a copy of the page to read and complete. Follow up by having each child create a similar page about himself. After each child shares his paragraph with the class, collect and laminate the papers. Then place them in a center—along with a wipe-off marker—so students can solve the puzzles during free time. *Joanie Brillant—Gr. 4, Bechtel Elementary, Okinawa, Japan*

```
t x p z y w p d t e d f v u d
z e l t l l m m p s t u v w x
y z a a n b c d e f g h i j
k l o c o u n t r y m i n o p
q r e h h s t w u v u x y z j
a b s i c e d o e f g t h i e
j k l l m r o p q r e s t a
g o l d e n r e t r i e v e r
c o l l e g e u v w x n y z s
a b c d e f s o n s g h i j k
l m n o p t r a v e l i n g q
r s t u v h u s b a n d w x y
z a b c d o n e f g h i j k l
m n o p q b r s t u v w x y z
a b c d e b f g h i j k l m n
o p q r s y t u v w z t z a b
```

Hello! I'm Mrs. Cox, your new <u>teacher</u>. I grew up in the <u>country</u>. I was an <u>only</u> <u>child</u>. Growing up, I thought about becoming a <u>nurse</u>. But in <u>college</u>, I decided to become a teacher. I have taught for <u>sixteen</u> <u>years</u>. I have a <u>husband</u>, <u>two</u> <u>sons</u>, and a <u>golden</u> <u>retriever</u> named Taffy. My <u>hobby</u> is <u>traveling</u> to different <u>places</u> in the United States and the world.

New-Class Gallery

Get to know your students better with an **art and writing** project that becomes a decorative display! First, use a favorite computer program to print a graphic of an attractive picture frame. Make a copy of the picture frame for each student, leaving space below the frame for the student to write a paragraph. Direct each student to draw and color a picture of herself doing something she enjoys in the space inside the frame. Then have her add a paragraph about her likes, dislikes, hobbies, and family in the space below the frame. Direct the student to share her work with the class. Then arrange the papers along a classroom wall to create a picture-perfect gallery of your new class! *Neal Dickstein—Gr. 5, Ethel McKnight School, East Windsor, NJ*

"Seed-sational" Math

Use this mouthwatering **statistics and graphing** activity to help students get better acquainted during the first days of a new school year! Have each student eat a slice of watermelon and save the seeds. Next, have each child share one fact about herself for each seed saved. After everyone has shared, divide students into groups of four. Have each group list the total seeds collected by each group member in order from least to greatest and find the data's mean, median, mode, and range. Afterward, give each group a sheet of construction paper and glue. Have each group make a pictograph of the seeds collected by its members using its own seeds. (See the example.) Then display the graphs on a bulletin board titled "Statistics and Graphing Are 'Seed-sational'!" *Marsha Schmus—Grs. 3–5 Gifted and Talented, Chambersburg, PA*

Seeds Saved	
● = 2 seeds	
Group Member	**Number of Seeds**
Aisha	● ● ● ● ● ●
Brent	● ● ● ● ●
Ali	● ● ● ●
Katie	● ● ● ● ● ●

September

September Journal Topics

Looking for thought-provoking journal topics for students to write about during the month of September? Then give these **writing prompts** a try!

- Labor Day is the first Monday in September. What job do you *not* see yourself having as an adult? Why?

- Other than being round, how are pennies, hamburger patties, and tires alike?

- If you had to choose between having a computer and having a TV, which would you choose? Why?

- If your bedroom were ever destroyed by fire, what three things from it would you miss the most? Explain.

- Imagine yourself 35 years from now. Describe how you think you will look.

- National Honey Month is observed during September to honor beekeepers and honeybees. What would be the advantages of having a bee for a pet? The disadvantages?

- Which is more fun: planning a party or going to someone else's party? Explain.

- What would you do if you suddenly realized that you'd accidentally thrown away your parents' only set of car keys?

- Which is more valuable to you: your sight or your hearing? Why?

- If you met someone who had a piece of spinach stuck between her front teeth, what would you do? Explain.

- September is Self-Improvement Month. What three traits do you think you most need to improve? Explain.

- What would be the advantages of having every country in the world use the same unit of money? The disadvantages?

- What would you say to your best friend if he or she had just lost your school's spelling bee?

- Imagine that your teacher is a robot. What would you most like to program this machine to do? Explain.

- How might life change if there were no television shows on after 8:00 P.M.?

- What ten adjectives best describe your favorite kind of candy?

The reproducibles on pages 258-259 were written by Ann Fisher, Mill Hall, PA.

Triple (and Quadruple) Trouble!

Mr. Jones knows he's in for a challenging year. He's just been given the names of the boys and girls who are in his upcoming class. The problem? He's discovered he will have not one, not two, but *three* sets of triplets! In addition, he'll have a set of quadruplets in his class!

Help Mr. Jones combine all of the boys' and girls' names below into a class roster. List all of the students' names in alphabetical order on the blanks provided, last names first. Check off each name as you write it. The list has been started for you.

boys

Paul Hawkes

Austin Whitted

Thomas Brown

Josh Whitman

Timothy Brown

James Green

Bryan Billings

Scott Black

Kyle Simon

Jonathan Groth

Daniel Young

Steven Black

girls

Kelsie Mitchell

Jill Green

Lisa Grove

Tiffany Brown

Melinda Briggs

Sally Black

Cassie Hartman

Amber White

√ Jennifer Adams

Stephanie Black

Becka White

Sylvia Tyson

Jessica Green

Caitlin White

Mr. Jones's Class

1. *Adams, Jennifer*
2. _____
3. _____
4. _____
5. _____
6. _____
7. _____
8. _____
9. _____
10. _____
11. _____
12. _____
13. _____
14. _____
15. _____
16. _____
17. _____
18. _____
19. _____
20. _____
21. _____
22. _____
23. _____
24. _____
25. _____
26. _____

Bonus Box: Alphabetize *cycle, hors d'oeuvre, gym, school, tsunami, wrangle, gnash, phrase, gist,* and *gab* by the way they are pronounced—not by their spellings. Hint: *Phrase* (frāz) is first.

Clock Calculations

Got some spare *time* on your hands? Then celebrate National Clock Month (September) with these clock calculations!

You know that if it's now one o'clock, in three hours it will be four o'clock. As a number sentence, you write this:

$$1 + 3 = 4$$

Simple, right? But suppose it's 11 o'clock. In three hours it will be two o'clock. So the number sentence is written this way:

$$11 + 3 = 2$$

Interesting, huh? When you solve clock math problems, it's helpful to look at a real clock and think about how the hands move on the clock face.

Use the clocks below to help you add:

 1. 3 + 7 = _____   2. 12 + 4 = _____   3. 10 + 6 = _____   4. 5 + 8 = _____

Now that you have the hang of it, try these:

5. 2 + 9 = _____   6. 12 + 6 = _____   7. 7 + 7 = _____   8. 8 + 8 = _____

9. 10 + 8 = _____   10. 12 + 12 = _____   11. 3 + 13 = _____   12. 9 + 14 = _____

Ready to subtract? For 4 – 5, think this way: It's four o'clock now. What time was it five hours ago? Answer: 11.

13. 5 – 5 = _____   14. 3 – 6 = _____   15. 10 – 12 = _____   16. 9 – 4 = _____

17. 2 – 7 = _____   18. 1 – 6 = _____   19. 12 – 12 = _____   20. 1 – 14 = _____

21. Did you notice some interesting patterns in clock math? What number on a clock acts like a zero in regular addition and subtraction? _____

Bonus Box: To avoid the confusion between morning and evening hours, some clock faces are divided into 24 hours. Suppose a 24-hour clock chimed once the first hour, twice the second hour, and so on until it chimed 24 times the 24th hour. How many chimes in all would you hear during 24 hours?

Celebrate the Season

Fall

7r2 = 8 cubes
3)23
-21
 2

Look at All That Sugar!

Open students' eyes to just how much sugar is in their favorite candy bars with this fun-to-do **math and writing** activity. Obtain two boxes of sugar cubes. Also, ask each student to bring in the nutrition label from his favorite candy bar. Give each child crayons or markers, glue, and a 12" x 18" sheet of white drawing paper. Then have him follow these steps:

1. On the drawing paper, illustrate your own version of a funny monster.
2. Predict the grams of sugar in your candy bar. Then check your prediction against the sugar content on your candy bar's nutrition label.
3. Glue the nutrition label to your monster's hand.
4. On your drawing, divide the sugar grams listed on the nutrition label by three (the approximate number of grams in a sugar cube). Round your answer to the nearest whole number. Then glue that number of sugar cubes to your monster's belly.
5. Write a paragraph explaining what you learned and attach it to your paper.

Arrange students' papers in a display titled "Look at All That Sugar!"
Linda Hess—Gr. 4, Green-Fields School, Woodbury, NJ

Superbly Descriptive Pumpkins

Stretch students' vocabularies with this seasonally superb **vocabulary-building** activity. Ask students to bring in pumpkins of any size or shape. (Provide extras for students who forget or are unable to bring them.) Next, type a double-spaced list of adjectives, such as the one shown. Cut the words on the list apart, fold the strips in half, and place them in a trick-or-treat pail. Divide students into groups of four; then have each child choose a pumpkin and draw an adjective from the pail. Direct the student not to share her word with anyone outside her group and to look it up in a dictionary to get a clear understanding of its meaning. Then have her use acrylic paints and other art materials along with her group members' suggestions to decorate the pumpkin in a way that suggests her adjective. Conclude by having the groups take turns guessing the adjective that each pumpkin represents. Extend the activity by having students classify the adjectives into categories, such as those that describe attitudes and those that describe behaviors. *Carol Thompson—Gr. 5, Aragon, GA*

lovesick

lovesick	sarcastic	awestruck	deceitful
taciturn	conceited	petrified	boorish
horrified	intellectual	glamorous	humble
boisterous	sickly	timid	amiable
sheepish	despicable	eccentric	avaricious
flamboyant	rancorous	livid	dazzling
ecstatic	gaudy	incredulous	morose

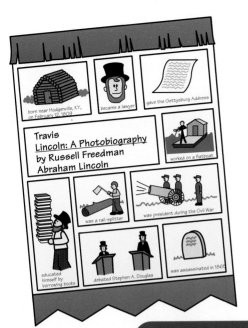

Biography Banners

This eye-catching **book report project** is perfect for sharing biographies! Have each student draw ten squares and rectangles on a 12" x 18" sheet of white drawing paper. In one shape, have him write his name and the title, author, and subject of his biography. In each of the nine remaining boxes, have the student use words and pictures to provide some of the following information about his book's person: talents, accomplishments, hobbies, failures, challenges, family, life span, residence, and other interesting facts. For a finishing touch, have the student add colorful construction paper fringe to the top and bottom of the banner. Showcase the finished projects in a display titled "Beautiful Biography Banners." *Julia Alarie—Gr. 6, Essex Middle School, Essex, VT*

Thanksgiving

Perky Turkey Centerpiece

Make perky turkeys the center of attention on your students' Thanksgiving Day tables with this creative **art and writing** project! *Carla Walker—Gr. 5, Monte Vista Elementary, La Crescenta, CA*

Materials for each student: 12" x 18" sheet of construction paper, six 9" x 12" sheets of construction paper (2 sheets each of a different color), 2" x 12" strip of red construction paper, 1" square of yellow construction paper, ruler, scissors, glue, stapler, black marker

Steps:

1. Starting on the 9-inch side, accordion-fold three 9" x 12" sheets (one of each color). Staple the folds of each fan together at one end. Glue the fans together at the edges to form one large fan (the tail feather).
2. Cut one 9" x 12" sheet in half lengthwise so that it measures $4^1/2$" x 12". Glue together the short edges of one half sheet to make a cylinder (the turkey's body).
3. Cut the remaining $4^1/2$" x 12" piece in half to make two $4^1/2$" x 6" pieces. Starting on the $4^1/2$-inch side, accordion-fold and staple each piece as in Step 1 to make two small fans (feathers).
4. Cut the two remaining 9" x 12" sheets of paper in half to make four 6" x 9" pieces. Starting on the 6-inch side, accordion-fold and staple each piece as in Step 1 to make four medium-sized fans (feathers).
5. Starting at one end, roll up about five inches of the 2" x 12" red strip and glue it to the remaining portion to form the turkey's head. Tuck and glue the remaining part of the strip under the rolled portion to form the turkey's wattle.
6. Make the turkey's beak by folding the yellow square in half to make two triangles. Glue the beak to the head. Draw two eyes. Then glue the head and wattle to the body.
7. Glue the body to the center of the 12" x 18" sheet of paper. Glue the left and right edges of the tail feather to the base behind the body. Glue one edge of each of the smallest feathers to the inside edge of both sides of the body and base. Glue a medium-sized feather behind each small feather in the same way. Glue the two remaining medium-sized feathers to the base behind the tail feather.
8. Write a Thanksgiving poem on the base.

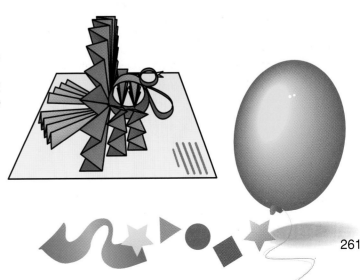

Season your October and November lesson plans with these top-notch writing prompts!

October Topics

- October is Computer Learning Month. What new thing would you like to learn to do with a computer? Why?
- Which event gets you more fired up: being invited to a friend's sleepover or having a sleepover at your house? Explain why.
- What annoying habit do you have that you wish you could break? What could you do to stop?
- Having fun doesn't have to cost any money. Describe five fall activities you could do with your family this weekend that would not cost any money.
- Lots of people like to read mysteries. Why do you think they're so popular?
- If Christopher Columbus were to visit the shores of the New World today, what four things do you think would surprise him most? Explain your answers.
- What type of shoes do you prefer to wear: sandals or sneakers? Why?
- How would you describe an ice-cream sundae to a martian?
- If a day were suddenly 12 hours long instead of 24, how would this affect you?
- If a scarecrow could suddenly talk, what might be the first three things it says?
- *Halloween* spelled backward is *neewollah.* What two things would create a crisis in your school if they were accidentally done backward? Explain.
- Would you rather buy a Halloween costume or make your own? Why?

November Topics

- If you were to suddenly become weightless, what would you want to do first? Why?
- How might school be different if there were no books, papers, or pencils?
- Explain what you think poet Ralph Waldo Emerson meant when he wrote, "The only way to have a friend is to be one."
- Do you think it's easier to write a report or make a speech? Explain.
- Would a turkey make a good pet? Why or why not?
- Which would you rather do: fish for an answer or a compliment? Explain.
- Suppose an aunt you don't see often visits your home and constantly calls you by your cousin's name instead of your own. Explain what you would do.
- What would you do if you started to pay for a new CD and realized you didn't have your wallet? Explain.
- What would be the advantages of going to school an hour longer each day? The disadvantages?
- "A book is a friend," according to an American proverb. Do you agree or disagree? Why?
- Describe a menu that a turkey might like to gobble up on Thanksgiving Day.
- Think of your two favorite book characters. How are they alike? Different?

The reproducibles on pages 263-265 were written by Ann Fisher, Mill Hall, PA.

Autumn Imagery

Autumn—what a beautiful time of the year! Colorful leaves and cooler temperatures signal the end of summer and hint at the winter ahead.

A *diamanté* (dē ə män tā) is a rhinestone, an imitation gem that looks like a real diamond. A *diamante* is a special type of poem. See if you can write diamantes about autumn that sparkle like diamonds! Read the two examples below; then follow the instructions.

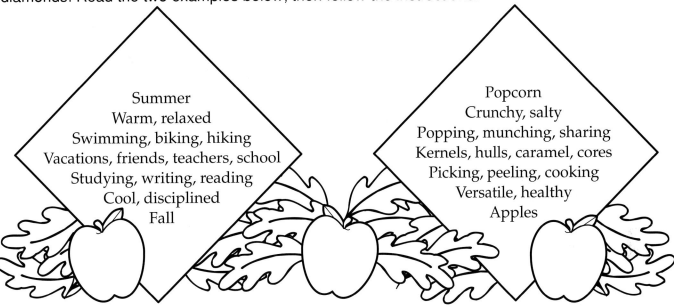

Summer
Warm, relaxed
Swimming, biking, hiking
Vacations, friends, teachers, school
Studying, writing, reading
Cool, disciplined
Fall

Popcorn
Crunchy, salty
Popping, munching, sharing
Kernels, hulls, caramel, cores
Picking, peeling, cooking
Versatile, healthy
Apples

Notice that each diamante has two different nouns—one that begins the poem and one that ends it. The first example is about two different seasons. The writer uses words to describe summer that are nearly opposite those used to describe fall. In the second example, the nouns are two fall foods.

Directions: Study this form for writing a diamante.

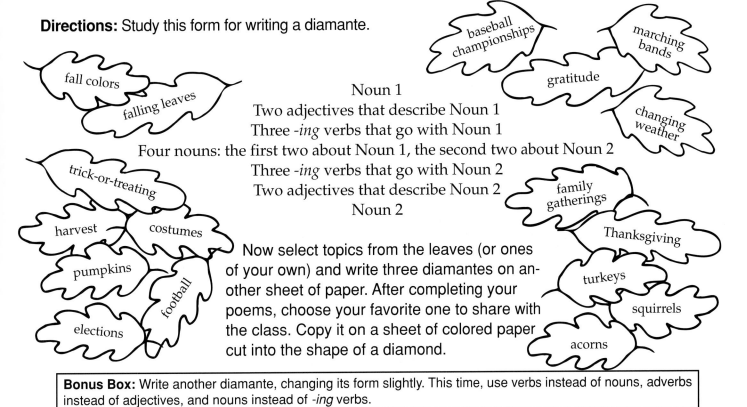

Noun 1
Two adjectives that describe Noun 1
Three *-ing* verbs that go with Noun 1
Four nouns: the first two about Noun 1, the second two about Noun 2
Three *-ing* verbs that go with Noun 2
Two adjectives that describe Noun 2
Noun 2

fall colors
falling leaves
baseball championships
gratitude
marching bands
changing weather

trick-or-treating
harvest
costumes
pumpkins
football
elections
family gatherings
Thanksgiving
turkeys
squirrels
acorns

Now select topics from the leaves (or ones of your own) and write three diamantes on another sheet of paper. After completing your poems, choose your favorite one to share with the class. Copy it on a sheet of colored paper cut into the shape of a diamond.

Bonus Box: Write another diamante, changing its form slightly. This time, use verbs instead of nouns, adverbs instead of adjectives, and nouns instead of *-ing* verbs.

Peter's Pumpkin Patch

Peter has just picked the 12 plumpest, most-prized pumpkins in his entire pumpkin patch! He has decided to make them into jack-o'-lanterns for a dazzling Halloween display. Help him decorate the pumpkins. Draw features on the 12 pumpkins so that

- $\frac{1}{2}$ of the pumpkins have stems
- $\frac{1}{12}$ don't have noses
- $\frac{3}{4}$ are smiling
- $\frac{1}{6}$ have ears
- $\frac{5}{6}$ have hair
- $\frac{1}{4}$ have square eyes
- $\frac{1}{6}$ have eyebrows
- $\frac{1}{3}$ have triangular eyes
- $\frac{1}{4}$ have square noses
- $\frac{2}{3}$ have round noses
- $\frac{1}{4}$ are frowning
- $\frac{5}{12}$ have round eyes

Bonus Box: If Peter picked 48 pumpkins and used the same fractions above in decorating them, how many pumpkins would be frowning? Have round eyes? Have hair? Have triangular eyes?

Time to Be Thankful

Thanksgiving is a special time, a time to remember all of the people and things in your life for which you're thankful. On the photos in the cornucopia, draw some of those things and people.

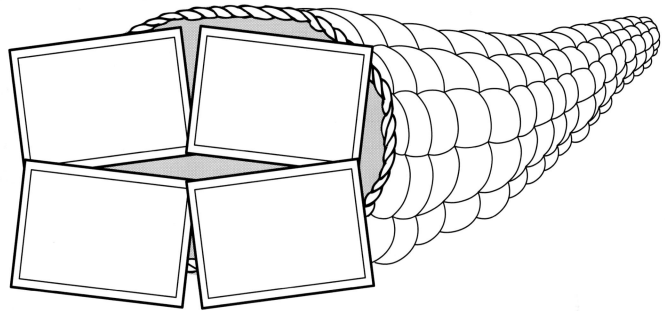

Now complete the puzzle below. Follow each step in the directions very carefully. Then write the new result in the blank. When you're finished, you'll discover a phrase that describes something we all do at Thanksgiving!

1. Begin with THANKSGIVING. _____THANKSGIVING_____

2. Remove all the vowels. _____THNKSGVNG_____

3. Add the word *COB* between the second and third letters from the left. _____

4. Remove the third and sixth letters from the right. _____

5. Switch the fourth and fifth consonants from the left. _____

6. Add the word *LESS* between the fourth and fifth letters from the right. _____

7. Move the fourth letter from the right so that it is the first letter from the right. _____

8. Add the word *BUY* after the fourth consonant from the left. _____

9. Remove the sixth letter from the left. _____

10. Add the word *OUR* after the letter *Y.* _____

11. Remove the second letter from the left. _____

12. Change the fourth letter from the right to an *I.* _____

13. Move the first letter on the left so that it becomes the fifth letter. _____

14. Switch the second consonant and the second vowel from the left. _____

15. Add spaces after the fifth and ninth letters. _____

Bonus Box: How many words of four or more letters can you make from the letters in *Thanksgiving?* Don't include *thanks, giving,* or any plurals.

Celebrate the Season

December

Yogurt-Lid Ornaments

Put students' **measurement and art** skills to work creating eye-catching Christmas tree decorations! *Arminda Feldkamp—Gr. 5, Seneca Grade School, Seneca, KS*

Materials for each student: old Christmas card or piece of wrapping paper, $3\frac{1}{8}$" plastic yogurt lid, scissors, glue, ruler, 10' length of crochet thread, 14" length of crochet thread, access to a hole puncher

Steps:
1. Trim away the outer edge of the plastic yogurt lid to make a three-inch circle. Then make half-centimeter cuts around the circle's outer edges.
2. Cut a $2\frac{1}{2}$-inch circle from the front of the Christmas card or the wrapping paper. Glue the cutout to the uncut part of the plastic circle.
3. Knot one end of the ten-foot length of crochet thread. Slide the knot between the edges of any cut on the plastic circle so it is on the circle's back side.
4. Wrap the thread across, down, and up between the edges of every seventh slit until there is no more string, creating a woven pattern around the illustration as shown. When finished, tuck the end of the thread under the threads on the back.
5. Punch a hole in the lid as shown.
6. Double the 14-inch length of thread and push one end through the hole in the lid. Knot the two ends together to form a loop for hanging.

"Tree-rrific" Book Reports

Assign students a December **book-report project** that decorates the classroom and puts everyone in a holiday spirit! Have each student read a holiday novel (or read one aloud to your class). When he has finished reading his book, give the student a sheet of green poster board on which you've traced a Christmas tree pattern. Have the student cut out the shape, take it home, and decorate it as creatively as possible, adding real lights, ornaments, or Christmas scents if desired. Require each tree to have five student-made ornaments, each displaying a different scene from the book, and a tree topper that includes the book's author and title. Also have the student attach a written book summary to the back of his tree. After students share their projects with the class, post the festive projects on your classroom walls. As an alternative to a Christmas tree, have students decorate poster board wreaths with cutouts that depict the book scenes. *Wendy Patterson—Gr. 5, Pigeon Forge Middle School, Pigeon Forge, TN*

The Girls' Revenge by Phyllis Reynolds Naylor

December Project Guidelines

Mmmm...Math!

Combine **geometry and measurement** for a holiday math activity students will love! After gathering the materials listed below, arrange students in groups of four or five. Distribute the materials. Then guide students through the steps shown to create colorful cone trees that make yummy gifts! *Marty Brink—Gr. 5, Wateree Elementary, Lugoff, SC*

Materials for each group: can of white commercial frosting, 14-oz. bag of M&M's candies, jar of green sugar sprinkles

Materials for each student: sugar cone, round cookie (larger than cone's diameter), plastic spoon, twist tie, 18" piece of plastic wrap, metric ruler, copy of page 270, calculator (optional)

Steps:

1. Complete Part I of page 270 as directed.
2. Use the spoon to frost the top and sides of the cookie. Then place the cookie in the center of the plastic wrap.
3. Turn the cone upside down and place its base on top of the cookie as shown. Frost the cone. Then complete Part II of page 270 as directed.
4. Decorate the cone with M&M's. Then add green sprinkles.
5. Pull the corners of the plastic wrap up and gather them above the cone's point. Use the twist tie to hold the wrap in place.

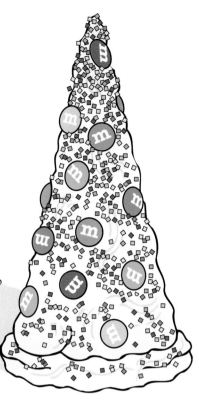

Spotlight on Human Rights

Observe Human Rights Day (December 10) with a **reading and summarizing** activity that sends students on a search for human rights violations. Share with students that the Universal Declaration of Human Rights, which was adopted on December 10, 1948, states that all people everywhere are entitled to basic human rights. Help students brainstorm a list of basic rights and freedoms that they feel all people deserve. Then divide students into small groups. Give each group a section of the newspaper, directing group members to search the section for an example of a human rights violation. Conclude by having the group write a paragraph that summarizes the situation and includes a suggestion for how it could be rectified.

Holiday Book Drive

Encourage students to think of others during the December holidays by having them participate in a worthy **book-collecting project.** Ask local florists, parents, and staff members to donate baskets that students can decorate with seasonal designs. Invite students in your class (or the entire school) to bring in used books for the drive. Also have your class make a supply of attractive bookmarks. Fill the decorated baskets with bookmarks and assorted books on a variety of topics and reading levels. Then distribute the baskets to needy families in your community as Christmas gifts. *Patricia E. Dancho— Gr. 6 Language Arts, Apollo-Ridge Middle School, Spring Church, PA*

Snazzy Snowmen

Invite friendly snowmen to invade your classroom with this cool **art and poetry-writing** activity! *Anita Miller—Gr. 5, Meadows Elementary, Topeka, KS*

Materials for each student: 6 squares of white paper (two 4" squares, two 6" squares, and two 8" squares), two 5" squares of black paper, 36" length of black yarn, colorful paper scraps, scissors, glue

Steps:

1. Cut two matching circles from each pair of white squares.
2. Cut two matching hats from the black squares.
3. Tie a six-inch loop at one end of the yarn.
4. Glue the snowman pieces back-to-back below the loop so that the yarn is sandwiched between the pieces. Leave a small amount of space between each body part as shown.
5. Use the paper scraps to decorate the snowman in a way that illustrates your favorite hobby, interest, sport, or book character.
6. Write a related poem on the largest body part.
7. Hang the snowman from the ceiling.

Skiing

Now I love to ski on snow-covered slopes.

Before, I was just too chicken!

But learning to do the snowplow

Has made me lots less panic-stricken!

by Annie

A Grand Ol' Flag

Celebrate Betsy Ross's birthday (January 1) with this **creative-thinking** activity. Share with students that, according to legend, Betsy Ross created our country's first stars-and-stripes flag. Explain the meaning of Old Glory's colors and design *(red for hardiness and courage; white for purity and innocence; blue for vigilance, perseverance, and justice; the stripes for the 13 original colonies; the stars for the 50 states)*. Next, have each student design on white paper a flag that represents his family, a team to which he belongs, or the class. Provide time for each student to explain the meanings of his flag's symbols and colors. For related activities on citizenship, check out the special unit on pages 128–132.

If He Were Alive Today...

Observe Martin Luther King Jr.'s birthday this year with an activity that develops **critical-thinking and research** skills. Share with students that Dr. King was a black civil rights leader who promoted nonviolent ways of achieving equal rights. Then have students consider what life would be like if Dr. King were still alive today by completing copies of page 273. Extend the activity by having student groups create timelines from 1968 to the present. On the timelines, have students include three to five events that Dr. King might have been a part of had he lived during that time period.

Seasonal Journal Prompts

Perk up your December and January lesson plans with **writing prompts** that are guaranteed to get kids' pencils moving!

December Topics

- December is National Stress-Free Family Holidays Month. Suggest five things your family could do to make this year's holidays more enjoyable and less hectic.

- December 3 is the anniversary of the world's first successful heart transplant. Do you think more people should be organ donors? Why or why not?

- The game of bingo has been around since 1929. Why do you think it's so popular?

- If you could design a new cookie cutter for the December baking season, what shape would it be and why?

- Suppose someone gave you a real gingerbread house. Describe what you might see, taste, touch, and smell in the house.

- Is it necessary to give a gift to every person who gives you a gift? Why or why not?

- What toys do you think are unsafe? Explain why you feel they are dangerous.

- If you could update the design of Santa's sleigh, what would you change? What new features would it have? Explain.

- Suppose that verses inside greeting cards could only be written in recipe form. Write the recipe you'd want inside your family's holiday card this year.

- The poinsettia is a favorite holiday plant. If there were no poinsettias, which plant would you choose to take its place during this season? Why?

January Topics

- Which New Year's resolution would you be more likely to keep: saving part of your weekly allowance or reading at least one book each month? Explain.

- Pretend that a state zoo is having a contest to name its newest polar bear cub. What name would you suggest and why?

- Which would you prefer to do with friends: sled down a snow-packed hill or ice-skate at a new rink? Why?

- Some people start feeling a bit blue during January. Why do you think that is so?

- Suppose that an ice storm caused your family to be without electricity for an entire weekend. How could you entertain a younger brother and sister during this time?

- Dr. Martin Luther King Jr. dreamed of equal rights and worked peacefully to achieve them. Why is it important for people to have dreams for the future?

- Would it be easier for you to admit a mistake to your parent or your best friend? Why?

- In what ways are playing sports and doing homework alike?

- How is laughter like good medicine?

The reproducibles on pages 270-273 were written by Ann Fisher, Mill Hall, PA.

Mmmm...Math!
Discover how yummy math can be by completing the tasks below!

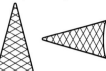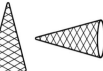

Part I

1. What is the name of the space figure each student has been given? _____

2. What is the diameter of the space figure's base in centimeters and millimeters?

   _____ cm   _____ mm

3. Define *radius*. _____

   _____

   What is the relationship between a radius and a diameter? _____

   _____

4. What is the radius of the space figure's base in centimeters and millimeters?

   _____ cm   _____ mm

5. Use the formula C = πd to find the circumference of the space figure's base in centimeters and millimeters.

   _____ cm   _____ mm

6. What is the length of the entire space figure (from base to vertex) in centimeters and millimeters?

   _____ cm   _____ mm

Part II

7. About how many centimeters is the diameter of a piece of M&M's candy? _____ cm
   Based on this approximate diameter, how many M&M's placed side by side would make a row equal in length to your answer to question 6? _____ M&M's

8. If 12 M&M's contain 3.5 grams of fat, how many grams of fat would be in 36 M&M's?
   _____ grams

9. If a package of plastic wrap contains 100 feet and 18 inches of wrap is needed to wrap a cone tree, about how many cone trees could you wrap? _____ trees

10. Using the prices listed below, calculate the total cost for a class of 30 students to make cone trees.

    Materials for a class of 30 students
    6 tubs of frosting @ $1.39 each   _____
    6 packages M&M's @ $2.29 each   _____
    6 jars of sugar sprinkles @ $1.29 each   _____
    4 boxes of sugar cones @ $1.49 each   _____
    3 boxes of plastic spoons @ $0.79 each _____
                                   Total   _____

The 12 Days of Math

Sing a round or so of "The 12 Days of Christmas" as you work these musical math problems! Show your work on another sheet of paper and then write your answers in the blanks provided. All of the gifts in the song are listed to help you. One more thing: You don't have 12 days to do these problems!

- a partridge in a pear tree
- 2 turtledoves
- 3 French hens
- 4 calling birds
- 5 gold rings
- 6 geese a-laying
- 7 swans a-swimming
- 8 maids a-milking
- 9 ladies dancing
- 10 lords a-leaping
- 11 pipers piping
- 12 drummers drumming

 1. There were 80 pears on the pear tree. One day the partridge became very excited about Christmas and knocked off $\frac{1}{2}$ of the pears. The next day he knocked off $\frac{1}{2}$ of the remaining pears. How many pears were left on the tree? _____

 2. The turtledoves were annoyed by all the leaping and drumming, so they decided to peck on the heads of the lords and drummers! How many heads must each dove peck? _____

 3. Suppose that all of the birds in the song are in your backyard. If you're blindfolded and select 1 bird, what are the chances that it will be a partridge? _____

 4. Each calling bird called 3 more calling birds to join the group. How many calling birds are there now? _____

 5. Each gold ring is worth $245.00. Each ring also includes a diamond worth $1,200.00. What is the total value of the 5 rings? _____

 6. The dancing ladies plan to share equally any eggs laid by the geese. Suppose each goose lays 1 egg a day for 30 days. How many eggs will each lady receive? _____

 7. How many more people than animals are included in the song? _____

 8. If each maid milked 3 cows a day, how many cows would the group milk in a week? _____

 9. The dancing ladies danced from 5:00 P.M. until 7:30 P.M. and then from 8:30 P.M. until midnight. How many hours in all did they dance? _____

 10. The dancing ladies and the leaping lords went to a fancy ball in fancy carriages. Each carriage holds 3 people. How many carriages were needed? _____

 11. If all the lords, pipers, and drummers are men, then how many more men than women are in the song? _____

 12. A pair of drumsticks costs $8.95 plus $0.45 tax. How much would it cost to buy each drummer a pair? _____

Bonus Box: Groups of drummers want to take groups of maids to a dance. What is the fewest number of groups of each that is needed so that everyone has a partner?

The Miracle of Hanukkah

At Hanukkah, Jewish people celebrate a miracle that took place over 2,000 years ago. They recaptured their temple and the city of Jerusalem from the Syrians. The temple was reconsecrated in a celebration that lasted eight days. The people relit the Eternal Light, finding only enough oil to last one day. Miraculously, the oil lasted for eight days! Today, Jewish people remember this great miracle and their ancestors' fight for religious freedom.

Directions: Think about eight miracles that you would like to see happen. Write a sentence about each one on a menorah candle. On the large center candle, draw a picture of a special event in your life that gives you hope for the future. On an index card, write a diary entry describing this event. Write about what you saw, heard, smelled, tasted, and felt. Tell why this day is so special.

Note to the teacher: Provide each student with a colorful 9" x 12" sheet of construction paper, an index card, scissors, and glue. Have each student cut out his menorah and glue it to the construction paper. Then have the student cut around the menorah, leaving a colorful border around it. Have each student attach his card to the bottom of his menorah.

What If...?

1. If Dr. King were alive today, what three main problems in our society do you think he would be trying to solve?

2. If he were alive today, do you think Dr. King would be holding a political office? If so, which one? If not, why not?

3. Which groups of people would Dr. King most likely be helping with equal rights today?

4. In his lifetime, Dr. King received many honorary university degrees. He was also chosen as *Time* magazine's Man of the Year for 1963. He won the Nobel Peace Prize in 1964. Dr. King was a minister, a speaker, and a respected civil rights leader. If he were teaching in a university today, what subjects do you think he might be teaching? Why?

5. If Dr. King were alive today, he would be happy with the progress made in some civil rights areas. Finish this paragraph starter, spoken by Dr. King: "I am so glad that..."

6. If Martin Luther King Jr. were alive today, do you think we would be celebrating his birthday this year? Why or why not?

Bonus Box: Dr. King gave his famous "I Have a Dream" speech in Washington, DC, in 1963. If he gave a speech today with the same title, what would it include? Write the opening paragraph of the speech.

I have a dream.

What if Martin Luther King Jr. were alive today? You probably know lots about Dr. King. He was a black civil rights leader who was born in 1929 and died in 1968. He was only 39 years old when he died. His birthday is celebrated each year as a tribute to his ideas on equal rights and nonviolence.

A lot has changed since the days of King's peaceful protests, but the world still needs equality and peace. Think about how Martin Luther King Jr. might affect our society if he were alive today. Read the questions on the right. Choose three to answer in short paragraphs. Write your paragraphs on another sheet of paper.

Celebrate the Season

Holiday and Seasonal Activities for the Classroom

February

Heart-to-Heart Talks

What would Derek Jeter and Babe Ruth say to each other if they could meet? Or Sojourner Truth and John F. Kennedy? Have students use their **research and dialogue-writing** skills to create such heart-to-heart conversations between famous folks! First, cut hearts of various shapes and sizes from colorful construction paper. Divide each heart in half by making a different puzzle cut. Then label each half with the name of a different famous person from history or the present, or with a literary character's name. Place the labeled halves in a bag and have each student draw one. Next, have each child find the classmate holding the matching half of his heart. Direct students with matching halves to research their two personalities and then write a conversation that could occur between the two. Display students' work, along with their heart halves, on a bulletin board titled "Heart-to-Heart Talks."
Kimberly A. Minafo, Pomona, NY

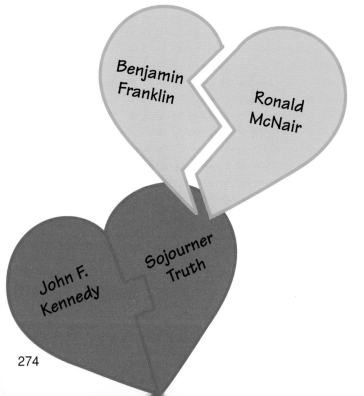

Category Match-o

Familiarize students with famous Black Americans and the areas in which their achievements were made with a fun-to-play **categorizing** game. Display the list of famous Black Americans shown. Discuss the names together, having students research any that are unfamiliar. Next, have each student draw a large five-by-five bingo grid on a 9" x 12" sheet of paper and label the middle space "Free." Then have students randomly program their grids with names from the list. For game markers, use peanuts in the shell in honor of George Washington Carver's work. During the game, hide the list from students' view.

Begin play by calling out any category. Have players cover the names they think fit that category. Continue calling out one category at a time until a player covers five names vertically, horizontally, or diagonally and calls out "Match-o!" Check the answers by having the player read the covered names aloud. If she is correct, reward her with a small treat. If not, continue play. After playing several rounds, invite students to munch their peanut markers!

Astronauts/Explorers • Ronald McNair • Mae Carol Jemison • Matthew Henson	**Athletes** • Jesse Owens • Jackie Robinson • Jackie Joyner-Kersee
Civil Rights Leaders • Rosa Lee Parks • Dr. Martin Luther King Jr. • W. E. B. Du Bois	**Musicians** • Louis Armstrong • Count Basie • Duke Ellington
Government Officials • Shirley Chisholm • Colin Powell • Thurgood Marshall	**Singers** • Ella Fitzgerald • Lena Horne • Nat "King" Cole
Scientists/Inventors • Benjamin Banneker • George Washington Carver • Garrett Morgan	**Educators** • Mary McLeod Bethune • Booker T. Washington • Benjamin E. Mays
Poets/Playwrights • Phillis Wheatley • Maya Angelou • Paul Laurence Dunbar	**Film/TV Personalities** • Sidney Poitier • Oprah Winfrey • James Earl Jones

Chinese New Year Story Plates

Welcome the Chinese New Year (February 12) by showcasing students' **art and narrative-writing skills.** Begin by displaying a piece (or a picture) of Blue Willow china. Explain that its drawings tell an ancient story about the daughter of a Chinese mandarin and the man she loved, who were changed by the gods into turtledoves to escape her father's wrath. (Or read aloud a picture-book version of the story, *The Willow Pattern Story* by Allan Drummond.) Next, give each child a paper plate and markers. Have the student use the markers to create a picture on the plate; then have her write a story explaining the illustration. After students share their plates and stories, display the items on a bulletin board titled "Gung Hay Fat Choy!" which means "Happy New Year!" in Chinese.

March

We're Marching Off To...

This March show students that **writing directions** is easy if they start off on the right foot! Give each student six to eight copies of a foot pattern like the one shown. Next, prompt the student to think about something she could instruct another person to do, such as brush his teeth. After the student writes a rough draft of her directions, have her write each successive step on a separate foot pattern as shown. Arrange each set of labeled patterns along a hall or bulletin board under a banner titled "What Are We Marching Off to Do?" Have students study each set of directions and guess the task being described. For more expository writing ideas, don't miss the activities on pages 46-50. *Kimberly A. Minafo, Pomona, NY*

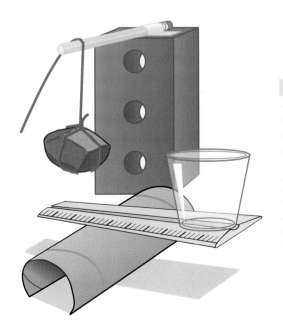

Leprechaun Traps

Invite students to use their skills in **science and descriptive writing** to capture some mischievous leprechauns! At the beginning of March, challenge each student to design and construct a device that could catch one of the wee creatures. Require that each trap include at least two different simple machines (lever, inclined plane, wedge, screw, wheel and axle, pulley). Also specify that the device be no larger than an 18" x 24" desktop and be built of easy-to-find items. After the traps have been completed, have each student write a paragraph describing how and why the trap should work. Then have him tape the paragraph to his project. Display the traps in your school's library on St. Patrick's Day. *Tiffany Giannicchi, Allegany-Limestone Central School, Allegany, NY*

275

Seasonal Journal Prompts

Looking for journal ideas for February and March? Then this splendiferous collection of **writing prompts** is just "write" for you!

February Topics

- February is National Children's Dental Health Month. What advice would you give a new dentist who is wondering about the best way to treat her younger patients?

- Suppose that the groundhog is afraid of shadows and the weather forecast is calling for a sunny Groundhog Day. What would you say to Phil to calm him down and prepare him for the big day?

- Do you think it's right for some athletes to be paid millions of dollars in salary when they only play a few months out of the year? Why or why not?

- If Cupid's arrow could send love to any particular group of people in the world today, which group would you have him aim for and why?

- What would you do if you opened a new box of chocolates and discovered that half of the candies were missing?

- Do you think that email will ever totally replace letters? Explain.

- If you spied a penny on the sidewalk, would you pick it up? Why or why not?

- Presidents' Day is celebrated on the third Monday in February. Do you think a woman will ever be elected president of the United States? Why or why not?

- What do you think the proverb "Birds of a feather flock together" means?

- Which do you prefer to take: an escalator, an elevator, or the stairs? Why?

March Topics

Can you help me with my homework?

- March can be a windy month. Describe five things you could do on a windless day that you couldn't do on a windy day.

- Which would your best friend rather do: fly a kite or make a kite? Explain.

- National Weights and Measures Week is the first week in March. If love and hate were actual objects, which would weigh more? Why?

- Which do you think would be harder for you to learn: sign language or a foreign language? Explain.

- Of all the holidays celebrated during the year, how would you rank St. Patrick's Day on a scale of 1 to 10 (with 10 being the highest rating)? Explain your rating.

- Describe an outfit you could wear to school on St. Patrick's Day that might win you the award for "Person Wearing the Most Green."

- How would you handle the problem of a classmate's calling you every night to get help with homework?

- March is International Mirth Month. How could humor make a tough subject—such as accidentally locking your parents' car keys in their car—easier to talk about?

- If you could ask first lady Laura Bush any question, what would you ask and why?

- What could you do to help a friend who's being bullied by someone at school? Explain.

The reproducibles on pages 277-279 were written by Ann Fisher, Mill Hall, PA.

An American Success Story

Madam C. J. Walker (born Sarah Breedlove) was America's first female self-made millionaire. She is the only African American woman in the United States National Business Hall of Fame. Her road to success was often difficult, but she never gave up. Complete the puzzle below to learn more about Madam Walker.

Directions: Cut apart the 15 boxes. Read the cause in the title box. Find the matching effect in another box and lay that box beside the title box so that the cause and effect are side by side. Then read the cause in the second box and find its effect in a third box. Continue until you have placed all 15 boxes side by side. When you're finished, you'll discover a word that describes Madam C. J. Walker. Look up the word's meaning and write it on the back of the last puzzle piece. Then tape the boxes together in order to make one long strip.

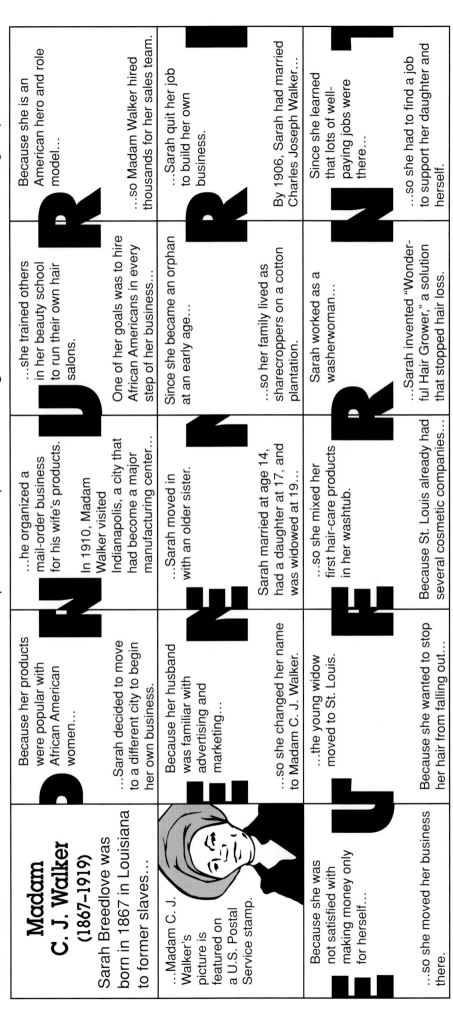

Madam C. J. Walker (1867–1919)

Sarah Breedlove was born in 1867 in Louisiana to former slaves…

...Madam C. J. Walker's picture is featured on a U.S. Postal Service stamp.

Because her products were popular with African American women…

...Sarah decided to move to a different city to begin her own business.

Because her husband was familiar with advertising and marketing…

...so she changed her name to Madam C. J. Walker.

...the young widow moved to St. Louis.

Because she wanted to stop her hair from falling out…

Because she was not satisfied with making money only for herself…

...so she moved her business there.

...she trained others in her beauty school to run their own hair salons.

...he organized a mail-order business for his wife's products.

In 1910, Madam Walker visited Indianapolis, a city that had become a major manufacturing center…

One of her goals was to hire African Americans in every step of her business…

...Sarah moved in with an older sister.

Since she became an orphan at an early age…

Sarah married at age 14, had a daughter at 17, and was widowed at 19…

...so her family lived as sharecroppers on a cotton plantation.

Sarah worked as a washerwoman…

...so she mixed her first hair-care products in her washtub.

...Sarah invented "Wonderful Hair Grower," a solution that stopped hair loss.

Because St. Louis already had several cosmetic companies…

Because she is an American hero and role model…

...so Madam Walker hired thousands for her sales team.

...Sarah quit her job to build her own business.

By 1906, Sarah had married Charles Joseph Walker…

Since she learned that lots of well-paying jobs were there…

...so she had to find a job to support her daughter and herself.

©The Education Center, Inc. • THE MAILBOX® • Intermediate • Feb/Mar 2002 • Key p. 312

Note to the teacher: Each student will need scissors and clear tape to complete this page.

Everybody Loves a Party!

Mr. Heart's students are busily preparing for their big Valentine's Day party, and everyone's pitching in! Read and solve each problem below. Write your answers on the matching hearts. Be sure to include A.M. and P.M. with each time.

1. Amy will bake cupcakes. She will begin at 3:30 P.M. and spend 15 minutes preparing the batter. If the cupcakes have to bake for 12 minutes, when will they be done?

2. Jon wants to perform a special song. He will practice 20 minutes every day beginning at 4:50 P.M. At what time will Jon finish practicing?

3. Rob will cut out paper hearts for decorations. Each one will take 4 minutes. If he begins at 11:30 A.M. and cuts out 12 hearts, when will he finish?

4. Maya and Josh will prepare fresh vegetables. They will begin at 4:10 P.M. and work for 55 minutes. When will they finish?

5. It will take Sally 13 minutes to make and then hang a streamer. She will begin at 5:15 P.M. and hang 4 streamers. When will she finish?

6. Matt offers to help Sally with 4 more streamers. (See problem 5.) Working together, the two of them can make and then hang a streamer in 8 minutes. If they begin at 7:05 P.M., when will they finish?

7. Brad will begin making valentines at 10:15 on Saturday morning. He will spend 5 minutes cutting out hearts for each card. He'll spend 6 more minutes decorating each card. If he makes 9 cards in all, when will he finish?

8. Mr. Heart left his home at 7:20 in the morning. He drove 10 minutes to a store, shopped 6 minutes for party cups, and then drove 8 minutes to school. When did he arrive at school?

9. It takes Kyle 2 minutes to blow up a heart-shaped balloon. If he starts at 11:45 A.M. and blows up 20 balloons, when will he finish?

10. Kelsie will begin decorating with balloons at 1:00 P.M. It takes her 4 minutes to hang each of 6 balloons from the ceiling. It takes her 1 minute to display each of the other 14 balloons. When will Kelsie finish?

11. A committee of students will begin welcoming guests 12 minutes before the party begins. If the party begins at 10:00 A.M., at what time should the committee be ready?

12. Cleanup after the party will take 35 minutes. If the party ends at 10:45 A.M., at what time will the cleanup be finished?

Bonus Box: Draw a clockface (without the hands) on your paper. Draw 2 straight lines across the face of the clock, dividing it into 3 sections, so that the sums of the numbers in the sections are the same.

Shamrock Shake-Up

A lucky leprechaun has visited your schoolyard, just in time for St. Patrick's Day! He left you and your classmates all these shamrocks, covered with words. What should you do with them? Look below!

Directions: Read the three words on each shamrock. Think about how you could use them together. Then complete _____ of the following activities, including number 1, on your own paper.

1. Choose a shamrock. Write an imperative sentence (command) using all three of its words. Then write an interrogative sentence (question) using the same three words.

2. Choose two shamrocks. Write a paragraph describing something lucky that you would like to happen to you. Use all six words in your paragraph.

3. Choose three shamrocks. Write a diary entry telling about the one person in the world that you'd consider yourself very lucky to meet. Use all nine words in your entry.

4. Choose two shamrocks. Design a billboard that advertises the new product "Luck-in-a-Can."

   Include clever slogans and all six of the words.

5. Choose one shamrock. Write a limerick (or another type of poem) using the shamrock's words as rhyming words.

Bonus Box: Get together with a classmate and read his or her sentences from number 1. Use the same three words that your partner used to write two sentences: a declarative sentence (statement) and an exclamatory sentence (exclamation).

©The Education Center, Inc. • *THE MAILBOX* • *Intermediate* • Feb/Mar 2002

Note to the teacher: Before making student copies of this page, fill in the blank in the directions to indicate the number of activities you want each student to complete.

Celebrate the Season

Holiday and Seasonal Activities for the Classroom

April

Recycled Words

Kick off Keep America Beautiful Month with a **vocabulary** activity that asks students to recycle words! Post a list of homographs such as the one shown. Explain to students that *homographs* are words that have the same spellings but different meanings. Also point out that homographs can represent different parts of speech (see the example). Have each student choose any ten words from the list and use each one in a sentence. Direct the student to skip one or two lines after each sentence and to underline each homograph.

Next, have each student trade papers with a classmate. Instruct each child to write a sentence on each extra line(s) that uses the homograph differently. Provide dictionaries for anyone who needs help. When a student gets her paper back, have her mark each homograph's part of speech as shown. For recycling ideas that are perfect for Keep America Beautiful Month and Earth Day, see pages 12-13.

n.
That pork <u>chop</u> looks mighty tasty!

v.
Seth had to <u>chop</u> wood for the stove.

bail	blaze	chord	file	scale
bank	boom	desert	foil	sock
bark	bore	down	lap	spell
bat	bound	duck	light	tick
bay	bow	fair	mean	tip
bit	chop	fell	reel	will

Laughing Matters

Strengthen students' **clarification-writing** skills during National Laugh Week (the first week in April) with the help of some fabulously funny photos! Direct each student to bring a funny photograph of himself to school. Have the student tape the photo to a construction paper square. Then have him caption the picture with a humorous sentence. Display the photographs on a wall or bulletin board for students to view. Then have each student vote for the photo he thinks is the funniest and write a paragraph giving at least three reasons for his choice. To vary the activity, have each student write a paragraph explaining the events that caused him to strike such a hilarious pose.

I was just trying to put my best foot forward!

May

May Day Poetry Cards

Celebrate the first day of May with a positively fragrant **poetry-writing** activity! Ask students to donate small flowering plants or stems (purchase a few extras from a local discount store). Have each student snip three blossoms and press them between sheets of newspaper for one week. While they wait, have each student use the format shown to write a poem about a springtime topic, such as gardening or baseball. After the flowers are ready, have each student complete these steps to create a lovely poetry card:

1. Paint one side of a sheet of watercolor paper. Let it dry.
2. Fold the watercolor paper in half. Cut an oval shape from its front.
3. Use Aleene's Tacky Glue to glue your pressed flowers onto an unlined index card.
4. Cut a piece of transparency film the same size as the index card. Place it over the flowers and glue it to the card at the corners.
5. Glue the flowers behind the oval cutout. Then copy your poem inside the card.

Marti Bierdeman—Gr. 5, Bolin Elementary, East Peoria, IL

I see...
I hear...
I feel...
I smell..., and
I taste...

Butterfly Symmetry

Bring new meaning to the concept of **symmetry** with the help of a bevy of beautiful butterflies! Have each student fold a 12" x 18" sheet of drawing paper in half and unfold it onto a newspaper-covered workspace. Direct the student to dribble black paint on one side of her paper up to the fold. Then have her refold the paper, press the two sides together, and open the paper so the paint can dry. Point out the symmetry of the paper's halves. Then have the student refold her paper and cut half of a butterfly shape along the fold. Finally, have her open her cutout and use colorful markers to decorate the wings, being careful to maintain their symmetry. Tape the completed butterflies to a window for a dazzling display. *Julia Alarie—Gr. 6, Essex Middle School, Essex, VT*

Ladybug Stationery

What could possibly make students buggy 'bout **writing letters?** Ladybug stationery they've designed themselves! Give each student a hole puncher, a white sheet of lined paper, a sheet of red construction paper, glue, and a black pen. Have the student punch holes in his red paper. Then have him glue the punched-out dots around the perimeter of his lined paper, spacing them evenly apart. When the glue is dry, have the student use the pen to turn each red dot into a ladybug as shown. Finally, have him pen a letter to his mom (or another older female friend) on his stationery. If desired, let the student decorate an envelope for mailing his Mother's Day note! *Valerie Frey, Lakeview Baptist School, Six Lakes, MI*

281

Spring right into April and May with these kid-pleasing **writing prompts!**

April Topics

- Which do you prefer: rainy days or Mondays? Why?

- If you were the governor of a state that bordered an ocean, what would you do to protect the ocean from pollution?

- Which are you more like: an ice-cream sundae or a single scoop of vanilla? Explain.

- If you had to choose a coin for our government to stop making, which one would you choose and why?

- In honor of Keep America Beautiful Month, your principal has removed all wastebaskets and announced that no paper can be thrown away for an entire week. Explain what you'll do with your used paper.

- Suppose your grandmother has never used a computer. How would you persuade her to buy a computer for her home?

- In your opinion, what is the most important letter of the alphabet? Explain.

- Which is more useful to you: a wall clock or a watch? Why?

- What age do you most look forward to being? Why?

- If your toes could talk to one another inside your shoe, what would each one say to the other?

May Topics

- If you could be photographed with a famous person (living or dead), who would you want to be photographed with? Why?

- Which of the senses would it be hardest for you to be without: sight, hearing, smell, touch, or taste? Why?

- If you could host your own talk show, which three people would you invite to be your first guests? Why?

- National Pet Week is in May. Which would make a better pet: an elephant or a gorilla? Explain.

- How do you think a mother cat or dog would like to spend Mother's Day? Explain.

- If you caught your younger brother or sister spying on you or reading your diary, how would you react? Explain.

- How would you explain to a three-year-old the difference between a flashlight and a candle?

- The first surviving *quintuplets* (five children born at a single birth) were born in May of 1934. How would your life be different if you had four siblings the same age as you? Explain.

- If you could change your birthday to another month, date, and/or year, would you? Why or why not?

- Memorial Day is observed each year on the last Monday in May to remember those in the military who have died. Should we have "sad" holidays such as Memorial Day? Why or why not?

The reproducibles on pages 283-285 were written by Ann Fisher, Mill Hall, PA.

No Joking!

Celebrate National Humor Month in April by completing some hilarious jokes! The jokes below are not very funny right now because some words are missing. Use context clues to choose the word(s) in the lists to complete each joke. Check off each word as you use it. You'll have two words left over.

Remember that the jokes will make sense and be funny only if you match the right words to the right blanks.

1. Why was Cinderella thrown off the baseball _____?
   Answer: Because she ran away from the _____.
2. Why did the _____ take a bath?
   Answer: So he could make a _____ getaway.
3. What's green and _____ a foot every three seconds?
   Answer: A frog with _____.
4. What lies at the bottom of the _____ and shivers?
   Answer: A _____ wreck.
5. Why wasn't the _____ afraid of the shark?
   Answer: It was a man-eating shark.
6. Which _____ has the most _____?
   Answer: Moo-souri.
7. Why did the _____ argue all the time?
   Answer: They couldn't _____ eye to eye on anything.
8. How does a _____ get to the _____?
   Answer: In a hambulance.
9. What do you get if you cross a parakeet and a _____?
   Answer: Shredded _____.
10. What do you call an owl with a sore _____?
    Answer: A bird that doesn't give a _____.
11. What does an eagle _____ with?
    Answer: A _____-point pen.
12. Why do kangaroo moms hate _____ days?
    Answer: Because the kids have to play _____.
13. Where should a 500-pound alien go?
    Answer: On a _____.
14. What happens if you tell a joke to a _____?
    Answer: It _____ up.
15. What's _____ and white and red all over?
    Answer: A _____ penguin.

hospital
hiccups
planes
mirror
write
team
jumps
throat
diet
blushing
ball
potatoes
ocean
walks
inside

black
robber
cows
tweet
rainy
cracks
pig
clean
bald
nervous
hoot
see
girl
lawn mower
state

Bonus Box: Some jokes are funny because they include *homophones*—words that sound the same but have different meanings and spellings. For example: How do you paint a rabbit? With *hare* spray! On the back of this page, write and illustrate a joke that includes a homophone.

Problem solving, estimating

Ernie's Earth Day

Ernie is trying to do his part to help the environment on Earth Day. He plans to collect recyclables from his neighbors. Then he will take the items to the recycling center. Study the map and its key. Then answer the following questions.

1. If Ernie collects all the empty milk jugs, how many will he have in all? _____

2. How many more newspapers than magazines are there to be collected? _____

3. All together, how many cardboard boxes and glass bottles can Ernie pick up? _____

4. Suppose Ernie collects all the glass bottles. If the recycling center pays him $0.02 for each bottle, how much will he earn? _____

5. One route from Ernie's house to the recycling center passes exactly 5 houses with about 300 total recyclables. Draw this route on the map without retracing any part of it. Then list in the blanks the items that Ernie could pick up. The first one is done for you.

50 MJ + _____ + _____ + _____ + _____ = _____

6. Another route from Ernie's house to the recycling center passes exactly 7 houses with about 850 total recyclables. Draw this route on the map without retracing any part of it. List in the blanks the items that Ernie could pick up. The first one is done for you.

125 AC + _____ + _____ + _____ + _____ + _____ + _____ = _____

7. Ernie's little sister, Erin, wants to help. She will use her wagon, which can hold about 175 items. Using a red marker, draw a route for Erin to take so that she stops at every house on her route to the center without picking up more items than her wagon can hold. List the items and the total that Erin can pick up.

_____ + _____ + _____ = _____

8. Ernie has time to make only 4 stops. Find a route that allows him to collect the most items. He may pass some houses without stopping, but he can't retrace any of his route. Using a blue marker, draw this route on the map. List the items in the blanks.

_____ + _____ + _____ + _____ = _____

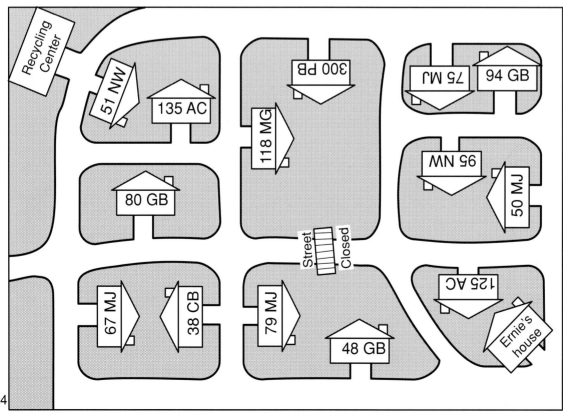

Key

AC = aluminum cans   GB = glass bottles   NW = newspapers
CB = cardboard boxes   MG = magazines   PB = plastic bags
   MJ = plastic milk jugs

©The Education Center, Inc. • THE MAILBOX® • Intermediate • April/May • Key p. 313

Note to the teacher: Each student will need a red marker and a blue marker to complete this page.

¡Celebrate Cinco de Mayo!

Cinco de Mayo is a lively Mexican-American holiday. The Spanish words *Cinco de Mayo* mean "fifth of May." This holiday commemorates a surprising battle fought on May 5, 1862. An army of 6,000 French soldiers tried to capture two forts in Puebla de Los Angeles, Mexico. However, a much smaller Mexican army of 2,000 soldiers fought hard and held the forts. The Mexican people did not gain full independence at this time. But the victory proved to the world that Mexico wanted the freedom to rule itself.

Want to learn more about how this fun-filled holiday is celebrated? Use your best detective skills to unscramble the sentences below. Be careful—there are five words that don't belong in the sentences. (They belong on another page about some other well-known holidays!) Just mark out those words. Then rewrite each sentence on another sheet of paper, using capital letters and punctuation correctly.

1. part many Americans in activities observe Cinco de Mayo fun take to
2. celebrate it's a people time to the of Mexico and friendship America between the
3. we parades and to speeches colorful valentines listen attend
4. white decorated red and are green in streets
5. red and the colors of the white Mexican green are flag
6. enjoy bunny people Mexican food traditional
7. include some of foods tortillas and special these guacamole
8. American special dances musical cities events are and held in many
9. famous guitars on musicians their sleigh play tunes
10. local play bands patriotic songs Mexican mask
11. around dancers twirl castanets and snap their
12. in last cities often for some several festivals days
13. Hall Los Angeles activities in the streets outside held City are in
14. the become a holiday has turkey celebration of heritage Hispanic

Bonus Box: Unscramble these popular Mexican foods: *ascto, drifeer nabes, tho lishice, norc saltirotl, daihensacl,* and *trobsiru*. Circle the foods you have tried.

Celebrate the Season

Holiday and Seasonal Activities for the Classroom

End of School Year

Compliment Quilt

Wrap up the school year with an **art and writing** project that's sure to warm the heart and spirit of every student! Gather the materials needed. Then guide students through the steps shown to create individual quilts that are pieced together with uplifting compliments. adapted from an idea by *Kimberly A. Minafo, Pomona, NY*

Materials for each student:
14" x 16" piece of tagboard or poster board
ruler
pencil
markers
copy of the nameplate pattern below
glue
pens with different colors of ink (gel pens work great)

Steps:
1. On the tagboard, draw an 8 x 7 grid of two-inch squares with a pencil.
2. Erase the penciled lines that form the grid's 26 outer squares to create a two-inch-wide frame around the remaining 30 squares.
3. Color the frame black or another color of your choice.
4. Glue a copy of the nameplate pattern in the center of the grid so that it covers the two centermost squares. Write your name on the nameplate with a colorful pen or marker.
5. Color each square to resemble a patchwork quilt. Avoid very dark colors.
6. Compliment yourself by writing a sentence such as "I am a good sister to Emily and Josh" in one of the squares. Use a pen for your writing.
7. Pass your quilt around the room so your classmates and teacher can write compliments about you (in ink) in the remaining squares.

Step 2

Nameplate

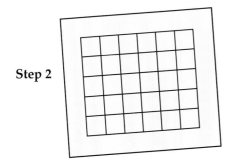

> *A Quilt of Compliments*
> *to warm the heart and spirit of*

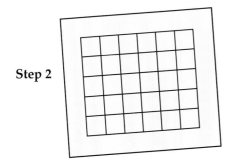

Beach Party Read-In

Kick off summer vacation with a "sand-sational" **reading motivation** celebration! On a designated day during the last week, invite students to come to school dressed in shorts, tropical shirts, sandals, and beach hats. Also allow them to bring beach towels, beach chairs, and small inflatable pool items, such as floats and inner tubes. Place beach baskets full of great books around the room. Enlist parents to help in serving a lunch of hot dogs, lemonade, and ice cream. Then spend the afternoon letting each beachcomber relax on his towel with a favorite book. Even Frankie and Annette would agree that it's a great way to close the books on another year! *Rebecca McCright—Gr. 4 Language Arts, Washington Elementary, Midland, TX*

Time in a Bottle

Capture students' favorite school memories with an **art and writing** project that doubles as a timely end-of-the-year display. Photograph each student (or have each student bring a recent photo from home). Then direct each child to cut two large identical bottle shapes from two 12" x 18" sheets of oaktag. Have the student glue her photo in the center of one cutout and fill the space around it with drawings of her favorite school memories from kindergarten through the current grade. Then have her write an essay about her memories and copy it neatly on the second bottle cutout. Finally, have the student connect the two cutouts at the top with a brad to make a booklet. Display the booklets on a bulletin board titled "If We Could Save Time in a Bottle…" *Donna DeRosa—Gr. 6, School #7, Belleville, NJ*

Popsicle Poetry

When the weather outside says it's summer, head outdoors with papers and pens for this creative **poetry** activity. Once outside, treat each student to a colorful Popsicle. After students eat their treats, collect the sticks and rinse them in a tub of hot water. Then dry the sticks and give one to each student (or distribute craft sticks instead). With students, brainstorm a list of adjectives that describe the Popsicles they just enjoyed, such as *frosty, colorful, slippery,* and *slushy.* Then instruct each student to write four words—a verb, a noun, an adjective, and an adverb—on each side of her stick. After collecting the sticks in a container, have each child draw one stick and use its words in an original poem. Be sure to bring along a box of baby wipes to clean sticky hands! *Patricia Dancho—Gr. 6, Apollo Ridge Middle School, Spring Church, PA*

287

Name _____

288

Countdown to Summer!

Hooray for summer! It's time to grab some ice cream, ride the surf, go for a swim, and maybe do a little gardening! But before you do, take a look at the following problems. Solve each one by making a list. Show your work and write your answers on another sheet of paper. Now get hopping—summertime's coming!

Ike's Ice-Cream Parlor
vanilla-chocolate-strawberry

1. Lulu wants to order 2 scoops of ice cream, with each scoop a different flavor. How many combinations are possible?

2. Lili wants to order a 2-flavor cone. How many combinations are possible? (Hint: In this problem, a cone with chocolate on top of vanilla is different from one with vanilla on top of chocolate.)

Mike's—The King of Ice Cream
**butter pecan   choco-chip
pistachio   lemon sherbet
raspberry swirl**

3. Henry wants a 2-scoop cone: lemon sherbet on the bottom and a different flavor on top. How many combinations are possible?

4. Harry wants a 2-scoop cone of any 2 flavors, as long as they are not the same. How many combinations are possible?

Spike's Ice Cream
chocolate
vanilla
strawberry
butter pecan
banana
choco-chip

Spike's Toppings
nuts
M&M's candies
sprinkles
cherries
chocolate syrup

5. LeAnn wants a 2-scoop cone of different flavors. How many combinations are possible?

6. LuAnn wants a sundae with 2 different flavors of ice cream and 2 different toppings. How many combinations are possible?

Shirley's Surf Shoppe

grizzly green   bongo blue   screaming orange   yoohoo yellow   three-alarm red   pink pizzazz

7. Bebe and Deedee want to rent surfboards. How many combinations of colors are possible? (Hint: They can rent the same color.)

Sue's Suits

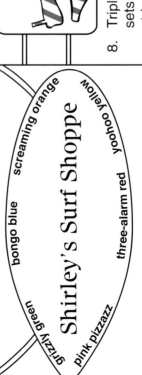

8. Triplets Sara, Fara, and Tara bought 3 sets of matching swimsuits: solid, striped, and polka-dotted. On Monday, Sara and Fara wore their striped suits and Tara wore her polka-dotted one. On Tuesday, each sister wore a different suit from the one she wore on Monday. How many possible ways could that happen?

9. Jess wants to plant carrots, tomatoes, and radishes. But when he went to the garden shop, carrot and radish seeds were sold out! Jess still wants to plant tomatoes and two other vegetables. How many combinations are possible?

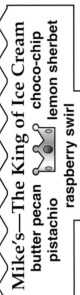

Gus's Garden Shop

beets   peas   carrots
lettuce   onions   tomatoes
         radishes

Bonus Box: Suppose you have 9 red socks, 7 green socks, and 5 blue socks in a drawer. If you reach into the drawer without looking, what's the fewest number of socks you must take before you're sure to get a pair of blue socks?

Name_____

It's Inventory Time!

Mr. Zane's classroom supplies are a mess! He has asked Jack and Jenna, two of his most organized students, to help him organize and store his supplies before summer vacation begins.

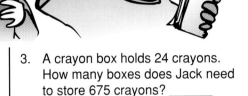

Read the problems below. Show your work on another sheet of paper. Then write your answers in the blanks provided. Jack and Jenna, and *especially* Mr. Z, are counting on you!

1. Scissors are stored in boxes that hold a dozen pairs each. Jack has more than enough scissors to fill 2 boxes, but not enough for 3. What is the fewest number of pairs he could have? _____ What is the greatest possible number? _____

2. Jenna found 34 new pads of paper, each with the same number of sheets. Which of the following could be the total number of sheets? Circle each answer.

1,190	1,800
1,300	2,520
1,700	2,720

3. A crayon box holds 24 crayons. How many boxes does Jack need to store 675 crayons? _____

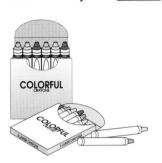

4. Jack needs to pack Mr. Z's beloved collection of 75 ceramic frogs. Jack can pack 2 to 5 frogs in a box. What is the fewest number of boxes Jack needs? _____ What is the greatest number of boxes he needs? _____

5. A package of red paper has 20 sheets. A package of green paper has 8 sheets. What is the fewest number of packages of each color Jenna could pack together so that she would have an equal number of red and green sheets? _____
_____
_____

6. Jenna wants to combine Mr. Z's paper clips and rubber bands and then divide them into identical sets. Jenna counted 150 paper clips and 180 rubber bands. Which of the following are numbers of sets Jenna can make with no leftovers? Circle each answer.

6	15	45
10	25	60
	30	

7. Jenna found 120 pieces of chalk scattered all about the classroom! Mr. Z wants them divided equally into boxes that have at least 10 pieces each, but no more than 20. List the different numbers of pieces of chalk Jenna could pack in each box.
_____

8. Jack counted 250 jelly beans in a jar sitting on Mr. Z's desk. Mr. Z wants the jelly beans stored in containers of 50 each. Mr. Z plans to give Jack and Jenna an equal number of containers and keep the rest for himself. How many jelly beans will Mr. Z get? _____
_____

9. Jack will arrange 30 desks in rows for Mr. Z. Each row will have the same number of desks. How many different ways can Jack arrange the desks?
_____
_____
_____
_____

10. Jenna spots this brainteaser in one of Mr. Z's teaching magazines: "Three different factors of 48 added together equal 33. What are they?" Can you help Jenna solve the puzzle?
_____
_____

Bonus Box: Which of the following numbers does not belong with the others? 56, 14, 40, 63, 35 _____ Explain why.

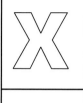

Easy As ABC

Remember the Alamo? Photosynthesis? Metaphors? Here's a neat way to recall some of the topics you studied this year. In each group of letters below, add a letter in the blank to complete a hidden word. Each hidden word has at least four letters and may have extra letters before and/or after it. The hidden words are topics or places you may have studied or read about this year. Some are proper names.

Circle each hidden word. Keep track of the letters you use by coloring them. Remember: You'll use each letter only once. The first one has been done for you.

1. FANUM __B__ ERFDY
2. GOSEN ___ ENCER
3. PRIWO ___ ERODS
4. SHADI ___ ITRAM
5. HUWIR ___ UOTEX
6. TOGRA ___ MARDS
7. CRASA ___ RICAM
8. IMPRO ___ UCTOR
9. AGALA ___ YSIST
10. YIPPA ___ TAHGO
11. WIERO ___ IONAL
12. PIZAL ___ LAINS
13. ISHOW ___ ALEST

14. TALAS ___ AMOTH
15. IKNEW ___ ORKAL
16. AVOWE ___ THAKN
17. BIMUS ___ LETEN
18. IFACT ___ RACMY
19. ADDNO ___ ENUST
20. SCOMM ___ FINCH
21. TRIND ___ ALBEX
22. ZILFO ___ CEDES
23. RASCI ___ NCEED
24. SQUAP ___ ATERZ
25. VASUB ___ ECTAN
26. GILSE ___ ERGYO

Bonus Box: Make five hidden-word puzzles like the ones above that include other topics you learned about this year. Give your puzzles to a friend to solve.

OUR READERS WRITE

Our Readers Write

Class Calendars

Reinforce computer and research skills with a project that produces a class set of calendars. Divide your class into 12 groups, assigning each group a different month of the year. Instruct each group to research to find school holidays, student birthdays, historical anniversaries, special events, and celebrity birthdays that occur in its assigned month. Then have each group use a computer program to design a calendar labeled with all the information. Make student copies of each month's page. Then have each student arrange the months in chronological order and staple them together from the back so he can easily pull off the top month.

Cori Collins
St. Gabriel, St. Mary, and St. Margaret Mary Schools
Neenah and Menasha, WI

| September 2001 | | | | | | |
Sun	Mon	Tue	Wed	Thu	Fri	Sat
						1
2	3	4	5	6	7	8

Picture-Perfect Frames

Transform unused CD jewel cases into attractive boxed picture frames. Simply replace a case's paper insert with a photo matted on construction paper. Open the jewel case a few inches to display the frame on a desktop or attach a length of magnetic tape to the back to create a magnetic frame.

Carolina Caddell, Laurinburg, NC

Journal Idea Box

Create this journal idea box to keep a full supply of interesting writing prompts at your students' fingertips. Label 3" x 5" tabbed index card dividers with categories such as "Family and Friends," "School," "Life," and "Miscellaneous"; then place the dividers in a card file box. Next, assign each category a different-colored 3" x 5" index card and program each card with several category-specific journal prompts (see the example). File the cards behind the appropriate dividers. Have each student select a card from the box when he needs a journal topic. To cut down on lost cards, attach a library card pocket inside each student's journal to store the card while in use.

Chana Rochel Zucker—Gr. 5
Beer Hagolah Institute, Brooklyn, NY

☐ I love my...
☐ My best friend...
☐ If I could communicate better with...
☐ I enjoy spending time with...
☐ Friends are...

Digital Thank-Yous

This technology project is the perfect follow-up to a guest speaker. Use a digital camera to take several pictures of a guest speaker during his presentation. Afterward, have a selected group of students use a computer to crop, size, and arrange the photographs on a document along with a note of thanks. Print out the page and have each student sign his name. Then laminate the thank-you and drop it in the mail. Next time you have a classroom visitor, select a different group to prepare the thank-you card.

Joy Tweedt—Gr. 6
Northwood Elementary
Ames, IA

Gifts on Display

Are you showered with artwork, pictures, and letters from students but have limited space for displaying them? Try filling a three-ring binder with clear sheet protectors from your local office supply store. Slip each gift inside a different sheet protector. You'll have a year's worth of memories in one easy-to-share book!

Jennifer Sagginario—Gr. 4
Santapogue Elementary
West Babylon, NY

New Concept Day

Generate student excitement for learning new concepts with this simple tip. Create a large, colorful sign that reads "New Concept Day!" Display the sign before each lesson introducing a new concept. Students will know to pay extra close attention to the lesson and may even try to guess the new concept before you begin!

Pat Forrester—Gr. 5, Pine Valley Elementary, Colorado Springs, CO

NEW CONCEPT DAY!

Personality Plates

Start the year—and end it—with this getting-to-know-you activity. Give each student a paper plate labeled with her name and an old newspaper or magazine. Direct the student to personalize her plate with cutout words that describe her. Allow each child to share her plate with the class; then post the plate on a bulletin board titled "Personality Plates." After you take down the display, store the plates until the end of the school year. On the last day of school, return each plate to its owner. Then have each student think about how she has changed over the year and share which words she would add or delete.

Steve Battles—Grs. 4–5
Butler Elementary
Springfield, IL

Crazy Creatures

Follow up an oceans unit by making these crazy creature projects! To begin, a student creates a crazy name for his creature such as "octisnake," "whalefish," or "crabphin." He then illustrates his creature on drawing paper and cuts out the picture. Next, the student cuts his creature in half and glues each piece to a 9" x 12" sheet of construction paper that has been folded into three sections as shown. Finally, the student writes a few paragraphs describing his creature (including what it eats, the part of the ocean it lives in, and how it protects itself from predators) and glues it to the center of the folded paper. Display the projects with the title "Crazy Creatures."

Tiffany Colasanti—Gr. 4
Hinsdale Central School
Hinsdale, NY

Teacher's Choice Award

Motivate students to turn in top-notch assignments with this easy-to-implement tip. Use a permanent marker to write "Teacher's Choice Award" on a supply of gold or silver stickers. While grading an assignment, place a sticker on any paper that you consider outstanding. When passing back the assignment, announce any Teacher's Choice winners. Explain what made each winner's paper stand out; then reward that child with a special Teacher's Choice pencil.

Teacher's Choice Award

Joyce Hovanec—Gr. 4
Glassport Elementary, Glassport, PA

Quote Me on That!

This back-to-school activity sets up the perfect open house icebreaker. On the first day of school, have each student fill out an interest inventory. Select one quote from each student's paper and write it on a separate sentence strip. On open house night, place the strips on a table. As parents arrive, challenge them to find their child's quote. Open house will be a hit, and you'll have information about your students to personalize lessons throughout the school year!

Lisa Stephens—Gr. 5
Centerville Elementary, Anderson, SC

Rewriting Rhymes

Let Mother Goose strengthen your students' vocabulary skills! Gather a collection of nursery rhyme books. Have each student copy her favorite verse on paper. Then have her mark through any word she wants to replace with an antonym, a synonym, or a homophone. After substitutions have been made, have the student copy her rewritten rhyme on another sheet of paper and write the total number of word changes at the bottom. Next, have students swap papers. Challenge each child to find her partner's changes and categorize them as shown. Make the activity more challenging by having students omit the number of changes from their papers.

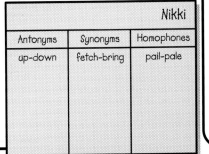

		Nikki
Antonyms	Synonyms	Homophones
up-down	fetch-bring	pail-pale

Kami Hayes—Gr. 5
Elk Plain School of Choice
Spanaway, WA

Classroom Promises

Do you involve students in developing your classroom rules? This year, try teaming up with your class to develop a set of student and teacher promises instead. Write the phrase "The students in [teacher's name]'s class promise to…" on a sheet of chart paper. Have students positively state helpful behaviors to finish the sentence. Then label another sheet of chart paper with "[Teacher's name] promises to…" and write your classroom responsibilities as the teacher. Type the completed lists into a single document and have each student sign one printed copy. Then give each student a copy and send another home to each family. What a great way to get your school year off to a positive start!

Kimberly A. Minafo—Gr. 4
Tooker Avenue Elementary
West Babylon, NY

Reading Pillows

Motivate independent reading with an incentive that's "sew" cool! At the beginning of the year, ask each parent to provide a 16-inch pillow form and two 18-inch fabric squares. (Purchase discounted material at fabric stores for students who may need it.) Set up a portable sewing machine in your classroom. Then have each child, with the help of a parent volunteer, sew a pillowcase to cover his pillow form. With their own personal pillows, your students will beg to curl up in a cozy corner with their favorite books.

Ann Mooney—Gr. 5
Nike School
Catawissa, MO

Good-Work Clothespins

Put your students in charge of their own good-work display with this nifty idea! First, have each student write her name on a wooden spring-type clothespin. Direct her to glue a small school photo of herself on another clothespin as shown. Then have the student decorate both clothespins with colorful markers. Next, string a clothesline in the classroom. Invite each student to clip an assignment that she is proud of on the line with her clothespins. As new work is completed, encourage students to change their special papers.

Julie Alarie—Gr. 6
Essex Middle School
Essex, VT

Stuffed Animals Project

Looking for a great class or schoolwide service project? Challenge students to clean out their toy boxes and bring in gently used stuffed animals. Ask a local dry cleaner to donate cleaning for the animals. After the toys are cleaned, have each student select an animal and write a brief story about it, including its name, likes, and dislikes. Have students copy their stories onto sturdy cards. Then punch a hole in each card and tie it around the animal's neck with ribbon. Hold a field trip to deliver the animals to a nearby nursing home. The residents will love holding the cuddly toys, and your students will enjoy an unforgettable experience.

Eva Miller
Nuckols Farm Elementary
Richmond, VA

Map Distortions

Use this hands-on activity to demonstrate how flat maps distort the portrayal of land and water masses. Give each group of three students an 11" x 18" sheet of paper. Have one group member sit in a chair while a teammate holds the paper across his face. Direct the remaining student to gently trace the sitter's face (from ear to ear and hairline to chin) with a marker. When everyone is finished, have one member from each group hold up her team's tracing. Then discuss how the obvious distortions in the tracings are similar to those found in flat maps.

Marie Altenburg—Gr. 6
Lindenhurst Middle School, Lindenhurst, NY

U.S.A. Leaves

Rake in plenty of geography and letter-writing practice with this fall bulletin board activity! After reviewing how to write a friendly letter, have each student write several letters to relatives and friends who live in other states. In each letter, have the student request that the recipient send him a leaf that is found in his area. Laminate the returned leaves; then label each leaf and post it on a bulletin board with a U.S. map. Connect each leaf to its home state with pushpins and crochet thread. What an "unbe-leaf-ably" great display!

Sharon Crosby, Saint Johns, AZ

Super Sentences Journal

Build sentence-writing skills with this simple-to-do idea. Place an inexpensive hardbound journal at a center. When you spot a particularly strong sentence on a child's assignment, mark it with a yellow highlighter. Then have the student copy the sentence in the journal, signing and dating the entry. Not only will students refer to the journal when they write, but you'll also have a supply of sample sentences to use during writing and grammar lessons.

Cheryl Dietz—Gr. 4, Holy Family Education Center, San Jose, CA

Halloween Treat Cups

Celebrate the Halloween season by making a patch of pumpkin treats. Provide a hot glue gun and the materials listed. Then have each student follow the steps shown to make a fun favor to take home. Or let your kids make the treats for a class of younger children in your school.

Materials for each student: small Styrofoam® cup, yellow and orange paint, paintbrush, small piece of sponge, black marker, yellow M&M's® candy piece, small treats for cup, piece of plastic wrap, length of orange ribbon

Steps:

1. Paint the bottom third of the cup yellow.
2. Paint the top two-thirds of the cup orange, leaving the rim white. Let the cup dry.
3. To make the face, add eyes and a mouth with the marker. With your teacher's help, hot-glue the candy piece to the cup for the nose. Sponge-paint the cheeks yellow.
4. Fill the cup with the treats. Then wrap it in the plastic wrap and tie it at the top with the ribbon.

Judy Wheeler, Wausau, WI

Heading Hint

If your students change classes, then they probably have a hard time remembering how each teacher wants them to head their papers. To eliminate this confusion, give each child a peel-off label for each class. Have the student place a label on the inside cover of each class's notebook; then have him write the appropriate heading on each label. When the student opens a notebook, he'll know instantly which heading to use.

Dulcy Leigh Wells—Gr. 6
Dan McCarty Middle School
Fort Pierce, FL

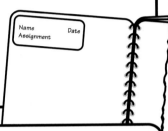

Rounding Reminders

Help your students remember when to round a number up or down with these sports-related reminders:

High Five: If the digit to the right is 5 or greater ("high-er"), round up.

Fourth Down: If the digit to the right is less than 5 (four or less), the digit to be rounded sits "down" and stays the same instead of moving up.

Wendy Morris—Grs. 4–5
Christ Lutheran School, East Point, GA

Touchdown Spelling

Watch spelling scores soar with this winning incentive! Cover a bulletin board with green paper; then use chalk to draw yard lines on the paper to resemble a football field. Give each student a page of clip art that features football players, cheerleaders, and other football-related figures. Have the student color and cut out each picture and label it with her name. Laminate the figures. When a student makes an outstanding score on a spelling test, let her display one of her cutouts on the board.

Felicia Sockey—Gr. 4, Pocola Elementary, Pocola, OK

Poetry Rocks!

Many older students don't cheer the prospect of studying poetry, but they just might when you use this fun activity! Ask each student to bring in a copy of the lyrics of a favorite song, emphasizing that it must be appropriate for school. After receiving approval from you, have each student copy the lyrics on a transparency. Then use the lyrics to discuss rhyme schemes, metaphors, similes, alliteration, onomatopoeia, and other concepts. Students will quickly see that poetry has been part of their lives all along and that it isn't so difficult to understand.

Pam Fassler—Gr. 6
Lincoln Heights Middle School
Morristown, TN

Tear Into Reading!

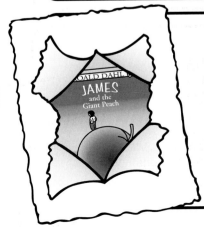

Encourage students to tear into books with this motivating display. Staple a variety of book jackets (student-made or real) on a bulletin board. Then cover the display with another layer of paper. After cutting a slit directly over each jacket, gently tear the paper and fold it back as shown to reveal the hidden jacket. Title the display "Tear Into a Good Book!"

Brenda A. Keller—Gr. 5
Canadochly Valley Elementary, East Prospect, PA

Good-Work Hoopla

Show off your students' best work with a display that's perfect for a classroom corner. Tie three lengths of fishing line to a Hula-Hoop® toy as shown. Attach the other ends of the lines to a coat hanger. Next, tie varying lengths of string around the hoop. Attach a spring-type clothespin to the end of each string. Then suspend the hanger from your ceiling and clip a student paper to each clothespin.

Lucretia Crowe, Vancleave, MS

Dear Doc

Wrap up a unit on the human body with this cool letter-writing activity. For each student, type a "Dear Doctor" letter that asks a health question (see the example). Sign each letter with an anonymous signature, such as "Sneezy in St. Louis." Give each student a letter; then have her use reference books to write a response as if she were a doctor. Display the letters on a bulletin board titled "What's Up, Doc?"

Anna Luetke
Divine Savior Lutheran School
Indianapolis, IN

25 Sneezy Street
Waterloo, IA 33333
October 15, 2001

Doctor Healthiman
Medical Center
111 Great Drive
Fitwell, NY 25555

Dear Doc:

I don't know what to do! I can't seem to stop sneezing. What causes sneezing anyway?

Sincerely,
Achoo in Waterloo

Birthday Lunch Bunch

Celebrate student birthdays with an idea that's easy and inexpensive. Once a month, invite students celebrating birthdays during that month to join you in the classroom for lunch. After students finish eating, let them have free time as they wait for their classmates to return from the lunchroom. It's a fun and easy birthday bash that your students are sure to love!

Michelle Bauml
Lake Jackson, TX

G Is for Gallon

Are your students somewhat muddled about liquid measurement? Then follow these steps to create a visual that will remind students in a snap.

1. Draw a large *G* to represent a gallon.
2. Draw four large *Q*s inside the *G* to represent four quarts.
3. Draw two large *P*s inside each *Q* to represent two pints.
4. Draw two *C*s inside each *P* to represent two cups.

Retha Taylor
West Jefferson Elementary
West Jefferson, NC

Good-Bye Slips

For an easy way to assess how your students' day went, give each child a good-bye slip several minutes before dismissal (see the example). Collect the completed slips and read them after students leave. This is a great way to help students communicate about problems or celebrate the positive things that have been happening to them.

Marsha Schmus—Gifted and Talented
Chambersburg, PA

Good-Bye Slip
Name (optional): _____
Date: _____
1. Today my day went (circle one)
   excellently
   pretty well
   not so great
2. The reasons for this were
   _____
   _____
3. I hope _____
   _____
   _____

Student Teacher Poster

Guarantee a great start to your student teacher's time with your class. Ask the student teacher to meet with you before her first day. Before this meeting, have each student create a poster that includes a recent photo and information about his interests. Also write a brief paragraph about each child summarizing his academic growth and other helpful information. Share these posters and paragraphs with the student teacher during your meeting. Then ask her to share a similar poster of herself with students on her first day. Students will love this activity and will bond even more quickly with your student teacher.

Cheryl Sykes Howe, Elon College, NC

Thinking Skills in Action

Spotlight important thinking skills with a display that stars your students! Label bright yellow lightbulb cutouts with the skills you want to highlight. Post the cutouts on a bulletin board. Whenever you catch students putting one or more of the skills into practice, take a photo. Then display the developed pictures near the appropriate lightbulbs on the bulletin board.

Debra A. Wilkins—Gr. 4
Gifted and Talented
Watchung, NJ

Analysis

Cells Demonstration

Use a popular children's toy to demonstrate an important concept about cells. Display a bucket of LEGO blocks. As a class (or in several small groups), have students build a structure with the blocks. Discuss how the LEGO pieces are the building blocks of the structure. Then point out that, in the same way, cells are the building blocks of all living things.

Sora Miriam Zucker—Gr. 5
Beth Jacob Day School, Brooklyn, NY

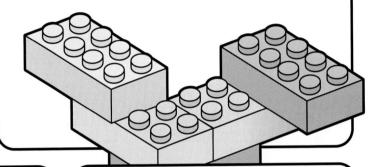

TNT Review

Review the previous day's lessons with an idea that's packed with TNT! Explain to students that in your class TNT stands for "Think, Neighbor, Talk!" After an important lesson, give students one minute to silently think about what was discussed. Then give each child one more minute to tell a neighbor what she remembers from the lesson. Finally, spend a few minutes talking as a group. To encourage sharing during this final part of the review, pass a ball or stuffed animal from student to student to signify a turn to talk.

Tonya Forbes—Gr. 5
Holy Angels School
Aurora, IL

Bulletin Board Letters

Imagine always having bulletin board letters when you need them. It can happen with this tip. Laminate a package of construction paper (one color). Then use a die-cutter to cut letters from the laminated paper: eight of each vowel and frequently used consonants and four of each remaining letter. Letter-perfect!

Stacie Squier—Gr. 6
Cornerstone Christian
San Angelo, TX

Brag Board

Here's an easy way to build a classroom community and create a great display at the same time. Title a bulletin board "Brag Board." Place a pad of self-sticking notes nearby. When a student wants to share an accomplishment or kind deed he's done, have him write it on a note and stick it to the board. Encourage students also to boast about a classmate and anyone else who has earned a spot on the brag board.

Jennifer Plocek
Hedrick Elementary
Lewisville, TX

I helped Dad build a doghouse this weekend!
—Mark

Kelli picked up my bookbag for me!
—Tara

Director's Chair for a Day!

This coupon entitles you to sit in the director's chair for a whole day! You can turn it in when you arrive at school.

Motivation Coupons

If your computer program includes a business card maker, you can motivate students in only moments! Decide on several rewards to offer deserving students. Then just type in the text, add a graphic, and print. If desired, laminate each coupon so it can be reused after a child turns it in.

Kelli Higgins
P. L. Bolin Elementary, East Peoria, IL

Shoe Bag Advent Calendar

This December give your students a surprise a day by transforming a shoe bag into a sturdy Advent calendar. Use a marker or glitter pen to number the bag's pockets from 25 to 1 as shown. Place an index card labeled with a small treat inside each pocket that corresponds to a school day. Include treats such as a guest reader, extra recess time, or a special snack. Each morning during December, ask a child to pull the day's card from the bag and announce the treat.

Kimberly A. Minafo
Pomona, NY

An Avalanche of 100s

No one will argue that December is full of distractions for students. Motivate them in a snap with this idea. When a student receives a 100 on an assignment, write his name on a paper snowflake. Then post the snowflake on a large wall space or hang it from the classroom ceiling. Challenge the class to fill your room with an avalanche of 100s between December 1 and the holiday break.

Sherril McMillan—Grs. 4–5
Brassfield Elementary
Bixby, OK

Exotic Words

To expand your students' vocabularies, try this word challenge. Display a sentence strip labeled with a category such as mammals, musical instruments, colors, birds, or clothing. Encourage students to use dictionaries and other references to find "exotic" words that fit the category (for example, *zither, lute,* and *cornet* as musical instruments or *mauve, taupe,* or *chartreuse* as colors). Have students write the words on index cards and then pin them to a bulletin board titled "In Search of Exotic Words."

Isobel L. Livingstone, Rahway, NJ

Class Photo Cards

Looking for an unforgettable holiday gift for your students? Take several group pictures of your class early in the year. In December, have the negative of your favorite shot developed into a photo card for each child. Be sure to have the card printed with a short greeting and the date (see the illustration). Then type a brief note to insert with each card. Both parents and students alike will love this classy keepsake.

Hope Armstrong—Gr. 6
Jefferson Elementary
Pierre, SD

Draft or Final?

If your students sometimes forget whether they're working on a rough draft or a final copy, try this helpful tip. Provide students with colorful lined paper for their rough drafts. Have them complete all final copies on white paper. No more confusion!

Carol Scharf—Gr. 4
Sea Gate Elementary
Naples, FL

Holiday Card Borders

Don't toss out your greeting cards after the holidays are history! Instead, cut off the front panel of each card. Then use the card fronts next year to create a holiday border around each of your bulletin boards.

Michelle Trubitz—Grs. 5–6
Brookside Upper Elementary, Westwood, NJ

Line Up and Learn

Do you assign each student a number to make record keeping easier? Then you've got an easy way to review math skills! Each time you want students to line up, give a direction, such as "All prime numbers line up" or "All factors of 12 line up" (see the other suggestions). Not only will you review important math concepts, but you'll also slow down students in a hurry to line up first.

Monica Bounds—Gr. 4
West Elementary
Jefferson City, MO

Suggestions
- all numbers that are evenly divisible by 2
- all multiples of 3
- all odd numbers greater than 10
- all numbers less than 4 x 5
- all numbers greater than the sum of ⁻4 + 20
- all numbers less than the number of inches in a foot

Fired Up About Poetry!

Turn a cold winter day into a party that celebrates poetry! Ask students to bring poetry books to school on a specified date. On the big day, help students decorate the back of a bookcase to look like a make-believe fireplace. Then gather around the roaring fire and read the students' favorite poems together. Serve hot chocolate and cookies to make this cozy celebration of poetry complete.

Elizabeth A. Ordway—Gr. 4
St. Joseph School
Danbury, CT

Stuffed Animal Announcements

Want your students to notice an important message you've written on the board? Prop a favorite stuffed animal near your chalkboard or whiteboard. Then draw a speech bubble near the toy's mouth and let him make your important announcement!

Isobel L. Livingstone
Rahway, NJ

CD Hall Passes

Don't throw away the junk mail CDs that fill your mailbox! Instead, recycle them to create durable hall passes. Use a permanent marker to label each CD with a destination in your school, such as the restroom, office, or library. Then tie a length of string through the hole to make a hard-to-lose hall pass necklace.

Cecelia Morris—Gr. 5
Maple Hill Elementary
Middletown, NY

Attention, Please!

Motivating students to take notes, focus on a lesson, or remember to bring items to school can sometimes be a challenge. The next time you need everyone's attention, grab a broad-tipped wet-erase marker (available at an office supply store) and write directly on your classroom windows! The ink wipes off easily, and you'll have everyone's attention in a flash.

Kimberly A. Minafo
Pomona, NY

Spelling Raffle

It's a sure bet that studying for a spelling test doesn't top your students' list of things they like to do. To motivate students to study their words, title a bulletin board "Super Spellers." Every week post the name of each student who made an A on the spelling test. The following Friday, put those names in a container and draw one winner. Award that child an automatic A on the day's test; then let him give the quiz to his classmates.

Heather Wagner—Gr. 5, St. Casimir School
Los Angeles, CA

Don't forget to study for tomorrow's science test!

Supply Lunchboxes

For a handy way to store supplies used during group work, label an inexpensive plastic lunchbox for each of your student groups. Stock the boxes with supplies such as crayons, markers, colored pencils, glue sticks, and scissors. Because the lunchboxes have lids, you'll cut down on the spills that often happen when supplies are stored in buckets or baskets.

Ami Hannawald—Gr. 4
Butler Elementary
Butler, OH

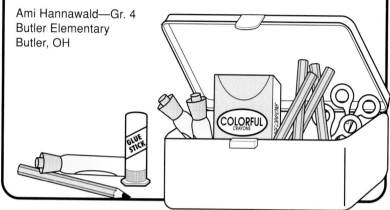

Buddy Up!

Use this idea to help your students learn to work well with others and get to know each other better. Each Monday divide the class into pairs, or buddies. Rearrange seating so buddies can sit beside each other. Then have each twosome work together during the week on tasks such as the following:

- Read orally to each other.
- Work together to solve a math problem.
- Check each other's assignment books.
- Note assignments for an absent buddy.
- Practice spelling words together.

Change buddies each week so that every child has the chance to partner with each of his classmates.

Debbie Wyzard—Gr. 4, Bethel Lutheran School, Morton, IL

Once Upon a Food Chain

Follow up a lesson on food chains with this creative activity! Ask your librarian to help you gather a variety of fairy tales and folktales. Read to students *The Three Billy Goats Gruff*. Point out the food chain that is illustrated in the tale: the green grass (producer) is eaten by the goats (primary consumers), who try not to be eaten by the troll (secondary consumer). After the discussion, have each student locate another story that includes a simple food chain (see the suggestions listed). Then direct the student to illustrate the food chain on a sheet of art paper. Display the finished drawings on a bulletin board titled "Once Upon a Food Chain."

Sharon Spadaro—Gr. 6
Trinity Middle School
Washington, PA

Suggested stories:
The Three Little Pigs
The Gingerbread Man
Jack and the Beanstalk
Little Red Riding Hood
Hansel and Gretel

Michigan

Pipe Cleaner Mobiles

Getting ready to make mobiles? Then trade in the coat hangers and yarn for a package of pipe cleaners! Have students follow these steps:

1. Draw and cut out shapes to include on the mobile. Label one shape with the mobile's title. Punch a hole in the top of each shape.
2. To create the base, insert a long pipe cleaner through a plastic straw.
3. Cut several pipe cleaners to various lengths. Attach each shape to one end of a pipe cleaner length as shown. Twist the other end around the base.
4. To create a hanger, twist one end of a long pipe cleaner around the base, pointing upward as shown. Bend the end to create a loop. Then tie a piece of string through the loop and hang the mobile from the ceiling.

Michelle Briegel—Gr. 4
MacGowan Elementary
Redford, MI

Class Birthday Candle

Wishing you could find an easy way to celebrate your students' birthdays? Divide a large paper candle into sections as shown, one per child. Starting at the bottom of the candle, label the sections in order with students' names and birthdates (including half birthdays for children with summer birthdays). On each child's birthday, cut his section from the bottom of the candle. Then write a message on the back of the section and tape a new pencil to it before presenting it to the birthday child.

Mary Kovacs—Gr. 5
St. Thomas More School
Allentown, PA

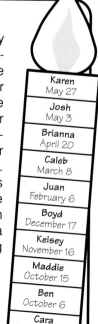

Karen
May 27

Josh
May 3

Brianna
April 20

Caleb
March 8

Juan
February 6

Boyd
December 17

Kelsey
November 16

Maddie
October 15

Ben
October 6

Cara
September 23

Your Writing Shines!

Encourage even the most reluctant student to share his written work with this inspiring incentive. Purchase a large pair of plastic sunglasses from a novelty store. Decorate the glasses with sequins, feathers, pom-poms, or other art supplies. When a student writes something that truly "shines," ask him to don the glasses—since he'll need to protect his eyes from the glare—and read his work to the class.

Natalie Hughes-Tanner
Ermel Elementary
Houston, TX

Computerized Spelling

Watch word-processing skills grow with this weekly spelling activity. Each week have each student type his spelling list in alphabetical order. Then have him insert ten new words of his choice in the alphabetized list, using various options to distinguish them from the assigned words (changing the size, using a different color or font, etc.). At the end of the year, have each student print his spelling list pages and compile them to create a personal word book.

Michelle Risengrant—Grs. 5–6
Wingate Elementary
Wingate, PA

Wrapping Up a Lesson

I liked…

I discovered…

I learned…

I was surprised…

I think I will…

I never knew…

I still wonder…

Looking for a productive way to wrap up a lesson, a visit from a guest speaker, or a video viewing? Display a poster as shown in your classroom. Then call on volunteers to orally complete one or more of the starters.

Jennifer Gunerman—Gr. 4
Klem Road North Elementary
Webster, NY

Sentence Patterns

Boost sentence-writing skills with this team game. First, write a pattern such as the one shown on the chalkboard. Divide the class into teams. Then give teams five minutes to fill in the blanks in as many different ways as possible. After each team shares its sentences, write a new pattern on the board and play again. For an extra challenge, require students to write specific types of sentences, such as declarative, interrogative, imperative, or exclamatory.

Isobel L. Livingstone, Rahway, NJ

_____, _____ _____ _____ _____.

Examples:
Mary, please take your seat.
No, I did not practice.
Well, Don really did call.
Oh, I didn't say that.

Assigning Projects

Try this tip the next time you assign a project to students. On scrap paper, list the steps and guidelines for the project. Then rewrite them in the same format as the project you're assigning. For example, if you want students to create a travel brochure, design your project handout to resemble a brochure. Want students to write a newsletter? Then show them how by writing the assignment in newsletter format.

Shawn L. Parkhurst
Canadian Academy
Kobe, Japan

Personality Profiles

Build self-esteem and an appreciation for differences with this easy art activity. Using an overhead projector, trace each student's silhouette on a large sheet of construction paper. Then cut out each tracing. Next, provide the student with scissors, glue, and discarded newspapers and magazines. Direct her to cut out words and pictures that reflect her interests and personality and then glue them to her profile. After posting the projects, challenge students to guess the identity of each profile.

Melissa A. McMullen—Gr. 5
Saint Patrick School
Newry, PA

What a Smartie!

Here's a smart way to display your students' papers! Glue strips of pastel construction paper around a paper towel tube. Then wrap the tube in plastic wrap, tying off the ends with string. Use a permanent red marker to write "Smarties" on the wrap as shown. Display the candy on a bulletin board titled "What a Smartie!" When a student earns a great grade on a test, tape a roll of Smarties candy to his paper. Then let the student remove the treat and staple his paper to the board. How smart!

Janine Every
Daniel Street School
Lindenhurst, NY

Waiting on the Web

Downloading new Web sites provides great teaching resources, but precious time may be wasted if a child just sits and stares at the screen while she waits. Make use of every valuable minute of classroom time by posting a list, such as the one shown, at your computer. Change the list of filler activities periodically so students will have new activities to choose from.

Kathy Yahr, Twin Hills School, Twin Hills, AK

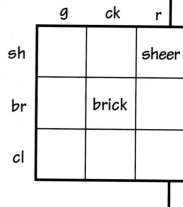

What Can We Do While We're Waiting on the Web?

- Count as high as you can by 4s.
- Play 20 Questions with your computer partner.
- Recite to yourself the states and their capitals.
- Use the letters in your name to spell as many different words as you can.
- Choose a classroom object. Write a list of words that rhyme with it.
- Create math problems with answers that equal today's date.
- List six-letter words that are all verbs.
- Practice your spelling words.

Missing Puzzle Pieces

If you have a collection of jigsaw puzzles in your classroom, you've probably faced the problem of stray pieces. The next time students finish assembling a puzzle, place a sheet of poster board atop the completed puzzle and carefully flip it. Then have students label the back of each puzzle piece (and the puzzle's box) with a code letter. Until all of the puzzles have been assembled and marked, place lost pieces in a box labeled "Strays." When a student realizes the puzzle he's working on is missing a piece, he'll know just where to look for it.

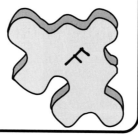

Betty Winslow, Bowling Green Christian Academy
Bowling Green, OH

Cereal Ads

Want to add some snap, crackle, and pop to persuasive-writing skills? Ask students to bring empty cereal boxes to school. Distribute one box to each student. Direct the student to study the information on the box and write an ad to persuade people to buy that cereal. After students share their ads, have the class vote on the most persuasive one.

Colleen Dabney
Toano Middle School
Williamsburg, VA

Word Grids Game

Pack lots of word practice in a little bit of time with this quick activity. Draw a grid, such as the ones shown, on the board. Have each student copy the grid on her paper. Then challenge students to fill each block with words that begin with the letter(s) on the left side and end with the letter(s) at the top.

Isobel L. Livingstone
Rahway, NJ

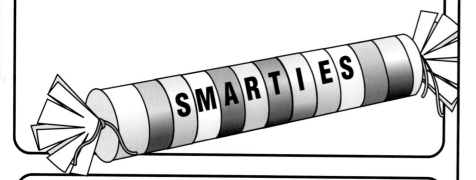

	e	l	m
s	sale		
t			team
f		fall	

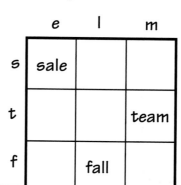

	g	ck	r
sh			sheer
br		brick	
cl			

Smile File

Use this idea to get ready for those days when you could use a little extra encouragement. Label a file folder "Smile File." In the file, place each complimentary note you receive from a student, parent, or co-worker. When your spirits need a lift, take a few minutes to read through the file. In no time, you'll be energized and ready for the next challenge!

Patricia E. Dancho—Gr. 6
Apollo-Ridge Middle School
Spring Church, PA

Skits in a Bag

Improved speaking and creative-thinking skills are in the bag with this nifty idea! With students, brainstorm 25 people, 25 places, and 25 actions (attending a birthday party, winning a contest, etc.). Write each item on a separate index card. Then place each group of 25 cards in its own labeled bag. For a fun Friday activity, divide the class into groups. Have a student from each group pull one card from each bag. Then challenge each group to plan and present an impromptu skit based on the cards. With practice, students will grow more creative and less self-conscious about performing in front of others.

Marsha Schmus
Shippensburg School District
Shippensburg, PA

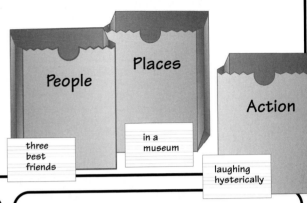

People

Places

Action

three best friends

in a museum

laughing hysterically

My Class Units Album

Wrap up each of your social studies, science, and thematic units with this picture-perfect activity! Collect a class supply of the small black photo albums that many businesses offer free with photo processing. At the end of each unit, give each student a 4" x 6" index card. Have him write the unit's name at the top of the card and write about and/or illustrate his favorite activity. Then have him insert the card in his album. At the end of the year, each student can take home a completed album that reminds him of all he's learned!

Michelle Biondo and Angela Renfro
Gladden Elementary
Belton, MO

Solar System
My favorite activity was when we made the planet models.
It was

Quick Cleanup

If your students change classes during the day, try this easy way to encourage them to spiff up your classroom before they leave. About two minutes before the class ends, let one student roll a die and announce the number rolled. Then direct each student to put away, pick up, or throw away that number of items before she leaves. In no time, your room will be ready for the next group of kids.

Julia Alarie—Gr. 6
Essex Middle School
Essex, VT

Disk Storage

Give students quick and easy access to their floppy disks with this super storage tip. Use a hot glue gun to attach two plastic book binders to a piece of cardboard so that they are about $2^3/_4$ inches apart. Then just insert the disks in the binders' slots as shown. Students will be able to locate their personal disks in a snap!

Karen Popovich, Spring Brook School
Naperville, IL

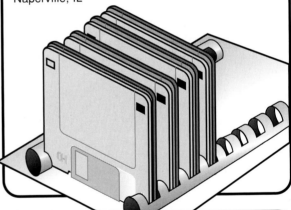

Displaying Good Character

Encourage good character with a motivating, no-fuss display. Each week label a tagboard strip with a different character trait and its definition. Post the strip on a small bulletin board and discuss the trait with the class. During the week, a student who thinks he exhibited that trait describes his action on a self-sticking note. Then he sticks the note on the display. A student can also write a note about a classmate he observed demonstrating the trait. At the end of the week, choose the best example of the characteristic and reward that student with a special prize.

Sherri Blevins—Gr. 4
Mt. Zion Elementary
Jonesboro, GA

Perseverance
not giving up; "stick-to-it" attitude

Mmmm...Matter Models

When your class is studying states of matter, ditch the standard water-and-ice model for this sweet substitute! Use an electric warming tray to melt sweetened baking chocolate, pointing out the change from a solid to a liquid. Then have each child use a plastic fork to dip a pretzel into the melted chocolate and place it on waxed paper. Students can observe the liquid chocolate changing back into a solid as it cools and hardens. If desired, let students dip different cookies and crackers into the chocolate and observe any other physical changes. Then let them munch on their yummy models!

Tracy L. Early—Gr. 5 Science, East Palestine Elementary, East Palestine, OH

Laughs Over Lunch

Let's Have Laughs Over Lunch!

Please join me for a special lunch next week on the day of your choice. We'll talk about these fun topics:

- *Why don't you ever seem to grow out of your least favorite shirt?*
- *Do you think people really begin to look like their pets?*
- *Who made up the rule that dessert has to be eaten last?*

You may choose a classmate to eat with us if you wish. Let me know which day you'd like to meet. I'm looking forward to our lunchtime together!

Mrs. Minafo

Do you have a student who's struggling with a personal or classroom challenge? Encourage this child by inviting her to a special lunch. Mail a card inviting the student to join you (alone or with a buddy) for lunch on a day of her choice. On the invitation, list three silly topics you plan to discuss during the meal (see the example). Then, during the lunch, discuss the questions, share a joke or funny book, and talk about anything else on the child's mind. The silly questions will help ease anxieties the student may have about eating with the teacher. Plus, the special meal may open a door for her to share about her particular struggle.

Kimberly A. Minafo
Pomona, NY

State Chalk Maps

If your school's playground includes an asphalted area, you've got the perfect place to review your state's geography! Divide students into groups of two or three. Then give each student a piece of sidewalk chalk and head outdoors. Direct each group to draw the outline of your state on the asphalt. Then periodically blow a whistle and announce a city or landform in your state. At your signal, each group must draw and label that item on its map. When the maps are complete, invite students to compare them.

Suzanne Funk—Gr. 4
South Mountain Elementary
Dillsburg, PA

Mystery Author

Encourage students to read their writing workshop pieces aloud with this mysterious incentive! First, secretly choose a number between one and the number of students in your class. Then post a sign-up sheet as shown. After volunteers sign up and share their work, announce the mystery number. Award the student whose sign-up number matches or comes closest to the mystery one with a special class privilege or treat. Not only will this simple incentive encourage reluctant students to volunteer, but it may also provide enough of a distraction to calm more nervous readers.

★ **Author Day Sign-Up Sheet** ★

1. Caleb Howard
2. Rujima Kalimenthieri
3. Aaron Thomas
4. Marcie West
5. Becca Coleman
6. Julia Kim
7. Todd Robinson
8. McKinley Trotman
9. Brittney Benson
10. Micah Hanes

Jill R. Bluth, Draper, UT

Web Site Address Book

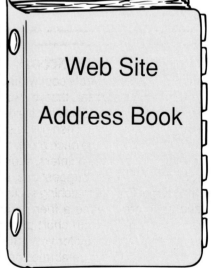

The Internet may be an educational wonderland, but remembering the addresses, user names, and passwords for your students' favorite sites can be a nightmare! Use this handy tip to put the information right at your fingertips. Purchase an inexpensive address book. Then write each site's name, address, user name, and password in the book, along with a kid-friendly description. Keep the book at your computer station for easy access.

Cheryl Norton—Gr. 4
Lake Dallas Elementary
Lake Dallas, TX

Class Yearbook

Don't wait until the end of the year to create this picture-perfect class book! Have each student glue a photo of himself in the center of a sheet of sturdy paper and divide the paper into four sections as shown. As a class, choose four topics—such as personal statistics, favorites, least favorites, and dreams for the future—to feature in the sections. After each child fills in the sections with the information selected, collect the finished pages. Then arrange them in alphabetical order behind a student-designed cover and bind them into a class yearbook. Not only will students love reading this yearbook (and the ones made by your previous classes), but you'll also have a handy photo reference for substitutes and student teachers.

Susan Keller—Gr. 5, Plumb Elementary
Clearwater, FL

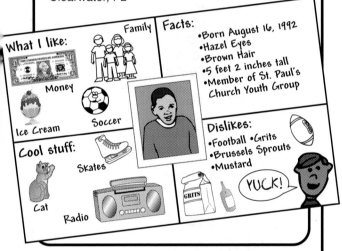

The Inside Scoop

End the year with a truly cool writing activity! Announce to students that you want them to give next year's students the inside scoop on being in your class. Then divide students into groups. Challenge each group to brainstorm a list of serious pointers, such as "Be organized," and silly suggestions, such as "Don't forget to wear matching socks!" Then have each group write a friendly letter to the upcoming class on chart paper. Post the letters in a hallway for your future students to read. Then celebrate the end of the writing session with an ice-cream party. One scoop or two?

adapted from an idea by Amy Evans—Gr. 4
Grace Christian School
Blacklick, OH

I Could Use a Hand!

1. Staple the handouts in the basket.

2. Return the hole puncher to Mr. Davis.

3. Clean up the crafts table.

4. Write tonight's homework on the board.

Helping Hands

Wondering what to do with students who arrive early or have to stay a little late? Place a sheet of paper labeled "I Could Use a Hand!" on a clipboard. Then place the clipboard in your supplies area. During the day, write on the list any nonurgent tasks that need to be done, such as returning borrowed supplies or stapling handouts. Then encourage early arrivals or late dismissals to tackle a task on the list. Simply check off a job once it's complete.

Kimberly A. Minafo
Pomona, NY

Buddy Book Reports

Looking for a motivating book report for the final weeks of school? Here's one students will cheer about! Allow each child to pair up with a classmate (one who reads on approximately the same reading level) to read the same book. Then have the twosome create the final book-report project together.

Carol Raupe—Gr. 4
Menchaca Elementary
Manchaca, TX

Balloon Bookmarks

Say, "So long!" to your students at the end of the year with this high-flying gift idea! For each student, cut a bookmark-sized tagboard strip. Decorate one side of the bookmark with stickers. After writing a special note to the student on the other side, punch a hole in one end of the bookmark and tie it to the ribbon of an inexpensive helium balloon. When the student is finished with the balloon, she simply snips the ribbon to create a tasseled bookmark.

Leslie Russell—Gr. 5
M. L. King School
Piscataway, NJ

Answer Keys

Page 41

1. is	6. brought	11. hung
2. began	7. drank	12. written
3. seen	8. fell	13. broke
4. throw	9. ridden	14. gone
5. froze	10. run	15. come

Page 43

Part 1
1. looks
2. smell
3. grew
4. sounds
5. seemed
6. remained
7. became
8. tasted

Part 2
1. became; Mary, president
2. seemed; mom, happy
3. sounds; idea, great
4. looks; She, fantastic
5. grew; teacher, impatient
6. smell; socks, terrible
7. remained; Jake, champion
8. tasted; dinner, delicious

Bonus Box
1. blue
2. red
3. red
4. red
5. red
6. red
7. blue
8. red

Page 59

Part 1
A. Sequence (blue)
B. Enumeration (green)
C. Generalization (brown)
D. Cause and effect (red)
E. Compare and contrast (purple)
F. Question and answer (orange)
G. Problem and solution (black)
H. Description (yellow)

Part 2
Answers may vary. Accept all reasonable answers.
a. Sequence
b. Problem and solution
c. Question and answer
d. Compare and contrast
e. Description
f. Sequence

Page 65

1. microbiology
2. microscope
3. microorganism
4. microwave
5. autobiography
6. autopilot
7. automatically
8. autograph
9. visit
10. evident
11. vision
12. video
13. invisible
14. substandard
15. submarine
16. submerge
17. subject
18. fragment
19. fractured
20. fragile
21. fraction
22. audible
23. audition
24. auditorium
25. audience

Bonus Box: Answers will vary.

Page 66
Answers may vary. Accept all reasonable answers.

Part 1
1. presweened: set in advance
2. unrikitic: not friendly
3. cozither: fellow pilot
4. bistellu: twice an hour
5. distroot: stop, do not continue
6. refeddled: built again
7. octaplinky: eight sided
8. prelelluped: approved in advance
9. overphrattered: priced too highly
10. regrup: start again

Part 2
a. 48
b. It has eight sides.
c. two
d. before
e. Stop the flight.
f. yes
g. before approaching the landing pad
h. Aliens from Pikky are unfriendly.
i. You can restart it.
j. because fuel is so expensive

Page 67
Answers will vary. Accept all reasonable answers.
Possible answers include the following:
1. ability to move
2. stopping
3. aware, knowledgeable
4. warlike, hostile
5. someone who is fleeing or trying to escape
6. speaking, vocal expression
7. ruling government, leaders
8. someone who is new at something, beginner
9. rising, increased
10. person who helps mankind
11. child, offspring
12. chief or main enemy

Page 70

1. tire	6. vault	11. right
2. rest	7. left	12. part
3. dip	8. play	13. toll
4. fire	9. tank	14. well
5. form	10. scale	15. log

Page 73

Part 1
1. MEOW—are
2. SQUEAK—is
3. MEOW—were
4. MEOW—are
5. SQUEAK—was
6. MEOW—are
7. SQUEAK—is
8. SQUEAK—is
9. MEOW—were
10. SQUEAK—was

Part 2
1. are
2. is
3. is
4. are
5. are

Page 82

Part I
1. N = 7
2. E = 24
3. L = 9
4. W = 0
5. B = 15
6. R = 3
7. O = 5
8. T = 1
9. T = 5
10. S = 15
11. E = 9
12. E = 0
13. H = 37
14. S = 0
15. T = 2
16. O = 23
17. E = 5
18. N = 0
19. T = 51

Part II
- property of one: E, T, H
- order property: N, B, O, S, O, T
- zero property: W, E, S, N
- grouping property: L, R, T, E, T, E

Part III
THE BOSTON NEWS-LETTER

Bonus Box: 1704

Page 83
1. $140
2. $168
3. $38
4. $356
5. $60
6. $24.75
7. $96
8. $126
9. $71.75; ($7.50 + $6.85) x 5 = $71.75
10. $59.50; ($5.50 x 4) + ($7.50 x 5) = $59.50
11. $180, $2,160; $540 ÷ 3 = $180; $180 x 12 = $2,160
12. $96.25; ($5.25 + $8.50) x 7 = $96.25
13. $40; $16 x 15 = $240; $240 − $200 = $40
14. $6,480; $540 x 12 = $6,480
15. $50.25; ($5.25 + $5.25 + $6.25) x 3 = $50.25

Bonus Box: $42 (regular price: 2 x $85 = $170, Brandon's price: 4 x $32 = $128, $170 − $128 = $42)

Page 86
1. $33 ÷ 3 − 3 = 8$
2. $5 + 55 x 5 = 280$
3. $9 ÷ 9 + 99 = 100$
4. $(77 − 7) x 7 = 490$
5. $(10 + 10) ÷ 10 + 10 = 12$
6. $(29 x 29) + (29 + 29) = 899$
7. $(12 ÷ 12) x 12 + 12 = 24$
8. $(72 x 72) + (72 ÷ 72) = 5,185$
9. $100 + (100 x 100) ÷ 100 = 200$
10. $505 ÷ 505 + 505 + 505 = 1,011$

Bonus Box: $(3 x 3)^2 ÷ 3 + 3 = 30$

Page 96
1. $5^1/_4$, $5^7/_8$
   Rule: add $^5/_8$
2. 9, $10^1/_2$
   Rule: add $1^1/_2$
3. 15, $17^1/_3$
   Rule: add $2^1/_3$
4. $11^1/_5$, 13
   Rule: add $1^4/_5$
5. $17^1/_8$, $20^3/_8$
   Rule: add $3^1/_4$
6. $18^5/_6$, $24^5/_6$
   Rule: add 1, add 2, add 3, add 4, etc.
7. $6^1/_2$, $5^1/_4$
   Rule: add $2^1/_2$, subtract $1^1/_4$
8. 20, $25^1/_2$
   Rule: add $^1/_2$, add $1^1/_2$, add $2^1/_2$, add $3^1/_2$, etc.
9. $11^7/_{10}$, $13^9/_{10}$
   Rule: add $1^1/_5$, add $1^2/_5$, add $1^3/_5$, add $1^4/_5$, etc.
10. $10^2/_3$, $12^1/_2$
    Rule: subtract $^2/_3$, add $1^5/_6$

Bonus Box: $23^5/_8$ ($1^1/_8 + 2^2/_8 + 3^3/_8 + 4^4/_8 + 5^5/_8 + 6^6/_8$ or in simplest terms: $1^1/_8 + 2^1/_4 + 3^3/_8 + 4^1/_2 + 5^5/_8 + 6^3/_4$)

Page 97
Measurements are to the nearest eighth.
1. $7^1/_4$ in.
2. 5 in.
3. $5^1/_8$ in.
4. $6^1/_4$ in.
5. $4^3/_8$ in.
6. 2 in.
7. $10^3/_4$ in.
8. $7^3/_4$ in.
9. $5^1/_4$ in.
10. $9^3/_4$ in.
11. $8^1/_8$ in.
12. $2^3/_8$ in.
13. $^1/_8$ in.
14. $1^3/_4$ in.
15. $2^1/_2$ in.
16. $1^1/_2$ in.
17. $13^1/_8$ in.
18. $10^3/_8$ in.
19. $15^3/_4$ in.
20. $12^1/_4$ in.
21. 11 in.
22. $15^7/_8$ in.
23. $16^1/_2$ in.
24. $11^3/_8$ in.
25. $17^3/_8$ in.

Bonus Box: A–G–I–E–C = $11^7/_8$ in. A–B–E–C = $16^7/_8$ in. A–G–I–E–C is shorter by 5 in.

Page 103
Step 1: 5, 7, 9, 12, 12, 14, 15, 17, 18, 20, 22, 23, 24, 27, 27, 27, 31, 33, 38, 39, 41, 43, 45

Step 2: Titles will vary.

Stems	Leaves
0	5, 7, 9
1	2, 2, 4, 5, 7, 8
2	0, 2, 3, 4, 7, 7, 7
3	1, 3, 8, 9
4	1, 3, 5

Step 3
1. 40
2. 23
3. 27

Bonus Box: 1st doghouse: 22; 2nd doghouse: 21; 3rd doghouse: 36; 4th doghouse: 14

Page 108

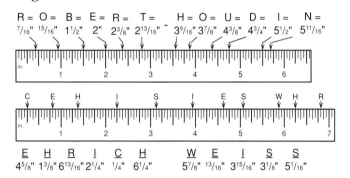

$R = O = B = E = R = T = \quad H = O = U = D = I = N =$
$\frac{7}{16}" \quad \frac{15}{16}" \quad 1\frac{1}{2}" \quad 2" \quad 2\frac{3}{8}" \quad 2\frac{13}{16}" \quad 3\frac{9}{16}" \quad 3\frac{7}{8}" \quad 4\frac{3}{8}" \quad 4\frac{3}{4}" \quad 5\frac{1}{2}" \quad 5\frac{11}{16}"$

$\underline{E}\ \underline{H}\ \underline{R}\ \underline{I}\ \underline{C}\ \underline{H} \qquad \underline{W}\ \underline{E}\ \underline{I}\ \underline{S}\ \underline{S}$
$4\frac{5}{8}" \quad 1\frac{3}{8}" \quad 6\frac{13}{16}" \quad 2\frac{1}{4}" \quad \frac{1}{4}" \quad 6\frac{1}{4}" \qquad 5\frac{7}{8}" \quad \frac{13}{16}" \quad 3\frac{15}{16}" \quad 3\frac{1}{8}" \quad 5\frac{1}{16}"$

$1\frac{5}{16}" = H \quad 1" = O \quad 4\frac{1}{4}" = U \quad 4\frac{13}{16}" = D \quad 5\frac{7}{16}" = I \quad 5\frac{3}{4}" = N \quad 2\frac{3}{16}" = I$

Bonus Box: $5\frac{4}{16}"$ or $5\frac{1}{4}"$

Page 109

12 cm = P	8 cm = T	5 cm = G	15 cm = T
40 mm = R	25 cm = I	17 cm = I	70 mm = I
22 cm = E	10 cm = D	10 mm = T	18 cm = O
35 mm = S	5 mm = I	90 mm = A	25 mm = N

Answer: prestidigitation

Page 112
1. likely
2. unlikely
3. likely
4. unlikely
5. unlikely
6. unlikely
7. unlikely
8. likely
9. 1
10. $\frac{5}{37}$
11. 1
12. 0
13. $\frac{8}{37}$
14. 0
15. $\frac{12}{37}$
16. $\frac{1}{37}$

Page 116
1. The Mediterranean Sea is located at the top of the map. The Red Sea is located east of the Nile.
2. The river runs through the middle of the map, fanning out into a delta when it reaches the Mediterranean Sea.
3. The Western Desert is west of the Nile. The Eastern Desert is east of the Nile.
4. The Upper Kingdom was south of Amarna. The Lower Kingdom was north of Giza and Cairo.
5. The three capital cities on the map are Thebes, Alexandria, and Memphis.
6. The Valley of the Kings is west of the Nile across from Karnak and Luxor.
7. Box 1: Monuments at Giza
   Box 2: Step Pyramid at Saqqara
   Box 3: Temples at Karnak
   Box 4: Temples of Ramses II at Abu Simbel

Page 121
Part 1
1. Pacific Ocean
2. Atlantic Ocean
3. Gulf of Mexico
4. Sierra Nevada
5. Cascade Range
6. Rocky Mountains
7. Appalachian Mountains
8. Great Lakes
9. Mississippi River
10. Alaska Range

Part 2
Quillayute, WA—blue
Astoria, OR—blue
Bishop, CA—brown
Bakersfield, CA—brown
Blue Canyon, CA—orange
Las Vegas, NV—brown
Yuma, AZ—brown and red
Phoenix, AZ—brown
International Falls, MN—yellow
Duluth, MN—yellow
Marquette, MI—orange and yellow
Sault Ste. Marie, MI—orange and yellow
Mobile, AL—blue
Pensacola, FL—blue
Tallahassee, FL—blue
Key West, FL—red
Fort Myers, FL—red
Miami, FL—red
West Palm Beach, FL—red
Syracuse, NY—orange
Caribou, ME—orange and yellow

Part 3
Answers may vary. Accept all reasonable responses.
1. Because California is one of the largest states, it has a wide variety of climates and land regions of different elevations. The state includes several mountain ranges, valleys of rich farmland, and desert areas.
2. Las Vegas doesn't receive much rain. Clouds that move eastward from the Pacific Ocean lose most of their moisture in California as they rise above the Sierra Nevada.
3. They are all near large bodies of water.
4. The hottest cities are located nearer to the equator (at lower latitudes) than the coldest cities. The coldest cities are farther away from the equator (at higher latitudes) than the hottest cities.

Background Information

1. Coming to America was exciting and scary for the adventurous colonists. Many people left Europe because they wanted a different and better life. Others left because they couldn't worship God as they pleased.
2. Most of the colonists came over as indentured servants. In exchange for working for someone without pay for five to seven years, they were given passage to America and were clothed and housed.
3. While traveling on a ship to America, colonists were crowded into a damp and cold space below deck. Days were spent sitting in a small space with nothing to do. Trips lasted two to four months.
4. Millions of native peoples lived in the New World before the colonists arrived. Some of them welcomed the colonists, while others sensed that their arrival meant danger.
5. The colonists' first houses were quickly and poorly constructed. Storms and fires often destroyed them.
6. The colonists' first homes were damp, dark, and comprised of only one big room. Calls of nature usually meant going outside since there were no indoor bathrooms.
7. Children often stood at mealtimes. The few chairs were reserved for the parents.
8. Most of the colonists didn't know how to farm. Some early settlements experienced a "starving time" during which food ran out.
9. Early colonists had to spend most of their time growing food and building homes. Because colonists had to make all their own cloth, which took a long time, clothing was scarce.
10. Colonial children had lots of freedom since adults were so busy taking care of basic survival needs.
11. Large families were common in colonial America. For example, Benjamin Franklin had 17 brothers and sisters.
12. Colonial children who lived in the first settlements were taught at home by their parents. In between all their chores, children were taught to read, write, and add.
13. Colonial children were expected to help out around the house from the time they were three. They were given simple chores that kept them from bothering their busy parents.
14. Colonists did not brush their teeth, resulting in many cavities. Teeth couldn't be filled, so they were pulled—sometimes by the town barber!
15. Christmas didn't become a major holiday until the 19th century. Many colonists worked on this day. Some went to church and enjoyed a special dinner.
16. African American slaves were not permitted to learn to read or write. People believed that if they did learn, slaves would get ideas about being free. Some slaves secretly learned to read and write.
17. Beer was the main drink for early colonists—even babies! It was watered down and contained only about one-half percent alcohol. Colonists avoided drinking water because of the fear of waterborne diseases and because water wasn't easy to get.
18. Both colonial men and women wore wigs. An expensive wig could cost as much as it would to house and care for a servant for one year.

Causes of World War I: a, e, g, k, o, p
Reasons USA Entered War: b, f
Results of World War I: c, d, h, i, j, l, m, n

Part 1

1. World War I ends.
2. Americans buy huge amounts of goods.
3. Factories increase production of goods.
4. Demand for products falls because people can't afford to keep purchasing them.
5. Warehouses and stores become full of products that go unsold.
6. People buy stock on credit to try to make more money.
7. Stock prices drop drastically. Many investors lose all of their money.
8. Many banks and businesses fail. Many people lose their jobs.
9. The Great Depression begins.
10. President Franklin D. Roosevelt proposes New Deal programs to end the depression.

"Conjuring Up Colors!"
Mixing together any two primary colors of pigment-containing media produces another color.

Red + blue = purple	Blue + yellow = green
Red + yellow = orange	Red + blue + yellow = brown

Answers to questions 1–3 will vary.
4. Mixing all seven colors and color combinations will result in black (or a nearly black color).

"Mixing It Up!"

Red + red = deep red	Blue + yellow = green
Red + blue = purple	Yellow + yellow = deep yellow
Red + yellow = orange	Red + blue + yellow = brown
Blue + blue = deep blue	All seven colors = black (or nearly black)

Predictions and recorded temperatures will vary.
1. Darker colors absorb more heat (radiant energy) and should have the highest temperatures.
2. Lighter colors absorb the least heat (radiant energy) and should have the lowest temperatures.
3. Answers will vary. Some light-colored materials could have a greater increase in temperature due to the thickness of the fabric.
4. Answers will vary. Possible variables include the thickness of the materials, the content of the fabric, or the type of weave.
5. Answers will vary, depending on the items chosen. Students could note that the only difference in the items should be color.

Bonus Box: A light-colored car would keep a person cooler in the Arizona desert because light colors absorb less heat (radiant energy). A dark-colored roof on a house in Maine would keep it warmer because dark colors absorb more heat (radiant energy).

Page 153

1. Answers will vary.
2. Yes, length makes a difference. The shorter rubber bands will have a higher pitch than the longer ones.
3. Yes, width makes a difference. The wider rubber bands will have a lower pitch than the narrow ones.
4. No, color does not affect the sound at all.
5. Yes, some rubber bands fit more tightly around the box than others. The tight-fitting rubber bands will have a higher pitch than the looser-fitting ones.
6. The thinner, tight-fitting strings would play the higher notes. The thicker, looser-fitting strings would play the lower notes.

Bonus Box: A long, wide rubber band has a lower pitch than a short, wide rubber band.

Page 158

Instructor Aves Birdy's Class
- vertebrate
- warm-blooded
- hatch from eggs
- breathe with lungs
- have a beak or bill
- have feathers

Mr. Mammalia's Class
- vertebrate
- warm-blooded
- feed young with milk
- breathe with lungs
- most have hair or fur
- most bear live young

Ms. Four-Fish's Class
- vertebrate
- cold-blooded
- breathe mainly with gills
- live in water
- hatch from eggs

Professor Reptilia's Class
- vertebrate
- cold-blooded
- breathe with lungs
- hatch from eggs (some bear live young)
- have scales

Dr. Amphibia's Class
- vertebrate
- cold-blooded
- breathe with gills or lungs
- hatch from eggs
- live part of life in water, part on land

Page 167

Assignment I: Mercury, 0.4 AU; Venus, 0.7 AU; Earth, 1 AU; Mars, 1.5 AU; Jupiter, 5.2 AU; Saturn, 9.5 AU; Uranus, 19.2 AU; Neptune, 30.1 AU; Pluto, 39.5 AU

Assignment II: Points representing each planet should be plotted as follows: Mercury, 4 mm; Venus, 7 mm; Earth, 1 cm; Mars, 1.5 cm; Jupiter, 5.2 cm; Saturn, 9.5 cm; Uranus, 19.2 cm; Neptune, 30.1 cm; Pluto, 39.5 cm.

Assignment III: The poppy seeds should represent Mercury, Mars, and Pluto. The grape should represent Jupiter. The mustard seeds should represent Venus and Earth. The peppercorns should represent Uranus and Neptune. The piece of M&M's or Skittles candy should represent Saturn.

Page 173

1. haul
2. hail
3. heat
4. hemisphere
5. hash
6. music
7. mosaic
8. motto
9. moonstruck
10. musty
11. sheer
12. siege
13. silver
14. signify
15. shirt
16. carbon
17. cease
18. candle
19. catastrophe
20. cappuccino

Riddle answer: Because his teacher told him the **test** was **a real piece of cake!**

Page 175

1. a gross; A gross (12 dozen) costs only $5.40, while 36 individual frindles total $9.
2. $155
3. $9,865
4. $437.50
5. yes; Those three items total $17.25.
6. $30,000
7. $153
8. Answers will vary. Several possible ways include the following:
   — three T-shirts, four notebooks
   — two baseball caps, two posters
   — one flag, one pair of sunglasses, one baseball cap, five notebooks
   — one dictionary, three frindles, one T-shirt, four notebooks, two flags

Page 180

Possible outcomes will vary. Accept all reasonable responses.
1. Lily's Aunt Celia is a U.S. spy against the Nazis.
2. Lily's cousin is a general in the navy.
3. Lily has written 14 books.
4. Lily's aunt is sick with frostbite.
5. Lily's dad is in the Secret Service.
6. Lily is going to row out to meet her dad and take Albert with her.

Page 181

1. note
2. kitten
3. kitten
4. note
5. note
6. kitten
7. kitten
8. note
9. note
10. kitten
11. note
12. note
13. kitten
14. kitten
15. note
16. kitten

Page 185

Accept all reasonable answers.

1. Green
2. Yellow
3. Red
4. Blue
5. Yellow
6. Yellow
7. Yellow
8. Yellow

9 and 10: Answers will vary. Possible conflicts include

- Meg doesn't like her appearance.
- People think Charles Wallace is dumb.
- Sandy and Dennys are upset with Mrs. Murry because she didn't wake them up during Mrs. Whatsit's visit.
- Meg gets angry at others who call Charles Wallace dumb.
- Meg gets in a fight with a classmate.
- Charles Wallace gets upset at Mrs. Whatsit for trying to get Mrs. Murry to serve the birthday caviar.

Page 186

Answers may vary. Possible answers include

1. composure, tranquility, peacefulness, calmness, calm, peace
2. huge, enormous, overwhelming, tremendous, stupendous, phenomenal, great, fantastic
3. carelessly, thoughtlessly, accidentally, heedlessly
4. disappoint, dissatisfy, fail, frustrate
5. gloomy, sad, depressed, dejected, down, blue, despondent
6. doubtfully, distrustfully, incredulously, cynically, skeptically
7. physical, material, concrete, real, tangible
8. emptiness, nothingness, oblivion
9. fleeting, momentary, brief, temporary, impermanent
10. angry, enraged, annoyed, aggravated, furious, mad, upset
11. mournfully, dismally, gloomily, dolefully, sorrowfully
12. messy, sloppy, careless, untidy
13. timely, opportune, favorable, auspicious
14. danger, threat, risk, peril, hazard
15. persistence, backbone, determination, endurance, spirit, spunk, nerve
16. charitable, accepting, patient, merciful, sympathetic

Bonus Box

1. void
2. unkempt
3. tolerant
4. tenacity
5. somber
6. serenity
7. propitious
8. prodigious
9. plaintively
10. menace
11. indignant
12. inadvertently
13. ephemeral
14. dubiously
15. disillusion
16. corporeal

Page 193

Note: The page numbers noted below are based on the version published by Aladdin Paperbacks, 1999.

	Word	Page #	Part of Speech	Match the Meaning	Meanings
Ch. 1–4	a. anxious	3	adj	4	1. ill will toward someone
	b. poacher	4	n	3	2. feeling of deep resentment
	c. spite	6	n	1	3. one who kills wild animals illegally
	d. grudge	23	n	2	4. worried
	e. ford	24	n	5	5. shallow part of a body of water
Ch. 5–8	f. misery	40	n	2	1. put out of place
	g. sly	43	adj	5	2. great unhappiness and suffering
	h. miserly	46	adj	4	3. tempt
	i. lure	56	v	3	4. stingy
	j. dislocate	58	v	1	5. tricky
Ch. 9–12	k. peaceably	65	adv	5	1. indirectly
	l. rabies	66	n	3	2. fight or object
	m. protest	71	v	2	3. disease of warm-blooded animals
	n. secondhand	81	adv	1	4. keeping apart from others
	o. solitary	84	adj	4	5. in a calm manner
Ch. 13–16	p. brewery	98	n	1	1. factory where malt liquor is produced
	q. unconscious	98	adj	5	2. near the inside of the body
	r. amble	101	v	4	3. move by digging
	s. internal	104	adj	2	4. walk or stroll
	t. burrowing	114	v	3	5. not aware

Page 258

1. Adams, Jennifer
2. Billings, Bryan
3. Black, Sally
4. Black, Scott
5. Black, Stephanie
6. Black, Steven
7. Briggs, Melinda
8. Brown, Thomas
9. Brown, Tiffany
10. Brown, Timothy
11. Green, James
12. Green, Jessica
13. Green, Jill
14. Groth, Jonathan
15. Grove, Lisa
16. Hartman, Cassie
17. Hawkes, Paul
18. Mitchell, Kelsie
19. Simon, Kyle
20. Tyson, Sylvia
21. White, Amber
22. White, Becka
23. White, Caitlin
24. Whitman, Josh
25. Whitted, Austin
26. Young, Daniel

Bonus Box: phrase, gab, gym, gist, gnash, hors d'oeuvre, wrangle, cycle, school, tsunami

Page 259

1. 3 + 7 = 10
2. 12 + 4 = 4
3. 10 + 6 = 4
4. 5 + 8 = 1
5. 2 + 9 = 11
6. 12 + 6 = 6
7. 7 + 7 = 2
8. 8 + 8 = 4
9. 10 + 8 = 6
10. 12 + 12 = 12
11. 3 + 13 = 4
12. 9 + 14 = 11
13. 5 – 5 = 12
14. 3 – 6 = 9
15. 10 – 12 = 10
16. 9 – 4 = 5
17. 2 – 7 = 7
18. 1 – 6 = 7
19. 12 – 12 = 12
20. 1 – 14 = 11
21. 12

Bonus Box: 300 (1 + 2 + 3...+ 24 = 300)

Page 264

Students should have decorated their pumpkins as follows:

6 with stems
1 without a nose
9 smiling
2 with ears
10 with hair
3 with square eyes

2 with eyebrows
4 with triangular eyes
3 with square noses
8 with round noses
3 frowning
5 with round eyes

Bonus Box: Twelve pumpkins are frowning, 20 have round eyes, 40 have hair, and 16 have triangular eyes.

Page 265

1. THANKSGIVING
2. THNKSGVNG
3. THCOBNKSGVNG
4. THCOBNSGNG
5. THCONBSGNG
6. THCONBLESSSGNG
7. THCONBLESSGNGS
8. THCONBUYBLESSGNGS
9. THCONUYBLESSGNGS
10. THCONUYOURBLESSGNGS
11. TCONUYOURBLESSGNGS
12. TCONUYOURBLESSINGS
13. CONUTYOURBLESSINGS
14. COUNTYOURBLESSINGS
15. COUNT YOUR BLESSINGS

Bonus Box: Answers will vary. Possible answers include the following: *hang, sing, sink, sank, task, stink, stinking, shank, shin, think,* and *tank.*

Page 270

Answers to questions 2 and 4–7 will vary, depending on the size of the sugar cone used.

Part I

1. cone
2. Answers will vary.
3. A radius is a line segment that has one endpoint at the center of a circle and the other on the circle. A radius is half the diameter.
4. Answers will vary.
5. Answers will vary.
6. Answers will vary.

Part II

7. 1; Answers will vary.
8. 10.5
9. 66
10. 6 tubs of frosting: $8.34
    6 packages of M&M's: $13.74
    6 jars of sugar sprinkles: $7.74
    4 boxes of sugar cones: $5.96
    3 boxes of plastic spoons: $2.37
    Total: $38.15

Page 271

Students' methods for solving some problems may vary.

1. 20 ($80 \times \frac{1}{2} = 40$; $40 \times \frac{1}{2}$)
2. 11 (10 + 12 = 22; 22 ÷ 2)
3. 1 in 23 (1 + 2 + 3 + 4 + 6 + 7)
4. 16 (4 × 3 = 12; 12 + 4)
5. $7,225.00 ($245.00 + $1,200.00 = $1,445.00; $1,445.00 × 5)
6. 20 (6 × 30 = 180; 180 ÷ 9)
7. 27 (8 + 9 + 10 + 11 + 12 = 50; 1 + 2 + 3 + 4 + 6 + 7 = 23; 50 − 23)
8. 168 (8 × 3 = 24; 24 × 7)
9. 6 (From 5:00 to 7:30 is $2\frac{1}{2}$ hours. From 8:30 to 12:00 is $3\frac{1}{2}$ hours; $2\frac{1}{2} + 3\frac{1}{2}$)
10. 7 (9 + 10 = 19; 19 ÷ 3 = 6 r. 1 = 7 rounded up to the nearest whole number)
11. 16 (10 + 11 + 12 = 33; 8 + 9 = 17; 33 − 17)
12. $112.80 ($8.95 + $0.45 = $9.40; $9.40 × 12)

Bonus Box: 2 groups of drummers, 3 groups of maids (The factors of 12 are 12, 24, 36, and so on; the factors of 8 are 8, 16, 24, 32, and so on; the least common factor is 24, which is 2 groups of drummers and 3 groups of maids.)

Page 277

Boxes should be taped together in this order.

1. **Madam C. J. Walker (1867–1919)**
   Sarah Breedlove was born in 1867 in Louisiana to former slaves...
2. Since she became an orphan at an early age...
   ...so her family lived as sharecroppers on a cotton plantation.
3. ...Sarah moved in with an older sister.
   Sarah married at age 14, had a daughter at 17, and was widowed at 19...
4. Since she learned that lots of well-paying jobs were there...
   ...so she had to find a job to support her daughter and herself.
5. ...the young widow moved to St. Louis.
   Because she wanted to stop her hair from falling out...
6. Sarah worked as a washerwoman...
   ...Sarah invented "Wonderful Hair Grower," a solution that stopped hair loss.
7. ...so she mixed her first hair-care products in her washtub.
   Because St. Louis already had several cosmetic companies...
8. Because her products were popular with African American women...
   ...Sarah decided to move to a different city to begin her own business.
9. ...Sarah quit her job to build her own business.
   By 1906, Sarah had married Charles Joseph Walker...
10. Because her husband was familiar with advertising and marketing...
    ...so she changed her name to Madam C. J. Walker.
11. ...he organized a mail-order business for his wife's products.
    In 1910, Madam Walker visited Indianapolis, a city that had become a major manufacturing center...
12. Because she was not satisfied with making money only for herself...
    ...so she moved her business there.
13. ...she trained others in her beauty school to run their own hair salons.
    One of her goals was to hire African Americans in every step of her business...
14. Because she is an American hero and role model...
    ...so Madam Walker hired thousands for her sales team.
15. ...Madam C. J. Walker's picture is featured on a U.S. Postal Service stamp.

Puzzle word: ENTREPRENEUR. An entrepreneur is someone who organizes and manages a business, taking responsibility for all risks involved.

Page 278

1. 3:57 P.M.
2. 5:10 P.M.
3. 12:18 P.M.
4. 5:05 P.M.
5. 6:07 P.M.
6. 7:37 P.M.
7. 11:54 A.M.
8. 7:44 A.M.
9. 12:25 P.M.
10. 1:38 P.M.
11. 9:48 A.M.
12. 11:20 A.M.

Bonus Box: The sum in each section is 26.

Page 283

1. team, ball
2. robber, clean
3. jumps, hiccups
4. ocean, nervous
5. girl
6. state, cows
7. potatoes, see
8. pig, hospital
9. lawn mower, tweet
10. throat, hoot
11. write, bald
12. rainy, inside
13. diet
14. mirror, cracks
15. black, blushing

words not used: planes, walks

Page 284

1. 271
2. 28
3. 260
4. $4.44
5. Answers may vary. One solution: 50 MJ + 75 MJ + 48 GB + 67 MJ + 51 NW = 291
6. Answers may vary. One solution: 125 AC + 50 MJ + 75 MJ + 300 PB + 118 MG + 135 AC + 51 NW = 854
7. 48 GB + 67 MJ + 51 NW = 166
8. 125 AC + 300 PB + 118 MG + 135 AC = 678

Page 285

Answers may vary. Suggested answers are listed below. The words in parentheses are the ones that are not used and should be marked out.

1. Many Americans take part in fun activities to observe Cinco de Mayo.
2. It's a time to celebrate the friendship between the people of Mexico and America.
3. We attend colorful parades and listen to speeches. *(valentines)*
4. Streets are decorated in red, white, and green.
5. Red, white, and green are the colors of the Mexican flag.
6. People enjoy traditional Mexican food. *(bunny)*
7. Some of these special foods include tortillas and guacamole.
8. Special dances and musical events are held in many American cities.
9. Famous musicians play tunes on their guitars. *(sleigh)*
10. Local bands play Mexican patriotic songs. *(mask)*
11. Dancers twirl around and snap their castanets.
12. Festivals in some cities often last for several days.
13. In Los Angeles, activities are held in the streets outside City Hall.
14. The holiday has become a celebration of Hispanic heritage. *(turkey)*

Bonus Box: tacos, refried beans, hot chilies, corn tortillas, enchiladas, burritos

Page 288

1. 3: v-c, v-s, c-s
2. 6: v-c, v-s, c-v, c-s, s-v, s-c
3. 4: ls-bp, ls-cc, ls-p, ls-rs
4. 10: bp-cc, bp-p, bp-ls, bp-rs, cc-p, cc-ls, cc-rs, p-ls, p-rs, ls-rs
5. 15: c-v, c-s, c-bp, c-b, c-cc, v-s, v-bp, v-b, v-cc, s-bp, s-b, s-cc, bp-b, bp-cc, b-cc
6. 150: 15 ice-cream combinations (see problem 5) x 10 topping combinations (n-M, n-s, n-c, n-cs, M-s, M-c, M-cs, s-c, s-cs, c-cs)
7. 21: g-g, g-b, g-o, g-p, g-y, g-r, b-b, b-o, b-p, b-y, b-r, o-o, o-p, o-y, o-r, p-p, p-y, p-r, y-y, y-r, r-r
8. 7:

Sara	Fara	Tara
pd	pd	str
pd	pd	sol
sol	sol	str
sol	sol	sol
sol	pd	str
pd	sol	str
sol	pd	sol

9. 6: t-b-p, t-b-l, t-b-o, t-p-l, t-p-o, t-l-o

Bonus Box: 18 (You could take all the red and green socks before taking 2 that are blue.)

Page 289

1. 25, 35
2. 1,190; 1,700; 2,720
3. 29
4. 15, 38
5. 2 packages of red, 5 packages of green
6. 6, 10, 15, 30
7. 10, 12, 15, 20
8. 50 or 150 (Jack and Jenna may receive either 1 or 2 containers each.)
9. 8 different ways: 1 row of 30 desks, 2 rows of 15 desks each, 3 rows of 10 each, 5 rows of 6 each, 6 rows of 5 each, 10 rows of 3 each, 15 rows of 2 each, 30 rows of 1 each
10. 24, 6, 3 or 24, 1, 8

Bonus Box: 40. All of the other numbers are multiples of 7.

Page 290

1. N U M **B** E R
2. S E N T E **N** C E
3. **Z** E R O
4. D I **G** I T
5. **Q** U O T E
6. G R A M **M** A R
7. A **F** R I C A
8. P R O D **U** C T
9. G A L A **X** Y
10. **U** T A H
11. E R O S I O N
12. **P** L A I N S
13. W **H** A L E S
14. A L A S **K** A
15. N E W **Y** O R K
16. V O W E **L**
17. M U S **C** L E
18. F A C **T** O R
19. V E N U S
20. C O M M **A**
21. I N D **I** A
22. F O R **C** E
23. S C I E **N** C E
24. **W** A T E R
25. S U B J E **C** T
26. E **N** E R G Y

Index